HOUSE OF CARDS

PSYCHOLOGY AND PSYCHOTHERAPY BUILT ON MYTH

ROBYN M. DAWES

THE FREE PRESS
A Division of Simon & Schuster Inc.
NEW YORK   LONDON   TORONTO   SYDNEY   SINGAPORE

THE FREE PRESS
A Divison of Simon & Schuster Inc.
1230 Avenue of the Americas
New York, NY 10020

Copyright © 1994 by Robyn M. Dawes
All rights reserved,
including the right of reproduction
in whole or in part in any form.

First paperback edition 1996

FREE PRESS PAPERBACK and colophon are trademarks
of Simon & Schuster Inc.

Manufactured in the United States of America

10 9 8 7 6 5

Library of Congress Cataloging-in-Publication Data

Dawes, Robyn M., 1936–
    House of cards: psychology and psychotherapy built on myth /
Robyn M. Dawes. —1st Free Press paperback ed.
        p. cm.
    Originally published: New York: Free Press; Toronto: Maxwell
Macmillan Canada; New York: Maxwell Macmillan International,
©1994.
    Includes bibliographical references and index.
    ISBN 0–684–83091–4(pbk.)
    1. Psychotherapy—Philosophy. 2. Clinical psychology—Philosophy.
3. Psychotherapists. 4. Clinical psychologists. I. Title.
[RC480.5.D38 1996]
616.89'14'01—dc20   96-12597
                                                                    CIP

ISBN 0-02-907205-0
        0-684-83091-4 (Pbk)

The cartoon depicted facing the title page is reproduced with the permission of
Sidney Harris.

Dedicated to the professional psychologists (and psychiatrists) I know who take research results seriously, in hopes this book will strengthen rather than weaken their clout.

The greatest enemy of the truth is not the lie—deliberate, contrived, and dishonest, but the myth—persistent, pervasive and unrealistic.
—John F. Kennedy

When ideas go unexamined and unchallenged for a long time, certain things happen. They become mythological, and they become very, very powerful.
—Edgar L. Doctorow

CONTENTS

PREFACE

As I argue throughout this book, behavior is influenced by multiple factors. My own decision to write the book has been motivated by two factors in particular: anger, and a sense of social obligation. At least, those are the two of which I am most aware. I have also had time, made available by an "in-house sabbatical" at Carnegie Mellon University after serving for five years as a department head, and I have been greatly encouraged by colleagues who have taken the time to review various chapter drafts.

Why is anger a motivation for writing this book? Because the rapid growth and professionalization of my field, psychology, has led it to abandon a commitment it made at the inception of that growth. That commitment was to establish a mental health profession that would be based on research findings, employing insofar as possible well-validated techniques and principles. At least, professional practitioners in psychology were to make clear to their clients and to society at large that they were proceeding in the absence of relevant scientific knowledge when none existed. What was never envisioned was that a body of research and established principles would be available to inform practice, but that the practice would ignore that research and those principles. Worse yet, far too much professional practice in psychology has grown and achieved status by espousing principles that are known to be untrue and by employing techniques known to be invalid.

Instead of relying on research-based knowledge in their practice, too many mental health professionals rely on "trained clinical intuition." But there is ample evidence that such intuition does not work well in the mental health professions. (In fact, it is often no different from the intuition of people who have had no training whatsoever.) Forty years ago, professionals could be excused for believing in the power of their own intuitive judgment, because at that time there was very little evidence concerning its accuracy one way or the other. That is no longer true. Today there is plenty of evidence about the accuracy of their intuition, and it's negative.

Thus, I am angered when I see my former colleagues make bald assertions based on their "years of clinical experience" in settings of crucial importance to others' lives—such as in commitment hearings, or in court hearings about custody arrangements, or about suspected child sexual abuse. I am particularly infuriated when they base these assertions on results of psychological techniques that have been proven to be invalid but that "I myself have found to be of great help in my clinical practice." Those are real people out there about whom the judgments are being made. Moreover, the people whose lives are affected—or their lawyers—may have great difficulty casting doubts on what such professionals claim, due to the pretense that some sort of science underlies the claims. Often that is not true. There really is a science of psychology that has been developed with much work by many people over many years, but it is being increasingly ignored, derogated, and contradicted by the behavior of professionals—who, of course, give lip service to its existence. An expert in a court room setting is supposed to be competent to present an opinion with reasonable certainty. But a mental health expert who expresses a confident opinion about the probable future behavior of a single individual (for example, to engage in violent acts) is by definition incompetent, because the research has demonstrated that neither a mental health expert nor anyone else can make such a prediction with accuracy sufficient to warrant much confidence. (Professionals often state that their professional role "requires" them to make such judgments, however much they personally appreciate the uncertainty involved. No, they are not required—they volunteer.)

Finally, such experts are costing society more and more, not only because they are proliferating but because their claim to be working on the basis of authoritative intuition is compatible with our naive ideas about what constitutes "expertise." Those who admire the expertise of medical doctors, for example, stress their powers of judgment and intuition, while simultaneously downgrading their heavy reliance on laboratory techniques and results that are well-validated but impersonal, like blood tests, biopsies, and X-rays.

I feel a sense of obligation because society has supported my research and has personally supported me sufficiently well that I do not, like some previous generations of university professors, have to take a vow of semipoverty to pursue my interests. Thus, I feel an obligation to tell people my view of what's going on. Moreover, I will attempt to educate not just by drawing conclusions but by sharing the research and reasoning on which I base these conclusions. For example, rather than simply cite the research studies that have concluded that professional psychologists (and other mental health professionals) do not "learn from experience," I have attempted to differentiate types of learning, to review the conditions under which these different types may or may not occur, and to demonstrate that the experience of mental health professionals does not allow learning of the type they claim to have had. For educational purposes, I have also attempted to make each chapter in Part One self-contained—even though I must then repeat some principles (for example, about the nature of retrospective memory) when they are applicable to different topics, and must occasionally cite the same references (for example, concerning psychotherapists' theoretical orientations).

I have tried to stick to the facts, at least those that appear most probable on the basis of research findings. The reader may, in addition, want to know about my own experience in the professional field. I started out as a graduate student in clinical psychology in 1958, but I switched to research (in the mathematical psychology program at Michigan) in 1960. My first year of clinical training—at the Ann Arbor Veterans Administration Hospital—was sufficiently successful that I was granted a U.S. Public Health Service fellowship in clinical psychology for my second year, and I started working at the University of Michigan hospital psychiatric unit. During my first year, I became increasingly skeptical that those of us responsible for patient treatment really knew what we were doing, and my many friends on the VA staff shared some of my skepticism. It was in my second year that I was introduced to the unwarranted arrogance of "clinical expertise," and I quit. (See my account in Chapter 5 of the conclusion reached from a single response to the Rorschach ink blot Test.) I had very little to do with professional psychology after that until I became acting co-head (1973), then acting head (1979), and then head (1981–1985) of the psychology department at the University of Oregon. This department had a professional clinical psychology program, in which a majority of its psychology students were enrolled; unlike most, this program shared my own research-based philosophy that our understanding of people's innermost problems and motives is limited, and that we should simply assist them on the basis of what we do know. For example, projective testing techniques—which supposedly provide great insight into people but that have been shown to be invalid—were not taught at the University of Oregon's program (although the students would often be inundated with such techniques later, when they went on their year's internship at places approved by the American Psychological Association).

As department head, I had many dealings with the American Psychological Association (APA),* especially because its bureaucrats in charge of accrediting clinical training were not always happy with the department's view that clinical training should be a part of general training in psychology. During the early 1980s, I was involved in a delicensing procedure (on the side of the defense). To my amazement, I was subsequently elected president of the Oregon Psychological Association, against which I had testified at the delicensing procedure. I served for three years on its board. (This book does not cover the delicensing hearing, because I do not feel competent to distinguish between what I know on the basis of public information and what I know on a confidential basis.) I have also had personal experience with mental health experts as a client—for example, as a single male parent who has raised a brain-injured daughter from age nine. (Observations concerning that experience as well as other personal experiences will be omitted from this book, for reasons of confidentiality and self-protection.)

After moving to Carnegie Mellon in the fall of 1985 to head an interdisciplinary department of social and decision sciences, I served for approximately two years on the APA's national ethics committee. I resigned after being outvoted six to one on a policy matter, but I was persuaded to go back on the committee by the APA's board of direc-

---

*The American Psychological Association and The American Psychiatric Association bear the same acronym. Unless otherwise indicated, APA refers to the American Psychological Association throughout this book.

tors after it supported my position. So I do know a great deal about professional psychology on a personal as well as a research basis, even though I do not practice it. I believe I am competent to judge, especially because those engaged in an activity themselves are often "the last to know."

Given my experience and my knowledge of the relevant research, I focus my discussion on professional psychology, not on psychiatry or professional social work. The research I cite, however, often has the same implications for these fields. I focus on psychology, because that is the field I know best.

I would like to thank my colleagues who read drafts of various chapters and made excellent suggestions. All of them are well-known researchers as well as friends, and I thus especially appreciate that they have taken time out from their own work to read and critique what I sent them. They are, in alphabetical order, professors Hal Arkes (Ohio University), Jim Davis (University of Illinois), David Faust (Rhode Island University), Baruch Fischhoff (Carnegie Mellon University), Steven Hayes (University of Nevada at Reno), George Loewenstein (Carnegie Mellon University), Paul Meehl (University of Minnesota), John Miller (Carnegie Mellon University), Alan Roberts (Scripps Clinic), and Martin Seligman (University of Pennsylvania). They are not to be held responsible for what I have written—especially not George, who was my severest critic.

Most especially, I thank my secretary, Carole Deaunovich, for being so superbly competent and tolerant.

I would also like to express my appreciation of my agent, Gerry McCauley, particularly for his doggedness, and of the Free Press editor, Susan Arellano, particularly for her (not always successful) attempts to keep my writing "cool" in discussing issues that leave me anything but cool. In addition, I am grateful to my copyeditor, Janet Biehl, for her energetic insistence that I express ideas (particularly mathematical ones) in as simple a manner as possible. While her multitude of comments did little to enhance my self-esteem, the book undoubtedly benefited—a more important outcome. I am also grateful for Loretta Denner's thorough and patient production editing.

Finally, I would like to express my gratitude to my partner, Mary Schafer, who was not a critic, for her love and multiple reinforcements—which are fully reciprocated (at least, the love is).

Part One

THE CLAIMS OF THE MENTAL HEALTH EXPERTS VERSUS THE EVIDENCE

Many people suffer from emotional distress—ranging from psychosis through severe addictions to mild depressions. Such distress has been labeled "mental illness" in our culture, and until the late 1950s it was treated primarily by physicians. Particularly since the early 1970s, however, the number of people claiming to be experts in alleviating emotional distress has increased dramatically; by the later 1980s there were more clinical psychologists than psychiatrists, and more psychiatric social workers than clinical psychologists. Except for the prescription of psychoactive drugs, treatment of emotional distress is provided primarily by these nonmedical people. The practice of psychology, which requires postgraduate training and a Ph.D. or Sc.D. credential, has been licensed (hence restricted) in every state and territory since the middle 1970s, and psychiatric social workers are now being licensed in a majority of states as well. Licensing allows people to collect third-party fees for their services from insurance companies and the U.S. government. Moreover, licensed practitioners are increasingly relied upon as "experts" in court proceedings involving custody disputes, diagnosis of emotional problems, factual issues such as whether a child has been sexually abused, and even judgments and predictions about future behavior—such as whether someone is likely to be violent, or whether a convicted murderer is "irredeemable" (and hence eligible for execution).

Emotional suffering is very real, and the vast majority of people in these expanding professions sincerely wish to help those suffering. But are they really the experts they claim to be? Is our society justified in granting them special status and paying them from common funds? Are they better therapists than minimally trained people who may share their knowledge of behavioral techniques or empathetic understanding of others? Does possessing a license imply that they are using scientifically sound methods in treating people or providing an "expert opinion"? Should their opinions be recognized in our courts as having any more validity than the opinions of anyone else? In particular, are their opinions any better than those of judges, who have been selected on the basis of their legal record to make tough social decisions? Can these mental health practitioners, for example, make a better determination of whether a young child has been sexually abused than can be made by a careful consideration of the evidence without considering their opinions?

These questions have been studied quite extensively, often by psychologists themselves. There is by now an impressive body of research evidence indicating that the answer to these questions is no. Those claiming to be mental health experts—including many psychiatrists—often assert that their "experience" allows them to apply principles of psychology in a better manner than others could, but the research evidence is that a minimally trained person applying these principles automatically does at least as well. Moreover, the research evidence indicates that—unlike a surgeon, for example—mental health practitioners don't develop skills in applying these principles through experience. Often, moreover, they don't even attempt a systematic application of principles, instead claiming to base their practice and judgment on "trained intuition," which presumably allows them to transcend or ignore these principles when they shouldn't. There are "scientifically based" practitioners who attempt to base what they do on these principles, but there is no system of assurance that others will do so as well in these rapidly expanding fields, and they don't. A license has become, unfortunately, a license to ignore the valid principles and generalizations that do in fact exist in the mental health areas (though not in impressive numbers). And when the practitioners ignore valid principles, they can even become outright dangerous to our civil liberties, as when they ignore what they presumably should know about the malleability of human memory or the suggestibility of young children. ("There was no really good evidence. It was the therapists' notes that convinced me she was guilty.")[1]

The purpose of Part One is to share with the reader the research basis for these negative conclusions. I will sometimes describe specific studies, sometimes rely on summaries of sets of studies. These results have very strong implications for public policy in the mental health area. We should not be pouring out resources and money to support high-priced people who do not help others better than those with far less training would, and whose judgments and predictions are actually worse than the simplest statistical conclusion based on "obvious" variables. Instead, we should take seriously the findings that the effectiveness of therapy is unrelated to the training or credentials of the therapist. We should take seriously the findings that the best predictors of future behavior are past behavior and performance on carefully standardized tests, not responses to inkblot tests or impressions gained in interviews, even though no prediction is as good as we might wish it to be. The conclusion is that in attempting to alleviate psychological suffering, we should rely much more than we do on scientifically sound, community-based programs and on "paraprofessionals," who can have extensive contact with those suffering at no greater expense than is currently incurred by paying those claiming to be experts. We might also be better off relying more on ourselves in addressing our own problems.

This section of the book is based on a philosophy enunciated by Paul C. Stern. A major policy goal of psychological and social science should be to "separate common sense from common nonsense and make uncommon sense more common."[2] The common sense that assumes trained people must possess unique skills simply because they claim to have them is common nonsense. In addition, the common-sense attitudes and beliefs that lead us to accept mental health practitioners in particular as experts must be understood as common nonsense. The uncommon sense to understand the issues involved in evaluating claims of expertise and to grasp the meaning of the research addressing these issues should become common sense. It is to this goal of separating sense from nonsense that the first seven chapters of this book are addressed.

CHAPTER 1

INTRODUCTION

Many people in the United States suffer from problems that the professions of psychiatry and psychology claim to address. People often feel emotionally distressed to the point of debilitation, and many behave in dysfunctional and destructive ways. The monetary cost of alcoholism, drug addiction and what is termed "mental illness" is enormous: an estimated $273.3 billion in 1988.[1] The personal cost is difficult to measure but is clearly also enormous. Public opinion polls indicate that people are aware of these monetary and personal costs and believe that they constitute a critical social problem.[2] As summarized in a recent *NewsReport* of the National Research Council:

> Mental disorders cause substantial disability in the United States. About one in five adults suffers from a diagnosable disorder, including severe mental illnesses, such as schizophrenia, affective disorders, and substance abuse. At least 12% of youngsters under the age of 18—a total of 7.5 million children—have a diagnosable mental illness. Mental disorders cost billions a year in disability and economic costs.[3]

So there are big problems. *The question is whether the services rendered by professional psychiatrists and psychologists provide solutions to those problems.* The answer proposed in this book is rather simple. There is some scientific knowledge about *some* mental disorders and types of distress and how to alleviate them. When psychiatrists and psychologists base their practice on this knowledge, they generally perform a valuable service to their clients. All too often, however, mental health practitioners base their practice on what they believe

7

to be an "intuitive understanding" of their clients' problems, an understanding they have supposedly gained "from experience." But when they practice on this intuitive basis, they perform at best as well as minimally trained people who lack their credentials (the topic of Chapter 2) and at worst as licensed, expensive (if inadvertent) frauds (the topic of Chapter 5).

The reason I reach these conclusions is that the ability of these professionals to alleviate emotional distress has been subjected to empirical scrutiny—for example, their effectiveness as therapists (Chapter 2), their insight about people (Chapter 3), and the relationship between how well they function and the amount of experience they have had in their field (Chapter 4). Virtually all the research—and this book will reference more than three hundred empirical investigations and summaries of investigations—has found that these professionals' claims to superior intuitive insight, understanding, and skill as therapists are simply invalid. What our society has done, sadly, is to license such people to "do their own thing," while simultaneously justifying that license on the basis of scientific knowledge, which those licensed too often ignore. This would not be too bad if "their own thing" had some validity, but it doesn't. What the license often does is to provide a governmental sanction for nonsense such as:

> "In my mind, I know what she was thinking and feeling at the time of her death"—a Harvard professor of psychiatry, quoted in the *New York Times*, October 21, 1987, p. A22. Where his "psychological autopsy" was allowed into testimony at the trial of Teresa Jackson for (psychological) child abuse following the suicide of her daughter in Fort Lauderdale, Florida

or, from a professional talking about incest victims,

> "It's so common that I'll tell you that within 10 minutes, I can spot it as a person walks in the door, often before they even realize it. There's a trust, a lack of trust, that's the most common issue. There's a way that a person presents themselves. There's a certain body language that says I'm afraid to expose myself. I'm afraid to be hurt."—Good Morning America's on-air psychologist on the CNBC program *Real Personal*, April 27, 1992 (after maintaining that "Probably one in four women, one in eight men, have been incested.")

If the only result were nonsense, it would not be so bad. There is a lot of benign nonsense in the world. Unfortunately, such nonsense like this can have a profound effect on other people's lives, and it is expensive nonsense.

Claims to intuitive understanding, like those in above quotes, leave potential clients incapable of distinguishing between service that has a true scientific base and service based simply on the claims of those providing the service. The professional associations have exacerbated this confusion by monitoring and sanctioning their members only for the consistency of their practice with their presumed power and status, not for whether that practice does any good or has any scientific justification. Thus, in a recent flap concerning a female Harvard psychiatrist whose client committed suicide, the focus of the professional board's inquiry was on whether she had sexual relations with him—not on whether encouraging him to regress to an infantile state so that she could "reparent" him had any known value for him or anyone else. The write-up in *Newsweek* treated the public to what various well-known psychiatrists and psychologists "said," "thought," or thought they "knew" about the case but nowhere was there reference to any *evidence* concerning the psychiatrist's mode of treatment.[4] The impression is created that psychotherapy treatment is all a matter of opinion or conjecture. It isn't, but many practitioners treat it that way, while the professional associations support them in doing virtually anything at all that appeals to their "clinical intuition," as if there were no knowledge. The professionals are immune so long as they keep their hands off their clients and don't do anything else that would offend their colleagues' sense of status or propriety, such as be arrested for homosexual solicitation in a men's room or plead *nolo contendere* to a charge of child sexual abuse in order to avoid being jailed as a sex offender.

Finally, the mental health professionals who claim expertise without a scientific base have apparently had a profound effect on our culture's beliefs about what constitutes a good life, what types of behavior are desirable, and—most important—how people "should" feel about the world (see Part II). The most pernicious of these beliefs is that adult behavior is determined mainly by childhood experiences, even very subtle ones, and particularly those that enhance or diminish self-esteem. Self-esteem, in turn, is believed to be an important causal variable in behavior, even though the California Task Force on the Importance of Self-Esteem could find no evidence of such a causal effect. Especially, low self-esteem is believed to yield, with unerring consistency, personally or socially destructive behaviors, so that people who wish to change their behavior must experience an elevation of self-esteem *first* (as the result of therapy or an esteem-raising self-help group) and attempt serious change in their lives only later. Again, the evidence for this beliefs is negative. What these beliefs do is discourage people from attempting to craft a decent life for themselves and instead encourage them to do whatever is necessary to *feel* good—about themselves. Sometimes such striving after "mentally healthy" feelings and attitudes simply result in ludicrous behavior (like clutching a teddy bear while proudly proclaiming oneself undoubtedly an incest victim, despite an inability to remember any credible instances). In general, however, this strategy is self-defeating, because it ignores the simple principle that much of our feeling results from what we do rather than causing us to do it.

By contrast, other professionals do base their recommendations on what is known, or on what is believed to be true on the basis of research findings. They do not offer grandiose and false advice to the general public about how to live, think, and feel. The simple reason is that their own scientific knowledge about human distress makes them aware of its limitations, and most of them are responsible enough not to pretend that these limitations do not exist.

THE GROWTH OF PSYCHOLOGY

As the problem of mental distress becomes ever more severe in this country, the magnitude and status of the professions claiming to have a solution also grow. Psychiatry, with its requirement of medical training and its emphasis on prescribing drugs, has approximately doubled in size in the past thirty years. In contrast, psychology has become big business. In this chapter, I will concentrate on the growth and practice of professional psychology, because it has had the biggest impact on the mental health field since the early 1970s, when clinical psychologists were first licensed as mental health experts. Clinical social work has also had a growing impact, somewhat later—as clinical social workers became licensed in many states through the 1980s. The practice of social workers is more akin to that of psychologists than of psychiatrists, for example, in concentrating on psychotherapy rather than the prescription of psychoactive drugs. In addition, there are other groups of people labeled "therapists." Consequently, while I focus on psychology in this chapter, many of my conclusions are applicable to these other growing professions as well, and I will note this applicability by referring to other mental health professionals as well as psychologists when appropriate.

An estimated $2.8 billion was spent in 1985 on the services of "office based, licensed, clinical psychologists," as opposed to $2.3 billion on services of office-based psychiatrists.[5] That $2.8 billion figure is based on an estimated 55 million contact hours at an average charge of seventy-five dollars per hour (now higher); it accounts for two-thirds of all nonmedical professional office-based charges in the mental health area. (The rest is accounted for by licensed psychiatric social workers and other mental health professionals.) The costs of nonmedical services for mental health, drug addiction, and alcoholism increased at an average rate of 13.9% from 1985 to 1988;[6] given that rate of increase, we can estimate that 1990 costs for office-based, licensed clinical psychologists were approximately $5.4 billion (as opposed to $4.2 billion for office-based psychiatrists). Similar extrapolation yields a figure of $2.7 billion for other licensed experts. Few people pay these costs out of pocket. Medical insurance, Medicare, Medicaid, and other government programs pay. That is, we all pay.

Psychological testimony is also often sought in legal proceedings, specifically those involving a person's competency to stand trial, sentencing, psychiatric commitment, divorce, child custody, and—most recently—allegations of child abuse in the absence of physical evidence or reliable witnesses. Allegheny County in Pennsylvania, for example, instituted a new procedure for all disputed child custody cases following the 1985 ruling in *Walsh v. Walsh*.[7] The parents and children in such cases are all automatically evaluated by a professional psychologist and by a social worker on a home visit as well. Parents who do not agree about custody arrangements can make no argument before a judge without undergoing such an evaluation first.

Not surprisingly, the cost and legal power of professional psychologists has been matched by their affluence. According to the most recent statistics published by the American Psychological

Association,[8] salaries of professional psychologists averaged $73,300 in 1989. Those with two to five years of professional experience averaged $54,068; those with five to nine years averaged $67,005; and those with ten or more years averaged $78,685. A survey taken by the Oregon Psychological Association in 1985 (which involved gross receipts rather than net salaries), when I was president of it, indicated roughly comparable figures. The subjects of this survey ranged from those who had been recently licensed to those who had already established a clientele and a reputation; Oregon at the time was experiencing one of the worst recessions in the country. (The Rand McNally listing of cities at the time had ranked the Eugene–Springfield area as the very worst urban area for economic opportunities.[9]) At board meetings of the Oregon Psychological Association, I was informed that the most common charge of established clinical psychologists in the Portland area was $125 per hour.

The cost, power, and affluence of professional clinical psychologists arises not solely from a belief in their expertise and efficacy but also from sheer numbers. The profession has expanded dramatically in the last thirty years. When I joined the APA in 1959, it had approximately 18,000 members, of whom only 2,500 listed specialties in clinical or counseling psychology.[10] When I quit in 1988, there were 68,000 members, approximately 40,000 of whom were in clinical or counseling.[11] By comparison, the American Psychiatric Association had 10,000 members in 1959 and grew to 34,000 in 1989[12]; assuming that a constant proportion of its members are engaged in practice, that is an increase by a factor of 3.4, while the proportion of American Psychological Association members in professional practice grew by a factor of 16. When I joined in 1959, there were no state procedures for licensing psychologists. Today there are licensing procedures and boards in every state and territory in this country and in every province of Canada. There were roughly 45,500 professional licensed psychologists in this country by 1985.[13] Since then, clinical psychology has doubled its numbers every ten years.[14] For comparison, the doubling rate of lawyers is twelve years,[15] of social workers fourteen years, and of psychiatrists twenty years.[16]

We are all paying for these services through insurance premiums and taxes. In most contexts in a market economy, payment for a good or service is based on a belief that it will work in a certain manner; for example, automobiles with antilock brakes and air bags are generally more expensive than those without because the purchaser has a belief that these safety features will work. If they do not work as advertised, or if they are not part of a car purporting to have them, the seller is liable to lawsuits and prosecution for misinterpretation and for misleading or fraudulent advertising. There is, in addition, some consumer protection for goods and services that purchasers cannot be expected to evaluate on their own without highly specialized training or that are offered primarily to those who lack general competence to understand. Thus, medical practitioners are licensed in every state, as are nursing homes.

UNJUSTIFIED GROWTH IN PSYCHOLOGY

The basic service that professional psychology claims to offer is the skilled application of a scientific understanding of human behavior and feelings, particularly as they relate to issues of mental health, and illness; psychotherapy offers unique skills as well. But as a group professional psychologists and other mental health professionals making the same claims do not possess a special expertise that allows them to provide this service. They are no better as psychotherapists than are others of comparable intelligence who are minimally trained (see Chapter 2); they do not have any special abilities in diagnosing mental distress and predicting human behavior, or in evaluating what causes particular people to behave and feel as they do (see Chapter 3); and they do not learn anything from clinical experience with distressed people that cannot be learned by reading textbooks (see Chapter 4). In fact, there is substantial evidence that the simplest statistical models do better than credentialed and experienced professional psychologists at predicting human outcomes. Moreover, the expertise of mental health experts is limited by the accuracy of the techniques they use; the accurate ones are easy to understand and master, while the ones purporting to require specialized training (like the Rorschach Ink Blot Test) are usually invalid. It follows that the licensing of psychologists in particular protects not the public but the profession (see Chapter 5). In fact, the social sanctioning of "clinical" techniques of dubious validity or proven invalidity through licensing them harms the public.

If research shows that the services of professional psychologists and other mental health experts are not what they are believed or assumed to be, why do these services not change? One answer is, of course, that taking the research findings seriously would call into question the affluence and power of the mental health professions themselves. There is, however, another important answer; the steady erosion of the profession's commitment to research findings as a basis for practice over the past thirty years. Professional medicine has moved in the exact opposite direction; starting with the scientific trials of the Salk polio vaccine in 1954, the systematic evaluation of possible new drugs and therapies has played an increasingly important role in determining practice; individual practitioners who ignore the well-publicized results of these evaluations are judged as harming their patients and can face charges of incompetence. To understand this erosion of commitment to research in psychological practice, it is necessary to know some of the history of the profession.

A BRIEF HISTORY OF PSYCHOLOGICAL PRACTICE

Sigmund Freud, who founded psychoanalysis, which led to the expansion of psychotherapy as a profession,[17] saw no reason why his techniques should be used only by medical doctors. Nevertheless, particularly in the United States, psychological evaluation and psychotherapy were considered to be medical specialties, so that prior to World War II only a few psychologists here and there engaged in what is now termed "practice." After the war many American soldiers returned home with psychological problems that were considered severe enough to require hospitalization, but there were not enough psychiatrists to staff the many Veterans Administration (VA) hospitals. This shortage was especially acute given government pay rates. The late E. Lowell Kelly of the University of Michigan proposed a solution: Allow psychologists to treat hospitalized veterans on a (near)-equal status with psychiatrists, who retained the ultimate medical responsibility. His rationale was that psychologists had a qualification that psychiatrists didn't: extensive research training. Thus, the psychologists would bring to the settings a competence different from that of standard medicine, and their unique contribution would be based on this competence. Practice would follow—not precede—research findings, even at a time when nonpsychiatric medical practice was less wedded to such findings than it is today. Kelly was successful in his lobbying arguments, and the field of clinical psychology was born.

Kelly was elected president of the American Psychological Association in 1956. As time passed, however, he became increasingly concerned that his vision had been abandoned, even as, after a period of ten or so years of steady growth, the profession exploded in numbers. Graduate programs proliferated, all appealing to a board of the APA for "accreditation." In 1971 the APA made a momentous decision. As evidence indicated that training in theory and research were unrelated to effectiveness as a psychotherapist, the association recognized a new degree, the doctorate of psychology without research training. It was abbreviated as a Psy.D., to differentiate it from the Ph.D., which is technically a "doctorate of philosophy" and which for years has implied not only relevant research training but the production of a dissertation that contributes new knowledge to the field of study. The recognition of the Psy.D. was provisional, pending an evaluation of the programs and the people graduating from them.

What happened, however, was rapid expansion. The original program at the University of Illinois no longer exists, but Psy.D. programs sprang up all over the country, and some of them—such as the Los Angeles branch of the California School of Professional Psychology— even obtained state and American Psychological Association accreditation to switch from granting a Psy.D. to granting a Ph.D. The finding that research training and competence were unrelated to effectiveness as a therapist received stronger and stronger research support, so that derogating research-based practice—as opposed to the "art" of psychotherapy—appeared appropriate to the profession. The fact that the research indicated that one's effectiveness as a therapist was unrelated to *any* professional training was ignored, especially when the question of whether to allow greater autonomy and status for the allied profession of psychiatric social work arose. People with Psy.D.'s became equal to those with Ph.D.'s within the profession through a phrase in most state licensing laws that required a Ph.D. from a program accredited by the APA "or equivalent training." The "fight" with the American Medical Association and the American Psychiatric Association to allow psychologists to be primary providers of mental health services was largely successful, perhaps in part by dint of sheer numbers. The original view that recipients of Psy.D.'s and now Ph.D.'s from professional schools were to function primarily as therapists was lost. These recipients now have equal impact with research-trained Ph.D.'s in influencing professional and public policy.[18]

Evolution continued along the same lines. The number of doctoral programs in clinical, counseling, and school psychology increased from about 250 in 1975 to almost 350 in 1989;[19] by 1979, about 25 percent of all doctorates awarded in clinical psychology were Psy.D.'s or Ph.D.'s from professional schools, and that percentage increased to 39 percent in 1987.[20] Starting in 1972, more degrees were awarded in the "health services provider" area than in the area of academic research, and by 1985 the ratio was almost three to one.[21]

During the expansion, the proportion of degrees in clinical, counseling, and school psychology granted by the institutions that a National Research Institute committee rated in the top 25 percent of graduate programs shrank from 37.5 percent in 1973 to 23.2 percent in 1983;[22] since this shrinkage was a consistent 1.4 percent per year unrelated to time, we can make a reasonable extrapolation to 13.2 percent in 1990. No exact figures are available, although Georgine M. Pion of Vanderbilt University—who has worked on many of the committees whose reports are cited here—gives a more optimistic estimate of "about 18–19% in 1987."[23] During that expansion, the rigor of the scientific training of practicing psychologists diminished. A person obtaining an advanced degree from an institution of lesser status does not *necessarily* receive poorer scientific training than one graduating from a place of higher status, or understand the scientific basis of psychology less well; there is a great deal of overlap in actual training and understanding. Nevertheless, proportions of psychology graduates from institutions of different status can be used as an indicator of quality and rigor of training. The figures, therefore, support the conclusions of Lee Sechrest of the University of Arizona, former head of its department, and a former president of the APA's division of clinical psychology:

Question: You have concerns about where psychology is headed. And yet every year thousands more psychologists are produced [with graduate degrees], most in applied areas.

Answer: One of the fundamental problems is that I don't think we are graduating thousands of psychologists. We are graduating thousands and thousands of practitioners who are peripherally acquaint-ed with the discipline of psychology.[24]

As we will see in Chapter 2, such peripheral acquaintance need not make for poor therapists. When, however, mental health practitioners in psychology present themselves as experts in legal proceedings, or in deciding whether child abuse actually occurred, or as in advising people about how to live, such peripheral acquaintance is a severe problem. The public trusts such experts on the assumption that they are applying valid psychological principles. But when the experts aren't even aware of these principles, their pronouncements are unsupported.

I know of no comparable changes in the quality of training for psy-chiatrists. Requirements of passing calculus, physics, biology, and organic chemistry for entrance to medical school have remained con-stant, however, and the first two years at most medical schools retain a highly academic ("scientific") curriculum. As one psychiatrist friend argues, biochemistry may not be nearly as important to psychiatric work as statistics would be, and much of the course work psychiatrists are required to take appears to be little more than drudgery. Such drudgery does, however, assure that the psychiatrists will have the intelligence and perseverance to succeed at these tough tasks. The topics they master may not be directly relevant to practice, but the qualities a person needs to master them may well be. Most of the major higher status graduate schools in psychology also require evi-dence of these qualities for admission, and their programs are intellec-tually demanding for students who intend to become professionals as well as for those who intend to enter research. Moreover, these pro-grams emphasize an approach to practice based on what is known sci-entifically.

Unfortunately, the lower status schools—*as a group*—do not emphasize research, and many of these professional schools select and train mainly on the basis of impressions of students' personal qualities. Graduates can emerge with little scientific training beyond a year's perfunctory course in statistics, centered mainly on how to enter data into a "canned" computer program. The APA has checklist require-ments for a program's accreditation, but satisfying such a list is a far cry from providing rigorous training. It is possible to argue that the individual is so complex, and human problems are so ineffable, and so on, that what therapists do is not amenable to scientific understanding—so that scientific understanding and training are irrelevant. But then there would be no justification for recognizing some people rather than others as having *scientific* expertise in the mental health professions, according them social status and pay on the basis of their purported application of scientific principles, or—most important— paying more attention to what they say than to what anyone else says.

There had been warnings of this situation. As far back as 1947, when the VA programs were just beginning to function, an APA committee on recommended training programs in clinical psychology wrote:

> It is important that this interest in research on the part of psychology continue, for as one surveys the scene the likelihood that the major burden of research will fall on the psychologist becomes clearer. If he [sic] permits himself to be drawn off into private therapeutic practice as has the psychiatrist, or into institutional therapeutic work as has the social worker, the outlook for research is dim in a field where the need is enormous. As had already been indicated, if a social need for therapy exists, then the need for research is even greater. The fact that there is not equal pressure for the latter is mainly due to the excusable but still short-sighted outlook of the public. The universities, with their more far-sighted orientation, *have a serious responsibility to develop research interests and abilities in the clinical psychologists they train.* The interest should be on research on the laws of human behavior primarily and on technical devices and therapy secondarily.[25] (italics added)

WHY RESEARCH AND RESEARCH TRAINING ARE SO IMPORTANT

One reason research training is so essential is that we do not know a great deal about the development and alleviation of emotional distress. Even in fields where we do know a great deal, research is essential to improving service. In gene therapy, for example, the noted researcher W. French Anderson urges caution in medical treatment: "Medicine is an inexact science; we still understand very little about how the human body works. Well-intentioned efforts at treatment with standard therapeutics can produce unexpected problems months or years later."[26] Anderson works, as do others in his field, with extreme caution and careful analysis of what is happening to patients undergoing gene therapy. But in the domain of psychological treatment we understand even less, and there are few "standard treatments," apart from drug therapy and social learning-oriented behavior modification.

It is possible to argue that since not much is known, evaluating psychological treatment should be equally vague and uncritical (a type of "characteristic matching," by which for years the yellowness of a root of a plant was interpreted as indicating that it might be beneficial in alleviating jaundice[27]). A more justifiable argument is that the less we know, the more scrupulous and careful we should be in applying and monitoring what we think we do know. That requires a knowledge of scientific methodology and a demand that conclusions rise to the challenge "show me"—a minimal requirement of science. One standard reply to this argument is to emphasize the *need* for mental health treatment, which leads to an implied ethic that "we (the intuitive "experts") must do *something*." But the very real need does not justify the pretense that the "something" we might wish to do— often, really "anything"—is necessarily valid or helpful, in the absence of evidence that it is in fact valid and helpful.

A second reason that research training is essential is that it is easy for people—everyone, not just therapists—to fool themselves into believing that they have great insight into the causes and alleviation of emotional distress. We believe that if we talk to people and get to know them "as individuals," we can understand them better than by using broad general principles and seeing how they should be applied. (Note that the latter is exactly the course pursued in general medicine, and there is empirical evidence that experts in physics and engineering pursue it as well.[28]) But the evidence indicates that this individualized understanding is often illusory. There is an apparent contradiction because in fact therapists who claim to have such individualized knowledge actually do help their clients. The contradiction is resolved by noting that the very same evidence that indicates that "insight" psychotherapy is effective does not reveal *why* it is effective; thus, somewhat paradoxically, the success of verbal therapy may not rely on the therapist's understanding of the client.

A third reason is that a commitment to rationality and scientific knowledge constrains the poorly trained and hence unskeptical professional from making extreme claims. Some of these claims are sheer nonsense—for example, a claim to be able to know what someone was thinking when she committed suicide, or to be able to tell within ten minutes whether someone has been sexually abused as a child on the basis of that person's general demeanor. Such claims are often believed. The Harvard professor who stated that he knew in his mind what Teresa Jackson's daughter was thinking in her mind when she committed suicide was allowed to testify as an expert in the Teresa Jackson child abuse trial, and Teresa Jackson was convicted. Many other mental health professionals claiming expertise are able—free of the constraints that an understanding of the evidence should provide—to testify whether a person was or was not "insane" during the commitment of a crime, not "insane" in the ordinary social sense of the term, which courts are as capable of judging as is anyone else, but in some supposedly scientific sense of the term. Moreover, the claims are often believed by the general public—often to the detriment of all involved. For example, the belief that schizophrenia and autism are due to a "schizophrenogenic" ("or iceberg") mother, who was unwilling to or incapable of providing the afflicted child with the affection required for normal development, has caused untold misery among the families of such disturbed children. How did that belief come about? From "clinical judgment," which was accepted because it is consistent with our "everyday intuitions." (Chapter 2 will detail the even more disturbing example of lobotomy as a "cure" for schizophrenia.)

One particularly pernicious result of the deemphasis on research has been a series of fads in the area of mental health. The most prevalent one as this book is written is an epidemic of diagnosing people as suffering from multiple personality disorder. This condition supposedly results from repressed child sexual abuse, or even from being raised by parents who practiced satanism—although belief in the existence of satanic cults (as opposed to belief in the KKK or the mafia) is based purely on "aided memories" of people in therapy or "support groups." (A well-publicized story of a satanic cult practice in Texas that led to ten murders was later retracted. It was a drug ring.)

To be sure, professional psychologists still *claim* that their practice is research based, whether or not it is in fact. In 1988, when the then-president of the APA was facing a revolt of research-oriented psychologists who threatened to form their own, research-based organization,[29] he said: "Our scientific base is what sets us apart from the social workers, the counselors, and the Gypsies."[30] And later: "The scientists are the jewels in our crown, and they will continue to be. So we're not going to give them up."[31]

CURRENT BUT UNJUSTIFIED SUCCESS

Having separated itself so far from its research base, how did professional psychology survive? One answer is through lobbying state and national governments for money and privilege. A great deal of money has been put into lobbying with positive results, which can be assessed by reading even randomly chosen issues of the APA *Executive Newsbulletin* or the *State Issues Forum.* Also, positive feedback arises from growth itself—just as the initial growth of VHS recordings led people to buy more VHS sets than Beta sets, which stimulated the growth of VHS recordings, and so on—even though the Beta technology may have been superior.[32] Moreover, salaries of professional psychologists are high, at least relative to salaries of research and academic psychologists. Finally, there is an intrinsic appeal to college seniors in doing "real clinical work" with "real people" after years of academic "preparation for life."

All these factors alone, however, cannot account for the successful growth of professional psychology. For example, lobbying pure and simple may have an effect when the numbers of people a lobby group represents is large relative to the individual legislator's entire constituency, or are "single-issue" oriented. But a hundred thousand professional psychologists and allied practitioners do not constitute such a group; they are geographically diffuse and hardly single-issue people.

Other lobbyists succeed by framing their issue in ways compatible with legislators' views of the world.[33] That is exactly what may account for the APA's lobbying success. Acceptance of what "authorities" claim about their own expertise is not a pathological syndrome, except at its extremes. Belief in authorities who really understand human life is therefore natural to us all. Haven't I myself cited Kelly and Sechrest as authorities? Moreover, as we will see in Chapter 7, authorities claim to be able to "explain" the individual life course, an ability that we all believe we have; yet research findings show that neither the authorities nor the rest of us can do this well, which may surprise the readers of the *New York Review of Books* as much as readers of *People* magazine. An observer cannot explain "why" people do what they do, and people themselves are often aware only of their after-the-fact rationalizations; few take careful notes based on "think aloud" ruminations at the time they make major decisions in their lives, and even if they did, many important factors influencing their behavior would not be included.

More specifically, professional psychologists and other mental health professionals employing the same procedures make the same "attribution errors" in their explanations that we all tend to make—overemphasizing the role of personality as opposed to situational factors in influencing the behavior of others, while simultaneously overemphasizing situational factors as opposed to personality in influencing our own behavior. We readily believe that when other people behave in ways we don't like, it's because they are "sick," but that when we behave in ways we don't like, it's due to the lousy home environment in which we were raised. That leads to the final impact of the claims of professional psychologists. They end up agreeing with the rest of us! Such agreement, of course, implies that they agree with each other as well, and then they can cite each other as additional authority figures.

FORENSIC PSYCHOLOGY WITH "PORTRAITS"

Let me illustrate these problems by an analysis of the presidential speech to the American Psychological Association at its 1990 convention.[34] The president who made it is a leading forensic psychologist. Although his presidential address was not delivered until 1990, he was the president who preceded the one who referred to the "jewel in the crown." His speech is a defense of psychological assessment in court settings. He makes many good points at the beginning when he discusses the presentation of results from well-standardized and validated tests. For example, the highest subtest score on an overall IQ test of someone subsequently brain-damaged cannot be used as an index of how well that person functioned prior to the damage. (Perfectly normal people as well will have some subtest scores higher than others, so that their highest score cannot be taken as a measure of their overall IQ, which is assessed by their average score.) He also stresses the importance of the reliabilities and validities (predictive accuracies) of the measures used.

Toward the end of the speech, however, the president pushes his own use of what he terms *psychological portraits* in court settings, by which he means detailed descriptions of a person's psychological functioning. First, he points out that the research evidence evaluating categorical judgments of professional clinicians yields negative results: "Research published much earlier showed that the type of one- or two-word differential diagnosis, characterizations, and predictions then extant were judged to be lacking in validity (Meehl, 1954, 1956, 1957). Reviews of more current studies (Dawes, Faust and Meehl, 1989), including an excellent recent update of the use of one's head instead of formulas (Kleinmuntz, 1990), reaffirm that conclusion."[35] He then dismisses such judgments in favor of what he terms "valid psychological assessment (portrait) findings."[36]

His evidence for their validity is two extreme cases. One is of a twenty-one-year-old woman who scored at the ninety-eighth percentile in aptitude tests and was Phi Beta Kappa in college. She subsequently suffered a serious head injury in an automobile accident and thereafter tested in the mentally defective range (third percentile) on intelligence tests. The other case he cites is of a man whose intellectual abilities were totally unchanged after exposure to neurotoxins in a workplace. (Not surprisingly, everyone involved agreed with the president's expert professional testimony that the first person had suffered extensive impairment as the result of brain damage while the second hadn't.) Using these extreme instances, he goes on to conclude that: "when such assessment is done well, it is patently obvious to all involved (i.e., juries, judges, and attorneys for *both* plaintiff and defense) that what such a psychologist-expert-witness concluded was valid (true) within the reasonable degree of certainty required in such litigation"[37] (italics in the original). Actually, however, he has made the reverse argument: Because it is patently obvious, it must be true. In other words, his claim that his judgment is valid is supported by the fact that everyone agrees with it, that is, by the lack of a need for his judgment—because the same judgment can be made without him. He misses the point that valid expert testimony in a court should be about matters that untrained judges and juries *cannot* evaluate without assistance.

He further supports his assertions by invoking social approval of such expert testimony: "in this regard, psychology is little different from medicine, engineering, or other professions. That is, professions in which practitioners (artisans) are judged by society to be valid (usable) for many services, despite the absence of the necessary research, primarily on the basis that common experience (of legislators, professional peers, patients, clients, and others) suggests some utility from their services."[38]

He has it backward. We trust engineers because we trust engineering and believe that engineers are trained to apply valid principles of engineering; moreover, we have evidence every day that these principles are valid when we observe airplanes flying. We trust doctors because we trust modern medicine, and we have evidence that it works when antibiotics and operations cure people. We do not, or at least should not, believe in the validity of a field as the result of first trusting a practitioner of it—and then concluding that "if she believes in it, it must be valid." There is enough history of wrongly trusting "professions" (like astrology, and the racial analyses of Nazi "scientists") that mere trust is not evidence of validity. An enlightened view demands a basis for trust. This president supplies none.

Most distressing of all, however, the president dismisses findings from research that has actually been conducted, and instead cites mere *hypothetical* findings from research that has yet to be conducted. As he himself points out, the research doesn't support his assertions: "They [Faust and Ziskin] correctly quote my belief that currently there is no body of research that indicates that assessment across the whole domain is valid or other than clinical art."[39] But he continues: "It is my hope that empirical research on such state-of-the-art psychological assessment will soon be undertaken. When it is, I firmly believe that research will reveal that acceptable levels of validity do now exist for these modern comprehensive psychological assessments and that it will serve as the requisite empirical basis for consensual agreement regarding the validity of such expert opinions currently being reached by attorneys for both the plaintiff and defendant for that subset of cases that I know first hand are being settled without going to court."[40]

But suppose his hope is not realized, and future research either is not done or does not reveal acceptable levels of validity? Moreover, there is little reason to believe that an overall judgment will have much validity when the components on which it is based have none, which in this context even the speaker himself admits. Then what? Are he and his colleagues to return to all the courts in which they have testified, apologize, and request new hearings for those involved? This approach to practice embraces a principle that I find unacceptable: Earn now, learn later—if at all. Compare this philosophy with the philosophy of extreme caution expressed by W. French Anderson, in the context of gene therapy about which a lot more is known already.

But the president presents the "portraits" anyway. Professional psychologists and other mental health experts are often willing to testify, and they have a profound impact on others' lives in the absence of any evidence that what they do is valid. Their supportive evidence is simply hypothesized, while negative evidence that has actually been collected is ignored. This form of reasoning can be termed *arguing from a vacuum*, because what is purported to be true is supported not by direct evidence but by attacking an alternative possibility. As we will see throughout this book, mental health professionals repeatedly argue from a vacuum to justify their practices.

The American people certainly deserve to have professional mental health experts in the court system only *after* evidence of their accuracy has been supplied, *not before*. We should demand more convincing arguments than this APA president presents. Lacking such evidence, he and his colleagues should be thrown out of court. But their licensing has allowed them in court, and the justification for their presence is based on exactly the type of arguments he presents. Unfortunately, these arguments are persuasive to many people, even though careful examination shows them to imply evidence that simply doesn't exist—the vacuum. They appeal to our uncritical intuitions. They sell. It is my hope that this book will convince the reader not to buy them.

BUT THE SCIENCE EXISTS, ELSEWHERE

The fact that the president cannot point to studies supporting his position does not imply that research psychologists have not conducted literally thousands of studies that have led to a "science of psychology." First, much progress in psychological knowledge has been in the areas of physiology, perception, thinking, judgment, behavioral control, and social beliefs, attitudes, and interactions.[41] Achievements are not limited to theoretical understanding but have applied uses as well. Many of these uses are so common that we do not even think of them as involving "social science": aptitude tests and public opinion polling are examples. These advancements may not have uniformly good consequences, but neither do those in other sciences, like nuclear bombs and medical devices that promote overpopulation and prolong life in a vegetative state or one of unrelenting and extreme pain. Aptitude tests that predict success in a racist environment may be used for racist selection to that environment; public opinion polls that accurately reflect voter sentiment may lead politicians to become subservient to that sentiment rather than do what they believe is right or strive to change that sentiment in a desirable direction. Nevertheless, aptitude tests do predict, opinion polls do reflect public sentiment, of course, on a statistical rather than a certain basis.

In psychology, however, knowledge that does cumulate, cumulates slowly. We do know some things about some conditions. We know that phobias and specific anxieties are not simply symptoms of a "deeper" disturbance, and hence that they can be addressed directly through behavioral means without the emergence of new symptoms. We know there is a strong genetic component in schizophrenia[42] and alcoholism.[43] The general wisdom based on actual scientific *studies* is that mild or moderate depression is best treated by a combination of behavioral, cognitive and drug approaches,[44] although evidence is accumulating that cognitive styles of blaming oneself for failure and crediting "luck" for success play a vital role in depression.[45] (We cannot be yet certain, however, that helping people to get over depressive symptoms as quickly as possible will be beneficial in the long term, in part because judgments of what is valuable or beneficial in life cannot be made on the basis of the standard categories for mental health or illness.)

Psychology has also developed a number of effective measurement devices and ways to predict future behavior. These devices are of the type that can be administered without much training, however, and do not require doctoral-level skill to interpret. Moreover, the best predictions are made on the basis of past overt behavior. It's not that people don't change—they do, sometimes profoundly. Rather, no personal skill has yet been developed—or assessment instrument devised—that allows us to predict who will change, when, and how.

Ironically, the reasons for this invalidity may be found in another area of psychological research—in human judgment and decision making. That area investigates people's systematic biases in making judgments and reaching decisions.[46] (These biases are covered in Chapters 3 and 4 of this book.) Such biases are particularly strong *either when judgments are made in the absence of a well-validated scientific theory or when they are evaluated without systematic feedback about how good they are.* Unfortunately both those conditions characterize the art of clinical prediction in professional psychology. These biases lead not only to invalid judgments of the type the APA president claims to be invalid but to an inference that the type of "portrait" judgments he espouses will be invalid as well. One particular problem stems from reliance on retrospective memory in the self-evaluation of judgmental accuracy when no careful records are kept or no scientific comparisons made. Retrospective memory is not only kind but also "makes sense" out of both the past itself,[47] for example, that if one is depressed, one's parents have been aloof, uncaring, and demanding, and our thoughts about past events and predictions made from them, for example, that "I knew it would happen all along"—even when past evidence indicates a contrary prediction was made.[48] Consequently, it systematically distorts the past and our past judgments in a way that makes the course of events appear to have been predictable and our judgments appear to have been good. The research supporting this generalization is so strong that editors of the National Academy of Sciences reports summarizing advances in psychology (see note 41) specifically exclude studies and "evidence" based on retrospective memory as providing nothing of scientific value.

It is precisely the biased judgments associated with lack of a well-validated theory, lack of systematic feedback, and reliance on retrospective memory that leads to what David Faust, himself a clinical psychologist, terms "the delusions of clinical psychology."[49]

STATISTICAL GENERALIZATION IN PSYCHOLOGICAL STUDIES

Some "scientific" studies in the mental health area involve experimental comparisons (see Chapter 2). Others are "correlational" studies in which factors vary and investigators examine the relationships between them. The critical difference between experimental and correlational studies is that in the former the investigator *manipulates* conditions, in as systematic a manner as possible, and observes what happens as a result—while in the latter the investigator allows conditions and results to vary naturally. Both types have passed the scrutiny of journal reviewers, whose rate of rejecting articles for publication generally ranges from 60 percent to over 90 percent.

All these studies have another characteristic in common: They report statistically stable trends and influences. None report results whose level of certitude approaches that of results in what people generally regard as established science. In the established science of medicine, for example, we have a fairly certain idea of what will happen if a cancer goes untreated, if an appendix bursts, or if an HIV infection establishes itself in the bloodstream. Such knowledge is probabilistic only in the sense that there will be a few exceptions—an occasional spontaneous remission of a well-diagnosed cancer, a rare benign response to peritonitis when a sac forms immediately around the infection, or an extremely slow progression from HIV infection to AIDS. The treatment of such conditions is less certain than the diagnosis—although its efficacy can be monitored in a way that provides fairly certain knowledge of what is happening, if not of the ultimate longevity of the patient. Other less certain knowledge lies "on the frontiers" of medicine. Similarly, we know enough about physics, astronomy and engineering to have experienced only two disasters in our manned space programs, although we do not know enough to be at all certain of the origins of the universe, a subject of much debate.

In psychology, however, we do not have this base of fairly certain knowledge. Even when we are fairly certain of a principle, its application remains probabilistic. Moreover, psychological principles themselves are established on a probabilistic basis. A cursory scanning of a successful empirical investigation indicates that it establishes at best only a "reliable" or "significant" statistical trend. A more careful reading indicates that this trend is established in a context of a great deal of variability. "Reliability," in psychology, means simply that we have good statistical reasons to believe this trend would be replicated if a similar experimental study or observational investigation were conducted in a context not too different from the study that originally established the trend. "Significant" means simply that we have reason to believe that the trend did not arise on a chance basis. (Ironically, the way we establish "significance" is to assume that only chance variation is operating, then prove that under those circumstances it is unlikely that we would have obtained a result as strong as the one we actually obtained. A phrase like "significant at the 1 in 1000 level" means simply that if the results were due to random processes, we would obtain a result as strong as the one we actually obtained only one time in a thousand.)

A further analysis of scientific studies of mental health practice indicates that there is always more unexplained variation in the results than there is variation that can be explained by the trend we believe the study has supported. Thus, when we assert that there is genetic influence in certain mental disorders, the basis of our assertion is that we can predict these disorders on the basis of genetic factors more reliably than we could on the basis of chance fluctuation. For example, studies find that the incidence of alcoholism is related to the alcoholism of the biological parents of children who have been adopted and is unrelated to the alcoholism of the children's adoptive parents. That does not mean that a child with an alcoholic biological parent, or even two, is more likely than not to become an alcoholic. Far from it—most children of alcoholic biological parents do *not* become alcoholics themselves. The study's conclusions mean simply that there's a trend, involving genetic constitution. Even in the face of well-established statistical trends, a child of alcoholic biological parents is most likely to turn out normal. The same result is found for children of schizophrenic parents, even though they are more likely to become schizophrenic than are people whose parents are not schizophrenic. In this context of variability (technically termed "unexplained variance"), about the closest we can come to making a prediction that a particular person will have a particular disorder is that identical twins of a schizophrenic individual have about a 50 percent chance of suffering from schizophrenia themselves.

The same principle of finding more unexplained variability than variability explained by an established trend also characterizes studies of the alleviation of emotional distress. We just don't know all that much about the causes of emotional distress, which is not to say that if we stick with what we do know, we cannot help people. When, for example, we find a trend that behavioral approaches are better at helping people overcome phobias than psychoanalytic ones, someone who is phobic would be well advised to try behavioral rather than psychoanalytic therapy—even though the differences in success rate are not great, and a particular individual might actually be better off with psychoanalysis. (Knowing which people would be better off with psychoanalysis would require further research—which might or might not yield positive results.) This unexplained variability is preponderant, and it is important to understand its existence. It is, in fact, the basis for a common argument from a vacuum that some psychologists make: "Because the research results indicate a great deal of uncertainty about what to do, my expert judgment can do better in prescribing treatment than these results." This judgment is then claimed to have "arisen from experience," without any evidence that the judgment yields more certainty than careful studies indicate is there. (In fact, such judgments that are opposed to research findings do worse; see Chapter 3.)

The statistical nature of generalizations in psychology and other social sciences can be masked by study conclusions indicating high reliability and significance. Both these factors are, however, a joint function of the effect size and the sample size in a given study.[50] Consider a hypothetical medical finding, based on a study of two samples of 10,000 people, that those who eat bacon at least once every two weeks have twice the rate of some dire consequence than do those who don't eat bacon—and that this finding is "highly significant." First, we don't know whether the two rates themselves are quite high or quite low in proportion to the general population, a result that is absolutely crucial to our decision about whether to enjoy eating bacon. Even if the rates are presented, however, they might be quite inconsequential for our decision making. For example, 8 dire consequences in the bacon-eating group (for a rate of 8/10,000 = .0008) versus 2 in the other group (for a rate of 2/10,000 = .0002) would yield a ratio of 4 to 1, a result of boardline significance. But we might not care much about a rate of .0008. (We have a 1-in-50,000 chance of being seriously injured or killed *every time* we go on an automobile trip.[51]) On the other hand, if the number of dire consequences were 10,000 (for a rate of 1.0) in the bacon-eating group and 2,500 (for a rate of .25) in the other, we might care a great deal about the rates.

It is important to keep in mind that even effects that are proudly proclaimed to be "highly significant" may be slight. It is especially important to keep that in mind when psychologists and their publicists tout results that have serious implications about life and desirable ways of living. One researcher group states that "it is generally accepted that a positive view of the self and positive mood state are necessary for adaptation and for persistence toward goals."[52] This statement is based on results of multiple studies that indicate a positive statistical relationship. But those findings do not imply that no one adapts, persists, or succeeds without being positive; some people may actually succeed because they believe that whatever they are trying to achieve is extremely valuable, or because they believe that putting forth the effort is the "right thing to do" or the only thing to do. (The term *necessary* in the foregoing quote is unfortunate, in my view.) In fact, the authors of this study themselves, in another section of the same paper, discuss the effects of unanticipated success,[53] which would be almost impossible if the former statement were interpreted to mean that feeling positive about an endeavor is absolutely necessary for its success.

Given all the variability in "the science of mental health and illness," responsible assertions must be of a ceteris paribus nature. Despite claims that pervade the popular media, for example, there is absolutely no scientific evidence that feeling good about oneself is a *necessary* condition for engaging in desirable behavior. Nor is there any evidence that feeling bad about oneself is *necessary* for engaging in undesirable behavior. There is a statistical correlation—that's all. But we are not even sure how to interpret that correlation. The behavior might lead to the feelings, or *vice versa*; or the influence behavior has on feelings might explain the whole correlation. Moreover, the correlation could change as people's beliefs and attitudes change, or even as their beliefs about how to interpret the same correlation change.

More important, the uncertainty of knowledge and its application in the mental health area means that *responsible professionals should practice with a cautious, open, and questioning attitude.* "Knowing" within ten minutes from the way a client walks that she was an incest victim as a child can easily lead a psychologist to ask questions that suggest to her that she must have been a victim. This suggestion in turn can lead the client to reinterpret inaccurately recalled instances of benign behavior toward her as indicative of abuse, which can lead her to conclude that abuse occurred when it didn't—perhaps based on a fully reconstructed memory of such abuse. That belief can lead the client to be alienated from her family and to adopt a stance of incompetence in the face of her own "recalled" childhood traumas. The resulting distress reinforces the therapist's conclusion that the client has suffered greatly from her childhood trauma, which she must now "live through"—occasionally with more improbable and bizarre details added—before she can function as an adult. "Authoritative" beliefs and statements about particular individuals are inappropriate and—because they are so often wrong—can be harmful. Those who seek the services of psychologists should be wary of any professionals who do not proceed cautiously.

Experts in court in particular should point out the statistical nature of psychological generalizations rather than paint a "portrait" of an individual or make causal statements about what led to what in an individual's life. Such causal statements are particularly common in civil suits, because the courts often demand proof of psychological harm. Psychological harm may be every bit as devastating as physical harm, but the question is how to establish it. To assess physical harm, we have well-validated theories about how the individual human body works and techniques for establishing malfunction—such as X-rays and blood tests—that transcend the self-report and behavior of victims. In contrast, to assess psychological harm, the evidence consists of the behavior and self-report of the victim, and the intuitive "art" of the examining psychologist or psychiatrist.

Does that mean we cannot assess psychological harm, even if it is considerable? No. In civil suits concerning exposure to harmful substances, we use statistical analyses to establish that the substances "caused" harm. We make an inference *from* the aggregate, such as an increase in the cancer rate of those exposed, *to* the individual, that is, to his or her cancer. In litigation about such exposure no responsible expert witness would claim to be able to tell exactly what led the particular victim's cancer to develop, or why it developed in one area of the body rather than another. Rather, he or she would testify based on these inferences from the aggregate. Similarly, a responsible psychologist or psychiatrist could cite statistical knowledge—saying "in general . . ."—and let the court apply the same rules for determining harm that it does in medical areas where the evidence is statistical rather than concrete.

Unfortunately, as indicated by the forensic psychologist's presidential address, that type of testimony is not what courts accept from professional psychologists, and it is not what professional psychologists present. Instead, a psychologist will most likely present a mythic statement about what caused what for the individual being evaluated, which will often be disputed by a professional psychologist on the other side. If the expert is not very persuasive in court, or if the opposition's expert is more persuasive, then what? Since the judgment is at best dubious in the first place, style of presentation may become of utmost importance.

ADVICE ABOUT HOW TO LIVE

Professional psychologists not only claim to have expertise they don't have, they claim to have insight into how people should think, feel, and behave. For example, the APA president who referred to the "jewel in the crown" stated in the fall of 1988, "We are all teachers. I think my clients see me as primarily a teacher. We have taught the whole culture. We didn't invent the woman's movement, but we have been among its most ardent supporters. I would like to get away from the medical model entirely. Our job is to bring knowledge to the world."[54] We can well ask what it is that professional psychologists have to teach. Without the "medical model," with its presumed expertise, what is left in mental health? The answer might be scientific knowledge. But the practice of professional psychologists is often *not* based on scientific knowledge, in fact flies in the face of such knowledge. What then do psychologists have to teach?

The answer is a belief system. Under the guise of advancing "positive" mental health—which certainly sounds fine and is consequently hard to oppose—the profession of psychology has propounded a simplistic philosophy of life. This philosophy maintains that the purpose of life is to maximize one's mental health, which is dependent wholly on self-esteem. Some psychologists, like Shelley Taylor, have "discovered" that self-esteem is more important even than realism: "Every theory of mental health" she asserts, "considers a positive self-concept to be the cornerstone of a healthy ego."[55] If the point of life is to maximize self-esteem, it follows that a positive self-concept is everything.

Thus, love, lust, friendship, doing the "right thing," accomplishment, leaving the world a little better or worse place than one found it, even behavior itself are all of importance only insofar as they impact mental health, which equals self-esteem. A wonderful person who does not happen to think particularly well of herself or himself (for whatever reason, such as a religiously based modesty or an absence of pride) is a failure. A conceited ass, in contrast, has good mental health. (The claim is made that such a person must be lacking in self-esteem *somewhere*—or there would be no need to be a conceited ass. Where that lack lies, however, is not specified. Once again, the argument from a vacuum.)

Part II of this book, which discusses the implications of this unidimensional view of life, is a bit speculative. The question of how much professional psychologists have to teach the rest of the population, outside the "medical model" domain, is basically one of value. While I personally do not accept the positivistic dichotomy of "fact" versus "value" as absolute,[56] it is nevertheless clear (to me, anyway) that a clinical view of life—even one that addresses the causes of psychological distress—cannot lead to conclusions about what constitutes a good life, any more than the fact that someone lived to age ninety-five without a single physical problem prior to a thirty-second heart attack implies that this person led a fulfilling or good life. Did Abraham Lincoln or Winston Churchill always think well of themselves? Not all psychological suffering is necessarily bad. People used to believe that "spiritual crises" could lead to greater understanding and maturity. A value-laden view, however, is simply defined out of existence by the teacher who advises us to do whatever is possible to maximize our mental health.

Unfortunately, this "maximize mental health" view also has some very negative impacts, both direct and indirect. The psychological analysis of the individual life—at least as it is currently practiced—often misses what is important in that life. Other qualities may be more important than freedom from conflict, distress, or self-doubt—or even from a well-recognized symptom of mental illness. Yet today "ill" people are treated with a paternalistic contempt, to the point that when such a person leads a remarkable life—as did Bertha Pappenheim, who was Joseph Breuer's and Sigmund Freud's patient "Anna O."—all they did that is admirable is explained, or rather explained away, in terms of their illness or their adaptation to the ill-ness.[57] "Mental illness is just like any other illness," like an ulcer, per-haps, but someone labeled as mentally ill is best advised not to tell others, because such "illness" carries a stigma. In fact, a plethora of mental health "experts" have to a large extent convinced the public that whether or not one is emotionally distressed can actually *define* whether or not one is a good person or is leading a desirable life.

Psychologists' contempt for the individual autonomy of their own clients can also be seen in their explanations of the lives of everyone else. They explain social problems in psychological terms, often to the detriment of solving or ameliorating them; it is the poor self-image of the impoverished American child that leads to a lack of academic skills, we are told, not the fact that these skills are taught for roughly half the number of hours per year in American schools than they are taught in a country such as Japan.[58] Mental illness is used to explain the problem of impoverished and homeless Americans, even though the broadest possible definition of mental illness would classify at most only one-third of them as "mentally ill."[59]

One result of the prevalence of these unwarranted assertions and theorizing has been to weaken people's trust in their own autonomy, in their own abilities to deal with the problems they confront in life. Once such belief is weakened, it is necessary to provide people with compensation in some way. One form of compensation is to encour-age them to have positive illusions to enhance their self-esteem (see Chapter 9). Without such illusions, people are supposedly so childlike that they could not function in the face of the uncertainties of the world (again, the derogation of autonomy). I will propose at the end of this book (Chapter 10) that we are actually a lot freer than the pro-nouncements of professional psychologists would have us believe we are, that we can decide what to do in our own lives, and that autono-my grows by exercising it. We do have choice. It is perfectly possible to function without illusions—and it must be kept in mind that the "teachers'" claims involve statistical generalizations about things as they are, not as they could be.

AND FINALLY, DRUGS

Another compensation that mental health professionals provide is drugs—again, to make people "feel good," as if that were a necessary condition for improving their lives. (The claim that people "need" drugs because they haven't solved their problems before taking them is another argument from a vacuum.) I am not talking only about the illegal street drugs—which at least make people high, or sometimes euphoric—but the psychoactive drugs that are now so commonly used in mental health practice to calm people. Sometimes these drugs are useful, even though they attack an individual's autonomy; there are certainly times when autonomy is a secondary concern. But at other times, they have led to such severe debilitation that autonomy became impossible, as when patients develop *tardive dyskinesia* (uncontrollable shaking, which can be permanent) as a result of using neuroleptic drugs. (The estimated rate of tardive dyskinesia is 10 to 40 percent, depending on length of use and age of patient[60]). Drugs can also be addictive. They must be used with great care, and the burden of proof that they are needed lies with the person advocating their use, not with the person who argues against or resists that use.

Currently, drug prescription is controlled by the medical profession. Psychiatrists, not psychologists, prescribe drugs, although many psychiatrists do so on the basis of recommendations by psychologists. The medical community, for its part, at least recognizes that drugs should be prescribed with great care, although physicians often do not exercise such care (as indicated by current concerns about the overprescription of drugs for the elderly in nursing homes). For several years now, the top priority of the professional groups within the APA has been to obtain drug prescription privileges for clinical psychologists. That is to say, exactly those people (represented by the APA's "practice directorate" and an advisory group called the Association for Professional Practice) who mistakenly believe that they can make valid judgments on the basis of "my experience" are the ones who now want prescription privileges. Of course, they want the profession to require that graduate students take some courses in psychopharmacology, but certainly not full medical training since it is not *directly* relevant.

Because there are so many more clinical psychologists than clinical psychiatrists, success in this endeavor could quite literally glut the country with people giving out drugs and people living under their influence. The major APA spokesperson claims that extending prescription privileges to psychologists would actually reduce the amount of drug prescription. Aside from containing the contradictory premises that drugs are both good (so more people should be allowed to prescribe them) and bad (reducing prescriptions would be a good thing), the argument that drug prescriptions will be lessened by radically increasing the number of people who make money by prescribing them might most kindly be termed naive.

There are critics who believe that psychologists should not obtain prescription privileges. Jeffrey Rubin, for one, points to the potentially devastating side effects of drugs currently in use.[61] One psychologist's response to Rubin is to proclaim the problem "exaggerated" because drugs can be "safe and effective when used properly."[62] That sounds fine, but what isn't safe and effective "when used properly"? Exactly how are these drugs to be "used properly"—and how is the person prescribing them to know they are still being "used properly"? (For example, tardive dyskinesia often isn't evident until the neuroleptic drugs are withdrawn.) The "proper use" answer is vacuous without a specification of *what constitutes proper use*—a research question.

Furthermore, why is it so incredibly important to ameliorate or stop the symptoms that these drugs address immediately—if even at the expense of stupefying the patient? Here a value-laden answer is once again disguised as a "clinical" one, with the assertion that the drugs are "necessary." Certainly, patients should be allowed to choose to risk the side effects if symptom alleviation is of sufficient importance to them. But how many patients are given that choice? The decision is made for them in the vast majority of instances, especially for people in institutions.

The push for drug prescription privileges continues, however—and with some success. Professional psychologists are now permitted to prescribe psychoactive drugs to people in the military and to Native Americans receiving services from the Bureau of Indian Affairs.[63] As the title of an article in the *APA Monitor* proudly stated: "On privileges issue, field is tilting to 'yes.'"[64] If nothing else, I hope this book will tilt the field in the other direction, at least for psychologists.

CHAPTER 2

PSYCHOTHERAPY

The Myth of Expertise

I had therapy cases I just botched, and yet they got better. Other cases I did great, and yet the patient deteriorated. I wondered what was going on here.

—Lee Sechrest[1]

Psychotherapy works overall in reducing psychologically painful and often debilitating symptoms. The reasons it works are unclear, because entirely different approaches may work equally well for the same problem or set of problems. Recovery is a *base rate* phenomenon. That is, in predicting the likelihood that a particular individual will recover, we can do little better than by predicting from the overall rate of recovery; we have no insight into exactly why some people get better while others don't. We do, however, know something about psychotherapist characteristics that make it work. Therapists in verbally oriented therapies, we know, should be "empathetic," while those using primarily behavioral techniques should have some knowledge of behavioral principles.

We also know that *the credentials and experience of the psychotherapists are unrelated to patient outcomes*, based on well over five hundred scientific studies of psychotherapy outcome. In fact, it is partly because psychotherapy in its multitude of forms is generally effective that I am writing this book. Having it more generally available is socially desirable.

THE NEED FOR SCIENTIFIC STUDIES TO EVALUATE EFFICACY

The scientific evaluation of psychotherapy is a fairly recent activity. The profession's own resistance to evaluating itself stemmed partly from its psychoanalytic origins. Freud's basic idea was that distressing psychological symptoms result from "the return of the repressed" in a debilitating form (*not* from repression per se). Adults defend against unacceptable needs, wishes, and feelings—which in childhood may have been quite conscious—and keep them from consciousness by means of "defense mechanisms," which are themselves unconscious, specifically, an unconscious part of the "ego." If during childhood these defense mechanisms are not well constructed, or if certain experiences such as sexual seduction by an adult or persistent fantasies about it make it particularly difficult for the developing person to prevent these needs, thoughts, and wishes from impacting him or her, they may express themselves as psychiatric symptoms. For example, Freud's patient "Dora's" coughing fits were thought to express both her wish to engage in oral sex with her father (perhaps after observing him engaging in that activity with his mistress) and her revulsion at the wish.[2] (Freud, ever the Victorian moralist, believed that the father's engaging in oral sex provided conclusive proof that he was impotent, which supported Freud's further conclusion that some hereditary constitutional factors were involved in the development of neurotic symptoms.)

Only through prolonged psychoanalytic sessions leading to a "transference" to the therapist of the patient's childhood reactions to parents and other significant adults can the defense mechanisms, and the impulses they are attempting to keep from consciousness, be understood. The therapist is extremely passive during psychoanalytic sessions, both to encourage this transference and to avoid premature "interpretations" of either the defenses or the needs; premature interpretations would lead to a "resistance" from the patient that would discourage rather than encourage insight. With eventual insight comes an ability to "sublimate" the unacceptable impulses in socially constructive ways (sublimation itself being a type of defense mechanism). Such sublimation can occur without the help of a therapist or psychoanalyst; for example, when the modern psychiatrist George Vaillant[3] discussed the men whose lives he followed in terms of the "maturity" of their defense mechanisms, sublimation was considered the pinnacle. Unlike Freud, Vaillant concluded that defense mechanisms evolve throughout adult life as well as childhood, and that final maturity cannot be well predicted from earlier life. An example of sublimation, according to Vaillant, was a man he studied who had channeled his rather intense anger into productive political activity and writing.

This psychoanalytic approach takes a long time ("interminable" according to some of its critics). Moreover, if a symptom is directly addressed before the patient is able to deal with it effectively, the theory runs, a new symptom will appear in its place, because the "basic issue" remains unresolved. The term used was *symptom substitution.* Subsequently, studies indicated that contrary to Freudian theory, symptom substitution did *not* generally occur. Another claim was that only the therapist—and perhaps eventually the patient—could understand the true nature of the patient's problems and their possible resolution and evaluate the efficacy of the process.

Let me share an anecdote that illustrates this claim. In 1966 (when I had joint appointments at the Ann Arbor VA Hospital and in the psychology department at the University of Michigan), a former colleague at the hospital, Dr. Lawrence J. Bookbinder, was investigating the use of behavioral techniques to alleviate some of the more distressing psychological symptoms that the psychiatric patients suffered. One afternoon in the coffee shop of the psychology department, I discussed Bookbinder's work with two professors who were considered central to the department's clinical program. They agreed that there was no evidence of symptom substitution in these patients, but they made the remarkable assertion that the mere elimination of symptoms is irrelevant to the question of whether a patient is "cured." I argued that being freed of a really debilitating symptom would lead to an enhanced quality of life that in turn could alleviate other psychological problems. For example, many of the men at the hospital suffered from impotence, and the inability to have a good sex life was very painful to them. I was about to stress the importance of positive feedback among different symptoms, between symptoms and feelings, and so on. But my senior colleagues interrupted. It didn't matter whether a man was actually impotent or not, they said. What was important was the total meaning for that man of impotence as such. That meaning could be assessed only through prolonged therapy; the actual physical fact of regaining sexual potency would be important only if it resulted from the transference process and greater self-understanding. In fact, it didn't even matter whether the impotence went away at all, they said, as long as the transference was successful. Only a truly expert therapist could evaluate whether it had been successful.

It is indeed very difficult to "get inside" someone else to determine unambiguously whether that person has benefited from any form of psychotherapy. But eliminating a symptom that is of crucial concern to the client really does matter. I agree with Hans Strupp that "a global judgment of [psychotherapy] outcome, which is analogous to a still photograph of an object in motion, must always remain exceedingly difficult and elusive" and that outcome judgments are "contingent on *values* placed on human behavior." But it is exactly a value-laden outcome for which the client (or insurance company, or government) is paying. Procedures—whether they are medical techniques or social programs—must be evaluated on the basis of certain indicators like blood pressure or infant mortality rate that nonetheless do not in and of themselves tell us the "whole story." A perfect one-to-one relationship between observable indicators and the global process in which we are interested is difficult to establish, but not having one available should not be used as an excuse to avoid evaluating what is happening by assessing these indicators. As Eugene Meehan points out, these indicators must be chosen wisely; infant mortality rates cannot be used to evaluate the quality of nursing home care to use his example.[5] But we must insist that a procedure such as psychotherapy be assessed in a way that allows the outside observer to reach a conclusion about its effectiveness. In psychotherapy, symptom remission is a prime candidate for such an indicator, as it is in medicine. What medical doctor would proclaim a patient "cured" without relief of painful symptoms? In fact, after my conversation in the coffee shop, the studies that have been conducted used symptom remission as the primary criterion of cure or improvement.

These studies are very important simply by virtue of the fact that they involve outside observers evaluating the efficacy of psychotherapy. The philosophy that only the individual therapist can tell whether improvement in a client has occurred is flawed. In the first place, the unsystematic judgment of a therapist is as subject to bias as is the unsystematic judgment of anyone else, including clients. The problems of unsystematic judgment are well documented, especially those of retrospective memory. Therapists, thoroughly committed to a profession—and perhaps to a particular technique—may well be "the last to know" when their efforts are ineffective. In the second place, evaluation without involving the patient's own feelings and behavior (that is, symptoms) ignores lessons from the history of mental health treatment. Mental patients were long treated in a cruel and unusual manner when practitioners disregarded their protestations that they did not want a "treatment" thrust on them; only later did the practitioners conclude in hindsight that many of these treatments were indeed poor or cruel. "Treatment" has included the use of chains, scalding baths, lobotomies, insulin shock, and now narcoleptics that can lead to tardive dyskinesia. Given this history, mental health professionals should be extremely careful before deciding that a treatment is "effective." The current approach is, as we know, much more enlightened—just as every previous generation knew that its approach was much more enlightened than previous ones. This conclusion is valid only when based on evidence.

It is even possible that treatments are biased by two attitudes that psychologists themselves hold but don't want to admit even to themselves: They don't like what the emotionally disturbed do and want to distance themselves from them. These attitudes could well bias psychologists' unsystematic evaluations of cures. Mental health professionals must reach their conclusions with extreme care, in a way that would convince a skeptic (again, a criterion implicit in almost all demonstrations that we term "scientific"). They owe that extreme care to people who seek professional help for themselves and alleviation of their problems, who trust those claiming to have expertise in mental health.

The question, then, is how to reach legitimate conclusions about the effectiveness of therapy. A number of deficient ways have certainly led to bad conclusions. One method that at first glance does not seem deficient is to search among therapy clients for examples of "success" and argue for the efficacy of therapy on the basis of this success. The problem with this method is that some people who experience distress will get over it whether they are in treatment or not. Having improved, these people will search for a reason for the improvement, as will their therapists. Not surprisingly, both client and therapist may well agree that the reason was psychotherapy. There is no way of evaluating that conclusion, because the client cannot compare what did happen with what would have happened if therapy had been unavailable. This simple objection illustrates an important logical fallacy. We do something in a particular situation, and something else follows. Was that something else caused or even influenced by what we did first? If we conclude that it was, we must have in mind a *hypothetical counterfactual*, or some idea of what would have happened if we had not done what we did. It is hypothetical because we can never be certain "what would have happened if." Nevertheless, we can evaluate the effect of what we did do only by comparing it with what we believe would have happened if we hadn't done it.

In most of our everyday functioning, we don't use hypothetical counterfactuals to confirm simple beliefs that we consider self-evident. Most of us believe that we know where our home is located, for example, because when we go there, it is there. We never check our belief by going to some other location—perhaps randomly chosen—when we wish to go home to verify that our home *isn't* at this other location. This absence of a check illustrates a "confirmation bias" in our everyday beliefs, a bias that generally serves us quite well. Most emotional disturbances are not fatal, and as our life situations change, we develop new ways of coping and thinking about them; our feelings of distress or happiness also vary. Where is the hypothetical counterfactual in the examples of "successful therapy"? Nowhere. Both therapists and clients nonetheless often cite such successes as "proof" of the effectiveness of therapy.[6]

Despite their uselessness, however, instances of success continue to be cited as "evidence" for the effectiveness of therapy, even by psychologists. For example, a writer maintains in *American Psychologist*: "Suppose you test artistic ability before and after therapy. Should you predict a difference between treatment and control [that is, no-treatment] groups? Not at all! Predict that your measure will increase only for the successful subgroup. After all, you do not want to predict an increase for the failure cases."[7] I leave it to the reader to figure out the validity of "predicting" success only for those cases later found to be successful.

A more common way to establish a claim for therapeutic effectiveness is to treat a group of people and find that in general they are better off after treatment than they were before. Here, the hypothetical counterfactual is that they would have remained the same without therapy. But there are serious flaws with this. For starters, we don't know that they would have remained the same. A much more subtle flaw is technically termed a *regression effect*. That is, processes appear to "regress" from less likely states to more likely ones simply because the more likely ones are likely to occur at later points in time. For example, people are not often extremely happy (or extremely unhappy). It follows that when they are, they are less likely to be as extremely unhappy (or happy) later—no matter what happens in the meantime. Because most people enter therapy when they are extremely unhappy, they are less likely to be as unhappy later, independent of the effects of therapy itself. Hence, this "regression effect" can create the illusion that the therapy has helped to alleviate their unhappiness, whether it has or not. In fact, even if the therapy has been downright harmful, people are less likely to be as unhappy later as when they entered it.[8]

To understand regression effects in general, suppose we toss a coin twice, and it falls heads both times. We toss it two more times. We expect fewer heads on these second two tosses; specifically, we expect that the probability that we will get two heads again is only 1 in 4; we will get one head and one tail (in either order) with a probability of 1 in 2, and two tails with a probability of 1 in 4; thus, our expected number of heads on the second two tosses is only one. Does that mean that coins "catch up to themselves" (a belief termed "the gamblers' fallacy")? No. It simply means that when we get an unusual result one time in a random process, we are unlikely to repeat it. This regression to 50 percent heads is, of course, probabilistic, because the probability is only 1 in 4 that the two heads will be repeated in the second two trials, but they *can* be. Similarly, if a fair coin has landed heads 9 times in 10 trials, the probability that there will be fewer than 9 heads in the next 10 trials is 99 in 100, but there is still a chance of roughly 1 in 1000 that it will land heads all 10 times in this subsequent set of 10 trials.

I am not claiming that life is a toss of a coin (any more than it is a river). The point of the example is that when there is any random component whatsoever, and we pick a group on the basis of being unusual in some way or other, we get a regression effect. It is, moreover, not even necessary to hypothesize a random component in what is being observed. All that is necessary is that the variables studied are not perfectly correlated. Not everyone realizes that illusions can result from regression effects. The best way to receive an award for "noted improvement" in academic work in some grade and high schools is to do terribly the previous semester; for example, an Israeli fight instructor has protested to psychologist trainers[9] that he "knows" punishment works better than reward, because: "I've often praised people warmly for beautifully executed maneuvers, and the next time they almost always do worse. And I've screamed at people for badly executed maneuvers, and by and large, the next time they improve."

The direct relevance of regression effects to evaluating psychotherapy is that people often enter therapy at times when they are particularly unhappy and distressed. But if their problem is one that varies over time rather than having a consistently downward course, regression effects alone could result in "improvement"—and an illusion that the improvement is due to psychotherapy: "If treated, a cold will go away in seven days, whereas if left alone, it will last a week." Emotional distress is certainly more serious than a cold, but even serious emotional distress will vary over time. Since such variability implies an imperfect relationship between outcomes at two different points in time, regression effects are to be expected. In fact, they occur even within a condition: "Of particular significance was the fact that those scoring highest on symptom reduction after SD were those whose symptoms were initially more severe, and who were less promising candidates for conventional types of therapy."[10] Of course.

The best way to evaluate the efficacy of therapy, however, is to compare a group of people who receive therapy with a group who don't. That is to say, as in any such scientific experiment, there must be an *experimental* group and a *control* group. The two groups must be equivalent when they begin therapy, moreover, so the comparison cannot be between people who seek out therapy and others who don't seek it out but who all have the same symptoms. People who seek out therapy will likely be more motivated to get over their problems than those who don't, which will skew the results. Even a highly sophisticated statistical control cannot establish equivalence on this most important characteristic—whether individuals seek out therapy. The result is a *self-selection bias.*

, That bias occurs in other domains as well. For example, there was considerable concern in 1989 about whether abortion may have bad psychological effects. C. Everett Koop, the surgeon general, testified in Congress that the studies attempting to assess this possibility were not done well enough to reach any type of firm conclusion. As some critics pointed out,[11] such studies *cannot* reach a firm conclusion in a society in which women are free to choose to have abortions or not— because having one is confounded with a desire to have one, and not having one is confounded with a desire to carry the pregnancy through to birth. (I'm not claiming that all women who want one necessarily obtain one, or that all who desire to have a baby necessarily do not have one; the point is that the two groups of women in general are not equivalent on the basis of this crucial factor of choice.)

The effects of self-selection can be quite subtle, and they often occur in contexts in which they would not "reasonably" be expected. In medicine, for example, a late 1970s study of the drug Clofibrate which is used to lower mortality from coronary heart disease, found that those who took the prescribed dose of Clofibrate 80 percent or more of the time had a 15 percent mortality rate within the next five years, as opposed to a 25 percent mortality rate for those who took the prescribed dose of Clofibrate less than 80 percent of the time. But people who took a placebo 80 percent or more of the time also had a 15 percent mortality rate, while those who took the placebo less than 80 percent of the time had a 25 percent rate.[12] It is unlikely that a placebo effect could influence a five-year mortality rate; more likely, those who adhered to the recommended medical treatment by taking the pill consistently took better care of themselves in other ways than those who didn't. In studies evaluating psychotherapy, the possibility of self-selection among subjects is quite prominent. People who are highly motivated to get better will not only seek out therapy but will engage in other activities that will help their condition more than those who aren't highly motivated. Thus, studies may well reveal nothing when they conclude that those seeking psychotherapy do better than those who do not.

The solution to this problem of self-selection is to evaluate psychotherapy in the same manner that drugs are evaluated. Volunteers for a study are *randomly* divided into an experimental group which is given the treatment, and a control group, which is not; the outcomes for these two groups are then compared. Such random assignment of individuals to groups does not guarantee that the two groups will not differ in ways relevant to the outcome. It merely creates a statistical expectation that the two groups will not differ. Larger sample sizes produce more likelihood that the experimental and control groups will be alike. This approach is called a *randomized experiment* in the social science literature and a *randomized trials experiment* in the medical literature, where it is most commonly used. What happens is that the control group provides the hypothetical counterfactual against which the outcome for the experimental group can be compared. The logic is explained well in Sinclair Lewis's novel *Arrowsmith*; the most widely publicized randomized trials experiment was that on the Salk polio vaccine in 1954.[13]

In psychotherapy, randomized experiments often involve randomly selecting people for a control group and promising them that they will receive treatment after a specified period of time—a "wait list control." Classical medical randomized control experiments do not do this. Another difference is that many medical experiments involve a *placebo control*, in which subjects in the control group are given a placebo and neither group is told whether they are the experimental or the control group. Such experiments are termed *double-blind* experiments because both the people in them and the people evaluating them are "blind" to whether they are in the experimental group or in the control group.

It is hard to develop a double-blind experiment in psychotherapy. Both the subjects and those examining the subjects are generally aware of whether they have received therapy. In psychotherapy, moreover, many of the criteria used to assess the success of treatment rely on the self-report of the subject, for the simple reason that much treatment is aimed to alleviate the emotional distress that the subject has experienced. Such self-reports could easily be biased by subjects' knowledge that they had or had not received psychotherapy. For this reason self-reports are rarely used without considering other outcome criteria as well.

Such randomized experiments are very necessary in evaluating treatments for emotional disorders. Studies that did not conform to the principles of randomized experiments have had dubious results. In one study the investigator concluded that of 136 people given a promising new treatment, 98 improved, 23 were somewhat improved, and only 12 failed to improve.[14] In a second study, 228 people given the same treatment were dichotomized into two groups: "improved" versus "the same or worse." One hundred and fifty-one could be classified in the first group, only 73 in the second.[15] (The numbers do not add up for reasons we'll see presently.) Let me describe the promising new technique that was being studied:

> After drilling a small hole in the temple on each side of the skull, the surgeon then inserts a dull knife into the brain, makes a fan-shaped incision through the prefrontal lobe, then downward a few minutes later. He then repeats the incision on the other side of the brain. . . . The patient is given only local anesthetic at the temples—the brain itself is insensitive—and the doctors encourage him [sic] to talk, sing, recite poems or prayers. When his replies to questions show that his mind is thoroughly disoriented, the doctors know that they have cut deep enough into his brain.[16]

How was "improvement" determined? By the lobotomists themselves casually talking to the patients at some later time. "I am a sensitive observer," one said, "and my conclusion is that a vast majority of my patients get better as opposed to worse after my treatment." The reason the numbers didn't add up was that the other patients had died on the operating table—three in the first study mentioned, four in the second. Where was the control group? Nowhere. Every patient who was believed "eligible" for the horror of being lobotomized underwent the operation. In fact, without doing anything even remotely close to a scientific examination of the procedure, the doctors performing it advocated its widespread use. After performing more than twelve hundred lobotomies, one doctor stated that while he had previously maintained that he "wouldn't touch them unless they are faced with disability or suicide," he had come to believe that "it is safer to operate than to wait" and that lobotomy "would be considered in a mental patient who fails to improve after six months of consecutive failure."[17] Moreover, the technique itself was "improved." The description quoted above refers to prefrontal lobotomy. It was later replaced with transorbital lobotomy, a safer operation that involved gently lifting the patient's eyeball from its socket, sticking in a thick needle behind it, and then as before manipulating it to destroy the same brain tissue until the patient becomes incoherent—the "ice-pick operation." More such "improvements" were envisioned before the American Medical Association put a stop to it. The more the doctors performed this treatment, however, the more confident they became. Their main concern was to find a new—better—variant of the treatment, rather than determine the efficacy of the basic treatment itself. The last to know!

The effects of such lobotomies are well illustrated in the movies *Francis* and *One Flew Over the Cuckoo's Nest*. I myself have observed their devastating results. The first patient with whom I attempted psychotherapy had taken off all her clothes one day and run around the streets of her home town screaming, "My father is the handsomest goddamn drunk in [X], Pennsylvania!" She was subsequently hospitalized and then was lobotomized within six *weeks*. She often continued to shout, "My father is the handsomest goddamn drunk in [X], Pennsylvania," but she would not take off her clothes or otherwise express her clearly ambivalent and partially sexual feelings toward her father, because she would immediately forget what she was shouting about. Unable to concentrate for more than ten seconds at a time, she was unable to obtain a job outside the hospital or live with relatives. She had, in effect, been sentenced to life imprisonment for having expressed her feelings in a socially inappropriate way. Although lobotomies are now greatly reduced, destructive techniques are far from ancient history.[18] I direct the reader to Jeffrey Masson's description of the "direct therapy" techniques of John Rosen. These techniques included harassment, and in some cases imprisonment, of clients in order to force them to "air out their problems"; Rosen didn't lose his license to pursue them until 1983.[19] Or consider the "reparenting" technique of the Harvard female psychiatrist mentioned in Chapter 1.

My point is that mental health professionals can all too easily do what was done to my patient if they don't subject their cherished techniques to the type of scientific scrutiny found in randomized experiments. And the less they use such scrutiny, the more confident they will become that they are doing good. *All* mental health practitioners are susceptible to an overinflated belief in their own position, and they should constantly subject themselves to the discipline of testing their ideas empirically or reading about others' tests of them. Medicine learned that lesson well when the widespread practice of removing children's tonsils in the late 1930s and early 1940s was subject to scrutiny by Harry Bakwin.[20] He found that although a majority (61 percent) of children in the New York School System in the 1930s and early 1940s had had their tonsils removed, there was no correlation whatsoever between the estimate of one physician and that of another regarding the advisability of tonsillectomy when a sample of the remaining 39 percent of the children were examined,[21] of whom 45 percent were said to be in need of having their tonsils removed (as were 46 percent in a later screening of those children who passed *this* screening). Eighty children had died each year as a result of the anesthesia administered for tonsillectomies. Findings such as these have led medicine, especially medical school professors, to appreciate the importance of systematically checking clinical judgment, for example through employing randomized clinical trials. Mental health professionals would be well advised to follow medicine's example.

STUDIES THAT EVALUATE EFFICACY

Randomized experiments evaluating the efficacy of psychotherapy began appearing occasionally in the scientific journals during the 1960s. One impetus for them came from psychologists' increased use of behavioral techniques, in which specific behaviors were targeted for change through the use of reinforcement principles. Since the whole point was to change these behaviors, the efficacy of the techniques was easily evaluated, and randomly selected (usually wait-list) control groups could be easily evaluated as well. As professional psychologists proliferated—and their fees soared—the "only the therapist knows" philosophy became increasingly difficult to maintain.

In 1977, Mary L. Smith and Gene V. Glass published a famous article in *American Psychologist* that concluded that psychotherapy is very effective. They summarized the results of 375 studies of psychotherapy effectiveness that had purported to use random assignment to experimental and control groups.[22] The summary technique they used, termed *meta-analysis*, first determined the average difference in each study between the experimental and control groups on some outcome variable that the therapy attempted to address (like behavior, self-report of anxiety or depression, or assessment of psychological functioning by "blind" observers). These differences were measured in terms such as subjects' well-being or reduction of symptoms. Each difference was assessed after therapy had ended for the people in the experimental group and at the same time for those in the control group. Smith and Glass treated the overall differences found in each single study as single units, computed their means (averages), and then analyzed these means.

One of their concerns was whether the average difference between the means for the experimental group and the means for the control group on the measures of well-being or symptom reduction were positive. These mean differences were computed separately for each study. In general, they were positive. In fact, the average of the means for the experimental groups on the various measures examined was on the average at the seventy-fifth percentile of the control group distribution. Making standard statistical assumptions,[23] Smith and Glass found that someone chosen at random from the experimental group after therapy had a two-to-one chance of being better off on the measure examined than someone chosen at random from the control group. That is a very strong finding—stronger, in fact, than findings for most medical procedures and for comparisons of healthy versus deleterious lifestyles.[24]

Smith and Glass's critics soon weighed in. Meta-analysis, they argued, compares apples and oranges. The various problems of clients seeking therapy differ across various studies. Some are acutely anxious, some are depressed, and some are even schizophrenic. The outcome measures differ. The therapeutic techniques employed differ. The therapists differ. The measures used to evaluate outcomes differ. Consequently, meta-analysis was criticized as sloppy. But the forms of the overall phenomenon being evaluated—psychotherapy—differ in all these respects as well. In order to generalize about fruit, it is perfectly appropriate to combine apples and oranges. In order to generalize about psychotherapy, it is perfectly appropriate to combine different measures of improvement that assess changes important in overcoming different psychological problems. Moreover, the particular contexts of the experiments may be more important in psychology than in medicine. The functioning of the human body seems less subject to specific temporal, social, and chance factors than is psychological well-being. It may then be quite reasonable to treat each study rather than each subject as the unit about which to generalize, even though standard statistical theory is less applicable to sampling diverse and ill-defined studies than to sampling people (or other units) from a homogeneous and well-defined population.[25] In fact, the same diversity that makes statistical generalization dubious may well be a necessity in psychology and the allied social sciences.

Smith and Glass's meta-analysis not only presented impressive evidence about the efficacy of psychotherapy; it concluded that three factors that most psychologists believed influenced this efficacy actually did not influence it.

First, they discovered that the therapists' credentials—Ph.D., M.D., or no advanced degree—and experience were *un*related to the effectiveness of therapy.

Second, they discovered that the *type* of therapy given was *un*related to its effectiveness, with the possible exception of behavioral techniques, which seemed superior for well-circumscribed behavioral problems.[26] They also discovered that length of therapy was unrelated to its success.

The professional psychology community hailed Smith and Glass's overall finding but not the three subsidiary findings. A series of studies was thereafter conducted to indicate that at least the first finding was inaccurate. But these studies failed to refute Smith and Glass.

I became involved in the field of meta-analysis after reading Smith and Glass's paper. At the time I was skeptical of it because while the authors of the studies they had reviewed claimed to have used random assignment, I found that many of them didn't. As we have seen, the subjects of a scientific study must be assigned randomly to experimental and control groups to avoid the self-selection problem. In fact, however, several experimenters who purported to have done random assignment actually chose the control group members randomly from people who were *similar* to those seeking therapy, but not on the basis of seeking therapy itself.

One experimental group, for example, consisted of students with poor grades seeking help to improve their study habits and attitudes toward academic work through group therapy. The control group in this study consisted of randomly selected students with equally poor records—but who, for all the experimenters knew, might have given up or even left college altogether. Self-selection can be much more subtle than this. For example, in one study comparing a group therapy approach to juvenile delinquency with the standard probation officer "treatment," the experimenter randomly assigned subjects to the experimental (group therapy) group and the control (probation) group. Any of those assigned to the group therapy group who stopped attending the group therapy sessions would be returned to having to see their probation officers. These subjects soon discovered that their absence from group therapy sessions would not necessarily be officially noted, and many dropped out. When the experimenter compared the overall success rates (lack of subsequent arrests), of the two approaches, he found little differences between the experimental and control groups. But, he concluded, group therapy can meaningfully be evaluated only for those who attend group sessions. When he compared only those who had good attendance records with the control group, he did find a difference in favor of the group therapy treatment. The problem with this comparison is that we don't know who in the control group *would* have attended sessions regularly *if* they had been assigned to the experimental group. Thus, there is no hypothetical counterfactual. Moreover, it is reasonable to hypothesize that the more motivated people in the experimental group were the regular attendees, so that the latter comparison involves self-selection. The situation is exactly analogous to the Clofibrate study. The Smith and Glass analysis, however, involved only a single overall measure of study quality, in which violations of truly random assignment were just one component. I thought it possible that the overall average effects were due to the inclusion of studies that didn't have true random assignment, an effect that Smith and Glass's single measure would have obscured.

When I was on sabbatical leave at the University of Michigan in the academic year 1978–79, Janet Landman (then a graduate student) and I collaborated on a project to check out self-selection in the studies Smith and Glass summarized. We obtained the list of studies from Smith and Glass, which had since been augmented to include 435. We omitted all unpublished studies, such as doctoral dissertations, on the grounds that they had not been subjected to the scrutiny by presumably disinterested peers that is required for publication. We sampled every fifth study on the remaining list, for a total of sixty-five. We read each study independently to judge whether there had been random assignment to the experimental and control groups. We never discussed studies with each other before making our independent judgments about them. When we compared our judgments, we found that our agreement rate was high; we disagreed on only three of the studies. (While that constitutes 95 percent agreement, a better statistic for evaluating agreement is the "phi-coefficient," which was .90.) After resolving these disagreements through discussion, we concluded that only 42 of the 65 studies (about two-thirds) had used the true random assignment that the authors claimed.

The studies we examined were remarkably diverse. One studied a "country club" for alcoholics that didn't serve liquor. Another studied a "general resource person" in an intensive care unit serving people who had experienced heart attacks. This person randomly selected one of each two patients admitted, explained to them in detail the literature given on their bedside table about successful living following a heart attack, and offered to work as a liaison with their families, to explain the consequences and challenges to them as well. (No "depth" therapy was involved). The differences between the experimental and the control groups on physiological measures indicating recovery were impressive. The most common conditions being treated in the studies were behavioral anxiety and phobias (which some critics, not being chronically anxious or phobic themselves, dismiss as trivial), but depression and even chronic schizophrenia were treated in others. Measures of success varied according to the problem, but the results were similar.

Landman and I analyzed these studies in the same way Smith and Glass had analyzed the studies in their original article, and we compared our results with the results we would have obtained had we analyzed all sixty-five studies. Much to our surprise, our results were virtually identical to those of Smith and Glass based on their whole sample of 435. That is, it didn't matter whether the studies had had true random assignment.[27] As I later told the Oregon Psychological Association, I had become a "reformed sinner"—someone who had originally been ready to ascribe the apparent effectiveness of psychotherapy to methodological flaws in the studies supporting it but who had now become a "true believer."

WHAT THE STUDIES SHOW ABOUT THERAPIST EFFECTIVENESS

The results of such analyses, however, also imply that the credentials and experience of the therapist don't matter. This result is rather unpleasant for professionals who require years of postgraduate training and postdoctoral experience for licensing to perform therapy, and who would like to restrict practice to those who are licensed. In the years after the Smith and Glass article was published, many attempts were made to disprove their finding that the training, credentials, and experience of therapists are irrelevant. These attempts failed. The abstract of a review by Jeffrey S. Berman and Nicholas C. Norton summarized such results:

> [A recent review] concluded that patients treated by paraprofessionals [people minimally trained] improved more than those treated by professionals. However, this provocative conclusion is based on inappropriate studies and statistical analyses. The present review omitted problematic studies and organized the data to permit valid statistical inference. Unlike [earlier authors listed] we found that professional and paraprofessional therapists were generally equal in effectiveness. Our analyses also indicated that professionals may be better for brief treatments and older patients, but these differences were slight. Current research evidence does not indicate that paraprofessionals are more effective, but neither does it reveal any substantial superiority for the professionally trained therapist.[28]

In other words, the professionals are no different from the paraprofessionals in the effectiveness of their treatment. Furthermore, consistent with earlier summaries of studies they and other authors had examined:

> In a first set of analyses, we examined whether the relative effectiveness of professionals and paraprofessionals might vary for different types of problems and treatments. When we classified studies according to the four most commonly occurring categories of patient complaint (social adjustment, phobia, psychosis and obesity), we found no reliable differences [between professionals and paraprofessionals] among the separate effect sizes. . . . We also failed to detect any systematic differences when we divided the studies into five forms of treatment (behavioral, cognitive-behavioral, humanistic, crisis intervention, and undifferentiated counseling).

And:

> Similarly, there were no statistically significant differences [again, between professionals and paraprofessionals, *not* between experi-

mental and control groups] between four different sources of outcome (patient, therapist, independent observer, and behavioral
indicator).

Perhaps the most famous study supporting this conclusion was performed by Hans Strupp and Suzanne Hadley.[29] They recruited as therapists university professors who had no background in psychology and
randomly assigned clients either to them or to professionally trained
and credentialed psychologists. In all, they assigned fifteen clients to
the professionals and fifteen to the professors. The clients were those
whose problems, as Strupp and Hadley put it, "would be classified as
neurotic depression or anxiety reactions. Obsessional trends and bor-
derline personalities were common." The professionals charged higher
fees, but they were no more effective as therapists than the professors.
The only slight difference was that after therapy the clients of the
professionals tended to be a bit more optimistic about life than those
of the untrained professors, but they didn't function any better on any
of the multiple measures the investigators evaluated. While this difference may result from the current professional belief that optimism
is an important criterion in mental health (perhaps *the* criterion, see
Chapter 9), it could also have arisen on a chance basis.

Other reviews indicate that the level of experience of professional
therapists is unrelated to their efficacy.[30] Consistent with such "it
doesn't matter" findings, William Miller and Reid Hester published a
highly influential review indicating that the intensity of professional
treatment does not matter even for people with the problem of alcoholism.[31] Miller and Hester summarized all the studies in which alcoholics were randomly assigned to inpatient or outpatient treatment.
Some of the inpatient programs involved prolonged stays in institutions devoted to radical changes in lifestyle, beliefs, and attitudes. But
there were no differences in outcomes between inpatients and outpa-
tients. Nor did Miller and Hester find any relationship between the
length of treatment and outcome. In fact, nothing worked better for
alcoholics than a minimal treatment involving detoxification and one
hour of counseling!

This result contradicts results of studies or other types of therapy, in
which a "dose-effect" relationship between length of psychotherapy
and outcome has been established; approximately 50 percent of

clients are measurably improved after eight sessions and 75 percent after twenty-nine.[32] The disturbing possibility also remains, however, that *few or none of the programs Miller and Hester studied did any good at all.* That possibility would be consistent with the results of the first randomly controlled experiment on alcoholism treatment, published in 1967 by Keith Ditman and his colleagues.[33] In that study, chronic drunk-driving offenders were randomly assigned to a psychiatric treatment clinic, to an Alcoholics Anonymous program, or to a no-treatment control group. In the subsequent year, 68 percent of those who had been assigned to the clinic were arrested again, as were 69 percent of those who had been assigned to Alcoholics Anonymous, but "only" 56 percent of those who had been assigned to no treatment were arrested again. (Most probably, these were statistical variations reflecting no stable difference in outcome.)

Our society now views alcoholism, especially drunk driving, as sufficiently serious that we do not consider assigning people to a no-treatment control. We take a similar approach to juvenile delinquency, which may be a mistake.

Believers in professional training, credentials, and experience for psychologists have responded to these study results in basically three ways. First, they combine an attack on the studies themselves with an appeal to hypothetical studies that have not been conducted. Even Strupp and Hadley used this familiar argument-from-a-vacuum at the conclusion of their paper about the equal effectiveness of untrained university professors: "Professional psychologists, by virtue of their training and clinical experience, are clearly much better equipped to deal with the vagaries and vicissitudes encountered in interactions with most patients."[34] There, "most patients" means the ones Strupp and Hadley *didn't* study. There is no support for that statement among the patients they *did* study.

Michael Lambert, David Shapiro, and Allen Bergin make the same argument in a broader form in the 1986 *Handbook of Psychotherapy and Behavior Change*: "Although the failures in this literature generally to show unique therapeutic effectiveness for trained professionals are sobering, these studies are flawed in several respects."[35] But *all* studies are "flawed in several respects." Psychology is a difficult field in which to conduct a good study, let alone one without any flaws at all. Are we to ignore what all these admittedly flawed studies indicate in common? Ignoring them would make sense only if they were all generally flawed in the *same* respect, but they aren't. Without such common flaws, it is extremely improbable that all the separate and unrelated flaws would lead to the same conclusion. No specific common flaw has been found or even proposed that would systematically bias the results against the professional. This absence poses the biggest problem for those attempting to ignore their implications: namely, that there is no *positive* evidence supporting the efficacy of professional psychology. There are anecdotes, there is plausibility, there are common beliefs, yes—but there is no good evidence. The reader wishing details about the studies is referred to the Lambert, Shapiro, and Bergin article.

A second, related defense of professionalism in psychology has been to postulate "interaction effects"—that is, that the outcomes for the professionals might be different from those of the paraprofessionals depending on the types of clients they treated or the types of techniques they used, while simultaneously there is no difference overall. The expertise of professionally trained therapists, for example, is said to be required for more seriously disturbed clients, who were in a minority in the studies conducted. One critic of Miller and Hester's analysis of the alcohol program studies suggested that inpatient and prolonged treatments may be required for more severe alcoholics, whereas Miller and Hester analyzed only programs that serviced a high proportion of less severe alcoholics.[36] This critic then presented an argument about why more intensive treatments would be good for the more severe alcoholics.

The problem with his suggestion, however, is that he fails to make a simultaneous argument about why the more intensive programs would be *bad* for the *less* severe alcoholics. If one treatment program is better for one class of patients, then—to be equally effective for all patients combined—it must be worse for some other class of patients. That's simple arithmetic. If the average of one set of numbers is zero and some of the numbers are positive, then some of the other numbers in the set must be negative. The presence of less severe alcoholics in the more intensive programs could obscure these programs' superiority for the more severe alcoholics, but it would not wipe out their overall superiority—*unless* these programs were simultaneously inferior for the other, less severe alcoholics. The one exception to the Berman and Norton finding quoted earlier was that "professionals were somewhat more effective in studies using short term treatments."[37] Logically, however, given no difference overall, they had to balance this with the finding that "paraprofessionals were somewhat more effective in studies involving longer therapies, as was found."

The type of interaction that would lead to a zero effect overall is technically termed *disordinal*, or *crossed*.[38] If one type of treatment or therapist, say, an experienced professional, is better for one type of client, while another is better for another type, this has severe implications: it implies that a professional therapist is worse for some clients than other types of therapists.[39] If so, it is extraordinarily important to discover who those clients are before employing professional therapists rather than paraprofessional ones. No such attempt has been made.

Occasionally, therapists may be more effective when they are using a technique that they believe to be superior than when they are using one in which they have less faith but that they have adopted for experimental purposes.[40] Reid Hester and his colleagues compared the efficacy of two treatments for alcoholism: Alcoholics Anonymous (AA), with its traditional "disease" model and emphasis on spiritual recovery, and traditional counseling.[41] They randomly assigned clients to these two treatments. They found that the treatments had equivalent effects overall. Six months after treatment was over, however, those clients who *before* entering treatment had expressed the view that alcoholism was a disease rather than a bad habit were much more likely to be abstinent if they had received the AA treatment rather than traditional counseling; conversely, those clients who had expressed the view that alcoholism was a bad, addictive habit were much more likely to be abstinent if they had received traditional counseling rather than AA. (Since there was no no-treatment control group, it is not possible to determine whether the clients were actually harmed by receiving a treatment incompatible with their pretreatment views.)

Some theorists have taken the negative findings on therapist credentials quite seriously. Advocates like Jerome Frank and Hans Strupp propose that psychotherapy works due to "nonspecific effects."[42]

Nonspecific effects are those that result from "the quality of the relationship" between client and therapist. This idea is supported by the finding that good psychotherapists tend to be empathetic, trustworthy, and warm.[43] In one study, William Miller, Cheryl Taylor and JoAnne West found that therapists' "accurate empathy," as they assessed it, accounted for 67 percent of the variability in their success with problem drinkers, while therapists' years of experience accounted for only one percent.[44] Unfortunately, some studies that support the importance of empathy, unlike this one, do not assess empathy independently of client outcome. For example, one investigator chose above- or below-average therapists by assessing client success and then concluded that the above-average therapists were more empathetic because their clients, who were successful, rated them as higher on empathy than the unsuccessful clients rated their therapists. That is about like predicting success on the basis of observing who is successful. (This study will not be referenced here.)

Even the existence of the correlation between empathy and success, however, does not explain the process of success or failure, and given that some therapies that are not based on relationship variables (like some behavior modification techniques) are successful, the interpretation that their success too must be based on some unevaluated quality of relationship remains speculative. My own favorite speculation, in contrast, in based on Hamlet, who in his famous soliloquy speaks of "taking arms against a sea of troubles." (That's a wonderfully mixed metaphor, because "taking arms" literally means putting on armor, and armor leads to quick drowning, as demonstrated when the Dutch once destroyed an invading Spanish army by luring it into the lowlands and opening up the dikes. But futility is not the point here.) The implicit message is that taking up arms against troubles does some good psychologically even if it does not fully "by opposing end them." When people enter therapy they are making a choice to deal with their problems rather than simply feel overwhelmed by them.[45] Being placed in a wait-list control group may deprive people of that opportunity, temporarily at least. (Again, such people may choose to deal with their problems in other ways, as do people in medical randomized trials experiments. These are meant to evaluate the superiority of the experimental treatment, not to prevent those not given it from attempting to get better in other ways.) If only the *motive* to enter therapy were important, then experimental groups and wait-list control groups would do equally well. If only the quality of the client-therapist relationship were important, then we would not expect behavioral techniques to do so well. I suggest it may be the actions of the clients themselves in "taking up arms"—that is, in doing something about the problems addressed in therapy—that result in a change in life itself that has a "therapeutic" effect. In other words, while therapy generally succeeds, the same success might be obtained by other means as well.

There are three additional factors that might contribute to therapist efficacy. First, the therapist is an "outsider" to the client's life and therefore may be less apt to take certain attitudes, procedures, and constraints or possibilities for granted. The therapist will also feel less bound to justify the client's past behavior than the client does (a *sunk cost*)[46]—and hence is less likely than the client to wish it repeated (to prove that it really was wise, despite its lack of success). Second, any change that breaks or stops self-defeating or socially pernicious positive feedback (a "vicious circle," often between behavior and feelings) may be a therapeutic one, and entering therapy may provide the "initial kick" to break an ongoing loop.[47] Thoughts, behaviors, and feelings are interrelated, and *any* technique that leads to a positive change in one of them (or in the body itself) may (*may*) lead to positive changes in the others as well.[48] If, for example, I act less uptight and hostile than I previously did as a result of establishing good rapport with a therapist, others may shun me less than they previously did. The pleasant and even close relationships I go on to establish may not only improve my "mental health" themselves, but they may also encourage me to be more relaxed about facing up to my problems and more energetic in attempting to overcome them. (Note that this model does *not* postulate that one must "work through one's problems" *first* and begin changing only later.) Third, therapy may begin a process of seeking out changes in one's environment or lifestyle that can be helpful (although conservative psychoanalysts "require" that clients not make radical changes in their lives—like getting married, having children, getting divorced, or changing vocations—while they are in analysis).

But I myself am arguing from a vacuum here, because I have no direct measure of the therapeutic effect of actively dealing with problems, or evidence of its efficacy. The most defensible answer to the question of why therapy works is, *We don't know*. We should do research to find out, and indeed many people are devoting careers to just such research. But we do know that the training, credentials, and experience of psychotherapists are irrelevant, or at least that is what all the evidence indicates. The horrible irony is that by supporting licensing, income, and status for credentialed practitioners, the mental health professions have treated variables that really don't matter as if they did matter. Much greater good could come from finding out what does matter, then from supporting the professional and social clout of those who can provide it.

The discussion in this chapter has been limited in two ways. First, it concerns the efficacy of only psychotherapy, not drug therapy. Research findings about the qualifications of effective psychotherapists do not address the question of who is better or worse at prescribing drugs. Outcome studies assessing the efficacy of various drugs generally treat the drugs themselves as the phenomenon to be evaluated, such as lithium for manic depression. To my knowledge, there have been no studies on how the effects of drugs are related to the qualifications, experience, or personal characteristics of the doctors who prescribe them and presumably monitor their effects—perhaps an interesting area.

The second limitation of this discussion is that most, although not all, studies involve treatments that clients freely choose. The clear exception is chronic patients in mental facilities. Gordon L. Paul and Anthony A. Menditto summarize what is known at this writing: "We do know what works best for chronically disabled patients with excesses in maladaptive and psychotic behavior, deficits in adaptive functioning, or both (a comprehensive social-learning program). We do not yet really know what works best for less extensively disabled, acutely admitted, or revolving-door patients, particularly in inpatient programs involving short to intermediate stays."[49]

A third limitation is that the criterion used to assess both the efficacy of therapy and the irrelevance of therapists' training and experience has uniformly been a reduction or cessation of symptoms in the client. In the coffee shop debate, I argued in favor of using this criterion. Certainly, symptoms are important, particularly to the person experiencing them. But mental illness is an *illness*, the nature and cure of which cannot be assessed by simply observing symptoms, is it not? And are not symptoms mere "surface" manifestations of a deeper underlying pathological process? A process that itself could remain basically unchanged even if the symptoms were reduced, much as a palliative cancer treatment can relieve the pain without slowing its inevitable destruction of the patient? Isn't the only way to assure that the symptoms won't reappear to eradicate or stop the disease process itself? In brief, if mental illnesses are true illnesses, mustn't there be a better way to establish whether people are cured than by noting whether their symptoms have been reduced or eliminated?

WHAT EXACTLY ARE WE STUDYING?

Questions about the nature of "illness" and "disease" cannot always be answered, even in the area of medicine, let alone psychology. Is AIDS a disease, or is the real disease the HIV infection that leads to AIDS? Or perhaps the disease is the opportunistic infections that kill the patient after the immune system has been virtually destroyed? Is high blood pressure a "silent disease," as advertised on television, or is it a condition that increases the probability of other diseases arising, such as heart attack or stroke—which would probably occur eventually without high blood pressure if the person lived long enough? For that matter, are heart attack and stroke truly diseases? If they are, should every degenerative condition that increases with age, like farsightedness, be labeled a "disease"? What about the natural decrease in vigor with age?

It is tempting to dismiss such questions as "merely semantic." But given the widespread belief in this culture that "mental illness is just like any other illness," questions such as these must be addressed rather than finessed. We cannot conclude, moreover, that psychotherapy alleviates mental illness and that the training, credentials, and experience of the therapist are irrelevant without clarifying the relationship between symptom reduction and the "illnesses" involved.

Myron Rothbart and Marjorie Taylor have beautifully explained a distinction between "natural" versus "artifactual" categories that may help us here.[50] "Natural" categories are those that appear to exist outside arbitrary human definition or convention, while "artifactual" categories are those that humans clearly define. Thus, the natural category "ulcer" is an ulcer is an ulcer, while the artifactual category "political liberal" may vary according to historical circumstance and the views of the person using the categorization. Children as young as nine will object that the statement "the doctor turned the skunk into a rabbit" makes no sense (as opposed to the statement that "the doctor made the skunk look like a rabbit"). But no one will object to the linguistic sense of the statement "the Democrat Ronald Reagan became a Republican." Rothbart and Taylor are particularly concerned with whether social categories are believed to be natural or artifactual; how, for example, people react to the statement that "the Jew converted to Christianity and therefore was no longer a Jew." Some anti-Semites and some conservative Jewish people might find that such a statement makes no sense. The distinction between natural and artifactual can be applied here to various categories of mental illness—and in fact to the whole broad class "mental illness" itself. Do we—should we—regard forms of mental illness as natural categories, and what about the whole broad class itself?

Inalterability is one criterion by which natural and artifactual categories are distinguished, but as Rothbart and Taylor point out, it is not the only one. An ulcer can go away and be transformed to normal tissue, after all. Another criterion is the number of inferences we can make about a thing once we know to what category it belongs. Once we have determined that a whale is a mammal rather than a fish (natural categories), we can infer that it does not lay eggs but gives live birth to its young. Once we know that stomach problems are due to an ulcer rather than to stomach flu, we can infer that the new drug treatments will do better than aspirin. In contrast, a liberal "Republican" and a conservative "Democrat" (artifactual categories) may hold more political attitudes in common than do liberals and conservatives within the same political party. There are, then, a number of criteria for distinguishing between natural and artifactual categories. Moreover, the distinction is not absolute. A similar approach may be found in the work of William Chaplin, Oliver John, and Lewis Goldberg, who argue that we distinguish between "personality states" (like being angry) and "personality traits" (like being an angry person).[51] In general, personality traits are considered to be stable, long-lasting, consistent across situations, and internally caused, while personality states have the opposite characteristics, but the difference is absolute only for extreme instances of traits and states—such as "domineering" versus "infatuated." In contrast, "concealing" and "transparent" can be regarded as traits, states, neither, or both. So it goes with natural versus artifactual categories.

Rothbart and Taylor admit that they cannot fully justify the distinction on philosophical grounds or even on philosophy of science grounds, but that in point of fact people do make the distinction. Here they reject the philosophy of positivism, which maintains that categories are determined by a single defining characteristic ("please define your terms") and that disagreements about category membership can arise only because people are attending to different empirical information or have used different defining characteristics to categorize this information. Moreover, which characteristics people use may be a matter of taste. People who persist in arguing with each other about whether something belongs in a particular category (say, about whether a particular action is "heroic") are simply confused, because they have access to different information or else they are using language differently. It follows that scientific categories follow from linguistic conventions, although scientists have adopted conventions on the basis of consistency with observation and theory. This view was first challenged by Ludwig Wittgenstein, who argued that instances of categories form "family resemblances"[52] (consider— his example—the number of activities we label "games"), and it has since been challenged by people who believe that categorization follows from certain nearly universal human activities. (For an excellent example, see George Lakoff's *Fire, Woman and Dangerous Things*.[53]) Consistent with their rejection of positivism, Rothbart and Taylor present no defining characteristic by which the broad class consisting of natural categories can be distinguished from that consisting of artifactual categories.

So are the categories of mental illness—such as schizophrenic, manic-depressive, hysteric, antisocial personality, neurotic—natural or artifactual categories? Are they related through "family resemblances," or are they best understood by looking at extreme examples? Do they form the same types of categories as physical illness, types that most of us believe do form natural categories?

George Vaillant defines mental health in terms of adaptation to problems (which he distinguishes from "adjustment"), and hence he sees forms of mental illness as forms of failure to adapt.[54] He maintains that adaptation and nonadaptive failure can properly be viewed in medical terms, as can the defense mechanisms of the subjects whose lives he studies and the level of "maturity" of those defense mechanisms. Vaillant claims that both the defenses and their level of maturity constitute natural categories, although perhaps more in the sense of family resemblance than of clear definition. He admits the difficulty of his approach when he notes that "the American Psychiatric Association had, with my blessing, *voted* that homosexuality no longer be classified a mental illness" and asks "how can anyone be voted sick or well, unless the critics of organized psychiatry are right, and mental health is just a cultural illusion?"[55] At the other extreme, Thomas Szasz, Jeffrey Masson, and others regard psychiatric categories as nothing more than socially constructed ones that derogate behavior or people we don't like.[56] But even if "schizophrenia," "manic-depression," and "alcoholism" are social conventions by which we describe socially disapproved behaviors, what about the "postlobotomy syndrome" from which my patient suffered? It had a fairly well-understood cause, physiological nature, set of associated behaviors (symptoms), and course over time (unchanging).

These last are the four criteria that H. Tristram Engelhardt, Jr., proposes as the criteria for determining whether something is a physical disease.[57] None of them alone defines a physical disease. Rather, it is their *convergence* that defines one. In order to term something a physical disease, we must know something about its cause, its physiology, its symptoms, and its course—particularly how it responds differentially to different treatments. For most conditions that we term "mental diseases" psychologists do not require knowledge of physiology, the second criterion; in fact, some people have maintained there isn't physiology involved (although most psychologists believe that different feelings and behavior are associated with different physiological states. Recent discoveries about the importance of endocrine secretions in the brain tend to support that belief, as does the existence of pleasure and pain centers). If we found a convergence between the other three criteria—cause, symptoms, and course—we would be generally comfortable in regarding the condition as a "natural" category of illness.

Do we find such a convergence? The answer is very simple: Sometimes we do and sometimes we don't. It depends on the type of behavior, the symptom syndrome, and the emotional disturbance we are considering. Although there is clear evidence of genetic influence on schizophrenia and alcoholism, for example, even with these conditions, all that is inherited is a tendency. Such problems "run in families," and studies of adopted children—and of twins raised apart—indicate that familial influences are genetic rather than environmental. But genetic influences that yield a tendency to schizophrenia also yield a tendency to other problems labeled "mental illness" as well.[58]

The American Psychiatric Association, through its various diagnostic manuals, has attempted to develop categories based on symptom clusters (syndromes), to point to some of the conditions defined in this manner that many of us would accept as natural ones, and then to treat all the categories in the manuals as if they were unambiguously natural—except for categories voted in or out, or categories that contain a clear gender bias. For example, the same behavior can lead to the label "antisocial personality" if the subject is a male and "histrionic" if the subject is a female.[59] This positivistic attempt to "locate" people on various "axes" is justified not by showing that these locations result in categories that allow us to accurately predict how people will behave with or without different treatments, but by demonstrating that when diagnostic experts are sufficiently well "trained" in using the manuals, they unsurprisingly agree about how to label people. Placement in the categories has also become necessary to receive third-party reimbursement for services. (I know several people whose psychiatrists or psychologists have actually apologized for their official diagnosis: "I have to label you this way in order to be reimbursed. Please don't pay too much attention to the label." Imagine a medical doctor apologizing for labeling an ulcer an ulcer, explaining that the label is a matter of convenience for being reimbursed!) At the other extreme, Szasz and Masson claim that the labels are nothing but pejorative, and they easily point to examples where the labels indeed are used in this manner—with the same ease with which advocates of the psychiatric diagnostic manuals point to examples of distress that appear to fall into clearly natural categories.

My point is very simple: Establishing that one particular category of mental illness is natural or artifactual does not imply much about whether other categories are natural or artifactual, or about the nature of mental health and illness categories in general. This point leads to one very clear conclusion: *The broad class of categories of mental illness is itself not a natural category.*

As with personality traits (like "domineering"), it is difficult to propose either a clear definition or a family resemblance among mental illnesses. There are characteristics that lead us to classify something as a form of mental illness, just as there are characteristics that lead us to classify something as a personality trait. Three important mental illness characteristics are: (1) the behavior of the individual appears to the observer sufficiently dysfunctional and maladaptive in certain specific ways that the observer is prone to believe that the condition forms a natural category of maladaptiveness; (2) the individual suffers emotional distress to the point that they feel unable to do "what they want to do"; and (3) the individual's behavior is derogated by others. We do not require strong convergence between the three characteristics (as we do in the characteristics outlined by Engelhardt for concluding that something is a medical disease). For example, someone who is labeled a sociopath (antisocial personality) may not suffer much emotional distress (although it is not clear how much we gain by the label as opposed to the simple description that the individual does not experience the same demands of conscience, or guilt if society's norms are violated, that most people do). It also is important to note that emotional distress, the second characteristic, does not refer to unhappiness per se. As we will see, extending the conception of mental illness to simple unhappiness can easily result in an infantile and basically unethical philosophy of life. What is necessary is that the emotional suffering must be experienced as debilitating.

These three characteristics may lead to some insight into the nature of mental illness, and how the various parties involved rely on different ones. The American Psychiatric Association's diagnostic manuals concentrate on the first characteristic (observer's judgment of dysfunctionality). Clients who are seeking help rely on the second characteristic (subjective feelings of incompetence); critics such as Szasz and Masson concentrate on the third characteristic (derogation by others). But exclusive reliance on only one of these characteristics leads not only to ignoring the others but to ignoring the fact that all three taken together have a positive statistical relationship in society as a whole. To appreciate this positive relationship, imagine that it did not exist. That would mean that people who behaved in a specified way that led an observer to believe that they suffered from a natural category of maladaptiveness would experience no more emotional distress than others, and that their behavior would be judged to be no less desirable than the behavior of others. Perhaps more important, it would mean that there was no statistical relationship between extreme personal distress and behavior that others judged to be undesirable. Imagine a society in which these conditions existed, in which there was no relationship between how well people felt about themselves and how much others approved of their behaviors. The positive relationship among these three characteristics challenges the diagnostician's claim to "objectivity," the client's claim to being concerned only with relief from distress, and a critic's claim that the whole conceptualization of mental illness merely involves derogating people and, at the extreme, depriving them of their civil liberties.

What all three characteristics have in common is an emphasis on symptoms. The clearest evidence that certain types of mental illness are natural categories is that the tendency to develop them is at least partly genetic. Currently, we can't do anything about an individual's genes, so cure and alleviation involve helping the individual to be as free of symptoms as possible. When we speak of someone as being a "schizophrenic in remission," we mean the symptoms have been effectively alleviated—just as we continue to consider someone "a diabetic" even though the individual maintains a normal blood sugar level as the result of taking insulin. (Interestingly, we don't talk of some other conditions as being "in remission," even though we could; for example, gout results from an inherited kidney deficit that results in high levels of uric acid in the blood,[60] but we do not speak of someone who avoids gout altogether by taking allopurinal daily to reduce blood uric acid level as suffering from "controlled gout," or "gout in remission." Taking the pill might, in contrast, be described by someone sympathetic to Vaillant's approach as involving "successful adaptation" to a genetic predisposition. We do not, however, analogously speak of "a schizophrenic" who is symptom free as having "successfully

adapted to schizophrenia"—a failure perhaps reflecting the third characteristic of mental illness, the pejorative one.)

The American Psychiatric Association's attempts to define mental
illnesses so clearly and precisely that they all appear to form natural
categories also involves symptoms, or in this case symptom clusters.
The person experiencing mental distress to the point of debilitation is
certainly also concerned with symptoms. Finally, of course, the person
who derogates another as "mentally ill" does so on the basis of symptoms. Thus, symptom elimination or reduction is a perfectly fine criterion to use in evaluating the efficacy of treatment.

The emphasis on symptoms is also compatible with the basic tenets
of a free society, although taking away others' freedom on the basis of
a "medical" judgment isn't. People decide whether to seek treatment
and what type to seek. If liberty is restricted, it must be on the basis of
overt behavior that leads to a *social* judgment that the person cannot
function freely, which a judge—not a professional psychologist or psychiatrist—is best able to make and is socially mandated to make. In
fact, in seeking even medical treatment, it is the person's free choice
to do so that is important. We may coerce Christian Science parents
of diabetic children to give them insulin, for example, only on the
grounds that the children themselves are not capable of making an
informed choice. We do not coerce Christian Scientist adults who are
diabetic to take insulin. A doctor who honors a "living will" implicit-
ly accepts the personal autonomy of the individual to decide what sort
of medical treatment to seek. Moreover, most of us seek treatment for
symptom relief. Even when we undergo an annual or biannual physical examination, which could lead to the discovery of a disease that
"only the doctor" can know about or understand, we do so to avoid or
forestall the development of later debilitating symptoms or death.
Symptoms are important.

The view that symptoms aren't important, expressed in the coffee
shop conversation described earlier, has been parodied by my Oregon
colleague Al Siebert, himself a clinical psychologist.[61] The symptoms
of paranoid schizophrenia, he says, include a belief in one's own extraordinary ability to hear, see, and understand things other people
don't. A professional who judges that a person who does not freely
seek help with psychological distress is in fact suffering from a form of
mental illness also believes in his or her own special sensitivities. The

diagnostician is sensitive to the individual's problems of which the individual himself or herself is unaware. Do we wish, Siebert then asks, for the mental health and court systems to be controlled by paranoid schizophrenics? If not, we must pay quite serious attention to the individual's own autonomy in seeking help, what it is the individual wishes to change as the result of the help, and the form of help desired. Again, symptoms—especially as experienced by the individual—are of utmost importance. The fact that the conclusions of this chapter are based on symptom elimination or reduction in no way limits their scope.

MULTIPLE STUDIES VERSUS THE LATEST BREAKTHROUGH

Critics of my argument may well be able to drag out a single study, or even several, that appear to contradict my conclusions. As I pointed out earlier, however, the generality of my conclusions is dependent on multiple studies conducted on multiple problems in multiple contexts. It would take a *substantial* body of new research to overturn the conclusions presented here. In this respect, psychology and allied social sciences are different from many physical sciences. Psychologists deal (correctly, in my view) with apples and oranges, and we do not abandon our theories on the basis of a single contradictory finding or two.

In contrast, in the physical sciences, Lewis Thomas writes: "In the fields I know best, among the life sciences, it is required that most expert and sophisticated minds be capable of changing those minds, often with a great lurch, every few years. In some branches of biology, the mind-changing is occurring with accelerating velocities. The next week's issue of any journal can turn a whole field upside down, shaking out any number of immutable ideas and installing new bodies of dogma, and this is happening all the time. It is an almost everyday event in physics, in chemistry, in materials research, in neurobiology, in genetics, in immunology."[62]

Perhaps he exaggerates a bit in saying this radical change is an "everyday event." But with the possible exception of the study of the physiology and functioning of the human brain, psychology cannot be characterized the way Thomas does the other fields. There are a lot of promises made about impending "breakthroughs" in appeals for funding of the scientific work in psychology and allied social sciences, but in the past breakthroughs have been few and far between. A single new study or two do not provide a breakthrough, in general, particularly not in understanding the nature of human emotional distress, its precursors, and its alleviation. Perhaps that is why many people view these areas as not involving "true science." At any rate, a new finding or set of findings that would turn the whole field I have discussed "upside down" is extraordinarily unlikely to occur.

This closing section of assurance and caution is "defensive," but there is a lot to defend against. Both professionals and the general public are frequently informed of new "discoveries," "techniques," or at least new "understandings" of emotional distress and its alleviation. Such claims make good press. People are interested in them. Researchers hint at such claims to obtain grants and to lobby that more governmental money should be allocated for such grants. Retractions of claims made in the past (such as the inability to find any such thing as "the addictive personality"—see Chapter 7) seep into the research literature and textbooks with little public fanfare and occasionally with no impact—even on the practice of the professionals.

Most responsible scientists adhere to an ethic of not publicizing their research findings until after their work is accepted by a peer-reviewed scientific journal, hopefully one with high standards of subjecting claims to rigorous scrutiny. But in psychology claims are often made on the basis of research that is simply bad. Let me give a concrete example. A member of the board of directors of the Oregon Psychological Association who was deeply concerned with child sexual abuse told me on several occasions that a wonderful new test had been developed that would allow psychologists to predict who was likely to abuse children. Once this test had been published, it could be used to screen all mental hospital patients in the state to determine who was at risk for engaging in such destructive behavior. This test was published, and it was terrible. The test developer had combed through 399 items from the MMPI (Minnesota Multiphasic Personality Inventory, a standard personality test to be described in detail later) "short form" to discover eleven items that differentiated a sample of ninety-three child abusers from a sample of thirty-seven non–abusers. Tossing 399 separate coins would probably have done almost as well.[63] The result was a test that should never have been used, but it was taken seriously. The winter 1986 issue of *Oregon Psychology* described the test, with the concluding comment that "the small size of the 11-item *Ic* scale is easily scored and requires little additional time and no special clinical training for effective use." Those "in charge" clearly did not understand how horribly inappropriate the test would be if used as a screening device. If someone had asked one of the board members, they would have been assured that psychologists *do* now have a way of identifying likely sex offenders, with a method "hot off the press." Such claims should not be believed.

I'm not maintaining that we never discover anything important, or even striking. The whole point of research—which I strongly support—is to make such discoveries. What I am maintaining is that the process is slow and full of dead ends, and the reader should evaluate new claims in light of the substantial body of negative research such as that reviewed in this book.

CONCLUSIONS AND IMPLICATIONS

Psychotherapy works. The magnitude of its positive effects is greater than the magnitude of many physical treatments, deleterious lifestyles, and changes in those lifestyles. Those who believe they have problems are encouraged to try it—especially if they have been unable to change their behavior by simply "willing" a change.

There is no reason, however, to seek out a highly paid, experienced therapist with a lot of credentials. If verbal therapy is sought, paraprofessionals are equally effective, especially empathetic ones. If the problems appear to require behavioral modification, as do phobias and lack of impulse control, a paraprofessional who understands behavioral principles is as effective as a highly credentialed professional. But success in therapy is far from assured, even though it works overall in a statistical sense. Someone who is dissatisfied with their current progress in therapy should not be inhibited about changing therapists or mode of treatment. (The therapist that is abandoned may attribute this decision to the depth of the client's pathology, but so what.) In particular, the results of the Hester et al. study of alcoholism treatment should be kept in mind. These results provide evidence that compatibility of a treatment approach with the client's views and beliefs before entering therapy may be an important factor in its success; clients may often be in a better position than the professional to choose a treatment modality and therapist. (For myself, in choosing a professional psychologist I would want one of the 30 percent of APA members who reads one or more of its scientific journals.[64]) Statements from professionals that they "know" much better than the client what is "needed" may often best be politely ignored—especially when these statements are made after minimal contact, followed by a standard diagnostic label. If verbal therapy is sought, find someone empathetic. Unfortunately, I have no good advice about how to judge whether someone is empathetic before getting to know that person.

CAVEAT EMPTOR

It takes a long time to do a study of the effectiveness of a particular type of psychotherapy or of psychotherapy in general. It requires examining many clients and many therapists, often over a period of years. Most of the studies on which I have based my conclusions were initiated years ago, even when the results have been published only recently. But the quality of the training of clinical psychologists, a major group of therapists studied, has deteriorated rapidly in the past several years. That might not mean much, given that training and credentials don't predict therapeutic effectiveness; but along with the decreased quality of training has come an explosion in numbers that assures that there will be more poor therapists around in the 1990s than at the time when the studies were initiated. A greater concern is that many new ideas and therapies have been initiated that are at best characterized as ideologically based or faddish (see Chapters 5 and 6). There are therefore more therapists who base their practice on such ideologies and fads, of which the reader should beware.

CHAPTER 3

PREDICTION AND DIAGNOSIS

More Myths of Expertise

> There is no controversy in social science which shows such a large body of qualitatively diverse studies coming out so uniformly in the same direction as this one. When you are pushing 90 investigations [as of 1991 closer to 140], predicting everything from the outcomes of football games to the diagnosis of liver disease and when you can hardly come up with a half dozen studies showing even a weak tendency in favor of the clinician, it is time to draw a practical conclusion.
>
> —Paul E. Meehl[1]

Much of the success of verbal therapy is influenced by the personal qualities of therapists and how they relate to clients. Much of the success of behavioral psychotherapy is influenced by therapists' understanding of the basic principles of behavior change, which are not too difficult to grasp. Much of the success of all therapy may be influenced by the fact that the client is taking action and no longer feels helpless in the face of disruptive emotional pain. Clear findings that psychotherapy works in general and that the training, credentials, and experience of the therapist are irrelevant to its success give rise to these speculations.

Nevertheless, a well-trained and experienced professional psychologist or similar professional may better understand what people—particularly distressed ones—are like, why particular individuals act and feel as they do, and how to diagnose individual problems, however much of a hodgepodge the resulting classification system may be. If so, then the professionalization of the mental health field, the fees, its status, and its public acceptance may all be justified.

Professional psychologists in particular behave as if they understand. Thirty-five percent of them appear in court.[2] Many have hospital admissions privileges, including involuntary hospitalization. They are deeply involved in diagnosing people in mental health facilities and in their offices, and they are often seen in the media providing explanations of why someone (from the latest serial killer to Saddam Hussein) did this or that, or offering advice to listeners about what to do and how to feel, and above all, when to seek psychotherapy. Moreover, they are well remunerated for such services.

The claim is that professional training yields understanding, not just about people in general but about the single individual in all her or his uniqueness. Statistical generalizations can be found in textbooks but an understanding of single individuals in all their complexity cannot.

UNDERSTANDING AND PREDICTION

To evaluate this claim, we must first decide what it means to understand another individual. Certainly, it means more than creating a "good story" about why particular people do what they do and feel as they feel, or about why this or that happened or is likely to happen. Good stories may be psychologically compelling, but they are not necessarily valid. Going beyond the good-story criterion of understanding requires some knowledge of the world and its workings. How do we obtain that knowledge? This complex philosophical question can be transformed into a slightly simpler one: How do we know that we know?

The question of establishing the validity of our knowledge may appear equally complex, but answering it does allow us to establish criteria for knowledge. If we truly know something, these criteria must be satisfied. The criterion with which this chapter will be concerned is the *ability to predict*; that is, we know something is the case if we can predict that in given situations it will hold true. Predictability is not synonymous with knowledge—a horribly complex, ad hoc system that could predict would not involve as much knowledge as a theoretically justified simpler one that didn't predict quite so well.[3] Nor is predictability the only criterion we use to assess whether we have knowledge. Such an aesthetic notion as "beauty in one's equations" may be a criterion. (See Dirac's discussion of Schrödinger's wave equations.[4]) But a crucial test of understanding is the ability or lack of ability to predict. Prediction need not be perfect, but it is found in all branches of science. Even sciences not involved with the future, such as paleontology, make predictions of what will be discovered when certain evidence is examined, such as new fossil evidence. Making sense of evidence already gathered is an extremely important activity in science, but it alone is not enough.

In the last chapter I discussed the crucial role of randomly controlled experiments in evaluating a treatment or therapy. A person who claims that a treatment is effective must demonstrate that it has an effect in comparison to a hypothetical counterfactual, obtained through construction of a randomly constituted control group. This "show me" criterion may have been extremely important to the development of scientific demonstration in Western civilization, beginning with the Renaissance rejection that an assertion about the universe or people could best be proved by referring to the Bible or to Aristotle. "Show me" is basically translated into "show me what will happen next" when we require prediction.

The demand to "show me" can also be quite subtle. In the late 1840s for example, Dr. Ignaz Phillipp Semmelweis noted that the rate of death from "childbed fever" among mothers who had given birth in a ward serviced by physicians was almost four times as high as mothers in a ward in the same hospital serviced by midwives.[5] The deaths tended to occur in women in the same rows of beds. Semmelweis wondered whether the reason was that they were attended by the same doctor. The doctors didn't clean their hands, even after returning from dissecting a cadaver in the morgue, because such practice was considered to be unmanly. Or perhaps the effect was psychological, since after a priest administered last rites to a dying patient, he went down the line of beds ringing the "death bell." At Semmelweis's request, the priest stopped ringing the death bell in the hospital, but the mothers continued to die in rows. Semmelweis then demanded that his colleagues and assistants wash their hands in a solution of chlorine of lime before they examined a woman or delivered her baby. Over the next fifteen months, the death rate fell from 12 percent to 1.2 percent. After participating in a republican street demonstration in 1848, however,

Semmelweis was fired from his hospital post. His successor stopped the silly requirement of hand washing, and the death rate rose to 15 percent. We would be more certain that the changes in death rate were due to hand washing if he had required the doctors to wash their hands in some randomly picked rows but not in others. Semmelweis happened nevertheless to be correct, and he tested it in a way that allowed him to present evidence to a person who demanded "show me." Unfortunately, the medical people at the time were not as impressed as we believe in retrospect that they should have been. The old practices were retained until the 1880s, when Dr. Joseph Lister understood the importance of Semmelweis's experiments. In the meantime, Semmelweis had lost his sanity, begun accosting people on the streets to warn them to stay away from doctors who didn't clean their hands, and died in a mental institution in 1865.

A happier example of the "show me" approach is provided by R. W. Wood, a professor of physics at Johns Hopkins University and "an inveterate perpetrator of pranks and hoaxes."[6] After Wilhelm Roentgen's 1895 discovery of X-rays—which could be broken down into alpha, beta, and gamma rays—physicists were eager to discover other sorts of radiation as well. In 1903 one of the most distinguished physicists in France, René Blondlot, announced that he and his laboratory colleagues had discovered a new type, which he labeled an N-ray in honor of the University of Nancy, where he was a professor. These rays, he announced, were emitted from the sun; others found that they were emitted from the human body as well. Wood and others were unable to see the N-rays when they attempted to duplicate Blondlot's experiments, and eventually Wood visited the laboratory at the University of Nancy, presumably to find out what he was doing wrong. When he was shown various ways N-rays could be created, he couldn't see them, although his hosts could. The N-rays had to be generated in the dark; one device involved passing light through a prism. After one demonstration Wood—the prankster—surreptitiously removed the prism from the device and asked for a repeat demonstration. It was repeated. He again failed to see the N-rays, but his hosts again did. So much for N-rays.

The Semmelweis and Wood stories illustrate an important point: The test of a claim requires a *comparative* demonstration. Death rates should decrease when the doctors clean their hands; the scientists should observe the N-rays when the prism is in place and not when it has been removed without their knowledge. To test professional psychologists' claims to understanding, therefore, we require not only an assessment of their predictive powers but a comparison of the accuracy of their predictions with that of some other means of prediction. After all, professional psychologists can predict with great certainty that the reader of this book will eat something within the next twenty-four hours. So, however, can anyone who has made casual observations of life. The question is what is the appropriate predictive method for making a comparison.

ACTUARIAL VERSUS CLINICAL
PREDICTION: THE METHODS

The answer may be found in the fact that professional psychologists claim to be able to make predictions about individuals that transcend predictions about "people in general" or about various categories of people. This is the opposite of the *actuarial* predictions used by insurance companies; such predictions are made on the basis of the actuarial tables, which for example compile accident rates on the basis of age, gender, marital status and past driving record. A claim to understand individuals in a "clinical" manner involve going beyond noting their membership in a broad class. The result is *clinical* prediction.

Other psychologists generally accept statistical analyses and generalizations as a critical part of their work (except those using computer simulation). Social psychologists study how people in general or at least in particular cultures behave in certain social circumstances—such as in solitude, in cohesive groups, in groups of strangers, with or without communication. Cognitive psychologists study how people think, the principles of "intelligent thought," and even principles of artificial intelligence. Personnel psychologists use certain selection or training procedures to try to improve human performance. Health psychologists study ways people can be persuaded to adopt healthy habits, sometimes modifying these ways on the basis of characteristics of the people to be persuaded. These psychologists specifically regard each individual subject they study as a representative of the population about which they wish to generalize, rather than attempting to make a specific prediction about that individual viewed apart from that population. Such claims are of a statistical or actuarial nature. Where professional psychologists differ is in their claim to understand the single individual as unique rather than as part of a group about which statistical generalizations are possible. They claim to be able to analyze "what caused what" in an individual's life rather than to state what is "in general" true. There is some overlap, and not all professional psychologists claim to understand the individual per se. Those that don't, however, are not found engaging in the activities that the evidence reviewed in this book indicates are mythologically rather than scientifically based.

Psychologists who are not involved with professional practice often make statistical generalizations based on categorizing people and circumstances. In addition, many of their predictive rules evaluate variables by numbers that have a clear directional relationship to the outcome to be predicted; such predictions use numerical scales. Thus, a grade-point average is a number that summarizes a high school student's performance; the higher the number the better the performance *in general* and the greater the likelihood of success in college. A high grade-point average in college, in turn, predicts success in graduate or professional school. Aptitude and interest tests are constructed so that higher numbers predict better performance, just as most medical indices relate higher numbers to greater seriousness of the disease or disease process. Moreover, some psychological variables have a "natural" directional relationship to the criterion of interest (for example, the number of a person's past criminal convictions are used to predict success on parole), just as some physical variables do (such as blood pressure in hypertension or leukocyte count in Hodgkin's disease). Occasionally, variables have a relationship to the criterion to be predicted shaped like an inverted U—such as in personnel contexts where moderate levels of aggressiveness are best, or physical ones where moderate blood pressure or a certain ratio of weight to height is desirable. If degree of deviation from maximal desirability is substituted for the original variable, this deviation has a clear directional relationship to the outcome to be predicted.

Predictions are made from numerical variables by using statistical techniques to develop weighted averages of the numbers that minimize error of prediction; this is known as a weighted average. (An ordinary average of a set of numbers is their sum divided by n, the number on numbers in the set; for example, the average of 3, 4, and 8 is equal to 3 + 4 + 8 = 15 divided by 3, or 5. Forming such an average is equivalent to weighting each number by the fraction 1/n and then summing the resulting products; for example $(3 + 4 + 8)/3 = (1/3)x3 + (1/3)x4 + (1/3)x8 = 3/3 + 4/3 + 8/3 = 5$. Note that when summing across the n numbers, the sum of the "weights" of 1/n by which they are multiplied is equal to 1. A weighted average is different from an ordinary average only in that the weights by which each number is multiplied need not all be equal to 1/n; they must still, however, sum to 1. In the present context, these weights are chosen by a statistical method to yield the best possible prediction of the criterion of interest.) Occasionally, variables are hypothesized to "interact," which can be incorporated into statistical prediction by multiplying the values of the variables involved and determining the best weight for this product. But as we have seen, such interaction effects are rare in psychology and other social sciences because they imply that predictions about one variable depend on other variables. In general, that is not true; higher grade-point averages in high school, for example, do predict greater probability of success in college, no matter what the student's Scholastic Aptitude Test (SAT) scores were, and higher scores predict a greater probability of success no matter what their grade-point average happens to be. There are exceptions to this general statement—for example, that caffeine helps "impulsive" people perform cognitive tasks in the morning and hampers their performance in the evening—while the opposite is true for "controlled" people.[7] Such exceptions are rare.

The two bases of actuarial prediction in psychology, thus, are categorization and the construction of weighted averages of continuous variables. Both examine *aggregates* of individuals to determine the best categories or way to weight numbers in forming their weighted average. Both accept error of prediction, which is to be minimized rather than abolished.[8] In fact, the statistical models themselves specify the amount of error to be expected when the resulting actuarial formulas are applied to new cases of prediction. Again, the movement from aggregate to particular is common to medical endeavors such as evaluating drugs, vaccines, or new forms of treatment. Moreover, as in such studies, attempts to determine effects on particular individuals—interaction effects—can be made only when these individuals are grouped with others in terms of a common characteristic.

In contrast, the extreme form of the "clinical" approach is to attempt an "inside" understanding of the particular individual viewed in isolation—hence, in all her or his "complexity"—rather than as a member of an aggregate.

This approach was recently summarized in a 1992 *American Psychologist* article.[9] The authors say that experts' knowledge consists of experience and practice that "involves accommodating previous understanding to the uniqueness of a particular clinical situation." This accommodation is *not*, however, explicit—that is, "a compilation of independent facts or sets of rules. Rather, it is a dynamic and contextualized understanding that is the result of the interaction of cognitive patterns or meaning gestalts with environmental cues." The authors justify this approach by referencing work on medical and chess expertise. In its extreme and less responsible form, this approach is expressed as "on the basis of my experience, I just know" (see Chapter 1).

The problem with this argument is that it *begins* by assuming that practicing clinicians have an expertise similar to that of medical diagnosticians and chess grandmasters, rather than by establishing this similarity empirically. But this similarity is not at all self-evident. Medical diagnosticians use a great deal of explicit knowledge—resulting from diagnostic tests—to "build intuitive expertise," and most chess grandmasters have studied roughly fifty thousand chess games.[10] We define "expertise" in terms of what experts accomplish, not in terms of how they go about their task. How well do these mental health experts do in comparison to actuarial predictions? Since understanding is not equivalent to prediction but necessarily implies it, we can ask whether professional psychologists make predictions that are better than predictions based on statistical models not involving professionals. A related question is whether the clinical approach is superior to the actuarial approach in a number of fields—including medicine, business, criminology, accounting, livestock judging, and so on. These questions have been extensively studied by psychologists themselves. The answer to them is no.

ACTUARIAL VERSUS CLINICAL PREDICTION: THE RESULTS

The first comprehensive review of whether statistical prediction or clinical prediction is superior appeared in 1954 in Paul Meehl's *Clinical Versus Statistical Prediction: A Theoretical Analysis and Review of the Literature.*[11] Meehl reviewed approximately twenty studies that compared the two methods for predicting such outcomes as academic success, response to electroshock therapy, and criminal recidivism. In no comparison was the clinical prediction superior to the statistical prediction. In predicting academic performance, for example, a simple linear weighting of high school rank and aptitude test scores outperformed the judgments of admissions officers in several colleges. In predicting the success of electroshock therapy, a weighting of marital status, length of psychotic distress, and a rating of the patient's "insight" into his or her condition outperformed one hospital's medical and psychological staff members. In predicting criminal recidivism in several settings, past criminal and prison record outperformed expert criminologists.

Meehl was concerned primarily with the statistical versus clinical methods for integrating information; thus, he primarily compared instances in which both types of prediction had been made on the basis of exactly the same data. (He also insisted that the accuracy of the statistical model not be checked on the same data on which it was derived—or that the sample size be so large that it not appear superior due to chance fluctuations.) Twelve years later, Jack Sawyer published a review of about forty-five studies; again, in none was clinical prediction superior.[12] Unlike Meehl, Sawyer also emphasized studies in which the clinician had access to more information than that used in the statistical model—such as studies that included interviews of people about whom the predictions were made conducted by experts who had access to the statistical model information prior to the interview. But such interviews didn't improve the clinical predictions. In fact, the predictions were better when the opinions of the interviewers were ignored. Moreover, in the few studies where the professional clinicians were given the actuarial predictions and were asked to "improve" on them, they did worse than the actuarial predictions; that is, prediction was better if their "improvements" were ignored. Sawyer concluded that even if some inputs of the clinicians were found to be valid, they should be incorporated within a statistical model, along with the other predictors, in what he termed a "mechanical" way. After Sawyer's review, similar evidence continued to mount. That led Paul Meehl in 1988 to reach the conclusion quoted at the head of this chapter. Later, he, David Faust, and I summarized even more studies in an invited article for *Science*, which was published in March 1989.[13]

A topic covered since the publication of Meehl's book is the prediction of whether the final diagnosis for an inpatient in the Minnesota hospital system will be one of "psychosis" or "neurosis." A patient diagnosed as psychotic is one who has lost touch with external reality (as in schizophrenia); a patient diagnosed as neurotic is one who is in touch with external reality but suffers from possibly immobilizing internal emotional distress.

Upon entering a Minnesota hospital, each patient filled out the Minnesota Multiphasic Personality Inventory (MMPI), a test consisting of 567 items with which the patient must agree or disagree. Some of the items have clearly psychological content—for example, "at times I think I am no good at all" and "my sex life is satisfactory" and "at times I have been so entertained by the cleverness of some criminals that I have hoped they would get away with it." Others have no apparent psychological implications, like "I like mechanics magazines" and "I believe in law enforcement." The items were chosen on the basis that their answers would differentiate between patients with a clear problem and "normal" people (often, unhappily, chosen from people visiting the patients, such as relatives). Thus, depressed people are more likely to answer "yes" to the statement about feeling worthless than are normal people. It also turns out that paranoid people are more likely than others to like mechanics magazines. The patient's answers to all the questions lead to an MMPI "profile" (to be distinguished from "portrait") of ten scores, each of which indicates the degree to which the patient's answers are consistent with one of ten different types of pathology. Constructed in the late 1940s, the MMPI quickly became—and has continued to be—the most widely used test given to psychiatric patients and others for "screening" purposes, both in and outside mental institutions.[14] Numerous studies have been conducted to establish the statistical relationship between the resulting profiles (or profile "types") and various types of psychological problems and personality and behavioral disorders.[15] In addition, the "clinical art" of profile analysis has been practiced and taught by professional psychologists.

In the early 1960s, Lewis Goldberg obtained access to the results of more than a thousand MMPI tests that had been given to patients in several Minnesota mental hospitals upon admission. Goldberg also had access to their final diagnosis as neurotic or psychotic. He developed a simple statistical formula based on the ten MMPI scores to predict this final diagnostic categorization. The formula, applicable to all the patients in all the hospitals, was roughly 70 percent accurate when applied to equal-size groups. Goldberg then presented sets of these profiles to professional psychologists with varying credentials and experience and asked them to judge whether each patient would have been diagnosed neurotic or psychotic. These people ranged from graduate students in clinical psychology to experienced professionals with a reputation for being expert in MMPI profile interpretation. None of them could surpass the 70 percent accuracy mark; occasionally, some did on some samples, but they could not repeat their superior performance on other samples. In one study, Goldberg and Len Rorer even presented professionals with the results of the statistical formula to help them in their judgment, but they did worse than the formula itself.[16]

Goldberg's studies, in which the statistical formula and the clinical judgment were based on the same data (the ten scores), have been criticized on the grounds that in some of the hospitals the MMPI results themselves could have been influential in determining the final diagnosis. But no reason has been presented as to why that possibility should be more helpful to the statistical formula than to the professional clinicians implementing their "art." At the Ann Arbor VA Hospital in 1966 and 1967, I myself encountered another type of criticism. I had instituted a procedure whereby the profiles of all entering patients were automatically scored using the Goldberg formula. Whenever the clinicians in the hospital found a patient who had clearly been misclassified by this formula, they pointed that error out to me, sometimes gleefully—such as when it classified an actively hallucinating, psychotic individual as neurotic. They were silent about the errors they made that the formula didn't; perhaps they did not even note them. The result was that their memory was biased against the formula and in their own favor. I was confidently assured that the formula didn't work as well as I had maintained, at least at the Ann Arbor VA Hospital—as if the clinicians' memory of a small sample of patients were a better basis for establishing the formula's validity than a sample of more than a thousand patients analyzed systematically. (When I pointed out this possible bias in their evaluation, my colleagues would good-naturedly agree that it presented a problem, but none were motivated to do a systematic study of the accuracy of their *own* judgment, even on the small sample available.)

Cases where the professional psychologist has information in addition to that used in the statistical formula—but still makes worse predictions—may be found in almost any evaluation of unstructured interviews. In one Second World War study, personnel psychologists predicted performance of navy recruits in the military elementary school that these recruits attended before receiving specialized training. The personnel officers had access to the recruits' high school records or aptitude test scores, or both. They made predictions about how well the recruits they interviewed would do in the elementary schools they attended. R. F. Bloom and E. G. Brundage studied a sample of more than 37,000 recruits attending various schools and discovered that the predictions of the personnel psychologists were consistently worse than predictions based on the high school ranks, or aptitude test scores, or a combination of the two, to which these same psychologists had access.[17] This consistently poorer prediction of interviewers compared with statistical models based on predictive information available to them has been replicated again and again. Certainly the interview is valuable, but only as a way of discovering information that is truly predictive—which is best then analyzed by using a statistical model. The "clinical art" of interpreting interview results yields poorer accuracy than is obtained by combining this information "mechanically." Yet "experts" continue to interview, make predictions, and express great confidence in the validity of their predictive judgments. ("The more I do this, the more I learn and the better I am.") The practice of basing selection for jobs and academic or professional programs on such interviews is especially popular, again despite the evidence. By now, however, the results of new research on this practice are quite predictable. At a recent convention of the American Psychological Society, Thomas Gehrlein and Robert Dipboye presented a paper whose abstract reads as follows:

> Interview research has largely ignored differences among interviewers and incremental validity [the degree to which an interviewer may improve upon the information in the interview statistically

combined]. These issues were examined in the context of college admissions. SAT's and high school rank were the best predictors of freshmen GPA. No evidence of [incremental] validity was found for the interview at the aggregate level or at the level of the individual interviewer. Contrary to expectations, experienced interviewers were no more valid than inexperienced interviewers. Results cast doubt on recent suggestions that interviewer-level analyses provide higher estimates of validity.[18]

This paper was not news. It would have been news only if the results had turned out differently. It simply refuted the suggestion that previous studies had underestimated the predictive validity of interviews by pooling results across interviewers.[19] Using the argument from the vacuum "logic" that by now should be familiar to the reader, the previous studies had made this suggestion to criticize results that the authors didn't like, but they provided no positive evidence that their suggestion might be correct. Gehrlein and Dipboyle presented evidence that it wasn't.

In fact, entire programs of interviews have been evaluated and found to be invalid. In April 1979 the Texas state legislature required that the University of Texas Medical School at Houston enlarge the size of its entering class from 150 to 200 students from Texas. The previous 150 had been selected by first examining the credentials of approximately 2,200 students and determining which 800 were best qualified. These 800 were then invited to the Houston campus, where they were interviewed by a member of the admissions committee and one other faculty member. The interviewers had submitted written assessments to a central committee, each member of which rated the applicant on a scale of 0 (unacceptable) to 7 (excellent). These rankings were averaged to obtain a combined ranking of all 800 students; the Houston ranking together with the rankings of the other three medical schools of the University of Texas were compared with the applicants' rankings of these schools by a computer program that guaranteed mutually highest choices. All 150 applicants who ended up coming to Houston were in the top 350 as ranked by the interview procedure. About ten dropped out and were replaced by applicants from lower ranks, to obtain the 150 students desired. When the school was required to add an additional 50 students to its entering class, all that were available had originally been ranked between 700 and 800. Forty-three (86 percent) of the students with these rankings had not been accepted by any medical school, inside or outside the Texas system.

No professors at the school were told which students had been among the first 150 chosen and which were the 50 chosen from the bottom of the rankings. Robert DeVaul and colleagues later compared the performance of those originally chosen with these 50.[20] There were no differences in the performance between these two groups by the end of the second year, by the end of their clinical training (fourth year), or after their first year of residency. "No differences" in this context does not mean "no significant differences" but rather no differences at all. For example, 82 percent of each group was granted the M.D. degree, the proportion granted honors was equivalent, and so on. DeVaul and his colleagues concluded that the interviews—the sole method for obtaining the final rankings—were a total waste of time. A similar conclusion had been reached earlier in a smaller study in which medical students whom Yale rejected on the basis of an interview and who went to another medical school were compared with those whom Yale had accepted but nevertheless went to the same schools.[21] There were no differences in their performance at these other schools. (By looking for differences only within schools, the authors controlled for the possibility that those Yale rejected may in general have gone to easier schools than those Yale accepted.)

It is of more than minor interest to note that 86 percent of those ranked low (700–800) by Houston on the basis of interviews hadn't been accepted anywhere else either. Apparently, some people are consistent at not creating a very good impression in an interview, but the impression they do create has no relationship to their success in medical school and beyond. Moreover, the fact that the interviews didn't predict performance in the two "clinical" years of medical school or in the first year of residency counters the standard hypothetical argument that although interviews may not predict success in academics, they may—"must"—predict success in interpersonal relationships. An interview situation ("impress me") presents a unique task to the interviewee; succeeding in this task apparently implies very little about how people will succeed in later tasks essential to success in professional work or anything else. Certainly first impressions are important, but the qualities that impress interviewers are apparently quite different from those that impress co-workers and supervisors.

The interviewers involved in the medical school studies were not professional psychologists, but the clinical approach they took is the same. It not only combined information on an intuitive rather than an explicit statistical basis but collected a great deal more information than would be combined by a valid statistical model. *In the area of psychological evaluation and prediction,* there are no studies of which I am aware that support the validity of this approach, no matter who employs it. Information added to the two or three most predictive variables does not help. Information that isn't predictive on an actuarial basis actually hurts. The one effect this additional information does have is to increase confidence in prediction, while at best leaving accuracy unchanged.[22] (Studies in medicine and business, which will be covered shortly, are a bit more equivocal.)

Before leaving this subject, I must describe one other interview study because it has such important social implications. In Pennsylvania, offenders who have been sentenced to maximum prison terms of two years or longer are considered for parole by the board of probation and parole after they complete half their maximum sentence. The decision to grant or withhold parole is based on a four-step process. First, the correctional staff writes a summary evaluation; second, a parole case analyst adds an opinion; third, a parole interviewer interviews the candidate and makes a recommendation to the entire parole board; fourth, the parole board makes a yes/no decision. The interviewer is either a parole board member or a specialized hearings examiner who has access to the previous reports of the staff and the analyst.

The parole interviewer interviewed 1,035 inmates between October 1977 and May 1978; 743 of these were subsequently considered by the parole board. Six hundred and twenty-nine (84.7 percent) were granted parole. In all but one of these cases, the decision of the parole board was identical to the final recommendation of the interviewer, who also made 4- or 5-point ratings on prognosis for supervision, risk of future crime, risk of future dangerous crime, and assaultive potential. In a one-year follow-up study, John Carroll and his colleagues compared the accuracy of prediction of the parolees' behavior based on the interview ratings with that of prediction based on simple background factors such as number of previous convictions.[23] (This information was also available to the interviewers and was shown to be correlated with their clinical judgments.)

The parole board considered about 25 percent of the parolees to be failures within one year of being released, for reasons such as being recommitted to a prison, absconding, being apprehended on a criminal charge, or committing a technical parole violation. The interviewer ratings had predicted none of these outcomes; the largest correlation was only .06. In contrast, a three-variable model based on the type of offense that had led to imprisonment, the number of past convictions, and the number of noncriminal violations of prison rules did have a modest predictability, correlating about .22, a result consistent with earlier findings that actuarial predictions based on prior record predict with a correlation of about .30 across a large number of settings.[24] When parolees were convicted of new offenses, the seriousness of their crimes was correlated .27 with the interviewers' ratings of assaultive potential, but a simple dichotomous evaluation of past heroin use correlated .46.

None of these correlations is particularly high; first, the sample is highly select, being limited to those who have been convicted of a crime; second, not all the parolees who committed crimes were caught. Third, these types of behaviors are not as predictable as we believe they are or would like them to be. The difference in the effectiveness of actuarial versus clinical prediction is, however, quite clear.

Moreover, this difference is quite consistent with comparisons of actuarial versus clinical methods for predicting violence.[25] An important qualification: The best prediction in general is that neither violence nor criminal behavior will be repeated, no matter what.[26] Although the general "base rate" prediction is that people will *not* repeat problems, judges—professional and nonprofessional alike—have a bias to believe that repetition is common. The studies show that judgments about who *is more likely* to repeat are much better made on an actuarial basis than on a clinical one. The same principle holds even for predicting involuntary termination from a police force.[27]

Actuarial methods have also been shown to be superior to clinical ones in assessing intellectual deficit due to brain damage. For example, when Leli and Filskov studied diagnoses of progressive brain dysfunction, they found that a diagnostic rule derived from standard tests of intellectual functioning correctly identified 83 percent of the new cases. But groups of inexperienced and experienced professional clinicians working from the same data correctly identified only 63 percent and 58 percent of the new cases respectively. When the clinicians were given the results of the formula, they did better (68% and 75% correct identifications respectively), but neither group matched the 83 percent accuracy of the formula. The clinicians' improvement appeared to depend on the extent to which they used the formula.[28]

In fact, in a series of studies David Faust and his colleagues discovered that professional psychologists could not even detect young adolescents who were faking brain damage on standard intellectual tests after being given virtually no instructions about how to do it other than "to be convincing."[29] Even when the faked results were sent to the professionals with an equal number of results from truly brain-damaged individuals and the professionals were truthfully told that there was a 50 percent chance that the test results they saw were faked, they still could not detect the fakes.[30] These professionals listed themselves (in the American Psychological Association directory or in the *National Register of Health Service Providers in Psychology*) as specialists in "neuropsychology"; many of them had had advanced training; and some of them had been awarded a special status of expertise called a "diplomate." Yet less than 10 percent recognized the faked results. Moreover, if anything there was a *negative* relationship between experience and ability to recognize the fakes—not, however, a statistically significant one. The usual criticism was made that the studies were flawed because neuropsychologists do not usually interpret test results without seeing the clients—yet this critique, as usual, lacked any positive evidence that the neuropsychologists would have done any better if they had seen the clients.[31] A more interesting criticism came from a famous neuropsychologist who, when told that the proportion of diplomates in the study was roughly equal to the proportion in the field, said to Faust, "Well, they couldn't really have been good neuropsychologists. Anyone willing to participate in your study could not have been competent."

Despite such poor showings and despite consistently poorer predictive and diagnostic performances than statistical analyses of test results make, a majority of neuropsychologists indicated in a 1988 survey that they preferred to use nonstandard methods—that is, intuitions—to reach judgments about intellectual deficit over statistical formulas.[32] These results have profound implications for court testimony about intellectual deficits that are alleged to have arisen from accidents or chemical exposure that might have resulted in brain injury, and for psychological "portraits" of the parties involved.

Studies of medical judgments are more mixed in their results, although when clinical judgments and statistical formulas are based on exactly the same input information, the formula once again makes superior predictions. Before Hodgkin's disease was controllable, for example, the late Hillel Einhorn studied how well judgments of the severity of the disease process as established from biopsy predicted survival time.[33] All 193 patients in the study died; the number of days of survival after the biopsy was the criterion studied. Three doctors, one an internationally recognized authority and the other two his "apprentices," rated nine characteristics of each biopsy that they believed were related to severity. They also made overall ratings of the severity of the disease process. While severity judgments are not identical to judgments about how long patients will survive, they should certainly be strongly related (in a negative direction, i.e., the greater the severity the less the survival time). Einhorn developed actuarial formulas—ones involving weighted averages of the numerical ratings of the doctors—to predict survival time from the nine characteristics for a sample of 100 patients the doctors had examined and then checked the accuracy of these predictions using these same formulas on the remaining 93. The doctors' overall judgments of severity were totally unrelated to survival time, but the formulas were. Einhorn's study demonstrated that the doctors' ratings of the biopsy characteristics provided potentially useful information in predicting survival time, but that only the statistical combination of these ratings actually predicted it. (Once when I talked about this study at a formal lecture, a dean of a prestigious medical school suggested that if only Einhorn had studied Dr. So-and-so, the recognized "world's expert," he would have discovered that a doctor's overall ratings could be quite accurate. I couldn't say so there, but the doctor was in fact Dr. So-and-so.)

A similar outcome has been found in studies comparing diagnoses of heart attack made respectively by doctors and a computer program in an emergency room. The doctors and the program were equally good at spotting a heart attack when it was actually present, but the program was superior to the doctors in diagnosing the absence of a heart attack when there was in fact none.[34] Statistical formulas have also been found to be superior to clinicians in predicting future heart attacks.[35] On the other hand, the predictions of a statistical formula (the APACHE-2) have been found to be inferior to predictions made by doctors who were board-certified in internal medicine, who were the "critical care fellows," and who "had seen the patient, obtained a history, and conducted a physical examination, as well as reviewed the pertinent laboratory and roentgenogram data available."[36] In another medical study, doctors were superior to a formula when they had more information than that used in the statistical models and when they had personally examined the patients.[37]

In the business context of predicting bankruptcy, a formula has been found to be superior to the judgment of bank loan experts, some of whom were highly paid by banks that loaned billions of dollars a year.[38] In a study predicting sales, however, managers outperformed the statistical formula.[39] In the bank loan study, the predictions of both the actuarial formula and the bank loan experts were based on the same information; but in the sales study, the managers "also had inside information" in addition to the information used in the statistical prediction. Thus, in both the medical and the business contexts, exceptions to the general superiority of actuarial judgment are found when clinical judges have access to more information than the statistical formulas used. Perhaps if this information had been incorporated into the formulas, they would have again been superior. In fact, that has happened. Unlike APACHE-2, a new statistical formula, APACHE-3, outperforms doctors in predicting death within 24 hours on an intensive care unit.[40]

These findings are not compatible with our intuitions about the validity of our intuitions. They challenge the expertise of professional predictions, and if professionals cannot predict the future well, how can the rest of us? Moreover, the findings appear to be "dehumanizing" in that they "reduce people to mere numbers." (But nothing in the statistical approach makes claims about what it means to be human; rather, the question is how to predict. In fact, the valid statistical approach involves a greater recognition of the role of autonomous choice than does the invalid clinical approach which is based on the incorrect assumption that an expert can tell so much about you that you really have no choice.) And, of course, these findings are an affront to the self-image of the purported experts themselves.[41]

The above findings concern areas in which prediction is often made on an intuitive basis rather than on the basis of well-accepted scientific principles. Professional psychology is just one of those areas, as illustrated by the variety of predictive problems studied. Mental health professions in general rely heavily on "intuitive" understanding, the accuracy of which is belied by the inferiority of predictions based on it. Yet mental health professionals who rely on intuition are among the few who "glorify" it, as opposed to using it as a first step in knowledge—which is then made as explicit and subject to scrutiny as possible through scientific study.

The preference for intuition over research data can be found in the reception given to a paper published in Science by David Faust and Jay Ziskin, which was devoted mainly to forensic psychologists' prediction of violence in legal settings.[42] The authors pointed out that the best prediction is that people will *not* be violent; they mentioned studies that demonstrated the superiority of statistical prediction in determining the *relative* likelihood of violence—that is, which people are more violence prone, although all are more likely not to be violent than to be violent. They reviewed literature showing this superiority in other areas in which psychologists and psychiatrists testify as well. The response was fast and furious.

First, the president and president-elect of the APA wrote to Science, claiming to speak "on behalf of 90,000 members of the American Psychological Association," disputing the conclusions of the article.[43] Since they could not dispute the conclusions of the research studies, they instead accused Faust and Ziskin of making a one-sided presentation and of ignoring the role of the court in deciding upon the validity of expert witness testimony in the "battle of the experts." But the whole point of having experts testify is that they express opinions "with reasonable certainty" ("to assist the trier of fact") about matters that the court cannot on the assumption that their claimed expertise has some validity. Hence, the evidence for this validity is of the greatest importance. The court is in no position to assess the validity of the purported science as a whole; researchers are, and that is exactly what Faust and Ziskin did.

Later, the *APA Monitor* presented a good reason for ignoring the research in favor of intuition.

> Further argument against Faust and Ziskin's conclusion was made by Russ Newman, director of legal and regulatory affairs for APA Practice Directorate, who pointed to a North Carolina brief arguing that testimony from a neuropsychologist should have been admitted. . . .
>
> A neuropsychologist had examined a man who had been injured by a log that fell on his head. The neuropsychologist found evidence of impairment and recommended that the man not drive, but the Industrial Commission in North Carolina would not admit the psychologist's testimony because he was not a physician. Instead, it relied on the testimony of a neurologist who found no evidence of impairment. The man later was involved in a car accident that killed two people. Observed Newman, "This contradicts the idea that you should throw out this testimony."[44]

Citing a single instance of a prediction that came true establishes nothing at all. In fact, in this case we don't even know that the prediction came true, because we are provided with no information about the accident; for all we know, it was entirely the responsibility of the other driver. This reliance on a single instance does, however, illustrate both the depth of the professionals' reliance on intuition and the fallacy of intuitive thinking. It is overly influenced by citing single, vivid anecdotes that are compatible with an intuition already held.

OBJECTIONS TO THE FINDINGS, AND THEIR IMPLICATIONS

In contrast to the highly emotional objections to the Faust and Ziskin paper, the objections to our companion *Science* paper on clinical versus actual prediction (Dawes, Faust, and Meehl[45]) relied not on anecdotes but on arguments. (We had to answer these objections in four revisions of the paper before it was finally accepted for publication.) Here, I would like to list the major objections to empirical results showing the superiority of statistical prediction and counter them, because many may occur to the reader as well.

The first objection to findings like Faust and Ziskin's and other findings is that each separate study evaluated has specific flaws, or their data could be interpreted in an alternative way that supports the validity of clinical prediction. But once again, this is merely a possibility, not a demonstration (the ubiquitous argument from a vacuum). It is possible, for example, that the judgments of personnel experts who interview people can retrospectively be found to have been valid if their judgments are ignored and the people they think will perform poorly are allowed into a program, even though among those admitted into the program their evaluations do not correlate with success. When predictions of violence on a psychiatric ward made by psychiatrists and psychologists are subjected to study and are found to be poor, it is possible that their predictions were poor because those patients they predicted would be violent were carefully watched as a result and hence had less of an opportunity than others to be violent. It is possible that the judgments of parole interviewers can be shown to have been valid if only they had been ignored. The problem with using these diverse objections as a basis for questioning the overall result concerning the superiority of statistical prediction is that each involves a *separate* alternative explanation for each result, and we would have to conclude on the basis of these separate explanations that they all independently but simultaneously accounted for the direction of the results, rather than accept a single principle that accounts for that direction. That's extraordinarily unlikely.

A second objection to negative findings is that the people studied were not true experts. This objection is based, however, on defining "expertise" in such an extreme way that it could characterize only a tiny percent of the professional prognosticators that most of the public believe can make valid clinical predictions. James Shanteau has found some evidence for the validity of intuitive clinical experts when they are defined as the very few people at the top of a field— but the fields were livestock judging and accounting, where there are well-known principles combined with systematic feedback, not psychology.[46] Lewis Goldberg also found some evidence for the validity of the judgments of a *single* expert (now dead), but his study otherwise demonstrated that psychologists and their secretaries were equally skilled at distinguishing between the responses of schizophrenic and brain-injured individuals on the Bender-Gestalt Test, in which people are asked to copy two-dimensional geometric figures.[47] David Faust informs me that one widely recognized neuropsychologist has actually conducted empirical studies to demonstrate that his judgments were valid in a particular area before testifying in court. The point is, however, that the clinical people whose predictions were studied in the investigations I summarized earlier include a sizable proportion who are recognized "experts." While, moreover, many of the studies also involved "apprentice experts" such as graduate students, they did no worse than the purported experts who were training them.

A third objection is that there was no well-defined population of "expert predictive tasks" from which investigators like ourselves randomly or systematically sampled. Thus, how is it possible for us to have reached a statistical generalization? There are basically four responses to this objection. The first is that in psychology and allied social sciences a generalization from a "qualitatively diverse" set of studies may be stronger than one from studies with a clear common characteristic, even though the usual tools of statistical generalization are not as applicable.[48] The second is—as Meehl points out—that it is time to reach at least a *practical* conclusion concerning the superiority of statistical prediction, which I am trying to do in this chapter. The third response is that hypothesizing that a new task could show superior prediction for the clinical approach does not imply that it will (the vacuum, again). And even if it did, so what? Such a finding would not imply either that the generalization was wrong or that the practical conclusion should be modified. Finally, these studies do have a common characteristic. They all involve the need to integrate incomparable information (e.g., characteristics of a biopsy) often from diverse sources (e.g., background information and test information, such as a grade-point average and an SAT score). As I will argue later in this chapter, statistical formulas are particularly good at such integration, while people are particularly bad at it.

A fourth and very common objection is that the predictive tasks presented to the clinical experts are not "ecologically valid." On this basis, Erin Bigler criticizes the studies of Faust that showed neuropsychologists unable to detect faked brain damage in test results.[49] In the "real world," Bigler argues, the neuropsychologists would see the clients as well as test results. But this objection ignores the fact that judgments like those based on test results are essential *components* of more ecologically common evaluations. I claim I can play Prokofiev's Third Piano Concerto brilliantly, even though I can't. You ask me to play scales and find that I do so unevenly, even with an occasional wrong note. When you then conclude that my claim was false, I object that you have not provided me with an "ecologically valid" task. After all, there aren't many scales in Prokofiev. You would be wise not to accept my objection.

A closely allied objection is that many judgments of a truly intuitive nature are "gestalt" ones, in which the whole is more than the sum of its parts, but the required task involves mere components. The implication is that these studies deny the existence of such gestalts. Not true—there is nothing in the studies that denies their existence. Certainly, a great many percepts, judgments, and patterns in life (say, a melody) have gestalt characteristics, but as with piano playing, a deficient part does not an integrated whole make. There is nothing in gestalt characteristics that can "rescue" a bad judgment about some component of the predictive task, the way a person might perceive an entire circle even though there is in fact a tiny gap in it. There is, for example, no reason to believe that the parole interviewer can accurately assess the civic-mindedness of a parolee while simultaneously doing such a poor job of predicting whether the parolee will be arrested and convicted of another crime while on parole.

Yet another closely allied objection is that, if not gestalts, truly important outcomes are ineffable. "Success," for example, means more than receiving a degree, keeping out of jail, or staying alive. "True" success or failure in life can't be measured, so there is no point in trying to compare predictions based on "mere indicators." But there is no positive evidence that clinical professional judgment does any better at predicting the ineffable than it does at predicting the "effable" (again and again and again, the vacuum). Second, it's hard to achieve the ineffable in the absence of "effable" outcomes of the type most commonly used as criteria. It is, for example, extremely difficult to savor the ineffable in life if you're "effably" dead, or to entertain any ineffable sense of occupational success after being "effably" fired repeatedly. Moreover, inability to cope with one's chosen profession is hardly trivial for the individual, and a crime is an extremely severe outcome for the victim.

The major objection to our negative findings, however, is one important for the remainder of this book: The results appear to contradict our intuition that life both is and should be much more predictable than the outcomes of the studies indicate.

But why would we then believe in high predictability in general in such contexts? First, people have good cognitive reasons for seeking predictability in the world, and success in this search is, according to many theorists, the "function" of cognition. A belief that predictability exists when it does not may often create more harm than a belief that we can't predict when we can,[51] but a general bias to believe that the predictability is present in the world may certainly be adaptive. Moreover, we apparently have a compelling emotional need to believe in such predictability. A world that is not predictable cannot be a "just" one that provides us (good people) with the "entitlements" (good outcomes) we deserve.[52] (But no one wants a world that is *perfectly* predictable, which would be a dull one. Nor do we want a world that is *overly* just, in which everyone guilty of a bit of bad behavior or suffering from a touch of neurosis would be haunted with a fear of retribution.) Having cognitive and emotional needs for predictability, however, does not imply that it exists in every context we seek it.

AN EXPLANATION OF THE FINDINGS

Why is statistical prediction superior to clinical prediction in the contexts studied? Some of the reason have to do with the desirable characteristics of such formulas. They are specifically designed to discover a pattern in contexts of variability—the signal distorted by noise. The statistical formulas combine the information optimally to detect the pattern. Moreover, small differences in weights due to variability do not result in large differences in the predictions the formulas make. In fact, as long as the predictive variables themselves are positively related, small differences in combination rules (e.g. the weights applied in constructing weighted averages) result in predictions very similar to those provided by the optimal combination rules. When, for example, weighted averages are used to predict, random weights applied to standardized variables yield predictions very similar to those provided by the best possible weights.[53] Finally, the weighted averages provided by statistical formulas automatically involve the comparison of psychologically incomparable predictors.

People, in contrast, have great difficulty combining qualitatively distinct or incomparable predictors. How, for example, does someone reviewing an applicant for medical school combine information about a past college record with a score on the Medical School Aptitude

Test? In order to do so well, it is necessary to know about both the distributions of these predictors and their predictability—information that is not available to the judge on an intuitive basis, but that forms the basis of the statistical prediction. Similarly, how can an interviewer integrate information about past job history with a self-reflective statement about ambitions, talents, and goals? How does a clinical judge integrate a positive test result in a medical test or an unusual response to a Rorschach Ink Blot Test with knowledge that a disease indicated by such results is extremely rare?

Such integration cannot be done on an intuitive basis. Instead, clinical judgment is often based on a number of cognitive "heuristics" rules of thumb. The first heuristic is to search one's memory (including memory of one's training) for instances similar to the one at hand. This heuristic is termed *availability*.[54] Unfortunately, availability can be quite biased by selective exposure, selective recall, vividness of the instance or category recalled, and so on. A second heuristic is to match the cues or characteristics with a stereotype or a set of other characteristics associated with a category—a heuristic termed *representativeness*.[55] The degree to which something matches a category, however, does not indicate how probable it is. For example, our stereotype of someone addicted to intravenous drugs is that such a person smokes marijuana; hence, marijuana-smoking is a characteristic that matches our stereotype of an intravenous drug addict—even though people who smoke marijuana are far more likely *not* to use intravenous drugs than to use them, let alone be addicted to them.

Availability and representativeness are the heuristics that most commonly lead us to make poor judgments, but they are not the only ones. Since these heuristics have *some* validity in the judgments reviewed in this chapter, the clinical judges generally do better than chance, but they do not do as well as a careful choice among possible relevant factors and determination of how they should be combined, which is done automatically by a statistical model. (For a bitingly humorous description of these heuristics in action, see Paul Meehl's essay "Why I Do Not Attend Case Conferences."[56] In such conferences people spend a great deal of time in "free association," making judgments about patients being discussed by comparing them to a previous patient or a prototypical patient—or sometimes even a relative—on the basis of a single common characteristic, combining biased availability and biased representativeness.)

As illustrated in the Einhorn study involving Hodgkin's disease and longevity, however, the expert human judge does have a very important role to play in making predictions: choosing the variables that *might* be predictive and coding them. Just as people without medical training cannot code the characteristics of a biopsy, people without some training in psychology cannot devise tests that may be predictive of success in a job or academic setting. Here is the valid role of expertise. Once the variables are chosen and then constructed or coded, they should be studied to discover exactly how good they are at predicting outcomes. That's what statistical "science" is all about: subjecting ideas to public scrutiny in a way that will convince the critic who demands "show me." The resulting statistical formulas, moreover, need not be "rigid" (a common criticism of them); they may be modified to incorporate new information as it becomes available. That's the antithesis of the "only I can tell and I can't explain how" approach of much expert testimony in court settings.

OVERVIEW AND IMPLICATIONS

The superiority of statistical formulas in predicting gives rise to what can be termed a "base rate" psychology. People's behavior and feelings are best predicted by viewing them as members of an aggregate and by determining what variables *generally* predict for that aggregate and how. That conclusion contradicts experts' claims to be able to analyze an individual's life in great detail and determine what caused what. Unfortunately, it is exactly the individualized-causality type of analysis that is most expected of professional psychologists and other mental health professionals. This expectation arises not only from our intuitive beliefs about the world but from these psychologists' own declarations about their abilities. As David Faust once phrased it, such declarations should be viewed *versus* the demonstrations of what professionals can actually do.[57]

Moreover, as we have seen, the inability to predict implies a lack of understanding—not because understanding and prediction are synonymous but because a claim to understanding implies an ability to predict. Evaluating the efficacy of psychotherapy has led us to conclude that professional psychologists are no better psychotherapists than anyone else with minimal training—sometimes than those without any training at all; the professionals are merely more expensive. Moreover, in predicting what people will do, clinicians are *worse* than statistical formulas, and statistical formulas are *a lot* less expensive; even developing them is now no great expense, given the availability of inexpensive computer time. One criticism of the statistical formulas is that they may have to be constructed, modified and tested in each separate context in which they are used, but there is evidence that across similar situations there is "validity generalization."[58] It is a great pity that so much effort has been expended in repeating the same result, and raising and countering the same objections to that result, effort that could have been expended on using that result to develop better statistical formulas that will make better predictions. When our *Science* paper appeared, one critic (whose letter to the editor was not published) concluded that what the results implied was that psychologists and psychiatrists should be trained to use the standard psychiatric diagnostic manuals more reliably. Then maybe these clinicians would do better. Why not instead put our efforts into improving the method we know to be superior by developing better statistical models? That should benefit almost everyone—except, of course, the people who are being highly paid to make inferior predictions. But the general public is more important than they are.

THE ETHICS OF PREDICTION

One objection to these conclusions that I personally find particularly distressing—in fact, infuriating—is that making predictions about people using statistical formulas is "dehumanizing," that it treats people as "mere numbers." There is nothing in the approach that implies a judgment about what people *are*; the point is to make the best possible predictions, which can then be used to everyone's benefit. Moreover, the statistical model can be made public, open to scrutiny, and modified appropriately. It can even be shared with the people about whom predictions are made, so that they know how it is they will be judged.

Let me give an example of this openness. A study at the University of Oregon's Psychology Department indicated that a simple (weighted average) statistical model combining past record, test scores, and a crude rating of the selectivity of the students' undergraduate institution predicted later faculty ratings of how well students had done in graduate school better than did the ratings of the admissions committee at the time the students were admitted. This same model could also be used to reject 55 percent of the applicants the committee rejected anyway on the basis of its members' clinical judgment, *without rejecting any applicants whom the committee considered and accepted.*[59] My colleagues and I decided that this finding concerning automatic elimination was of sufficient importance that it should be incorporated into the admissions process—both to save the psychology faculty from the meaningless work of evaluating applicants who had no chance of being admitted, and to save those candidates themselves the work, expense, and heartache of applying to a program to which they had no chance of being admitted.

Before implementing this automatic screening procedure, I checked it out the next year, even though from a statistical perspective it appeared to be extremely valid.[60] It was, after all, a radical procedure. What I did was to inform the other members of the admissions committee that the procedure was being implemented and that they were being asked to make judgments about only those who had passed the initial screening that eliminated the 55 percent. I deceptively passed on to them for evaluation any applicant who appeared to have particular strengths not reflected in past performance or test scores. None of my colleagues noticed this deception (or, upon learning the reason for it, complained about it afterward). Nor were any of those applicants who wouldn't have passed the screening given a rating by any of the other committee members high enough to have any chance of being admitted. The reason was that for every applicant below the cut-score who had a particular strength, there was at least one above that score who had a comparable strength, and there was no reasonable or ethical reason for admitting the former applicant in preference to the latter.

Lewis Goldberg, when he was head of the same admissions committee, subsequently informed potential applicants of the revised formula that was being used for screening: the Average Graduate Record Examination score plus grade-point average multiplied by 100.[61] Potential applicants were informed that if their score were less than 950, they should not waste their time and energies applying; they were also informed of the probability of their being admitted with particular scores above that level. While this procedure was met with some cries of "dehumanization," our opinion in the department was that being perfectly open and honest with the applicants—by providing them with as much information as possible about their chances of being admitted—was highly ethical. (Of course, the number of twenty-five dollar application fees to the university went down.) We were also able to implement an affirmative action program on the same basis, openly and explicitly.

Let me contrast such a procedure with an interview-based one that I have described in a previous book:

> A colleague of mine in medical decision making tells of an investigation he was asked to make by the dean of a large and prestigious medical school to try to determine why it was unsuccessful in recruiting female students. My colleague studied the problem statistically "from the outside" and identified a major source of the problem. One of the older professors had cut back on his practice to devote time to interviewing applicants to the school. He assessed such characteristics as "emotional maturity," "seriousness of interest in medicine," and "neuroticism." Whenever he interviewed an unmarried female applicant, he concluded she was "immature." When he interviewed a married one, he concluded she was "not sufficiently interested in medicine," and when he interviewed a divorced one, he concluded she was "neurotic." Not many women were positively evaluated on these dimensions, which of course had nothing to do with gender.[62]

There's the problem. The ineffable, intuitive clinical judgment is very difficult to challenge—at least, not without an extensive statistical study to assess its bias. A professional psychologist who claims in court that a particularly devastating "clinical judgment" is based on years of experience and cannot be explicitly justified can be challenged only on irrelevant grounds—such as training, years of giving similar testimony, demeanor, and so on. In contrast, a statistical model may be challenged on rational grounds because it is public.

Moreover, there is no need to include in such models variables that we consider inappropriate or lacking in merit. For example, I myself am opposed to use of paper-and-pencil "honesty tests" and personality tests for job placement, even if they do predict. People in such settings should be judged on what they have done and what they can do.

Past behavior provides an indicator of the former, and aptitude or achievement test performance an indicator of the latter. Unlike personality or honesty tests, the subject taking an aptitude or achievement test understands that there is a correct answer (such as to a short mathematics problem) and strives to obtain it. But what is the correct answer to a question about how one should respond to a valued employee who steals five dollars? According to the test scoring, the correct answer is to fire that employee. But if the person taking the test doesn't think that is the best solution, that person is scored for dishonesty.

The bottom line is a happy finding. In a majority of situations, an individual's past behavior is the best predictor of future behavior. That doesn't mean that people are incapable of changing. Certainly many of us do, often profoundly. What it does mean is that no one has yet devised a method for determining who will change, or how or when. Professional psychologists cannot predict that. (If any have been able to do so, it has been kept secret from the research literature.) But if we are responsible for anything, it is our own behavior. Thus, the statistical approach often weights most that for which we have the greatest responsibility.

CHAPTER 4

EXPERIENCE

The Myth of Expanding Expertise

[It is] important, perhaps imperative, that psychology
begin to assemble a body of persuasive evidence bear-
ing on the value of specific educational and training
experience.

—American Psychological Association, 1982[1]

The empirical data indicate that mental health professionals' accuracy of judgment does not increase with increasing clinical experience,
just as their success as psychotherapists does not. There are good logical and empirical reasons why experience does not help in this
context, even though we may all "learn from experience" in other
contexts. Moreover, there are good psychological reasons why the
professionals incorrectly believe that experience does enhance their
purported expertise, when it doesn't. The major reasons involve selective recall, selective interpretation, and assumptions about what is
likely to be true even though it isn't observed.

Why does the American Psychological Association believe that
assembling "persuasive evidence" is imperative, as expressed in the
quotation that opens this chapter? The reason is not that evidence
wasn't assembled, but that the evidence assembled was negative. The
body of evidence at the time about psychologists in particular indicated that there was little of any value in their training and experience
for their practice. In 1989, Howard Garb summarized the evidence in
a *Psychological Bulletin* article[2]: Professional clinicians make somewhat
better judgments than do nonprofessionals, but that can easily be
explained in terms of differences in such characteristics as intelligence
and by the fact that people who have learned how to use valid techniques employ them better than people who haven't learned to use
them. That's not a surprising conclusion, but what may be surprising

is that once the rudiments of the techniques have been mastered, their accuracy does not increase with additional experience using them. That is a very important finding. Any selective advantage that the professional has over the nonprofessional lies in their mastering the basics of a valid technique or two. They learn, for example, that the proper source books about the *statistical* evaluation of MMPI profiles will help them evaluate those profiles. They learn the principles of a particular behavioral technique, which leads to its proper use, and such techniques work.[3] *The accuracy of the judgment of professional psychologists and other mental health workers is limited, however, by the accuracy of the techniques they employ.* That's no different from any other applied field, but what has happened in psychology is that for intuitively compelling reasons, the myth has arisen that through experience per se a professional can develop accurate use of a "pet" technique that research has shown to be invalid, such as the Rorschach Ink Blot Test. Moreover, however often professional psychologists disavow the "medical model," the myth has arisen that the continued practice of a valid technique results in improvement, by analogy with medical procedures such as surgery. The research evidence supports neither of these myths.

Garb's generalization that experience does not improve performance was based on a survey of the research literature evaluating the performance of clinicians who employed a broad variety of techniques. One area in which we might expect there to be an exception is in evaluating neurological impairment. Measures of specific types of intellectual functioning have been carefully devised over many years. Ever since the success of tests of general intelligence used to screen United States military recruits in World War I, psychologists have been interested in differentiating various types of intelligence and intellectual functioning. Along with tests of overall "level" of intelligence (IQ), tests to evaluate specific types of intellectual abilities have proliferated, and many of them have been well validated. The use of such tests to evaluate the results of brain injury has likewise proliferated, and indeed many tests considered in isolation do determine abilities that are associated with such injury. Using such tests to determine how someone's abilities have *changed* as the result of brain injury is much more difficult, except in those few cases where the same test was administered prior to the damage—and even then any changes in performance must be evaluated with reference to the inherent degree of instability in the test results and to any factors other than the injury that might have occurred in the meantime. Given that they generally use such valid tests, neuropsychologists evaluating brain injury might well be expected to benefit from experience in their trade.

Not so. In a recent study (published after Garb's review) Faust and his colleagues asked "a nationally representative sample of clinical neuropsychologists" to evaluate the written results of tests of ten people known to have suffered from specific types of brain injury, or known to have suffered none.[4] Faust and colleagues concluded:

> Except for a possible tendency among more experienced practition-
> ers to overdiagnose abnormality, no systematic relations were
> obtained between training, experience, and accuracy across a series
> of neuropsychological judgments. Comparable results were obtained
> when analysis was limited to the top versus bottom 20% (in terms
> of experience) of the sample. This and other studies raise doubts
> that clinical neuropsychologists train and practice under conditions
> conducive to experiential learning.

Why did the American Psychological Association's committee believe it "imperative" to "assemble a body of evidence" for something that isn't true? The reason I propose is that the success of psychology and often mental health professions stems from the public's belief that experience *does* enhance professionals' performance. After all, it does in many other professions, and therefore it must in the mental health professions as well. But although professional psychology is proclaimed to be based on "the science of psychology," it nonetheless sees a need to provide evidence that experience enhances performance, rather than admit that it doesn't and implement changes in its practices accordingly. In fact, as the profession proliferates at an ever-increasing rate, providing this nonexistent evidence becomes "imperative."

Sadly, the association's statement has not yielded the initiation of a broad research program oriented toward findings that may help practitioners and their clients. Rather, it stands as a public admission that the profession has been rolling merrily along in the absence of such findings, and it reflects the degree to which the profession has lost its research base. The statement definitely does *not* take the form: "Research evidence has shown . . . [say, that the Salk vaccine works]. Therefore, we . . . [recommend its use]." It reflects the opposite approach to gathering evidence: "We do it . . . [say, recommend laetrile]. Therefore, it is imperative to assemble evidence . . . [that it works, even though it doesn't]."

I could end this chapter here, because the empirical bottom line has already been established: Appeals to experience per se are invalid because experience per se does nothing to enhance accuracy. There is not even a hint in the research literature that it does—just selective anecdotal evidence. But I would like to specify *why* experience per se does not enhance accuracy and then discuss why we might be incorrectly convinced that it does.[5] These sections will provide the reader with an understanding of why false claims are false, and perhaps an understanding of the nature of learning from experience as well. The reader interested only in the bottom line may wish to skip—or simply skim—the remainder of this chapter.

We all, of course, learn from experience. That is, we learn some things about certain matters from some types of experience. It is tempting to conclude that we therefore always learn from experience, independent of what is to be learned and the nature of the experience. Didn't Ben Franklin say that "experience is the best teacher"?

Actually, he didn't. He said that "experience is a dear teacher," following a discussion of the Book of Job, and he added, "and fools will learn from no other."[6] It is clear from both the context and the addition that "dear" in this context meant "expensive." (In the 1940s and early 1950s, the owners of some small farms in New Hampshire whom I knew were fond of misquoting Franklin and contemptuous of "book learning"; their land is now owned by a neighbors' sons who went to college instead of acquiring "experience.")

LEARNING MOTION SKILLS VERSUS LEARNING HOW TO CATEGORIZE AND PREDICT

Learning is a term so broad that it refers to a multitude of activities. To "learn from experience" means to develop a particular skill as the result of a particular type of experience. Skills learned may be intellectual (like medical diagnosis), physical (like walking), or a combination of the two (like athletic or musical performance, or even driving a car). We learn simple motor skills differently from how we learn such skills as categorizing, predicting, and differentiating what is important from what is unimportant in a complex pattern, all of which are critical to psychological practice. What sorts of skills are developed as a result of what sorts of experience? What are the characteristics of the experience necessary to develop various skills?

It is clear that we learn many motor skills from practice. Accomplishing some of these skills requires coaching, like swimming and playing the piano; others, however, are acquired through practice alone, like walking and sitting in a chair. In fact, some motor skills that are acquired "automatically" through practice can be seriously disrupted by coaching. It is very difficult to coach someone about how to sit in a chair, for example; an amusing exercise is to explain the process to someone in words, insist that they follow your instructions exactly, then watch both the person and the chair collapse on the first attempt to follow your instructions. Some skills, such as driving a car, consist both of parts that develop automatically and of parts that are coached. Steering in a straight line, for example, is accomplished by making tiny discrete adjustments of the steering wheel that are not made consciously.[7] (The "weaving" behavior of drunk drivers is often due to impairments in making these adjusting movements rather than to any visual problem.) The skill in making these adjusting movements is developed only through experience in driving; in fact, on the first driving lesson most complete novices alternate between going toward the ditch and almost crossing the center line—much to the surprise and consternation of their novice teachers, who themselves are often unaware of their own "tremorous" movements of the steering wheel. Driving skill is developed as the result of continuous and immediate feedback. Like sitting in a chair, driving a car could result in disaster for the person who follows explicit verbal instructions exactly.

Learning to sit in a chair and to drive in a straight line epitomizes our idea of how skills are learned intuitively and are improved with practice. Is clinical skill in the mental health professions of that nature as well? People often explain that clinical skill, too, is based on experience that leads to an ineffable feel about how to proceed, but it is not. Rather, it is a cognitive skill that most often involves conscious decision making on the part of the psychologist. Occasionally, a psychologist may make an impulsive or "intuitive" response to what a client does, but these occasions are rare. Moreover, because the psychologist does not experience feedback about the effects of such responses on either an immediate or a continuous basis, they cannot be "shaped" automatically, as in they are in motor skills. The skills of a clinician are more akin to concepts and categorizing (diagnosing) instances. In order to understand how experience can aid in the development of clinical skills, it is necessary, therefore, to consider how people learn to identify concepts and hence to categorize instances. Work in the area of how people learn to identify concepts has spanned several decades and shown *why* experience per se does not enhance accuracy of clinical judgment. Two conditions are important for experiential learning: one, a clear understanding of what constitutes an incorrect response or error in a judgment, and two, immediate, unambiguous and consistent feedback when such errors are made. In the mental health professions neither of these conditions is satisfied.

Consider first learning the skill of categorizing people—say, distinguishing between child abusers and non–abusers—on the basis of their psychological characteristics rather than their histories. The problem is to decide which people are in each category. Presumably, the person learning this skill is first presented with a number of people who have already been identified as one or the other; the learner is then asked to make judgments about subsequent people. Supposedly the person "learns" the correct assignment through a process of finding out which of these judgments are correct and which are incorrect. Learning how to diagnose cancer is done this way; first the medical student is presented with patients who have cancer and with others who have overlapping symptoms but who do not have cancer; subsequently he or she is asked to make a judgment about new people, then receives feedback about which judgments were correct and which were incorrect.

CAREFUL STUDIES OF LEARNING TO CATEGORIZE

How people learn to make such categorizations accurately has been studied in psychological laboratories. Simplified problems have been invented in which people are asked to distinguish between two categories of stimuli. The stimuli often used are much simpler than distinguishing between abusers and nonabusers, or between cancer patients and non–cancer patients. Rather, subjects are asked to distinguish geometric shapes that differ in shape, color, size and so on. The experimenter teaches the subject a concept—for example, that the pastel-colored shapes form a category—by requiring the subject to distinguish between instances included in the category and instances that are not included. Sometimes the category will be defined by a single characteristic of the stimuli, like pastel-colored geometric figures, sometimes by several characteristics combined according to a rule involving *and* or *or*—such as shapes that are both pastel colored and large, shapes that are either pastel colored or large. The simplest way of teaching the subjects the categorization is to require them to sort the stimuli into piles on the right or left; instances belonging to one category are supposed to be put in one pile, and those not belonging are to be put in the other. In many experiments, subjects make a choice about how to sort each stimulus, and the experimenter informs them about whether their choice was "correct" or "incorrect"—that is, whether the subject had sorted the instances according to the categorical rule the experimenter has in mind (for example, that pastel-colored shapes should be sorted to the left and other shapes to the right). Learning the correct sorting rule is thus equivalent to identifying the category. There are many variations on the basic experimental method; for example, the experimenter could present the subject with two piles of stimuli—one of instances of the category and one of instances not belonging to the category—and ask the subject to provide a verbal description of the category.

When this laboratory work was first initiated some forty years ago, it was described as involving *concept formation,* but this name was later changed to *concept identification,* because it is better described as identifying the concept the experimenter is attempting to convey than as forming this concept. (People have, for example, already "formed" the concept of a pastel color before entering the laboratory.) The work was also at first described in rather behavioristic terms; subjects' responses were said to be "shaped" through the "reinforcement" provided by the experimenter for each sorting response. In contrast, the terms used today are the ones I have used—the subject attempts to determine what the experimenter "has in mind." The reason for this change will soon become clear. In effect, concept discrimination involves the ability to distinguish the important characteristics that define a concept from the unimportant ones. This is precisely the problem facing a clinician in making a diagnosis or categorization.

Experiments were conducted that asked subjects to sort instances into categories. The standard outcome measure of the experiments was the proportion of correct sortings they made across all the trials. The outcome involved pooling correct versus incorrect responses across subjects to obtain this proportion; initial analysis of the outcome led to the conclusion that subjects learn gradually, much as we learn how to drive a car. For any given problem, the subjects' proportions of correct sortings increased on each trial. Moreover, the improvement in this proportion correct was itself proportional to its distance from 100 percent—for example, increased twice as quickly when the subjects were sorting at a 60 percent correct rate as when they were sorting at an 80 percent correct rate. This proportional improvement is the classic form of the "learning curve," which describes gradual learning; such gradual learning is consistent with the *law of effect*, which postulates that responses are shaped automatically through reinforcement without being influenced by the subject's ideas or hypotheses. Thus, early investigators concluded that concepts might be grasped automatically through reinforcement contingencies, much as a motor skill is gradually learned through consistent feedback about the results of practice. If this is how concepts are learned, then professional clinical psychologists may gradually come to form the concepts necessary for their practice and learn through experience how to categorize people and behaviors correctly.

There is, however, another interpretation of the results, one that can be described as involving *terminal insight*. The subjects in a sorting experiment may have ideas about the possible categorical sorting rule that the experimenter has in mind. The subjects guess what the rule is and sort accordingly. When they are told they are incorrect, they abandon that hypothesis and try out another ("maybe it's the large figures that belong on the left"). Thus, if their set of ideas about possible rules includes the one the experimenter has in mind—and the experimenter consequently reinforces as "correct"—they eventually identify the right rule. Once they have identified it, they stick with it, because from that point on they will be making correct sortings. Hence the phrase "terminal insight."

Note that the ideas of the subjects about what categorization rule the experimenter is employing is extremely important in this interpretation; that is, the subjects and the experimenter must share a "common ground" about how the instances might be categorized and about the messages conveyed by the experimenter's statements "correct" and "incorrect."[8] Moreover, and equally important, the terminal insight explanation implies that subjects will try new ways of sorting by distinguishing characteristics *only after they receive feedback that they have made an error* (as when a doctor discovers that what she had believed was a stomach cancer turned out to be an ulcer on closer examination). It follows that if the terminal insight model is correct, then mental health experts can learn correct categorizations only after they have discovered that they have made a mistake. Given the probabilistic nature of knowledge in this area, however, how can they ever be certain that they have made an error? In addition, the type of feedback that mental health experts actually obtain—as opposed to that of medical practitioners—tends to be chaotic, even in terms of the time interval that elapses between judgment and feedback, and sometimes it is nonexistent—the client just disappears. If the gradual learning model for categorization were correct, such ambiguous and chaotic feedback could be surmounted; given enough experience, it could yield learning. If, however, the terminal insight model is correct, then such feedback virtually precludes learning. Thus, for understanding how people learn to categorize from experience, it is critical to differentiate between these two models. I will now present the research evidence that compares them.

COMPARING THE GRADUAL LEARNING VERSUS TERMINAL INSIGHT MODELS

What would the pattern of learning look like according to the terminal insight model? When pooled across subjects, the proportion of correct sorting on each trial would be much the same as those predicted by the gradual learning model. In fact, if the subjects who haven't yet guessed what categorization rule the experimenter had in mind have a constant probability of doing so on each subsequent trial, the results are identical. Subjects who had already guessed what it was by the previous trial would continue to sort correctly, and a constant proportion of those who hadn't would now guess correctly. Once again, the degree to which learning improves on successive trials is itself proportional to the amount yet to be learned (that is, the discrepancy of proportion correct from 100 percent). The analysis is complicated somewhat by the fact that subjects have a fifty-fifty chance of being correct on a purely chance basis when they sort the instances, but the conclusion about the identical implications *when pooled across subjects* of the gradual learning and terminal insight models is unchanged.

These two models can, however, be distinguished. (It is *not* a matter of the ideology of the experimenter about whether to use a behavioristic or a mentalistic framework in analyzing results.) The method is to examine the responses of individual subjects. If the gradual learning model is correct, then each subject should show an increasing proportion of correct sortings across trials prior to her or his last sorting error. If, in contrast, the terminal insight explanation is correct, then each subject should be correct at a chance level (50 percent when there are two choices) prior to her or his last sorting error, because an error indicates that insight has not yet been achieved. Then, the appearance of gradual learning would be found *only* when pooling across subjects—who achieve insight on different trials of the experiment—whereas according to the gradual learning explanation, this gradual increase of being correct should appear within the individual subject as well. Analyzing individual response patterns in such experiments, the late Frank Restle, Tom Trabasso, and Gordon Bower found conclusive support for the terminal insight explanation.[9] Subjects' response patterns prior to the their last error were *stationary*, showing no increase in correct sorting. Moreover, the proportion of correct sortings prior to this last error was at a chance level. Insight appeared to occur suddenly, after a trial on which the subject was told that he or she had made an error. Again, because this insight occurred at different times for different subjects, the result was that pooling across subjects gave the appearance of gradual learning.

AN IMPORTANT STUDY OF LEARNING HOW TO IDENTIFY CONCEPTS

It is still, however, possible that subjects learned something prior to insight but that whatever they learned was not evident in their overt responses. To test this possibility, Trabasso and Bower developed an ingenious procedure termed an *alternating reversal shift*, in which the

correct response assignment (to the left versus the right) is often shift-
ed when the subjects have not yet identified the concept—so that it
would be impossible for them to learn gradually. Let me illustrate this
procedure with an example. Suppose the subjects are to learn to distinguish between pastel-colored geometric designs and other ones by
sorting the pastel-colored ones to the left. The first time the subjects
place a pastel-colored figure on the right or another to the left, they
are informed that they are incorrect. The second time they do that,
however, they are told that they are *correct*. The experimenters have
reversed the sorting task; so that the pastel-colored figures are now to
go to the right and the others to the left. Now, the next time the subjects place a pastel-colored figure on the *left* or another on the *right*,
they are told they are incorrect. On the error after that, however, they
are told that they are correct, and the sorting rule the experimenter
reinforces is reversed again—this time back to its original state. The
process continues, so that every second error is labeled as "correct"
and the sorting rule is reversed.

Now consider subjects who have not achieved insight into this pattern. Half the time they are reinforced by being told they were correct
when they place a pastel-colored design on the left or another on the
right, while half the time they are told they are incorrect for doing so.
According to the law of effect, these subjects should not be able to
learn at all. The "reinforcement" they receive is completely contradictory. But they do learn, and in fact they master the task after being
told they were incorrect the same number of times on the average as
the subjects who were *consistently* told they were correct for sorting
the pastel-colored figures to the left and the others to the right. That
result is quite consistent with the terminal insight model *without any*
learning at all prior to insight. When subjects make an error, they indicate that they have not yet considered the categorical rule that the
experimenter has in mind. Therefore, it doesn't matter whether the
experimenter changes which way the stimuli should be sorted.
Moreover, when subjects make an error, they abandon the hypothesis
they have in mind about the experimenter's rule and try another one.
It could be the correct one. Thus, far from learning this task as an
automatic result of being reinforced, the subjects learn *suddenly and*
only after having made an error.

At the time of Bower and Trabasso's important work, psychology itself was not free of behaviorist ideology. Thus, these investigators did not use the same mentalistic terms I have used here in describing their results. Rather, they developed a precise mathematical model about "hypothesis testing theory." (Interestingly, their model is quite similar to an earlier one termed "stimulus selection theory," which had been used to describe gradual learning without awareness.) Belief that concepts are learned according to a terminal insight process was, in fact, slow in gaining acceptance. For example, one investigator claimed that he had evidence contradicting such a model after conducting experiments in which subjects appeared to identify his concept gradually, but never succeeded perfectly. How, then, could the process be accounted for by his subjects' insight? Such insight, he argued, would have resulted in perfect performance, which he never found.

This subjects' task was to learn to sort ordinary playing cards into two piles depending upon whether the designs on their backs depicted a "unitary" object or a scene containing "multiple" objects. The subjects' average success rate was 75 percent at the end of the experiment, even for the subjects who were able to describe the rule correctly when asked what it was. This discrepancy between success rate and verbal insight apparently strengthened the experimenter's contention that the actual behavior could not be a consequence of insight but was perhaps developed according to the law of effect in parallel to the development of such insight. Spoilers, however, arrived on the scene. Don Dulany and Daniel O'Connell took the same playing cards and simply asked subjects to sort them to the right or left depending on whether the designs on the back were unitary or multiple.[10] The subjects achieved only an 80 percent success rate when these experimenters made the same distinction about what was unitary and what was multiple that the previous experimenter had made. The explanation for the earlier results, then, was not that the subjects had learned category membership through a process independent of their conscious hypothesis testing, but that the first experimenter had constructed categories that were so vague that subjects could describe them verbally without being any better than 75—80 percent successful in determining which instance (card) belonged to each. Looking at the back of some playing cards and attempting to decide whether the design—for example, a vase with flowers—is unitary or multiple might convince the reader that the distinction is extraordinarily vague.

Dulany and O'Connell's debunking experiment points to a very important conclusion. It is crucial in these concept identification experiments that subjects have a set of clear ideas about which rules the experimenter is apt to use *prior* to receiving the information about whether a particular choice is correct or incorrect. Hypotheses that do not exist can not be grasped. (In fact, this very principle led Plato to propose a heaven consisting of "pure forms" that must be recalled in order for a person to develop an understanding of such concepts as "virtue"—which must be defined in the same manner for a race horse as for a person.) A concept that is unknown to the subject—or that is sufficiently obscure that it does not "come to mind" as a possibility—cannot be understood by the subject simply by being told which stimuli belong to it and which do not.

IMPLICATIONS FOR "LEARNING FROM EXPERIENCE" IN THE MENTAL HEALTH FIELD

Now consider whether a psychological or psychiatric expert can learn a categorical distinction based on pure "experience." Generalizing from these careful experiments, we can conclude that such learning can occur only if categorical membership is based on a well-defined rule that can be understood prior to observing *anybody*, that is, prior to attempting to test this rule by applying it to instances. Otherwise, the professional is in the position of a medical diagnostician who is attempting to diagnose cancer on the basis of previous experience with cancer patients and those free of cancer without knowing what cancer is. Categorization—hence diagnosis and prediction—can be no better than the theoretical knowledge leading to the construction of well-defined categories.

Another important finding from the concept identification experiments has direct relevance to the learning through experience question. Recall that in these experiments *subjects identified the correct concept only after being informed that they were wrong.* Such explicit accurate feedback led them to reject an incorrect hypothesis and understand the correct one. The application to professional psychology is that even when a rough categorization does exist—as, for example, between "paranoid" versus "simple" schizophrenia—knowledge of what these categories are like and how to categorize individuals in them is gained through experience only when the learner judges incorrectly that an individual belongs to one category and then discovers through feedback that the individual belongs to another.

Now consider the statement that "I can identify child abusers because I have had experience working with fifty [or one hundred, or even five hundred] of them." Child abuse may have a fairly precise definition on the basis of actual behavior, but professionals who attempt to learn from experience to distinguish between abusers and nonabusers must—according to the learning-from-errors principle—have experience with people who *appear* to be child abusers but are *not*. Where does such experience come from? It is extraordinarily difficult to obtain; in fact, it is empirically impossible to obtain if one's contact is limited to people who actually are child abusers. It is also impossible to obtain by definition if the professional's conclusion that someone is a child abuser is assumed to be correct in the absence of supporting evidence.[11] Medical experts can claim to be able to recognize cancer without *extensive* experience in making erroneous judgments, but a clear definition of this "natural" condition (category) exists prior to the experience, as does the biopsy test to confirm whether it is present. This knowledge, in turn, results from previous research and biological knowledge. Compare that with knowledge about "the abusive personality." Categorical learning can occur in the absence of feedback about actual negative instances only when it is based on a "well-corroborated theory to make the transition from theory to fact (that is, when the expert has access to a specific model)," as Dawes, Meehl, and Faust put it.[12] Such models simply do not exist in the areas in which professional psychologists or psychiatrists most often make confident judgments—in courts—"as based on my years of experience." This experience is definitely *not* analogous to that in learning how to drive in a straight line or to sit in a chair.

Another characteristic of the concept identification experiments is that the subjects must receive immediate and correct feedback in order to identify the concepts. In fact, such feedback is important if people are to learn anything at all from experience—whether it is a concept, a general idea of how to deal effectively with people, or a motor skill. Even in learning to drive a car or sit in a chair, feedback must be immediate, systematic, and subject to a minimum of probabilistic distortion. But *the feedback most professional clinicians receive about their judgments and decisions is neither immediate nor systematic nor free of probabilistic distortion.* The immediacy problems are obvious: Lacking definitive procedures such as a medical biopsy, the correctness of the diagnoses and predictions that mental health professionals make often cannot be determined for years. Some are intrinsically impossible to evaluate, such as a judgment about who would be a better custodial parent. Knowing whether a good judgment was made would require not just feedback about what happened when one parent was granted custody but knowing what *would* have happened *if* custody had been granted to the other parent. But such hypothetical counterfactuals are unavailable.[13]

Even easily interpretable feedback, however, is probabilistic in three ways. First, the professional may or may not receive it, and its very existence may be biased in a particular direction—as when mental health workers notice people who return to an institution but do not notice those who do not; thus, "as any psychiatrist can testify, 'success' among the long-term mentally ill is a sometime thing."[14] (Somehow, I always thought that success was a "sometime thing" for any of us.) Even for practitioners outside institutions, as Courtenay Harding, Joseph Zubin, and Joseph Strauss point out, "there is no built-in system about eventual outcome success. They receive only the negative messages signaled by the reappearance of patients who have relapsed and often simply assume that those who leave 'uncured' are leading a 'marginal existence' somewhere."[15]

Second, feedback that is received lacks clarity or is rendered ambiguous by the operation of various confounds. Hence it is *intrinsically* probabilistic from the perspective of the professional. Human behavior and feelings are influenced by a multiplicity of incomparable factors, many of which are not known at the time when a judgment is made or that may exert an important influence only after that time.

Third, "self-fulfilling prophecies" arise when conditions that the professional may or may not have assessed correctly are influenced by the professional's own judgment. When a person is judged to be irredeemably violent and sentenced to death row, for example, this judgment itself may be a factor in facilitating later violence. When a seriously disturbed person is judged to be "in need" of hospitalization, this judgment may be a factor in worsening the person's condition. In such instances, no comparison is possible since the hypothetical counterfactual is missing—only here it is due to the professionals' own behavior (in judging the prisoner to be "irredeemable," and the seriously disturbed person to be "in need" of hospitalization), while the subsequent feedback is easily interpreted as indicating what would have happened anyway in the absence of the judgment.[16] (It is important to note that not all prophecies are self-fulfilling; for example, the prophecy that nothing bad will happen to me even though I take chances when I drive is a self-negating one.)

Such probabilistic feedback is a problem. Careful laboratory research has demonstrated that subjects cannot learn even the simplest task if the feedback about how well they are doing is sufficiently probabilistic.[17] Feedback "error" always hampers learning; how much depends on the nature of the task. Professional judgment in psychology is a difficult task, and the probabilistic component of the feedback after the judgment is made is enormous.

BUT THERE IS AN ILLUSION OF LEARNING

The fact that judgmental accuracy does not increase with experience is now (1992) being acknowledged in many journal articles; so is the efficacy of paraprofessionals as psychotherapists. Garb's review is an example.[18] Why, then, are so many professionals still convinced that their judgmental abilities are "honed" and enhanced by experience? So, unfortunately, are many courts, where a statement about years of experience is accepted as evidence of expertise. The answer lies in the feedback problem discussed above—specifically, in the biased availability of the feedback that the professional receives. These biases, as we have seen, include the lack of hypothetical counterfactuals, the probabilistic nature of the feedback, and the possibility of self-fulfilling prophecies.

But isn't constructing such categories (or mental illness) exactly what the diagnostic manuals are attempting? Yes, they are attempting it. Recall, however, that these categories have some natural characteristics and some artifactual characteristics—some more natural, some more artifactual. Those categories most easily classified as "natural" are those that involve genetic or other organic tendencies or "susceptibilities" that sometimes appear in overt form and sometimes do not. It is, for example, very difficult to diagnose schizophrenia or manic-depressive psychosis that is "in remission" other than on the basis of a previous diagnosis (and most probably a hospitalization). In contrast, those categories most easily classified as artifactual (like "histrionic" or "situational depression") are precisely those that have the largest amount of fuzz in their fuzzy boundaries. Much more important, however, is the problem that "by their fruits shall ye know them." If such categorization is important in treatment, why are untrained therapists as effective as those who have been trained in this categorization system? Why do simple statistical models predict better?

BIASES ENHANCING THE ILLUSION OF LEARNING

Some of the biases in feedback availability are also psychologically compelling and hence lead to a belief in the validity of learning, even as they result in its invalidity. The first bias is that instances where judgment turns out to be correct (even if on a purely chance basis) are often quite vivid. Such vivid instances are easily recalled by the professional and are shared with others. As such instances are "collected" throughout a career, their relative frequency is overestimated. Ironically, the more statistically improbable it is that a judgment would be correct, the greater the vividness of its success (perhaps yet another reason for derogating statistical formulas). Hence the greater impact of such instances over time as compared with more mundane judgments, which would potentially form a better basis from which to receive feedback, were it to be provided. Let me give an example of such a vivid instance.

Years ago a middle-aged man walked into a hospital complaining that he was growing breasts. The intake doctor noted that the man appeared depressed and asked why. The man answered that his mother had committed suicide earlier that week. The man was quickly referred to a hospital psychiatrist and subsequently placed on a locked psychiatric ward. The staff members on that ward, many of them psychoanalytically trained, were fascinated by the delusion of growing breasts following a mother's suicide. (The delusion was possibly related to the fact that the man, while married, had no children.) The man was given the usual psychological tests, including an intelligence test, the Rorschach Ink Blot Test, the MMPI (discussed in Chapter

3), and the Bender-Gestalt test, a test of copying simple geometric figures. A good friend of mine who was known as a Rorschach expert was asked, as a challenge, to interpret the results of these tests "blind"; he was told only that the man had an unusual symptom. (My friend undoubtedly assumed that it was of a serious, probably psychotic nature, since the man was in a locked ward.)

The staff meeting where my friend presented his interpretation of the results was crowded. He began by stating that on the basis of the Rorschach Ink Blot results, "I think there may be something organic [physically wrong] here." He asked if he could be told the results of the physical examination before proceeding. Actually, aside from the usual temperature, pulse rate, and blood pressure assessments, there had been no physical examination. My friend was immediately told about the man's breast-growing symptoms. He conjectured that the man might be suffering from an hormonal imbalance, and a complete physical examination of the man was ordered immediately after the staff meeting. It turned out that the man had Klinefelter's syndrome, which is brought about by having one Y and two X chromosomes, and he was indeed growing breasts, a common result of the syndrome. He had been quite thin all his life, and he had not happened to notice the breast development until the week of his mother's suicide. (The two X chromosomes also explained his childlessness, because such men are sterile.) After being given prescriptions to counteract the effects of this syndrome, the man was sent home (I hope with apologies for having been needlessly imprisoned for six weeks, but I cannot be sure). The story of my friend's successful diagnosis was repeated throughout the hospital and the nearby university, and he himself remembered it vividly when I talked to him about it more than twenty-five years later. But had my friend really learned from his experience with the Rorschach?

In fact, the Rorschach Ink Blot Test is not a valid test of anything it was supposed to assess at that time (see Chapter 5). There is simply no way of detecting Klinefelter's syndrome on the basis of what someone sees in a set of ink blots. That's it. But my friend didn't say that the man had Klinefelter's syndrome; he said—or is quoted as saying, anyway—"I think there is something organic." How many patients on that ward *wouldn't* have been found to have something organically wrong with them if they had been subjected to an intense physical examination? (It was my friend himself who subsequently diagnosed that the "something organic" was Klinefelter's syndrome, but only after extensive library work—not from experience with the Rorschach responses of men who had the syndrome.) Moreover, how many patients whose responses indicated a fair degree of disturbance wouldn't my friend have suggested had "something organic" wrong with them? (In fact, he may have considered that possibility more often than others did, since he once correctly diagnosed someone as suffering from an obscure psychotic condition brought on by an acute sensitivity to red wine.) Thus, the anecdote not only describes a single diagnosis, it does not provide *any* evidence for the idea that an experienced "Rorschacher" can use the test effectively based on that experience. Nevertheless, whenever I questioned the validity of the Rorschach to the people who were on the hospital staff or in the clinical program at the nearby university, they reminded me of this anecdote as a refutation of the research results I mentioned. This one single case was used as evidence that my friend—and hence all clinical psychologists—*did* learn from experience with the Rorschach, contrary to my claims and the empirical data that they don't.

(I'd like to make two comments about this anecdote before proceeding. First, anecdotes can be used as educational devices; we often remember them better than we remember general principles. In fact, I have right here used an anecdote to demonstrate that we shouldn't use anecdotes to establish generalizations. There is a crucial difference, however, between using an anecdote as an illustration and using it as a basis for generalization or as evidence. Another point this anecdote illustrates—again, a point established by research—is that once he was classified as a "mental case," the man's complaints were not taken seriously. He wasn't even asked to remove his shirt! If physicians paid no attention to the presenting symptoms of their patients who are not classified as suffering from a mental illness, they would soon lose their licenses or at least their clientele. It is, however, perfectly acceptable for a mental health professional to ignore what someone has to say once that person's problems have been classified as stemming from a mental illness or defect. Szasz is fond of finding cases—anecdotes, again—in which someone was ignored when claiming something that turned out to be literally true—such as that neighbors had killed and eaten someone.[19] Equally distressing is the implicit principle that we shouldn't take seriously what a disturbed person has to say. Recently, when I mentioned to a friend who is basically sympathetic to my view that people should feel as free to "shop around" for psychotherapists as for those providing any other service, she said that she thought this conclusion was questionable because "how can you expect someone who is seriously distressed to make a good choice?" My answer is, why shouldn't they? There is absolutely no evidence that emotional distress necessarily implies incompetence or an inability to judge what is helping or hurting in an attempt to alleviate that distress—any more than there is evidence that someone who has a severe physical problem cannot judge whether medical treatment is doing any good. Even many people who are seriously psychotic are out of touch with reality only *some* of the time about *some* aspects of reality.[20]

The second availability bias enhancing the illusion of learning from experience arises because professionals often can recall or cite specific instances in a way that creates feedback that is *consistent* but irrelevant. A professional notes that a majority of people who have a problem (say, neurosis) also have a characteristic "diagnostic" of that problem (say, recall of unhappy incidents in childhood). Another professional notes that women with breast cancer previously had high-risk breasts; still another notes that dyslexics had difficulty spelling. The relatively consistent association between the problem and the characteristic leads to the invalid conclusion that those with the characteristic will probably have the problem. No. The frequency with which people who have the problem also have the characteristic is *not* equivalent to the frequency with which people with the characteristic also have the problem. A vast majority of people who can recall unhappy incidents in childhood are *not* neurotic. Most psychotic individuals brushed their teeth as children, but tooth brushing does not predict psychosis, just as a vast majority of women with high risk breasts do *not* develop breast cancer, and a vast majority of those who can't spell are *not* dyslexic. Continually finding association by sampling only those who have the problem, however, often leads professionals to generalize from this select sample of people with the problem, which Paul Meehl, Gary Melton, and I—among others—have pointed out is an irrational generalization.[21] Careful laboratory studies have indicated that we all are prone to making this mistake, which Amos Tversky and Danny Kahneman have specified as resulting from biased availability followed by (what is technically termed) *representative* thinking, that is, making a judgment on the basis of the degree to which a characteristic matches a stereotype or category.[22] Professionals are no exception. Only practice based on knowledge, rather than impressions, can rectify the problem.

Let me give a rather striking example. In 1984 the rules and laws in Oregon regarding the licensing of psychologists were subject to review as a result of a state provision requiring the automatic reevaluation of them ("sunsetting provisions"). At that time, there were only a few legal exceptions to the rule stipulating confidentiality between client and psychologist. The major one was that if a psychologist had good reason to believe that a child was being physically or sexually abused, confidentiality was broken in the interests of protecting the child. The child welfare agency was to be notified immediately. The psychologist didn't require proof, just reasonable suspicion that the child was in danger; whether the child was actually in danger was to be determined by the state agencies, ultimately the criminal divisions. The purpose of this breach of confidentiality was to protect children.

Confidentiality was *not* to be broken, therefore, if the child was in no immediate danger—that is, if the incident or incidents had occurred years ago and the child was now grown, or if the family itself had provided protection by removing the child to a place where the allegedly abusive person could no longer harm the child. When the laws were being reconsidered, many professionals argued that the confidentiality rules should be changed to report *any* suspected child abuse, whether or not the child was in any current danger. The argument they gave was that "if there's one thing we know about child abusers, it's that they never stop on their own without therapy." When these professionals were asked how they knew that, the answer was that this was their opinion based on extensive contact with child abusers, or on that of other experts who had had extensive experience. How did they gain this experience? By engaging in psychotherapy with people who had been caught and mandated to have therapy with them from the court system. How likely was it that someone who had abused a child only once or twice would be caught? "Very unlikely" was the response. Thus, these experts' experience was *by necessity* limited to those who had the characteristics they claimed were true of all child abusers. (I am not maintaining that a large number of child abusers, or even any particular proportion, stop on their own. I have no idea how many do. What I am maintaining is that experience limited to those who haven't stopped on their own is an irrational basis from which to conclude that child abusers "always keep doing it until they are caught.") Moreover, it was by definition impossible for these abusers to stop without therapy, because they were already in therapy.

When I pointed out these experts' flaws in generalizing, they agreed with me that there was a "logical" problem with reaching the conclusion they did, but they would then produce the same argument with equal vehemence at the next meeting. Our own experience is indeed extraordinarily important in reaching conclusions; it can overwhelm logic, and we would in general be in great difficulty if we didn't pay attention to it. When, however, our experience is systematically biased, it forms a poor basis on which to learn. Again, there's nothing unique about professionals making such inappropriate conclusions. The same problem—and the same vehemence—can be found, say, among distressed children of alcoholics who attend groups of other distressed children of alcoholics, and who subsequently maintain that any children of alcoholic parents who don't admit to being very distressed are simply denying their feelings.

Ultimately, the confidentiality law was not changed, but perhaps more because it infringed on the prerogatives of a number of professional groups—including lawyers, psychiatrists, and ministers—than because the arguments for changing them didn't stand up to logical scrutiny. But whether it was changed or unchanged, the law was of dubious value anyway, because therapists had an ethical obligation not only to report suspicions of child abuse but to warn clients in advance that they would report these suspicions. They thereby effectively warned their clients not to say anything to arouse their suspicions. Although current evidence indicates that the area of sexual abuse may be an exception to the generalization that psychotherapy is effective (few controlled studies have been attempted[23]), this exception should not be generalized to the area of physical abuse.

The third bias toward the illusion of learning from experience arises when people inadvertently create their own experience and hence their own feedback. As we have seen, it is difficult to "learn" the validity of a judgment that someone is "irredeemable" or violent when that judgment itself leads to circumstances prone to encouraging violence, like placement on death row. What is "learned" in such circumstances is due to a self-fulfilling prophecy. A waiter, for example, "learns" that only well-dressed people give good tips, because having developed that initial hypothesis for whatever reason, he gives well-dressed people better service than poorly dressed ones.[24] These self-fulfilling prophecies can be particularly pernicious. For example, when I was head of a department, a friend in an important departmental position created immense chaos and ill-feeling through his extremely aggressive behavior. He would denounce people in public, threaten to resign, and so on. In one conflict he finished a telephone conversation with me by screaming that "the only way you get anywhere in this world is to push, push, push, push!" But that was true for *him*. His own aggressiveness had so alienated most of his colleagues that they wouldn't cooperate with him unless they were coerced to do so. But from his own perspective, he was reacting to them in the only reasonable way. (Fortunately, he quit his position eventually, and his much more positive characteristics—which were always evident in his behavior outside the university setting—came to predominate.)

On a broader level, self-fulfilling prophecies are part of some mental ailments. Depressed people often suffer from "negative cognitions" about themselves and their lives; they feel socially inferior and rejected by others. Unfortunately, these people are often correct—their sense of inferiority and rejection is brought about by their own "dysphoric" behavior, as pointed out and documented by James Coyne and his colleagues.[25] Depressed people are not a lot of fun to be around. Efforts of friends to express sympathy and to "talk them out of" their depression fail; subsequently, friends avoid them. Thus, an initial judgment of one's own inferiority can lead to behavior that provides compelling feedback that this judgment was correct. This sad process can end up like the famous cartoon of the therapist informing a mother that her child does not suffer from an "inferiority complex": "I'm sorry, Mrs. Jones, your son really is inferior." Sufficiently strong belief (for example, in one's inferiority) can in some circumstances create the reality (for example, of inferiority).

Self-created feedback can occur in professional practice as well. For example, I have an acquaintance who can be described in nontechnical terms as self-indulgent, conceited, and precious. He is a psychotherapist who has apparently achieved some sort of inner peace through labeling himself as having a "narcissistic character disorder." When he was talking about his private practice a few years ago to a group of other professionals, he made the startling assertion that he had concluded that the major psychological problem with American males today is narcissistic character disorder. This syndrome is tied to their being told as boys to be brave, he said, and in particular not to cry. After he realized that he himself had such a disorder, he had become increasingly aware that many of his male patients suffered from it as well. Virtually all of them had been told by someone at some point in their childhood that they should be brave and not cry. (What boy hasn't?) Once he had reached this conclusion about his clientele, he had developed a specialty in helping male narcissistic characters, and subsequently more and more of them had come to him for help. Hence his discovery that this syndrome is the major psychological problem faced by American males today.

All these availability biases are magnified by retrospective memory, on which most people—professionals included—rely to "learn from experience." Memory is, however, basically a *reconstructive* process, as we demonstrated in laboratory experiments as far back as 1930 by Sir Frederick Bartlett.[26] We attempt to "make sense" out of our recall of bits and pieces of our past ("memory traces") in terms of what we "know" to be true of the world today, by "filling in the gaps." Moreover, the general ideas that we evolve after filling in some gaps will influence our search for the other traces that we end up recalling. That means, for example, that our recall of stability and change in our own life is highly influenced by our implicit or explicit theories of human stability and change at present. If we are currently depressed, for example, and we believe that adult depression is brought about by the childhood experience of having aloof and demanding parents, it is easy for us to recall instances where our parents were aloof or demanding. We thereby form a judgment that our parents were generally aloof and demanding, which supports our judgment that we are currently depressed because of the way they treated us. Or, to take another example, if we are quite politically liberal as older adults, and we believe that people tend to get more politically conservative as they grow older, it is easy for us to recall some political attitudes in our youth that were even more liberal than our current ones. Such memories reinforce our belief that people tend to get more conservative as they grow older—even if assessments of our attitudes taken at various times in our lives demonstrate that we have actually grown more liberal.[27] That also means that we have a *hindsight bias* in which we not only conclude that we "knew it all along," but are unable to recall what we actually believed before an outcome was known.[28] We now have become experts in what did occur and hence suffer from the *expert's curse* in reconstructing what we believed before we knew the outcome.[29] (It is often hard for an expert to understand what someone with less expertise will think or judge, such as about a wine or an automobile.)

While our memories may be vivid, that does not mean that they are accurate; I myself often have a precise visual image of where something is, only upon checking to discover that this image is incorrect. Study after study has indicated how easy it is to manipulate what people "recall," studies that include careful checks to make sure that the subjects are not deliberately distorting.[30] The fact that something is recalled does not necessarily imply that it has happened. The naive idea that someone recalls something accurately, or can't recall it, or recalls it accurately but lies about it, is incorrect. We reconstruct the past. (This problem will be covered in greater detail in Chapter 6.)

The reconstructive nature of memory serves to enhance all the availability biases outlined above, because the past is recalled in a way that "validates" our current judgments. To be sure, professionals take notes, and charts of patient behaviors and feelings are available. But the professionals do *not* include in such notes or charts their *current* judgments concerning their clients. When they review such notes, it is all too easy to be subject to biased availability and to conclude that something that happened later "made sense" in the light of what the client said in the notes. As Baruch Fischhoff points out, we cannot learn unless we are *surprised* at what has occurred (again, the importance of the "error" in learning). The "creeping determinism of hindsight" makes us unsurprised, and we therefore cannot learn even in those contexts where some learning may be possible. Professionals relying on retrospective memory are no exception. This problem is exacerbated when—as is too common—the notes themselves are "upgraded" retrospectively, sometimes weeks or even months after the actual interaction with the client occurred.

THE MISSING WATCH

A mental health profession searching for expertise is like a man searching his house for a valuable gold and platinum watch that was crafted by a famous watchmaker. The man is sure that the watch is in the house somewhere. First, he searches the study (which here represents special expertise in psychotherapy). The watch isn't there, (studies actually conducted do not favor the professional psychologists), but maybe he has failed to look in the right places (perhaps studies in other problem areas or with more severe patients will). He also searches the dining room (perhaps special understanding is indicated by superior predictive ability). The watch is not there, either. He may not have looked as hard as he should (perhaps some other room will show the superiority of clinical to statistical prediction). Certainly the watch will be found in the master bedroom (learning from clinical experience will uphold the notion of expertise). Not there either, but again he hasn't looked in every conceivable nook and cranny. Perhaps it's in the den (agreement between diagnostic judges using the psychiatric diagnostic manuals may suffice).

It is "important, perhaps imperative" that the man find the watch. Why? Because he has used it as collateral for a large loan he took out to finance a business. Suppose he can't find it, or worse yet, suppose it isn't in the house, or worst of all, suppose it doesn't exist. Then the bank may call in the loan, and the business will fail. So the man keeps on looking for the watch, returning to places already searched, considering the possibility that it is in improbable places such as the bathroom or the balcony (panoramic "psychological portraits"). The problem is that as he searches in increasingly obscure and dark places, the light at the end of his flashlight (or is it the jewel in his crown?) keeps telling him it isn't where he is looking.

We've all made frantic searches for something, even returning again and again to places we've already looked. There's a bit of rationality in such searches, even in returning to look, if we know that we had the object in the first place and have at least a vague idea of where we might have lost it. What the man is doing, however, is acting as if he had the watch first by taking out the loan but only subsequently searching for it.

The man will no doubt continue searching, continue providing explanations about why his search may not have been thorough enough, and continue to search new rooms. The bank, however, won't put up forever with the argument from the vacuum that the search just hasn't been good enough yet. Professional psychologists all hold that loan through our third-party payments. In fact, it's not just a loan but a professional fee for the privilege of being told the watch exists, even though it is not yet found. Isn't it time to call in the loan?

CHAPTER 5

LICENSING

The Myth of Protecting the Public

The laws are intended to protect the public by limiting licensure to those persons who are qualified to practice psychology as defined by state and provincial [Canadian] law. The legal basis for licensure lies in the right of the state to enact legislation to protect its citizens. Caveat emptor or "buyer beware," is felt to be an unsound maxim when the "buyer" of services cannot be sufficiently well informed to beware, and hence states have enacted regulatory boards to license qualified practitioners. A professional board is a state or provincial agency acting to protect the public, not serve the profession.

—American Association of State Licensing Laws[1]

There are a multitude of reasons for licensing people who engage in medical practice. Psychotherapy, has often been categorized a medical procedure, but as we have seen, it lacks the scientific grounding that characterizes modern medicine. (Psychotherapy does have a lot in common with medical practices of centuries ago, some of which worked.) In this chapter I will concentrate exclusively on the licensing of psychologists—particularly those who practice psychotherapy or who proffer "expert" advice on psychological matters in courts, hospitals, and the popular press. I will discuss the licensing and social acceptance of other self-proclaimed experts in the next chapter, and also address the question of whether anyone outside the field of medicine who proffers mental health treatment should be licensed, and how.

Every state requires that practicing professional psychologists be licensed. In fact, in many states (like Oregon), it is illegal for people to refer to themselves as "psychologists" unless they are licensed, even if they do not provide a professional service. I, for example, am not legally a psychologist but a professor of psychology. In order to become licensed in most states, people must have a Ph.D. from a program accredited by the APA or an "equivalent" program, have a year of internship during graduate study (again from an APA-approved "or equivalent" program), have a year or two of postdoctoral supervised clinical experience, pass a national examination, and—in most states—convince their already licensed colleagues in an interview that they are capable. (See Chapter 3 on the validity of such interviews.)

The rationale to protect the public is fine. But the results are dismal. To understand the rationale and results, it is necessary to ask exactly who needs to be protected and from what. Otherwise, licensure is simply restraint of trade, that is, limiting psychology to professionals when we know (see Chapter 2) that others can practice it equally well.

THE NEED FOR PROTECTION

The major rationale for licensing is that some patients need protection. Who needs protection? People over whom psychologists have institutional power cannot make informed choices. Such people include residents of nursing homes, psychiatric hospitals, jails, and the military services. These people's lives are controlled by others, and the state has every right—in fact an obligation—to demand that those in charge be qualified. These custodians should meet certain educational requirements and adhere to certain standards of behavior. Psychologists who control residents in such institutions should certainly meet the standards of the APA's Ethics Code forbidding them to make sexual contact or financial arrangements with clients. Institutional settings, however, provide a poor rationale for requiring the licensing of psychologists. First, only about 9.8 percent of licensed psychologists work in such settings.[2] Second, the residents in such settings have little contact with those psychologists or with their psychiatrists; rather, their lives are controlled to a great extent by aides who are *not* licensed and who cannot currently be expected to be, since they are generally recruited on the basis of no qualifications whatsoever and are paid minimum wages.

The institutional control that the aides—not the professionals—have in such settings has been well documented. Those of us who have worked in such institutions have for years been struck by the degree to which patients are ignored by the "higher-level" professionals there. An intake interview resulting in a diagnosis is followed most often by a very brief daily monitoring of the patient's "progress," occasional discussions at staff meetings, and a final quick decision that the patient requires longer incarceration, or is perhaps "cured," or more likely is "in remission," and can leave (a decision often made after the insurance payments run out).[3] Until the early 1970s, however, systematic studies of what went on were lacking, although several sociologists such as Erving Goffman had made excellent unsystematic observation of patients' lives in such total institutions.[4] (Because such studies lacked "hard data," those who didn't like these observations or their implications could dismiss them as just "wrong" or "biased," while to others of us they appeared convincing.)

In the early 1970s, David Rosenhan of Stanford conducted a study to determine exactly what happens in mental hospitals.[5] Eight subjects, including himself, volunteered to be "pseudopatients" at twelve different psychiatric hospitals and to take careful notes about what happened in each. Each of these volunteer pseudopatients called up for an appointment, and when interviewed, they complained of hearing voices saying the words "empty," or "hollow," or "thud." "The choice of these symptoms," Rosenhan explains, "was occasioned by their apparent similarity to existential symptoms. It is as if the hallucinating person were saying, 'My life is hollow and empty.' The choice of these symptoms was also determined by the *absence* of a single report of existential psychosis in the literature" (italics in original).[6] Aside from falsifying their names and occupations, these volunteers all told the truth about their lives. Once they were admitted, often somewhat to their surprise, they stopped complaining of any psychological symptoms whatsoever and behaved in a normal fashion. All were diagnosed as schizophrenic and ended up being hospitalized from seven to fifty-two days, with an average of nineteen, before they were released. Throughout, all took copious and careful notes about what they observed and what happened to them.

Rosenhan was particularly impressed by several similarities in the records of these pseudopatients. First, other patients often suspected them of being normal, maybe even "plants," but none of the staff did. One cue was their note-taking, which the other patients often interpreted correctly as indicating that they were there to observe, but which the staff members ascribed to their illness. Second, the staff members did not take their attempts at conversation at all seriously. The staff averted their eyes when spoken to between 80 and 90 percent of the time and usually replied with only a word or two—even to a direct question—and left. (That finding is unsurprising to those of us who have worked in such institutions. Mr. Jones asks, "What can I do to get out of here?"; the staff member replies, "You know the answer to that," then reports at the next staffing that "Mr. Jones continues to deny the seriousness of his problems.")

The professionals at the top of the institutional hierarchy spent little actual time with the pseudopatients. "Average daily contact with psychiatrists, psychologists, residents, and physicians combined ranged from 3.9 to 25.1 minutes with an overall mean of 6.8 (six pseudopatients over a period of 129 days of hospitalization)," Rosenhan writes. "Included in this average time are time spent in the admissions interview, ward meetings in the presence of the senior staff member, group and individual psychotherapy contacts, case presentation conferences, and discharge meetings."[7]

This finding does not imply that no psychologists or psychiatrists anywhere do anything for custodial patients. Many are very helpful; a few are harmful. What it does imply is that there is no reason to single out psychologists as in need of licensing, as opposed to those who have much more daily influence over the patients' lives—the aides.

UNDERSTANDING OF PSYCHOLOGISTS' TECHNIQUES

The other major rationale for licensure is that those licensed use knowledge and techniques that those to whom they provided service cannot be expected to understand and evaluate. People who are intellectually incompetent, for example, cannot be expected to make an informed judgment about a variety of services, and they should be protected by holding the people who provide them with services accountable to state standards. The ability of the rest of us, however, to evaluate a service depends upon its nature. Many goods and services require technical knowledge that the ordinary citizen cannot be expected to possess. Few of us, for example, can evaluate new automotive devices such as antilock brakes in many cars, or determine for ourselves whether seatbelts and airbags would actually work in the event of a head-on accident. Because we cannot, the government requires that those providing these products be licensed to meet certain standards; they can be held liable if they fail to meet these standards and criminally liable if they do so deliberately. Nor can ordinary citizens be expected to be able to evaluate whether the architectural plans for a building are sound; thus, architects must be licensed in every state. Nor do ordinary citizens have enough knowledge of the law to practice it in the court system, although they may on occasion be allowed to represent themselves; thus, knowledge of state and federal law is measured by the bar examinations that lawyers are required to pass in order to practice. The field in which the need for licensing is most clear is medicine. The ordinary citizen cannot be expected to evaluate a medical diagnostic judgment based on a blood test or an X-ray, or whether an operation subsequently recommended is appropriate, or whether the person performing it has the skill to perform the operation in an acceptable manner.

An analogy is commonly made between psychology and medicine. "Mental illness" has been presented in our society as "an illness just like any other illness," and it appears to follow that people who provide services to ameliorate it—whether they are M.D.'s or Ph.D.'s or Psy.D.'s—should be licensed just like any other people who treat illness, including nurses. This presentation has been made largely to "destigmatize" emotional distress by holding that it is an "illness" and therefore nothing to be ashamed of. The constant repetition of the assertion, however, yields the belief that what psychotherapists and others do to alleviate emotional distress is similar to what medical doctors do to alleviate or cure physical disease. It yields the belief that licensed people use techniques that require years of training to master and are beyond the understanding of their clients. This inference is, however, true only for those who prescribe drugs. Nevertheless, constant repetition yields belief (see Chapter 7), in this case belief in a general principle from which specifics are inferred.

But the analogy between medicine and psychology is not a good one. A good analogy is one in which the specific components are really similar. Except as a rhetorical device—to alleviate stigma and enhance the status of the professionals dealing with distressed people—the implied similarity between medicine and psychology simply doesn't exist in reality. Emotional distress, whose various forms do *not* constitute a natural category, is often quite unlike physical disease, and how professional psychologists attempt to treat it is quite different from how medical doctors treat physical illness.

The medical analogy fails for another reason as well: Licensing may prevent incompetent people from intervening in other peoples' bodies for a fee (although there is no licensing requirement for writing best-selling books recommending outrageous diets), but it is clearly impossible to require a license for people to provide advice to others for a fee. Or at least it should be impossible, in a free society. The problem is that certain people and groups who do not advertise themselves as psychologists will nonetheless quite deliberately exploit emotionally distressed people. One such group of which I am aware advertised a weekend of "personal discovery" for those who wished it at no charge, conducted marathon group therapy sessions oriented toward "tearing apart" each new person who had taken up the offer, and then demanded thousands of dollars for subsequent weekends, on an escalating rate schedule. How could we prohibit such activity by licensing advice-giving, yet still have a free society? Our belief is that people can make commitments and spend their money as they wish—so long as they do not harm others.

Let's return to the rationale that professional psychologists should be licensed because the consumer cannot be expected to evaluate their services. Why should consumers who are legally competent to *choose* psychological services be unable to evaluate those services? We are not discussing consumers who are institutionalized and hence powerless to walk away from the service. Are people in outpatient therapy really incapable of judging whether they are benefiting from it or not? If professional mental health workers had techniques similar to X-rays and blood tests with which they could evaluate the condition of their clients, there would be a justification for licensing only those who could employ such techniques. But they don't have such techniques. If there were evidence that people who have been through the licensing procedure are better therapists than those who have not been, then there would also be a justification. But the evidence indicates that they are not better (see Chapter 2). If there were evidence that people who have been through the licensing procedure have a better understanding than do those who have not, then there would be a justification. But understanding implies the ability to predict, and the evidence is that statistical models predict better (see Chapter 3), and these statistical models—such as those used in interpreting the MMPI, the most commonly used test[8]—are in the public domain. If there were evidence that the experience gained along the way through the licensing procedure improved the use of valid techniques, then there would be a justification. But the evidence is that experience does not have that effect (see Chapter 4) once the basics of a valid technique are mastered. Licensing will certainly not prevent their proper use, but does licensing insure that valid techniques will be used in a valid manner? The answer, sadly, is no.

DOES LICENSING ASSURE QUALITY?

Even if licensing cannot be justified on the basis of protecting the public—people who have no choice or who cannot be expected to understand—there is the possible justification that it *assists* the public. It would, indeed, assist—if the practitioners who offer services under current licensing requirements were superior to those who are not licensed. A great deal of education and training is necessary in order to obtain a license. It seems plausible that those who receive such education and training would be superior to those who don't. For prescribing drugs, for example, we can at least hope that medical doctors' training in biochemistry, physiology, and medicine will make their choices better (in general) than those that people who have no such training would make. There is, however, a problem in any analogy between drug prescription and providing services of a purely psychological nature. The problem is that the education and training psychologists receive is not necessarily training in valid techniques or theories, but far too often is training in the *opinion* of someone with high status, opinion that may or may not have any scientific basis. This person in turn achieved status by being trained in the opinion of a previous high-status person. The student goes on to achieve high status as the result of the training and may later train someone else in the same opinion (usually slightly modified), and so on and so on. With a little bit of luck, or with planning on the part of the more responsible training programs, there is some scientific foundation somewhere in this self-perpetuating process. Otherwise, there is none. The problem is that licensing simply requires training—not training in something valid, or in something that works, or even in something that is not harmful, but simply training. As far as licensing is concerned, one can be equally well "trained" in the best-established techniques of behavior modification or in "repressed memory recovery through hypnosis."

To understand this problem, let us examine the APA's ethics rules,[9] which govern professional practice in almost every state. The use of psychological techniques is covered in a principle concerning *competence* (Principle 2). The preamble to the competence principle reads as follows:

> The maintenance of high standards of competence is a responsibility shared by all psychologists in the interests of the public and profession as a whole. Psychologists recognize the boundaries of their competence and the limitations of their techniques. They only provide services and only use techniques for which they are qualified by training and experience. In those areas in which recognized standards do not yet exist, psychologists take whatever precautions are necessary to protect the welfare of their clients. They maintain knowledge of current scientific and professional information related to the services they render.

That statement sounds fine at first reading, but at second reading it is not. Most important, it doesn't specify anything about what psychologists should *do* to insure "the maintenance of high standards." It doesn't say what psychologists should *do* with their "knowledge of current scientific and professional information," and the statement that "psychologists take whatever precautions are necessary to protect the welfare of their clients" "in those areas in which recognized standards do not exist" does not specify *what* those precautions are. (For example, It does not mandate the psychologist to share with the client the fact that he or she is employing a technique in an "area in which recognized standards do not exist.")

Nor do the components of the principle that follow this preamble mandate the use of valid techniques. Part A requires accuracy in representing training and credentials; Part B requires that teachers prepare well and that their presentations be "accurate, current, and scholarly"; Part C requires psychologists to *recognize* the need for continuing education (italics added); Part D requires psychologists to *recognize* differences among people (italics added); Part E requires an *understanding* of psychological and educational measurement (italics added); and Part F requires a *recognition* that personal problems may interfere with services provided (italics added) and that therefore psychologists should refrain from any activities in which these problems are likely to lead to inadequate performance or harm. (Assessed how? Remember that while therapy helps two-thirds of the clients, it leaves one-third worse off than if they had been in a control group. Were the personal problems of the therapist ever to blame in a particular case?) None of these rules govern what psychologists must actually *do*. The fact that only 30 percent of APA members in 1990 subscribed to any of its journals—aside from the *American Psychologist*, which comes with membership dues—implies a violation of Parts C and E,[10] but since all that is required is "recognition" and "understanding," not actual behavior, failure to know what it is going on does not constitute a violation.

For example, in an example published in the *Casebook on Ethical Principles of Psychologists*, the APA ethics committee censured someone for continuing, at the urging of a supervisor, to see a client who later deteriorated "because" she was believed to suffer from multiple personality.[11] The psychologist was censured on this post hoc basis because she hadn't had training in dealing with people with multiple personalities and hence had gone beyond her area of competence.

This somewhat purified example illustrates the one part of the competence principle that involves a real mandate: the requirement for training. But there is virtually no scientifically based knowledge about *how* to deal with multiple personality. So what is training? Is it being supervised by someone who *believes* they are expert in multiple personality and who is recognized by others as such an expert? Or is it perhaps attending a workshop or two run by such a person (most likely for a handsome fee)? How do such "teachers" come to be recognized as experts on multiple personality and to believe in their own expertise? The answer is: on the basis of their experience. As pointed out in Chapter 4, however, experience does nothing in the absence of scientific understanding and systematic feedback that allows the experience to be evaluated on the basis of this understanding. Thus, in areas where there is little or no scientific understanding, the training requirement does absolutely nothing whatsoever to enhance quality service. (Unfortunately, what it does accomplish is to make perfectly competent and conscientious therapists vulnerable to post hoc judgments that they strayed beyond their area of competence, while reinforcing recognition of "experts.")

Multiple personality is not the only area for which there is little or no scientific understanding. In fact, such areas are legion. Rather than allowing the therapists to do their best in those areas, however, and mandating only that they share the fact of their ignorance with their clients, the training requirement does precisely the opposite. It creates a pretense of knowledge where none exists, because the practitioner is required to "acquire" it. This pretense misleads both the clients and the general public, who support the whole enterprise through third-party payments. Many states require *continuing education* for maintaining a license, which makes the pretense even worse. Licensed psychologists go to workshops where someone "with extensive experience" tells them how to deal with a problem concerning which there is a minimum of scientific evidence or none—like how to tell whether a child has been sexually abused on the basis of the child's play with "anatomically correct dolls." Doll play is inadmissible evidence of abuse in the California courts "unless it can be shown to be generally accepted as reliable in the scientific community."[12] It isn't,[13] but this does not discourage those trained in interpreting doll play from making the usual vacuous assertion that "used properly" it can be helpful.[14]

Moreover, training in techniques "not generally accepted as reliable in the scientific community" abounds. One of my favorite training sessions was on how to "totally restructure your client's personality." The invitation I received began with a claim that sometimes it is my "responsibility" to undertake such a restructuring, in cases of extreme deviance—such as alcoholism or personality disorders—and it proposed to tell me how. Aside from the ethics involved ("I have decided to restructure *your* personality now that you have come to me for help"), we have no scientific knowledge of how to "restructure personality" or even of how to structure it in the first place. Another invitation I received was for a workshop providing knowledge of how to help clients overcome "co-dependency" on sex.

Licensing, which leads to the pretense of scientifically based knowledge where none exists, does not assure quality. Instead, it inhibits honesty. In particular, as Lee Sechrest (whose qualifications are described in Chapter 1) points out, it reinforces a human failure from which most of us suffer at least some of the time: a lack of "the courage to say 'we do not know how.'"[15] A license implies that its holder does know how. The license implies expertise in whatever the licensed person has been "trained" to do within the domain of "psychology." As Lee Sechrest points out,

> Court testimony is an example of what has happened. We [psychologists] drifted into it as a field. It started with psychologists talking about matters where they *did* have some expertise: measurement of intellectual functioning, descriptions of cognitive and behavioral impairment, and so on. Now psychologists can be "expert" on anything that can be defined as "psychology." That doesn't follow. Just because there are all sorts of things that are part psychological in nature—they involve behavior, beliefs, attitudes and so on—doesn't mean that we can claim to be experts in an area that involves these things without having to generate a scientific data base. Sexual abuse is an example. There are very few scientific data on the validity of the opinions that psychologists are giving. And psychologists can't just give an "opinion." Expert witnesses are forced to go beyond the data. Their fees depend on making these kinds of statements with a level of confidence that can't be justified given the state of our knowledge.[16]

A LICENSE TO USE TECHNIQUES THAT DON'T WORK

One pernicious effect of licensing is the pretense of knowledge in the absence of evidence. Worse yet, however, is the pretense that knowledge exists when there is evidence that this "knowledge" is incorrect. The history of the use of biofeedback to alleviate various disorders provides an example of such pretense. This history is recounted by Alan H. Roberts,[17] one of the first researchers to propose that biofeedback might be beneficial in alleviating such problems as headaches. He begins his history by pointing out that two articles published in 1969 raised the possibility that people could control their own autonomic emotional states through feedback involving systematic reinforcement methods, without any movement on the part of the person controlling these states. The first paper was written by the world-famous psychologist Neil Miller and was published in *Science*.[18] The second paper, by Joe Kamiya, was published in Charles Tart's book *Altered States of Consciousness*, an edited compilation whose chapters were not subject to the type of intense scrutiny required for publication in *Science*.[19] As Roberts points out, "First, some of the most important studies summarized in Miller's 1969 article were never satisfactorily replicated. Fifteen years after its publication, we still have no convincing evidence that the autonomic nervous system can be taught by operant [systematic reinforcement] methods independently of mediation by striate muscles [muscles people can move voluntarily]—this despite the fact that brilliant and dedicated scientists have spent years of their lives looking for missing data and trying desperately to replicate the findings." Moreover, "other work demonstrated that the alpha phenomenon [ability to control one's brain waves directly] might be artifactual and therefore might not be related to altered states of consciousness."[20]

It has been known for years—in fact, generations—that people can alter their autonomic states through changes in their *voluntary* activities, such as through relaxation or exercise. The question is whether biofeedback techniques can affect the autonomic nervous system directly. (There's some confusion here in the popular press about this. For example, a recent article extolling the virtues of "biofeedback" referred almost entirely to success involving relaxation techniques, labeling these successes as those of "biofeedback."[21] News that people can learn to relax—or to control muscles they rarely use—is not exactly new. Electronic feedback enhances the effectiveness of the techniques employed to obtain relaxation or control of seldom used muscles. But such feedback does not involve being "wired for a miracle," as one popular magazine article maintained.[22] The treatment employing this type of feedback is based on knowledge of the human muscle system—and the placebo benefits arising from addressing a problem. Again, see Roberts.[23])

Nevertheless, the Biofeedback Research Society that was founded in 1969 changed its name in 1976 to the Biofeedback Society of America, open to professionals as well as researchers—as if the existence of an ability to control autonomic responses through biofeedback had been proven to exist and was now available to alleviate emotional distress by training people in well-established methods to employ such feedback. As Roberts writes, "I attended the 1975 meeting at which this issue [opening up the society] was debated. The thrust of the debate was that the society could not survive solely as a research society. My clearest memory at the time is of a special meeting devoted to studies ostensibly showing that males could be taught [through biofeedback techniques] to raise the temperature of their testicles high enough to kill sperm and that this process could be used as a form of birth control."[24] While that may strike the reader as ludicrous, even more incredible claims have been made, as we will see. Roberts continues: "Even though I resigned from the society, I continued to be hopeful concerning the potential applications of biofeedback techniques,"[25] and he and his students continued to publish reports of apparent successes of biofeedback techniques—which neither they nor others were able to replicate. "Even so, I did not lose hope. We were faced [by the late 1970s] with literally hundreds of clinical studies purportedly showing that biofeedback techniques were clinically useful."[26]

To assess whether biofeedback might work after all, he and two colleagues, Donald Kewman and Sergio Guglielmi, "conducted double-blind studies to test whether biofeedback is useful in treating migraine headaches and Raynaud's disease, respectively. . . . Neither study produced evidence of specific effects, and some proponents of biofeedback became distressed. Kewman, Guglielmi, and I have been under attack (sometimes intemperate) ever since. When Kewman's paper was awarded a citation for excellence in research and presented at the 1979 meetings of the Biofeedback society, prominent clinicians in the audience attacked not only our methods *but also our ethics and morals*"[27] (italics added).

Professional psychologists are licensed to train people in biofeedback techniques. If we search hard for an excuse, we can find one. There have, at least, been *some* reports of successful results of using the technique—even though the people who published these results and others have all failed to replicate them. Worse yet, licensed psychologists and others in allied fields are permitted to use techniques that the research has shown unambiguously not to work—and they do so. Most commonly used are the "projective" techniques, of which the Rorschach Ink Blot Test is the best known.

A LICENSE TO USE SHODDY TESTS

The Rorschach Ink Blot Test is the test most highly recommended by professional psychologists,[28] and it is one of the most widely used. It is termed a *projective* test for reasons that will be clear shortly. Next to intelligence tests and the MMPI (both of which are *statistically* developed tests that are best interpreted *statistically*), such projective tests are those most commonly given.[29] While shorter-length projective tests—like drawing a person, completing sentences, or drawing a person, house, and tree—are slightly more common, the Rorschach has for years been the "badge" of the practicing clinician.[30] (Older readers may recall the award-winning performance of the late Susan Hayward in *I Want to Live*, in which a psychologist—played by Theodore Bikel—flashes ink blots at her, asks her what they look like, and confidently concludes that she is incapable of the murder for which she is ultimately gassed.)

The Rorschach Ink Blot Test consists of ten ink blots on cards roughly two-thirds the size of typewriter paper. Six of these blots are black or various shades of gray, and the remaining four are colored. The blots cover approximately half the area of the sheets; they are symmetrical about the middle of the paper when it is presented in a horizontal orientation, as it is to the person taking the test. These blots were originally produced by the psychiatrist Hermann Rorschach (1884–1992) for reasons unrelated to assessing personality structure or problems.

The person taking the test is presented with the cards one at a time and asked to say what it "looks like" to him or her. This instruction is purposely vague, in order to allow the subject to respond to the whole blot, large parts of the blot, or small details within it, and to base the response on the chosen part's form, shading, texture, color, or some combination of these properties. The subject is also free to respond to the white spaces surrounding each blot, or the white spaces within some of them. Finally, the subject is free to rotate the cards (but only after responding to the blot in the position in which it is presented), or even to turn the cards over to look at their backs.

After each response, the examiner asks the subject to explain the response by asking such questions as "Why does it look like a butterfly?" or "What makes that part look like two people having a political argument about whether Ronald Reagan was a good president?" or simply, "Tell me more." Moreover, subjects are urged to see more than one thing in each blot with queries such as "Anything else?" Throughout, the examiner is very careful never to challenge the subject's responses, or indicate approval or disapproval, or in fact to show any reaction whatsoever.

The theory behind the test is simple and compelling. The world contains ambiguous situations, and people respond to ambiguity in habitual ways that are dependent on their personalities, or "psychodynamics." The more ambiguous the situation, the more important are these habitual ways of responding. Because the ink blot supposedly has no structure whatsoever, it presents the subject with an ultimately ambiguous situation and hence is an excellent means of tapping these habitual response modes. Moreover, the content that people see in the blots may give valuable cues to what they "have on their minds" that they might not otherwise be willing to disclose. "Deep" psychological concerns and conflicts are free to be "projected" into the blots because these blots presumably have no structure; hence the Rorschach is termed a *projective* test. Responding to the purportedly structureless blots is supposedly analogous to dreaming—the form and content of which, as Freud and later Jung had suggested, can lead to insight about our unconscious needs and conflicts.

Just as the subject interprets the ink blots, the professional psychologist attempts to interpret the subject's responses. Supposedly, supervised experience gained in interpreting responses leads to greater skill in interpretation. Both the form and the content of the responses are interpreted. This interpretive process is as intuitively compelling as the "theory" underlying the test. One point that the examiner interprets is whether the subject attempts to integrate the entire blot into a single image, or uses only large parts of it, or attends only to small details. Use of the whole blot is supposedly indicative of a need to form a "big picture." Except in those rare cases where the entire blot can reasonably be viewed as a single image, this response supposedly indicates a tendency toward grandiosity, perhaps even paranoia—with a disregard for those aspects of reality that do not fit one's overall views. In contrast, responses based on tiny details of the blots are indicative of an obsessive personality—someone who attends to detail at the expense of more important aspects of life, perhaps in order to avoid them. Occasionally, the subject will form an image out of the white spaces around or within the blot. Because this "figure-ground reversal" goes beyond the obvious demand to attend to the blots themselves, a few such white space responses may be indicative of creativity, while too many (however many that is) may indicate an oppositional personality. Integrating different characteristics of the blot—like color and form—involves "ego strength" (for coping with disparate aspects of reality), but only if the integration is not an ad hoc one (like a "green zebra," or a zebra seen on the basis of a few black and white stripes). Being unable to produce a response upon seeing the first vividly colored blot indicates emotional lability, or a tendency to be emotionally reactive to situations that in others do not arouse strong emotions. Rotating the blot to see new things after several responses indicates flexibility—but only if the blot is rotated after several responses. (To believe one is free to rotate the blot immediately is indicative of poor reality testing.) And so on.

Moreover, the content of the imagery the subject generates is important. Many people see animals, but too high a proportion of animals indicates immaturity and lack of imagination. Human movement is a great thing to see, it means creativity, and high ego-strength again, but sex organs aren't. "Anal" responses from a male are indicative of homosexuality (except that the research shows that they aren't[31]); seeing figures that are part human and part nonhuman—satyrs, cartoon characters, witches—indicates alienation, perhaps the beginning of schizophrenic withdrawal from other people. Seeing "confabulated" scenes—those involving different images "thrown together" without regard to size or coherence, or those integrating something not present on the blot—is indicative of "poor reality testing." For example, a patient once told me that a blot looked like two Scotty dogs tearing apart a butterfly. It does. The response was a confabulated one, however, because the butterfly would have had to be as large as the dogs. Finally, seeing many things that other people can't may indicate outright schizophrenia (but seeing nothing whatsoever that other people can't may be indicative of "overcontrol." Gotcha!).

Giving and interpreting the Rorschach test is great fun. Moreover, the interpretations one makes are compelling, at least to the professionals who make the interpretations. For example, I once tested a very depressed man who responded immediately to the first blot that "it looks like a bat that has been squashed on the pavement under the heel of a giant's boot." Wow! A confabulated response indicative of extreme depression and feelings of being overwhelmed and crushed by forces beyond one's control. What response could possibly have been more "one-down"? The fact that the man was obviously depressed led me to believe in the validity of the Rorschach at that point. (I realized only later that I already knew that he was depressed and hence that the response provided me with no new information whatsoever.) Of course, if the man had been obviously psychotic, I could have focused on the confabulated nature of the response—that is, focused on the giant who is not on the blot—and if he had been violent, on his response's hostile nature. The Rorschach is indeed "projective"—for the interpreter.

Compelling as the theory is, compelling as the interpretations are, and as fun as the test is to give, it doesn't provide the insight about the subject that its users allege it provides. The number of responses the subject makes is roughly correlated with his or her assessed intelligence, or at least score on the standard IQ test, a correlation of .50 in a hospital sample I once studied. Then again, number of words the subject spoke in an interview may be equally correlated with intelligence. Seeing a lot of things that others can't see is in fact indicative of disturbance. Then again, making a lot of unusual responses to *any* set of personality test items is too (like responding yes to "I feel that my ideas may turn into insects," or "if there's any justice in the world, I'm in deep trouble," or even "I like mechanics magazines").[32] In fact, one Rorschach interpretation system developed in recent years does work (to some extent). It is a statistically based system termed the Exner System, developed by John E. Exner. Scoring is based mainly on the number and proportion of responses that are "bad" in one way or another.[33] This system presupposes that the blots actually do look like certain things, which is the exact *opposite* of the rationale for the Rorschach. As described in a recent 1992 review by Franklin C. Shontz and Patricia Green:

Exner's system requires uniformity of administrative, coding, and interpretive procedures. It encourages the use of the Rorschach as a standardized test rather than as a minimally structured instrument that takes advantage of the possibilities of the materials by allowing flexibility in administration, scoring, and interpretation. Thus, the Exner system may have transformed the instrument into something that its originator and many of its users might not wish it to be.[34]

While research indicating some validity for the Exner system is occasionally referenced as evidence for the "validity" of Rorschach testing per se, professional psychologists continue to project their interpretations of the subjects' projections in a clinical manner, as part of an overall "clinical assessment." As Shontz and Green point out: "None of the studies we reviewed specifically addressed the issue of what the Rorschach contributes to clinical assessment."[35]

The ability of professional psychologists is limited by the validity of the techniques they employ. That is true in medicine, engineering, and even military "science" as well. Nevertheless, one survey reported, "Clinicians indicated that personal clinical experience with a test was more important in their test-use decisions than pragmatic or psychometric limitations. In fact, clinicians repeatedly emphasized the subjective, insightful, and experiential nature of the testing process. Although the psychometric limitations of the tests were recognized, the tests were considered more valuable than suggested by reliability and validity studies, which were typically considered flawed or inaccurate."[36] This last rationalization should be all too familiar by now; the many studies whose conclusions are negative are dismissed as inadequate for this or that reason, and then a positive result is invented from the resulting vacuum—in the absence of any *actual* studies showing positive results: "The debate over the validity of the Rorschach has been lengthy and unresolved."[37] It has been lengthy, but it is "unresolved" only in the sense that professionals who still employ it do not accept the compelling evidence that the Rorschach doesn't work as it is supposed to. Nor do the other projective techniques.

How can I be so certain in my pronouncements about the Rorschach? Since the later 1930s, a standard book has been published every six years or so that reviews most of the commonly used test and measurement techniques in psychology. Termed the *Mental Measurements Yearbook*, its editors seek reviews from the leading experts in the field—without regard to whether these people are considered to be generally in favor of certain techniques or opposed to them. This yearbook was edited by Oscar K. Burros until his death in the late 1970s, and it has recently resumed publication. The Rorschach was reviewed in 1949, 1953, 1959, 1965, 1972, and 1978.[38] It and other projective techniques have been so thoroughly discredited that they are not even reviewed in the volumes that followed Burros's death. Prior to that time, each volume contained at least one unfavorable review of the Rorschach and one favorable review. Ironically, it is the *favorable* reviews that are the most damning. For example, in the first (1949) favorable review, Morris Krugman wrote: "The Rorschach withstood the clinical test well throughout the years and has come out stronger for it; on the other hand, attempts at atomistic validation have been unsuccessful and will probably continue to be so."

Here Krugman anticipated the argument made forty-one years later by the forensic psychologist who advocates "psychological portraits" (see Chapter 1). The argument is that simple predictions and categorizations that the test makes are invalid but that more complex judgments can be supported on the basis of a vacuum. No positive evidence that such judgments are valid is cited, but evidence is cited that the technique's use as a component in a "big picture" has withstood attacks based on the invalidity of the simple predictions.

The 1949 favorable and unfavorable reviews left open the possibility that future research could provide positive evidence of validity. Such evidence was not forthcoming when the next volume of the yearbook appeared, in 1953. There the Rorschach's defender, Helen Sargent, attempted to dismiss the continuing lack of positive results on the grounds that "the Rorschach test is a clinical technique, not a psychometric method." (Compare this statement with Shontz and Green's characterization of the Exner System thirty-nine years later.)

By the next edition, in 1959, many of the world's most eminent psychologists were lined up against the use of the Rorschach. Hans J. Eysenck quoted Lee Cronbach, one of the world's leading experts on psychometric testing: "The test has repeatedly failed as a prediction of practical criteria. There is nothing in the literature to encourage reliance on Rorschach interpretation."[39] Raymond J. McCall wrote, "Though tens of thousands of Rorschach tests have been administered by hundreds of trained professionals since that time [of the previous reviews], and while many relationships to personality dynamics and behavior have been hypothesized, the vast majority of these relationships *have never been validated empirically*, despite the appearance of more than 2000 publications about the test" (italics in the original; p. 154). McCall pointed out that in particular the number of human movement responses, which had been thoroughly investigated by then, is unrelated to anything.

In the 1978 edition, Richard H. Davis concluded: "The general lack of predictive validity for the Rorschach raises serious questions about its continued use in clinical practice" (p. 1045).

What did the Rorschach supporters write in the *Yearbook?* They cited no evidence whatsoever. Instead, they justified use of the technique on the basis that it is a "very novel interview" or a "behavior sample." Yet more recent reviews show only that the Exner System, the antithesis of "projective" uses of the Rorschach, has some validity. Why then does use of the Rorschach continue among licensed professionals? One obvious reason is that they are paid well for administering it. Another, however, was mentioned in the favorable 1972 *Yearbook* review by A. G. Bernstein: "The view that recognition [*sic*], the act of construing an unfamiliar stimulus, taps central components of personality functions is one that will remain crucial to any psychology committed to the understanding of human experience." I agree that the view is crucial to the *practice* of using projective tests, but is it a correct view? It yields a plausible belief that it should work. Such a belief provides a good rationale for seeking positive evidence that the Rorschach actually works. The evidence is that it doesn't work.

This evidence has finally had some impact. Professional psychologists are now being warned against using the Rorschach and other projective tests as a basis for court testimony. In the February 1991 issue of the *Pennsylvania Psychologist Quarterly,* the members of the ethics committee of the Philadelphia Society of Clinical Psychologists warn against its use in a court setting: "any psychologist who chooses to use instruments whose validity has not been demonstrated as predictive of desirable arrangements (for example, projective tests), should be prepared to be challenged on ethical grounds."[40] I ask, however: *If the use of an instrument (a projective test or any other) can be challenged on ethical grounds in a court of law, how can its use be ethically justified in any context at all?* My answer is that it can't.

I would like to offer the reader some advice here. If a professional psychologist is "evaluating" you in a situation in which you are at risk and asks you for responses to ink blots or to incomplete sentences, or for a drawing of anything, walk out of that psychologist's office. Going through with such an examination creates the danger of having a serious decision made about you on totally invalid grounds. If your contact with the psychologist involves a legal matter, your civil liberties themselves may be at stake. If you have been mandated to see the psychologist by a court order, quietly object to the test if possible, and ask to make an appointment later. Immediately consult a lawyer, who can be referred to the sources cited in this book or to the much more extensive reference list in Jay Ziskin's and David Faust's three-volume work.[41] Do not respond first, then object later. Any of your responses may be "interpreted" as indicating that you have an objection to the whole procedure based on some form of psychological pathology. This interpretation will be supported on a post hoc basis by the objection itself. That is, of course, self-serving for the psychologist involved.

Let me share an example of what can happen—it did happen. The last Rorschach test I myself ever administered was to a sixteen-year-old girl who had been hospitalized by her parents against her will. The parents' doctor had recommended hospitalization because the girl was dating a man over ten years older. Quite mature and smart, she responded well to the testing situation except for occasional periods of crying. She explained that she was very upset and depressed as a result of being in the hospital's locked ward. She became particularly upset whenever she couldn't answer a question in a manner she considered to be correct. Despite her negative mood and occasional long periods of inattention, which I carefully timed with my stopwatch, she obtained an IQ score of 126 (ninety-fifth percentile), and of the forty-one responses she gave to the Rorschach, forty were "good form" (that is, images that could clearly be discerned by an observer). The one exception was for ink blot card number eight. "It just looks like a bear. That's all. I can't explain." Card number eight does not look like a bear.

At the subsequent staff meeting, the head psychologist displayed card number eight to everyone assembled and asked rhetorically: "Does that look like a bear to you?" No one thought it did. He then "explained why" the girl had said it looked like a bear: She had been hallucinating. She was a "pseudo-neurotic schizophrenic" who knew how to appear normal even though she was often hallucinating, such as when she didn't respond right away—as I had so carefully documented with my stopwatch. (Incidentally, that's not what researchers who have proposed the term "pseudo-neurotic schizophrenic" as describing a natural category of schizophrenia mean by it.) Thus, the staff members should ignore the fact that she did not appear to be psychotic. The Rorschach had, in effect, "unmasked" her. (She had also drawn eyes looking to one side in the draw-a-person test, and she occasionally rocked in her bed when she went to sleep—evidence the head psychologist marshaled in support of his diagnosis.) When I protested that forty good form responses out of forty-one was actually a higher percentage than found among most perfectly normal people, the head psychologist replied that while I understood statistics, I failed to understand people. In particular, I failed to understand that "statistics do not apply to the individual." (Tell that to a smoker with lung cancer.) The patient was finally diagnosed as "schizophrenic" and sent home to her parents, because the particular setting where I was employed at the time was not one that could deal with schizophrenia. *The staff—over my objections—further agreed that if her parents were ever to bring her back, she should be sent directly to the nearby state hospital.* For all I know, she may well have been condemned to serve time in that snake pit on the basis of a single Rorschach response. But I don't know for sure. I quit.

WHAT A LICENSE ACTUALLY DOES

The first dictionary definition of *license* is: "official or legal permission to do or own a specified thing." By the third definition, however, we find that *license* can also mean "deviation from normal rules, practices, or methods in order to achieve a certain end or effect." State legislatures clearly had the first definition in mind when they developed licensure in professional psychology; their rationale was that there was a science of psychology whose practice should be licensed, as the practice of medicine, engineering, and architecture is licensed. Science, however, involves attending to empirical results, retaining only theories that withstand empirical tests of the type that would convince skeptics (see Chapter 3). If the rationale for licensing is the belief that it will require practitioners to be disciplined by science, then—as the experience with the Rorschach indicates—*license* has ironically and unintentionally taken on this third meaning. Like James Bond's "license to kill," professional psychologists have been granted a "license to ignore."

The "license to ignore" has very serious implications both for practicing professionals and for the rest of us who may be their clients. As
Paul Meehl writes:

> It is not a question of whether one abandons "scientific standards of
> proof" because one is operating in a clinical context where hard
> data may be hard to come by. It is more than that. It has ethical
> implications if I employ a diagnostic procedure which has repeated-
> ly been shown to have negligible validity to make life and death
> decisions about people and collect the patient's or the taxpayer's
> dollar for doing so.[42]

But the worst license of all is the license to make up one's own psychological theories, to make up one's own tests, and present the
"results" of one's fantasies in a legal setting as an "expert" witness. As
pointed out earlier by Lee Sechrest, this horrific type of license has now
been granted in the area of child abuse, particularly child sexual abuse.
It began with a gross overestimation of the incidence of child sexual
abuse. This overestimation has been reinforced by the definitional
ambiguity child abuse: it is variously defined as any sexual contact
before age eighteen with a person five or more years older, or as any
encounter with a "flasher" no matter how brief.[43] Meanwhile, when the
general public hears of child abuse, they think of actual forced intercourse or molestation. In a TV talk show, for example, such an image
may be reinforced by the presence, along with the "expert," of someone
who has in fact been horribly abused.[44] This overestimation of incidence is sometimes strengthened by assertions that people "forget" or
"deny" what actually occurred. The author of one particularly ludicrous
article simultaneously asserts one of five women is sexually abused as a
child and that half of these women forget the experience.[45] How could
the author possibly know such a thing? It would be impossible to conduct a general survey that could reach that conclusion, because such a
survey would require knowledge of actual abuse without relying on the
respondents' memories. Moreover, when the author concludes that one
of her clients who originally claimed not to suffer from abuse now
"remembers" it, how do we know that such memory is accurate? The
author of this article, it happens, has a private practice, which yields a
highly biased sample of available instances from which to generalize.

The next step in the creation of the child abuse fantasy has been to assert that "children never lie" (except, of course, when they deny being abused). One prosecutor, relying on psychologists' "expertise," is reported to have told a jury, "To believe a child's *no* is simplistic."[46] There is, of course, no evidence that children never lie, any more than there is evidence that adults never lie. As any parent can testify, children *do* lie—just as adults do. But then we are asked the rhetorical question, "Why would someone lie about something so important?" The implication is that people—including children—cannot be persuaded that important events occurred in their lives when they actually didn't. The implication underlies appeals to believe incredible stories of growing up in satanic cults that sacrifice babies and so on.[47] The fact is that much of what people "recall" couldn't possibly have occurred, but this does not deter those who argue that memories of particularly dramatic incidents must be accurate. Licensed psychologists themselves make this argument. In the area of child abuse, experiences that presumed victims have "recalled" include being parachuted from airplanes and molested on the way down, being forced to open graves of corpses who immediately spewed forth blood, and so on.[48] Another "recalled" a child care worker at a preschool taking the children to the music room, forcing them to defecate, and smearing their sex organs with the feces. Many of these "recalled" events are alleged to have occurred in the presence of other adults who noticed nothing unusual, not even the children's absence. In the music room story, no evidence was obtained from a chemical analysis.[49]

Even so, to the people who are doing the recalling, events that could not possibly have occurred are recalled with compelling vividness.

For example, my mother was always amused by her own vivid visual memory that when she cut her hand as a two-year-old and required stitches, they were administered with a sewing machine. One of the world's experts on human memory vividly recalled that he heard of the Japanese attack on Pearl Harbor in an announcement that interrupted a broadcast of a baseball game. Years later, he realized that the last games of the baseball season are in October, while the attack was in December. He still "recalls" the incident. He just knows that his recall is inaccurate.[50]

It is simply not true that people *either* lie *or* tell exactly what occurred *or* forget. People with the most rudimentary knowledge of psychology should know that recall is an active search process involving reconstruction of the past,[51] and that while the final memory may seem like a moving picture of what actually occurred, the process leading to this result is anything but a simple reactivation of the actual past. If professionally licensed psychologists were required to know psychology and to make their judgments in accord with what they know, they could not make confident statements about what occurred in their clients' past on the basis of what these clients have been guided to recall. Unfortunately, mental health professionals are themselves free to forget whatever they learned. (The "continuing education" requirement has nothing to do with continuing education in empirically established knowledge in psychology.) Hence they are free to make whatever judgments their own "clinical judgment" indicates. As Lee Sechrest points out, many have only a "peripheral acquaintance" with the science of psychology, and they act accordingly.

Especially horrible are the coercive and leading interviews that some professionals conduct with children whom they are convinced have been sexually abused. (See Ralph Underwager's and Hollida Wakefield's *The Real World of Child Interrogations*.)[52] The "expert" conclusion is that when the child finally says yes, this affirmation is proof that actual sexual abuse occurred. Fortunately, jurors—as in the L.A. McMartin preschool case—are sometimes more psychologically knowledgeable than the licensed experts are. In this case I agree wholly with the jurors. We will simply never know what happened, because after the leading and coercive interviews to which the children were subjected, there is no way of knowing for sure—least of all on the basis of their personal recall.[53]

Having exaggerated statistics and grossly misunderstood the nature of memory and the role that leading interviews can play in recall, some licensed experts then go on to provide lists of "symptoms" of sexual abuse that children may display. These lists often include the following symptoms:[54]

1. withdrawal or excessive daydreaming
2. poor peer relations
3. poor self-esteem
4. frightened or phobic reactions, especially with adults
5. a deterioration of body image

 6. feelings of guilt or shame
 7. "pseudomature" personality development
 8. attempted suicide
 9. exhibiting a positive relationship toward the suspected offender
10. regressive behavior
11. bedwetting
12. highly sexualized play
13. sexual promiscuity
14. overly compliant behavior
15. acting-out aggressive behavior
16. hints about sexual activity
17. sexual play with peers, toys, or themselves
18. excessive masturbation
19. sexually aggressive behavior
20. "age-inappropriate" understanding of sexual behavior
21. arriving early or leaving late from school without absences
22. lack of trust, particularly of significant others
23. lack of participation in school or school activities
24. inability to concentrate in school
25. sudden drop in school performance
26. extraordinary fear of males, particularly strangers
27. fear of being left alone
28. complaining of fatigue or physical illness
29. medical conditions such as pneumonia or mononucleosis
30. loss of appetite
31. clinging to parents
32. tics
33. hypervigilence
34. running away
35. irritability
36. difficulty with eye contact
37. extreme interest in fire
38. unprovoked crying
39. taking an excessive number of baths
40. suspiciousness
41. sleepwalking
42. sudden massive weight gain
43. sudden massive weight loss

44. excessive urination
45. confusion
46. nightmares
47. poor relations of a daughter with a mother
48. overdependence

This list includes, of course, virtually every behavior about which parents may be concerned—with the possible exception of homicide and psychosis—and even a few behaviors about which some parents are not concerned, such as an "age-inappropriate" understanding of sexual behavior (as determined by whom?) and "maturity" ("pseudo" or otherwise). As Underwager and Wakefield point out, this list bears a remarkable resemblance to lists of supposed symptoms of masturbation that were proposed around the turn of the century—an activity that is now considered harmless but that was then "corrected" with such drastic measures as binding the hands of young boys and surgically removing the clitoris of young girls.[55] The list also reflects a remarkably incorrect belief that perfectly normal boys and girls have no interest in sex.

After showing some of these "symptoms," the child who is suspected to be a victim is often asked to play with "anatomically detailed dolls" (ADDs) during or after an interview. Again, there is no scientific evidence that doll play has any validity in determining whether a child has been sexually abused. This lack of validity, however, does not prevent professionals from using the technique. One 1987 survey revealed that "of 92 child protective service agencies and 46 law enforcement departments in North Carolina, 94% of the protective service agencies and almost half of the law enforcement departments were currently using the dolls or anticipating using them in their investigations within the next year."[56] As Sue White and Gail Santilli point out, however, *only three articles* "have appeared in peer-reviewed journals as of 1988 despite the dolls having been used in sexual abuse evaluations from at least the late 1970s."[57] The studies in these three articles variously compared ten children believed to have been abused with ten who were believed not to have been, sixteen with sixteen, and twenty-five with twenty-five. In all three studies the children were asked to play with the dolls for thirty minutes. Otherwise, the procedures used, the categories of unusual play examined, the definition of *children* (the age ranges studied were 2–6, 5–8, and 3–8), and even the physical construction of the dolls themselves all varied. As critics pointed out, these studies "offer limited information about the scientific integrity of ADD's in child abuse evaluations. Some of the methodological problems that limit the findings include: small sample size; the nonblind status of other participants in the interview; the sexualized behavior of the nonreferred [normal comparison] control sample; the documentation of sexual abuse in the subjects by established criteria; the failure to establish interrater reliability in multiple interviews; and problems in establishing a replicable protocol."[58] This group of critics conducted a study of their own that corrected for most of these problems. In their study mental health professionals *failed* to distinguish between abused (for certain) and nonabused children. Their sample, however, was even smaller than previous ones—there were six abused and nine nonabused children.

In a more recent review of all studies published through 1991, which included those already mentioned plus some new ones, two colleagues and I discovered yet another problem, a very serious one.[59] The children suspected of having been abused generally came from poorer families living in poor neighborhoods, whereas the comparison children—generally those of acquaintances of the experimenters or chosen from preschools—were predominantly from richer families living in middle-class areas. Differences in doll play might therefore be accounted for—in part, at least—not only by differences in the cultures in which the children were raised but also by the physical differences in their homes. Because the researchers present only summaries of the background differences between the groups, and do not describe the homes, we cannot evaluate this possibly critical difference. Children who live in small homes or apartments with few rooms are more likely to observe adult sexual behavior than are those who live in larger houses.

Suppose, however, that even after further studies with adequate controls, there does appear to be some difference in the amount of sexualized or aggressive play between suspected abused and nonabused children. There would still be three important provisos to our reaching a firm conclusion. First, perfectly normal children often play with the dolls in ways that the "experts" believe are diagnostic of abuse, as a number of studies have indicated. While the actual rates of various behaviors involving sexuality differ across studies, they consistently conclude that about 5 percent of normal children around age five who are not even slightly suspected of having been abused will act out sexual intercourse between dolls when the dolls have an actual vaginal opening rather than the painted appearance of one, but over one-half will touch a penis, vagina, or anus.[60] (In a particularly distressing bit of "closed loop thinking," one researcher dismissed "sexualized" behavior on the part of one of the normal children by deciding that he might have been abused after all and reporting that to a child protection agency.) The "false positive" possibility—that is, concluding incorrectly that a nonabused child has been abused—in itself is distressing if there is no good evidence, apart from the doll play, of abuse.

The second proviso is that the suspect children in the studies have been made aware of sexual matters through discussions with their parents, through accusations involving people close to them, through interviews (often coercive), and—in cases of suspected group abuse—through conversations with their peers. To link doll play directly to abuse for such children is about as rational as attributing the slow movements of a heavily medicated psychotic person to the psychosis.

Finally, there is the possibility that factors independent of abuse (like "precociousness") lead to both the suspicion of abuse and to doll play that differs from "normal." Of course, an "expert" who believes that precociousness itself is a sign of having been abused will not consider such a possibility. But all the studies fail to demonstrate what is technically termed *incremental validity*, i.e., they fail to demonstrate that doll play provides any information over and above the information that already led some children to be suspected of being abused. Doll play is meant to distinguish those who were actually abused from those who were actually not abused in groups of children who are already suspected of being abused. Research that is interpreted as supportive, of doll play, however, actually only distinguishes between the suspected and the not-suspected.

Let me explain this difference by making an analogy. Suppose someone claimed to have a "test" of basketball ability. The person examines two groups of people. The first is a group of people suspected of being good basketball players—young adults who are tall, thin, and athletic. The second is a group of people suspected of being poor basketball players; the people in this group are the same age, but they are short, fat, and nonathletic. The test consistently distinguishes between the people in these groups. It tests how high people can jump, and only a small percentage of those in the short, fat, and unathletic "nonsuspect" group can jump higher than those in the "suspect" group of tall, thin, and athletic people. The test developer goes on to claim that the jumping test is an excellent indication of which people *within* the tall, thin, athletic group are better basketball players—and supports this claim by emphasizing the plausibility that jumping ability is important in basketball. Should we accept the claims made for this test? No, because among those who are *already* tall, thin, and athletic, how high they can jump pure and simple is probably only slightly related to how well they play basketball. Jumping ability *per se* would add little incremental validity for predicting basketball prowess—once we already know that these people are tall and athletic. Michael Jordan and other basketball stars often have superb jumping ability, but so do a lot of other people who can't play basketball very well, and a lot of people who can are not terrific jumpers.

On February 8, 1991, the APA's Council of Representatives endorsed a "Statement on the Use of Anatomically Detailed Dolls in Forensic Evaluations."[61] That statement read in part: "Neither the dolls, nor their use, are standardized or accompanied by normative data. There are currently no uniform standards for conducting interviews with the dolls." So how is it that APA members are permitted to use dolls for diagnostic purposes in such critical situations? The statement concludes: "Therefore, in conformity with the *Ethical Principles of Psychologists*, psychologists who undertake the doll-centered evaluation of sexual abuse should be competent to use these techniques." That, quite simply, is outrageous. It is blatantly unethical to use a technique unless one is competent to use it. (This is what distinguishes professionals from "the fortune tellers and the gypsies.") It is nevertheless entirely possible to be competent in the use of a technique that has no demonstrated validity whatsoever, in an extraordinarily important setting.

In contrast, the American Medical Association's ethics code strictly forbids physicians to use techniques that have no demonstrable validity, and in particular such techniques as the polygraph.[62] Such prohibitions protect the public. But support for detailed doll interviews "done competently"—when there is absolutely no evidence about how to conduct them competently—harms the public.

Although doll play actually distinguishes between suspect and non-suspect children rather than between abused and nonabused children, it follows that a majority of the children who are suspected of having been abused will be judged to have actually been abused. Thus, a diagnosis on the basis of ADDs can be termed "reliable," in the sense that different observers using the same test will reach the same diagnosis. The child has been sexually abused. The observers can even cite each other's opinion as evidence of this reliability. But this "reliability" is specious. If a bathroom scale consistently reads 300 pounds whenever Harry steps on it in the morning and 350 pounds whenever he steps on it in the afternoon, it is consistent ("it has test-retest reliability"). If there are two such scales that behave in exactly the same way (saying Harry weighs 300 pounds in the morning and 350 in the afternoon), their agreement could be cited as evidence of their consistency (they have "interjudge reliability"). The problem is that although they are indeed reliable, they are inaccurate.

In contrast to the reliable but inaccurate ADD, many other evaluations of child sexual abuse (whether or not they use doll play as a component[63]) suffer from unreliability. The experts simply disagree too much over the meaning of their results. For example, Thomas Horner, Melvin Guyer and Neil Kalter examined the opinions of senior clinicians at four clinics about whether a child called Melissa had been sexually abused by her father.[64] Their opinions were based on a presentation by Dr. W, who had interviewed Melissa alone about the alleged abuse, had interviewed her together with her mother, and had interviewed her together with her father. Dr. W had videotaped all the interviews, and sections of the tapes were shown to the senior clinicians during Dr. W's presentation. After the presentation, Dr. W led a discussion. The senior clinicians were asked to judge the probability that Melissa had actually been abused by her father at two separate points: immediately after the presentation but before the discussion, and then right after the discussion. Before the discussion, the clinicians' judgments ranged from five to seventy-five percent chance that Melissa had been abused; after the discussion, their judgments ranged from zero to 60 percent. A quarter of the earlier judgments was less than 20 percent, and a quarter was above 60 percent. I emphasize that this study was not based on a brief description or scenario but on the type of information and discussion that is used in court settings to arrive at authoritative pronouncements about abuse or lack of it as historical fact.

Given such a wide range of disagreement, these experts as a group cannot be accurate. Again, consider the bathroom scale analogy. If it is stepped on several times in succession and gives a radically different reading each time, it is not accurate. If two identical scales give radically different readings from each other, at least one of them is not accurate. There is no way of knowing which from the readings themselves. Moreover, they could both be inaccurate. What we can confidently conclude is that they cannot both be accurate.[65]

So experts disagree. A common response is, "So what? Don't other experts, for example medical ones, disagree?" Leaving aside for the moment the reasons that disagreement in the mental health area may be considered more damning than in other areas, let me point out that areas of expertise like medicine are based on validated scientific principles. A misguided expert's understanding and application of scientific principles can be challenged as misunderstanding and misapplication. In mental health, by contrast, experts base their opinions on an ineffable wisdom that accumulates through experience (see Chapter 4), or occasionally, on a transcendent ability to combine information that is actually of little or no validity (as in Rorschach results). Consequently, grounds for challenging the mental health expert's opinion on the basis of its particulars are not available; rather, it is mental health expertise itself that must be challenged.

The behavior of mental health experts in this regard would be ludicrous were it not tragic. It can result not only in the conviction of innocent people, but in disruption of the lives of children supposedly molested and in those children's belief for the rest of their lives that they were abused—whether or not they actually were. As Judge Robert Klein puts it, "what they have learned through the process of questioning over the span of time" they "now know to be fact." Further: "In fact, because the children now believe that such abuse occurred, they are unable to separate the facts from their learned experience and, consequently, their behavior is just the same as if they were abused. This abuse has become their reality."[66] Child sexual abuse is an awful thing. By having license to make up theories, symptom checklists, interviewing techniques, and tests of it, the purported experts in effect engage in it themselves. The fact that they are licensed provides no protection whatsoever for these children—quite the opposite.

Why are these practices tolerated? Perhaps a clue can be found in the policy statement from the American Academy of Child and Adolescent Psychiatry titled "Guidelines for the Clinical Evaluation of Child and Adolescent Sexual Abuse."[67] These guidelines advise: "The clinician needs to *decide*, based on history, an evaluation of child and parents, and review of corroborating evidence, whether or not any sexual abuse occurred" (italics added). I disrespectfully disagree. Such a decision is the business of courts of law. Child sexual abuse is a crime, and the questions of whether it occurred and, if so, who did it should be answered according to all the rules of evidence used in legal proceedings. Such a decision should not be a matter of "clinical opinion." Such opinion can, of course, assist a court, but only when it can provide evidence relevant to the facts in dispute. But "assistance" based on shoddy tests and assessments is no assistance at all.

Moreover, even the best psychological tests assess only feelings, predispositions, attitudes, capabilities, and so on—*not what actually occurred* (and often not what is likely to occur; see Chapter 3). In a child abuse case, what did or did not occur must be established in the way it is usually established, by examining witnesses, providing physical evidence, and by allowing critical scrutiny of this evidence through examination and cross-examination. A court that hears testimony from an expert who has already "decided" what actually occurred is faced with the problem of how it should reach a decision—about the validity of the expert's "decision." Courts, having no special expertise in the research concerning clinical judgment, are generally not equipped to address this problem. Instead, they rely on whether "professional judgment was in fact exercised" or "whether the clinician substantial[ly] departed from accepted professional judgment, practices, or standards."[68] Here, I agree entirely with Sechrest that when a real and responsible professional is asked to determine whether something happened when there is no way of knowing whether it did, the proper response is "I don't know." Licensing and the system of rules and procedures have instead encouraged a yes-or-no answer, in fact demanded one, even though they are constructed on the sands of shifting opinion rather than on carefully examined evidence for the validity of opinion. Yes-or-no answers have unfortunately become "standard professional practice."

Here again, I have advice for the reader: Take Judge Klein's words seriously. If the reader suspects a child of having been abused, do not permit that child to be examined by any licensed expert but a medical one. Otherwise the process of examination may well end with believing he or she was abused, even if no abuse actually occurred. Be particularly wary of allowing the child to be examined (other than physically) when a group of children are involved. The well-known "group polarization" effect—by which groups of people reach judgments more extreme than their individual opinions expressed before group discussion[69]—can easily be transformed into group hysteria when such a sensitive and emotionally laden issue as child abuse is involved. Moreover, if your child has been abused, do not accept the idea that it would be "therapeutic" for him or her to see the abuser prosecuted. There is no evidence to support that position, but there is evidence that children can become extremely upset if the person they have come to believe (rightly or wrongly) has abused them is found innocent, for example, as the result of invalid techniques used by "experts."[70] Later in life, the child may come to regret some of the things he or she was coerced to say. Try as calmly as possible to determine the facts in the same way you determine other facts, not on the basis of interviews and "tests" that have no validity—or on the basis of symptoms that could indicate almost any distress, including physical illness. The child's well-being is at stake here. Parents have the right to refuse to allow their child to be interrogated and tested. Exercise that right.

Once again, the worst can happen:

A San Diego couple, James and Denise Wade, had their 8-year-old daughter, Alicia, taken from them in 1989 after the girl was sexually attacked. Alicia said a stranger had abducted her, but welfare officials suspected James Wade; when she changed her story *after a year of therapy*—which the Wades say brainwashed her—he was criminally charged. Finally, DNA tests done by prosecutors not only excluded Wade but implicated a man already convicted of similar attacks. A judge declared Wade innocent, and, after two and a half years in foster care, the girl was returned to her shattered, bankrupt parents.[71] (italics added)

A LICENSE TO GO HAYWIRE

A California licensed psychologist, Edith Fiore, has developed a unique specialty that she shares with at least fourteen other licensed mental health practitioners around the country. She helps people overcome the ill effects of being abducted by extraterrestrials (ETs) who hypnotized the abductees so that they would forget the experience. The symptoms of these abductions, as well as the names of fourteen other experts in this field, are listed in her recent book *Encounters: A Psychologist Reveals Case Studies of Abduction by Extraterrestrials.*[72] Many of the people who were abducted were, of course, sexually molested by the ETs; on other occasions, the ETs used remarkable techniques to cure their abductees of chronic and sometimes seemingly fatal diseases. Some of the symptoms of such abduction, like sleep disturbances, are similar to those of people who have been sexually abused or who were raised in satanic cults and have subsequently "forgotten" the experience. Like other symptom lists, Fiore's includes symptoms that could be indicative of a wide variety of (sometimes rather serious) disturbances, like "inability to account for periods of time," "feeling monitored, watched, and/or communicated with."[73] Among the symptoms is listed an obsession with ETs and UFOs.

The therapy Fiore provided is remarkably simple. The ETs' attempts to make the abductees forget their experience cannot fully succeed. Using their own hypnotic techniques Fiore and her fourteen colleagues can help the clients recall the experience. The reason that the ETs' hypnotic attempt fails and the subsequent one succeeds is that:

> The subconscious mind has a memory bank of everything we ever experienced, exactly as we perceived it. Every thought, emotion, sound of music, word, taste and sight. Everything is faithfully recorded somehow in your mind. Your sub-conscious mind's memory is perfect, infallible.[74]

Here we have a striking example of the "license to ignore" gone haywire—in this case, to ignore virtually every study that has ever been conducted on the nature of human memory, especially those that show that memory under hypnosis is *not* more accurate than in a waking state.[75] The implications of these studies make it unsurprising that hypnosis produces "recall" of experiences involving ETs and UFOs, since one of the symptoms Fiore lists is obsession with ETs and UFOs. Bridie Murphy lives again, only this time she is sanctified by a state license.

Fiore and her colleagues are far from alone in their beliefs that people are abducted by ETs. Recently (1992), I received an unsolicited report in the mail from the Bigelow Holding Corporation. The introductory chapter of the report, written by John E. Mack (Harvard Medical School professor of psychiatry), begins by observing that a "Roper Survey, conducted between July and September, 1991, suggests that hundreds of thousands, if not millions, of American men, women, and children may have experienced UFO abductions, or abduction related phenomena."[76] He continues that "mental health clinicians should learn to recognize the most common symptoms in the patient's or client's history that they are dealing with an abduction case."[77] These symptoms include fear of the dark or of nightfall, repetitive nightmares, dreams about abduction, unexplained phobias or fears, and even the appearance for no apparent reason of small scars or cuts or bruises.

Five "key indicator" questions were included in this Roper Poll. The 5,947 adults were asked whether they had ever (1) wakened up paralyzed with a sense of a strange figure or presence in the room; (2) experienced a period of an hour or more in which she or he was apparently lost but could not remember why; (3) felt the experience of actually flying through the air without knowing why or how; (4) seen unusual lights or balls of light in a room without understanding what was causing them; and, (5) discovered puzzling scars on his or her body without remembering how or where they were acquired. Of those surveyed, 119 responded yes to four or five of these items. The authors of the Bigelow report conclude: "This is 2% of our sample, and it therefore suggests that 2% of adults in the American population have had a constellation of experiences consistent with an abduction history. Therefore, based on our sample of nearly 6,000 respondents, we believe that one out of every 50 Americans may have had UFO abduction experiences."[78] As they point out, two percent of the American adult population of 185 million constitutes 3.7 million people.

Knowing that people may be encouraged to say yes to any unusual question whatsoever, the researchers controlled for this by asking the respondents whether they had heard or seen the word *trondant* and known it had a special meaning for them. Only one percent of the sample answered yes, so the authors concluded that the positive responses to the other questions were not due to suggestion on the part of the questioners.

Finally, in defending their conclusion that 3.7 million Americans may have had an abduction experience, the authors propose that the reason many people want to dismiss the "massive weight of evidence" is *denial*.

> And from an emotional perspective, we have found that every-one—scientists, laymen, abductee, and UFO researcher alike— *wants* to deny the reality of such bizarre and unsettling encounters. Denial offers comfort and reassurance to anyone troubled by the possibility that the UFO phenomenon, as represented by thousands of UFO sightings, the photographs, radar reports, and abduction accounts might actually represent a non-human intelligence and technology. In this context it is only natural to prefer easy, unrea-soned denial to the effort of objective investigation.[79] (italics in original)

There are more things in heaven and earth than are dreamt of in my philosophy. That life exists outside the earth is certainly possible. It is less but still remotely possible that it evolved in the same man-ner (with the same extinctions) that life on earth did.[80] All the reported ETs are humanoid; a skeptic would claim that this similarity is evidence that the abductees' claims were influenced by popular cultural beliefs. But of course, such skeptics are "denying the reality of this horrible possibility. What I find more improbable, however, is that many of us in the general public want to have our Blue Cross premiums and tax-supported medical funds spent on licensed clini-cians who help people with the "post-traumatic stress syndrome" that results from ET abductions. Yes, people who suffer emotional distress that they believe results from such an abduction may be deserving of help or therapy—but not from people who corroborate for them that their current problems are due to an incredible past event. Those who convey this message, listed in Fiore's book, are all professional practitioners.

Despite the 3.7 million prospective clients claimed in the Bigelow report, the number of licensed practitioners who specialize in helping people "recover memories" of ET abductions is small. Many, however, are involved in helping clients recover memories of having been victims of sexual abuse as children, particularly incestuous abuse. These memories occasionally involve sexual orgies (it has been claimed that they occurred in various day schools) or even orgiastic parts of satanic cult practices.[81] The process of recovering such memories is distressingly similar to that leading to accusations of mass child sexual abuse or abduction by ETs. The clients who are quite often (but not always) women in their thirties or forties, suffer from a variety of common problems (like eating problems, or a temporary lack of interest in sex), often while they are getting a divorce. The therapist believes in her or his specially trained powers to "spot" people who have such problems as a result of childhood sexual abuse. Recall the claims of CNBC's expert on sex and family, that she can tell within ten minutes whether people are "survivors" of incest from the way they walk; see Chapter 1. Then, consistent with manuals and self-help books such as Ellen Bass and Laura Davis's *The Courage to Heal*, the client is encouraged to elaborate on a vague feeling that "something happened": to wit, "If you think you were abused and your life shows the symptoms, then you probably were."[82] The theory is that the childhood incestuous abuse has been totally "repressed," but that—once again—the memory exists intact in the unconscious and is expressed through body language and in the symptoms the client presents to the therapist. These symptoms are said to demonstrate that the client is now "ready" to recall the events explicitly because, in a somewhat skewed Freudian sense, they reflect both the event and this readiness. (Exactly why current distress, such as often occurs during marital problems and divorce, places a client in the fortunate position of being able to "face the facts" is not entirely clear.) Often, in addition to working with the client personally to help recover the memory, the therapist will advise the client to join a survivors' group.

Incest is a serious problem. The social taboo against engaging in incest exists in all human societies, except in a very few where rulers and kings and their families who are considered to have godlike characteristics are given license to engage in it. Incest occurs, and it undoubtedly can have devastating consequences, although the rate with which such devastation occurs cannot be estimated from the reports of therapists since, as a consequence of their work, they see only those people who are distressed. It is reasonable to assume that it never has entirely neutral or benign consequences. Thus, claims of recovered memory of incest must be taken much more seriously than claims of recovered memories from ET abductions.

The problem is so important that we should study these claims with great care. Even when we do so, however, they remain claims; the few published research reports that are alleged to support them are seriously flawed. In contrast, the professionals who are licensed to form their own opinions independent of the research findings—and other "experts"—are convinced that they are more than merely claims. For example, Bass and Davis report: "so far, no one we've talked to thought she might have been abused and then later discovered that she hadn't been."[83] Right there is reason for profound skepticism. There is no insight or technique in the mental health area that is infallible, that is, that does not lead to false conclusions on occasion. A claim that no false conclusions have ever been drawn immediately calls the claim into question, as, for example, should have been done with the claims for the remarkable success of transorbital lobotomy (see Chapter 2).

Let's examine the research. There has been none that even indicates the existence of Freudian repression, as opposed to ordinary processes of forgetting or motivated selective inattention. This latter process occurs when the existence of an event, such as bloody combat experience, is acknowledged, but some of its most disturbing details are recalled only later, perhaps as part of a "flashback." Even if repression does exist, we do not understand how it might work. That does not mean that such repression with later accurate recall is *impossible*. But, in contrast, there is a great deal of research that indicates the flawed nature of human memory, that its nature is reconstructive, and that events that literally never occurred can be recalled in great detail.[84] So let's move to specific research concerning recall of childhood sexual abuse.

First, the claims are held to be plausible because incest is claimed to be more common than is generally realized. The estimate that five percent of the population has suffered from sexual abuse as children (made by the National Center on Child Abuse and Neglect in 1986[85]) may be low, we are told, due to the "conspiracy of silence" that often follows such incest. If five percent is an underestimate, however, we don't know how much of an underestimate it is, and the jump from five percent to 25 percent is huge. Incest is also claimed to be more common than is generally realized because studies of people who are known to have suffered from it as children indicate that about one-third do not report it when they are questioned as adults, even under probing questioning.[86] That result may appear to support claims for an underestimation, but it actually does not. When we ask people about any event, there will be both those who did experience and do not report it ("false negatives") and those who did not experience it but do report it ("false positives"). It is the balance between people who erroneously fail to report the event and those who erroneously do report it that determines whether the reporting rate is an over- or underestimate of its true rate. That is particularly important to understand when the event is one that occurs in less than half the population, because then the smaller proportion of people who have not experienced it and who wrongly report it balance out the larger proportion of people who have experienced it and who do not report it.

The other main studies of the incidence of childhood incestuous abuse attempt to validate recovered memories by seeking actual evidence one way or the other. Unfortunately, the most frequently cited study as of this writing does not study the accuracy of these memories in a way that makes it possible to determine their validity.[87] First, the authors do not specify the criteria *they* (as opposed to their subjects) used for determining accuracy (not a trivial omission, given that other researchers would like to be able to check out their methods and conclusions). Second, they do not present interpretable statistics involving their validations, particularly on which types of criteria led to which conclusions; instead, they simply present anecdotes (case histories). Third, the study does not distinguish between subjects who recalled the incest all their lives and those who recalled it as a result of recovered memories. This distinction is absolutely critical to the question of the accuracy of such memories.

So we're still in the dark. At this point the practitioners involved could admit quite honestly, "We don't know whether these memories are accurate." (I myself would never proffer an opinion about a particular case without strong evidence, and I am not referring to evidence from psychological testing or interviews, which is not strong.) But the practitioners don't say, "We don't know." Instead, they claim they do know. The result is predictable: fury. There is the fury of the clients who are convinced that they have been abused, or rather "incested." We have a new verb in our language. They are furious at their parents. Then there is the fury of the professionals, who occasionally recommend that their clients take such actions as suing the parents, refusing to let them see their grandchildren, or ruining their reputation by letting mutual friends and acquaintances know about the newly discovered memories. In addition to fury, there is distress: the acute distress of the parents accused who believe themselves to be innocent. Many of them respond at first by asking if they can help in some way; when the professionals involved refuse to meet with them, as often happens,[88] they end up furious, too, wanting to sue the therapists. In fact, a new group called the False Memory Syndrome (FMS) Foundation by 1992 had a membership of about two thousand families, mainly parents who claim that they were falsely accused as a result of their children's "therapy." (By the end of the first half of 1993, the membership had grown to over 4,600.) The FMS Foundation disseminates information about the nature of human memory and about how to deal with retributive actions of children and their therapists, particularly their lawsuits.

Finally, there is the fury of the true believers at the skeptics who challenge them, particularly those of us who serve on the scientific advisory board of the FMS Foundation. We are accused of being antifeminist, of supporting denial (a charge we hear over and over again), and of not caring about incest.[89] We are accused, somehow, of being opposed to Anita Hill. We are even accused of making judgments about individual cases, when we actually do not. Irrational arguments are marshaled, such as "Why would anyone want to make this up?"—an argument based on the false belief that people variously tell the truth, do not remember, or lie, but never sincerely believe that they are telling the truth when they are in fact giving an inaccurate account of what occurred. A truly well-trained practitioner would know that this happens quite often, that people do seek explanations for currently unpleasant events, even the explanations themselves are unpleasant. A truly well-trained practitioner would know that explanations are easily influenced by current cultural beliefs, such as the importance of childhood events in the development of adult distress, even when such beliefs are wrong. A truly well-trained practitioner would understand the fallibility of human memory and its susceptibility to suggestion.

In particular, a truly well-trained practitioner knows not to make hypotheses that are impervious to evidence. But not only do many practitioners make such claims, they dismiss any contrary evidence as denial—for example, a sibling's claim that there was no indication of even minor distress at the time of the alleged event, or even evidence that the event couldn't have occurred when or where the client claims. Clients who subsequently recant—alleging they have been "brainwashed"—are dismissed as having "reentered denial." (One professional went so far as to testify in court—according to newspaper accounts—that the fact that her client referred to events that couldn't possibly have occurred only strengthened the conclusion that incest had occurred, because it is typical of incest victims to exaggerate.) Since a willingness to consider any contrary evidence would require questioning the accuser, such willingness in itself reflects a bias against the accuser, not to speak of women in general. The protestations of the members of the FMS Foundation are simply interpreted as an instance of denial—not as an understandable reaction of people who sincerely believe that their lives have been severely compromised, possibly even ruined, by allegations of events that never occurred. Perhaps some of them really are "denying" or "repressing" the fact that they really did commit incest, but their denial and beliefs are genuine. Ironically, the very same professionals who claim to have helped their clients get out of denial seem unsympathetic to parents who they think have the same problem.[90]

Again, let me emphasize that not all memories of childhood incest are false. A doctor who tells people who have suffered from fatigue for three weeks that they they are likely to have leukemia will be correct in a few cases. Some of the "correctly" diagnosed people may even go on television talk shows and attest to the doctor's wonderful diagnostic skills and perhaps say that the doctor has saved their lives by encouraging them to get early treatment. But it will not be a good diagnostic practice. I myself have severe doubts about the accuracy of the more radical claims, due to all the reasons outlined earlier—and due to the (literally unbelievable) lurid content of many of the memories.[91] (The counterargument is that the unusual amount of violence and even orgies or satanic ritual involved in these memories simply provides evidence about "why" they were repressed.) But I don't know.

The licensed professionals don't know either. Rather than admit they don't know, however, they "decide" that the memories are accurate. The result is not only fury and distress but widespread suffering, hate, and denunciation—all in the name of mental health. There is no evidence that the clients who recover the memories even feel better, however true or false these memories might be. While licensing has given professionals permission to proffer an opinion as if it were fact, it has apparently taken away from many of them ability to say three little words: "I don't know."

PATERNALISTIC GREED

The fact that some people are indeed distressed makes them susceptible to exploitation by nonlicensed people. Since an altruistic interest coincides with economic self-interest to restrict the trade of unlicensed profiteers, psychologists are particularly active in working to prevent such exploitation. Most states currently have no laws that would prevent any unlicensed person or group from offering advice for a fee, so long as that person or group does not fraudulently claim to be licensed. As I found when I was president of the Oregon Psychological Association during the licensing sunset and sunrise procedure, both psychologists and legislators are particularly concerned with limiting the activities of such exploiters: "Let's license not just the *name* but the actual *practice* as well!" After all, such restrictions on practice are found in medicine, engineering, and architecture. Why not psychology? Such restrictions would put many "lay therapists" who are not exploiters and who, as the research shows, are every bit as good as the professionals, out of business as well—thereby reducing the availability of therapy and raising its price. That, however, can be framed as an unfortunate side effect of protecting the public by restricting practice to stop exploitation.

Paternalistic altruism and individual greed combined in 1987 to yield a "model licensing law" passed by the APA's Council of Representatives. The stated goal was to have this "law" enacted into state laws in all American states and territories. What was the nature of this model licensing law? First, only people who had received degrees from one of the APA's accredited professional programs would be granted a license. Second, the license would cover not just the status of "psychologist" and an ability to receive third-party payments but the actual practice of psychology as well. *Practice* was defined as virtually any activity that involves opening one's mouth to give advice about any aspect whatsoever of human life or to help people in any way—whether or not a fee is charged. This practice includes some activities that do not work (like training in biofeedback). Moreover, practice "is not limited to" everything that might be considered to involve some sort of "psychology" or other in 1987. Let me quote.

> *Practice of psychology* is defined as the observation, description, evaluation, interpretation, and modification of human behavior by the application of psychological principles, methods, and procedures, for the purpose of preventing or eliminating symptomatic, maladaptive, or undesirable behavior and of enhancing interpersonal relationships, work and life adjustment, personal effectiveness, behavioral health, and mental health. The practice of psychology includes, but is not limited to, psychological testing and the evaluation or assessment of personal characteristics, such as intelligence, personality, abilities, interests, aptitudes, and neuropsychological functioning; counseling, psychoanalysis, psychotherapy, hypnosis, biofeedback, and behavioral analysis and therapy; diagnosis and treatment of mental disorder and emotional disorder or disability, alcoholism and substance abuse, disorders of habit of conduct, as well as the psychological aspects of physical illness, accident, injury, or disability; and psychoeducational evaluation, therapy, remediation, and consultation. Psychological services may be rendered to individuals, families, groups, and the public. The practice of psychology shall be construed within the meaning of this definition without regard to whether payment is received for services rendered. (See Section J for exemptions.)

Section J provides an exemption from being licensed to people teaching, engaging in research, or providing psychological services to organizations or institutions—provided that such activity:

> does not involve the delivery or supervision of direct psychological services to individuals or groups of individuals who are themselves, rather than a third party, the intended beneficiaries of such ser-

vices, without regard to the source or extent of payment for services rendered.[92]

What this awkward wording actually means is that professors and "organizational" or "industrial" psychologists who work for business organizations or government units are exempted. The rationale is that such people are not working for individual clients per se. That conception conflicts with the APA's Ethics Code, which specifies that the psychologist should be working for the individual being evaluated or treated. This in turn often conflicts with the actual practice of psychologists in giving court testimony—such as deciding that a convicted murderer is "irredeemable"—and with the practice of choosing people eligible for benefits like training or disability payments. Psychologists who decide that murderers should be executed as "irredeemable" or that injured people are undeserving of disability benefits can hardly be described as working in the best interests of these people, but according to the ethics rules, it is the person being evaluated who is the client.

The "model licensing law" is highly restrictive. Moreover, it proposes highly specialized training, at least to the point of receiving a Ph.D. degree or a substitute degree from a "practice-oriented" institution accredited by APA. There is no evidence to support the claim that restrictiveness benefits the public. It is totally unjustified.

CHAPTER 6

A PLETHORA OF EXPERTS AND WHAT TO DO ABOUT THEM

Professional psychologists are not the only people outside the medical profession who are licensed to practice. As of 1992, social workers are either licensed or certified in all states and territories; in twenty-seven states they are eligible for standard insurance reimbursement, dependent on the type of policy in only three and restricted to work in a clinic in only one.[1] In addition, various unlicensed people also present themselves to the public as experts in particular areas involving mental health, like rape counselors, alcohol counselors, and religious counselors. Some of these unlicensed or uncertified experts work on an informal basis (like leaders of private AA groups); some are hired by private or public agencies; and some simply "hang out a shingle," there being no law against untrained people calling themselves "therapists" so long as they do not misrepresent themselves as belonging to a particular profession. Many of these people perform valuable services as therapists, usually—unless they are trained in some particular behavioral technique—as empathetic and understanding listeners. Many of them are not very good therapists, and on rare occasions they are ripoff artists. As pointed out in Chapter 2, however, the success rate of minimally trained and paraprofessional psychotherapists is no different from the success rate of the highly paid professionals. (The ripoff artists were not included in the studies leading to this conclusion.) Does anything follow about the licensing or unique social status of professionals from this conclusion about their effectiveness as therapists?

Medical people must be licensed. They can dispense drugs. Moreover, the training in medical school covers principles of medical science, and although such leaders in the field as W. French Anderson may consider medical science "inexact," medical students must master it on at least a superficial basis. In psychology, by contrast, while there are indeed some well-established principles, obtaining a degree leading to a license often requires no more than a "peripheral acquaintance" with them (see Chapter 1). Licensing of psychologists doesn't work to protect anyone except those licensed. Now what about those not licensed? Like psychologists, they often justify their expertise on the basis of "experience." Like psychologists, they often use shoddy tests and propound theories that are based on ideology or fad rather than on empirical research findings or well-researched theory. The greatest use of anatomically detailed dolls to detect child sexual abuse, for example, is by self-proclaimed experts in the child protection agencies and by police and prosecutors, not by unlicensed and untrained counselors. People who specialize in "recovery" of repressed memories of being "incested" are as likely to call themselves simply counselors as psychologists.[2] Should all of them be licensed? Should none? Should they all be recognized as experts in court settings, or as experts in advising judges about custody arrangements? Should we pay any attention at all to what they have to say about alcoholism or obesity?

I will defer the difficult question of who *should* be licensed—that is, granted third-party reimbursement and recognized in our courts—to the end of this chapter. First, I want to deal with the question of whether those not currently licensed should be recognized as valid experts about the problems they address. Do they as a group have any expertise, aside from the simple human activity of listening empathetically and occasionally giving good advice?

Self-proclaimed experts' claims to competence can be very convincing. Those with the least training base their claims on their own personal experience with a particular mental health problem. This claim can be expressed in terms of a syllogism:

I have had the problem myself; I felt this way.
I did thus-and-so and overcame the problem (hence thus-and-so *caused* me to overcome it).
I have since had extensive interactions with people with the same problem.

Therefore, I understand the problem in its entirety. (For example, I know what anyone who wishes to overcome alcoholism must do in order to succeed.)

Now compare this type of personal experience claim with a scientist's or scholar's claim, which may also be expressed in the form of a syllogism:

I have studied the problem extensively.
I have studied alternative hypotheses about the nature, causes, and possible amelioration of the problem.
I have evaluated these hypotheses in light of the existing evidence.
I have tentatively concluded that some of these alternative hypotheses are better supported than are others.
Therefore, I understand *something* about the problem and how to address it (for example, that choosing an alcohol program consistent with one's beliefs is usually beneficial)—although new findings may always prove me wrong.

Suppose someone claimed to have a vaccine for HIV infection. Which type of person would be more convincing? I trust that the latter would be for most readers. A person's own experience with HIV infection would be viewed as irrelevant to that person's claim about the vaccine; knowing people who were infected, even treating them personally would also be considered irrelevant. Nor would we place much faith in someone whose evidence for the effectiveness of this vaccine was that it had halted progression from infection to AIDS just for himself or herself. We would want evidence about whether this person was thoroughly trained in biochemistry or molecular biology, in how to do laboratory experiments, in how to conduct medical randomized trials experiments to test the vaccine, and so on.

Problems involving psychological distress, in contrast, often appear as unique, individual, spiritual—that is, as personal. In dealing with such problems, we are more apt to accept the personal experience syllogism as valid, perhaps even as more valid than the scientist/scholar syllogism. We watch these people claiming expertise on the basis of personal experience on television talk shows. They are convincing. Moreover, we "know what they are talking about." But we often have only the vaguest understanding of someone who claims expertise on the basis of scientific study. We can accept the idea that we may not know much or even anything about science. But we do not easily accept the idea that we do not know a great deal about people. Thus, the person claiming expertise *about us* on the basis of the scientist/scholar syllogism is viewed with suspicion, while those who use the personal experience syllogism are not.

Thus, we are tempted to accept the personal experience claim as legitimate, but it is not legitimate. In previous chapters of this book, I pointed out the flaws in citing personal experience as the justification for a professional's claim to expertise. The personal experience of the nonprofessional is no different from that of the professional. Both are subject to availability biases, retrospective distortions, inappropriate generalizations, stereotypic thinking, and so on. A professional psychologist can claim—as I saw one do on television a few months ago—that *all* people who are depressed who do not receive treatment become suicidal, even though the claim was admittedly based on experience with depressed people who had become suicidal rather than on studying depressed people to see if they became suicidal without treatment. A nonprofessional AA leader can claim that he *knows* that following the twelve steps is the only way anyone can overcome alcoholism. Both can cite anecdotes from their own personal experience to support their claims. But neither should be convincing.

Not all nonprofessionals who invoke the personal experience syllogism state that they have had the problems themselves. For many, personal experience means experience with other people who have had the problem—often extensive experience. But the flaws of generalizing on the basis of such experience are the same as generalizing on the basis of oneself. Consider a group of purported experts on rape who appeared on television after William Kennedy Smith was acquitted of rape. Many stated that they wished they could have testified because they know how rape victims respond and could therefore have evaluated whether the accuser was truly a rape victim. Aside from the fact that this wish questioned Smith's innocence just after he had been found innocent, it illustrates a big problem with intuitive diagnosis. Perhaps these people really do know how rape victims respond. The problem in the trial, however, was to *distinguish* whether Smith's accuser was actually a rape victim or was not. The only relevant experience of an expert, therefore, would be in learning to distinguish among those claiming to be rape victims who were actually raped and who were not actually raped. All the experience in the world with women who were actually raped would not help in making this distinction. Because that was the experience of the experts (or at least what they claimed to be their experience), it was irrelevant. Again, as with diagnosing stomach cancer, the essence of a diagnosis lies in distinguishing between possibilities (like cancer versus ulcer). Unfortunately, where psychologists have failed is not in limiting the experience of their colleagues or others, but in teaching them that diagnosis is *differential* diagnosis, and that in general judgment to be meaningful must be *comparative*. That principle is often not understood intuitively, although occasionally it is. More than a peripheral knowledge of psychology helps in understanding it.

It is unfortunate that the public, as well as psychologists, often fails to accept the personal importance of an impersonal approach. What could possibly be of more personal importance to the person infected with HIV than the impersonal development of an HIV treatment? What could be more personally important to the graduate school applicants, parolees, and heart attack patients discussed in Chapter 3 than an improvement in impersonal, statistical prediction techniques? It would mean fewer failures in careers, fewer victims of parolees who return to crime, fewer failed parolees, better medical treatment, and so on. The fact that there is no "match" between the style (personal or impersonal) of addressing a problem and the personal importance of resolving it should not keep us from thinking clearly about it. More personal benefit can be obtained by the impersonal development of a vaccine or by an understanding of the importance of sterile medical procedures, than by a great deal of personal caring—however well-motivated—that doesn't do much.[3]

The greatest problem with alleged expertise based on personal knowledge is that it is subject to fads and ideologies. When a particular issue becomes prominent in society, people with experience in it become "experts." Others accept their personal experience claims on the basis of the incorrect inference that because there is a need for expertise, it must therefore exist. Naturally, it must then exist among those people claiming to have it. Such acceptance is common in situations of personal need, such as among people who have terminal cancer who want to accept the expertise of religious healers, imagery trainers, or people selling laetrile. Such acceptance can also occur on a societywide basis. For example, when the USSR developed the atomic and hydrogen bombs well before the time predicted by American policy leaders—and Communist political groups appeared to be capable of taking over Europe and Asia—this country experienced a surge of anticommunism that might best be described as hysteria. Immediately, senators (Joseph McCarthy in particular), former Communists (like Whittaker Chambers), and FBI agents who had infiltrated Communist cells in this country became "experts" on "the Communist menace." The House Un-American Activities Committee held well-publicized hearings concerning such trivia as Hollywood stars' attendance at Communist-sponsored peace rallies, which led to blacklists. Ordinary prudence and skepticism were often neglected or downgraded as "naive" and were even lambasted as "fellow travelers." Books were written (like Whittaker Chambers's *Witness*), fictionalized accounts of FBI informers were presented on television (for example, Herbert Philbrick in "Three Lives"), and people who "knew" denounced those who opposed the hysteria as "playing into the hands of the Communists"—just as those who now "know" about the terrible prevalence of incest denounce those who are skeptical as supporting pederasts, antifeminists, or even Satanists.

The anticommunist "experts" were not foreign policy analysts, political scientists, or historians. "Monolithic communism" they said, would endure forever unless we waged an all-out campaign to destroy it, no matter what that campaign did to our own Bill of Rights or to our sense of ethics in foreign policy. The anticommunist experts "knew" because they had had personal experience with communism. They were wrong—observe the fate of "monolithic communism" today. But they were persuasive at the time. Mental health concerns are paramount in our society today; we do not suffer from a shortage of food or materials or resources. We suffer because people are distressed, don't get educated, turn to crime in proportions far greater than in comparable countries, use drugs and become addicted to them, become alcoholics, become personally violent, and don't work very hard or take much pride in it. Naturally, nonprofessionals as well as professionals give us a great deal of advice about what to do about our mental health. And we accept personal experience as a basis for expertise when we shouldn't.

ABUSE

The subject of greatest current concern today (1993) can be described in a single word: *abuse*. We have come to understand that husbands physically abuse their wives, and incidentally vice versa, although usually with less devastating effects, parents abuse children physically and sexually, grown children abuse elderly parents, addicts (and even casual users) abuse drugs, and a large proportion of us abuse alcohol. All this abuse destroys people. Moreover, abuse is not limited to physical acts. Mental abuse as well can have devastating effects. We need to know as much as we can about abuse; therefore, there are people who claim to know about it.

I am compelled to state that I am not in favor of abuse, anymore than those who opposed Joe McCarthy in the early 1950s were necessarily procommunist. Moreover, I am compelled to state that I am in favor of ending abuse, just opponents of 1950s anticommunist hysteria were compelled to state that they did not want to see communism succeed. The very need to say that one opposes methods but not aims itself indicates the depth of our society's concerns about abuse.

We saw the flaws in professional psychologists' handling of sexual abuse in the previous chapter and the findings that early abuse statistically precedes later problems. These problems by no means *necessarily* follow abuse, or even follow it with a high probability. (Prolonged and extreme abuse as experienced by people who survived concentration camps for a number of years may be an exception.) Moreover, as we have seen, many of those claiming to have the greatest expertise in abuse—and who use the shoddiest techniques and tests to uncover or treat it—are *not* professional psychiatrists or psychologists. Somehow, we now have whole clinics of nonprofessionals specializing in different types and varieties of abuse, particularly sexual abuse.

Our obsession with abuse may have a personal down side. It can reinforce feelings of incompetence in individuals who believe they have been abused, and—more important—it can inhibit them from taking action to resolve *current* life problems they may have. There are instances of ongoing abuse with which victims really are incompetent to deal, such as children abused by their parents, frail elderly people abused by their grown children, and wives who cannot leave physically abusive husbands without facing poverty. I am concerned, however, with the current obsession with past abuse. There is simply no evidence that "past abuse will out" no matter what one's current situation is or what one does about it. A history of family violence during childhood is related to adult depression and relapse in general, but *not* for adults who are nevertheless free of chronic interpersonal stress.[4] The problem is that feeling and believing that one is a victim and hence incompetent can inhibit action. That results in a positive feedback effect, because acting to improve one's life—or failing to take such action—can have a profound influence on belief and feeling. An erroneous belief that past abuse necessarily has lasting effects can thus lead to drift and a worsening of the current lives of those who believe they were abused in the past. Often, those of us who question the wisdom of encouraging people to view themselves as victims are accused of "blaming the victim," and the conversation is supposed to end there. It shouldn't. We might better be accused of "blaming the adviser," and the ensuing conversation should concern advice, not victimization.

The past abuse obsession creates another problem. Since the perpetrator of the abuse is always someone else, that person is responsible for failing in our current selves if we think we have previously been abused. That can lead to blame. In ordinary circumstances, rightly attributed blame can lead us to take action to improve our situation.[5] (Occasionally not, as when victims, or relatives of victims, of police chases of someone else over something as trivial as speeding or a car theft are told to "blame the person fleeing, not the police"—while such chases continue and more people get killed.) But when the abuse or hypothesized abuse took place years ago, nothing to change the situation can result from the blame—although some "experts" urge those who believe they have been victimized to take such draconian measures as publicly accusing grandfathers on their deathbeds, on the grounds such "getting even" is "therapeutic." (Normally our society presumes innocence and believes that people should be given an opportunity to respond to charges or denunciations; some of the more rabid proponents of abuse everywhere, however, believe we should neglect such niceties—just as some of the more rabid anticommunists of the early 1950s did.) Blame itself doesn't do much unless it activates change. Where is the evidence that simply learning to blame—or hate—somebody is therapeutic? Before urging people to do such negative things, we should certainly demand convincing evidence that blame is therapeutic. But the evidence doesn't exist.

What we do have a great deal of historical evidence for is that people like to blame others and that great damage can be done when blaming gets out of control, specifically when it is focused on hurting those others rather than on benefiting ourselves. In the Middle Ages, Jews were said to be poisoning the wells during times of plague, and witches were said to be responsible for inexplicable physical problems and hallucinations and at bottom tools of the devil.[6] Just as the "power differential" of abusive parents or therapists over their children leaves their victims powerless, the devil is all powerful—unless some quasi-mystical exorcism can be arranged (in current society, psychotherapy). There's no devil to blame for child abuse, so it is increasingly common to ascribe demonic powers to real or alleged abusers. The satanic cultists who supposedly sacrifice babies are so extremely clever and powerful that they have consistently fooled the FBI, police forces, and investigative reporters, who find no independently corroborated physical evidence of their activities.[7] They are even said to have taken over the police and FBI.[8] Just as the Communists allegedly in the State Department in the early 1950s were so clever that they could never be found and may have taken over the department. The abusers are entirely responsible for the plight of those they have abused, they are to be blamed and hated, and they are so powerful that there is nothing their victims can do to improve their own lives.

Who is it that is most often believed to be incompetent as the result of past abuse? Women. While the CNBC psychologist in Chapter 1 announced that a fair proportion of men have been incested, her belief is a minority view. There's a great deal of consensus among self-proclaimed experts about the proportion of women who have been victimized. We now even read newspaper figures quoting a proportion of one in three women.[9] This view of woman as victim, whose mental health is thereby inferior to that of man, has a long and dishonorable history in psychiatry and psychology.

This implicit view of female inferiority can be found, among other places, in psychoanalytic theory. Freud did maintain that "biology is destiny," and psychoanalytic theory does imply that men and women are intrinsically different due to differing resolutions of the Oedipal conflict. For a male, a successful resolution involves giving up his desire to possess his mother by identifying with his father, who does in fact "possess" her. That meant, in Freud's time, identifying oneself as having mastery and becoming active and aggressive in a socially acceptable manner in a male-dominated society. Females, in contrast, can give up their early desires to possess the mother by becoming "Daddy's girl." They don't really have to "grow up" the way a man does, and in psychoanalytic theory, they generally don't. As Daddy's girl, they can concentrate on being cute and attractive—their supposedly proper role in society. Moreover, since their attachment to their mothers is never as directly sexual as that of little boys, they do not have to give it up as totally as little boys do; in fact, they can identify with their mothers with a lot less conflict—and hence less opportunity for maturity—than boys can identify with their fathers. Women can identify in part by becoming caring mothers themselves—again, their proper role in a male-dominated society.

What often goes wrong with men is that they cannot entirely give up their desire to possess their mothers; they might end up feeling too much tenderness for Mom, for example, so that they can have satisfactory sex only with women toward whom they do not feel tender. (Otherwise, it would be too incestuous.) In contrast, the female problem is that she might end up *too* attached to Dad. While Freud originally believed that female hysteria resulted from actual incestuous relationships or incidents with the father or with a related adult male figure in childhood, he later came to the much-disputed conclusion that memories of such relationships or incidents were actually wish-fulfilling fantasies of overly attached women. The feelings themselves were "repressed" because they were unacceptable. The women's fantasies, in which these unacceptable feelings were projected as coming from the father to the girl rather than vice versa, Freud said, were generally untrue memories that contain cues to actual present feelings. (Note that there is nothing in Freudian psychoanalytic theory about repressing memories of *actual incidents* in life, only about repressing one's own *feelings*. Note also that there has recently been a switch from Freud's absurd belief that all memories of incest were fantasies to the equally absurd belief that all fantasies of an incestuous nature indicate that actual incest occurred; "if you think something may have happened and you have the symptoms, it probably did.") When hysterical symptoms occurred, it meant that repression per se had failed to allow the woman to function normally, and the problem of the woman and her analyst was to analyze the symptoms to gain an understanding of these feelings so that they could be "defended against" in what George Vaillant later termed a more "mature" manner. (Again, according to standard psychoanalytic theory, it is not repression that leads to symptoms but rather its failure, in "the return of the repressed." That again has been switched to a belief that it is the repression itself that causes the problem and the only way to function is to reexperience the actual abuse in its totality—to learn to hate the perpetrator as much as he was hated when he betrayed the child's trust through his despicable acts. That switch involves yet another switch: For Freud, it was the adults who viewed incest with horror, a horror that arises only as the Oedipal conflict is addressed as we grow up. According to current popular belief, it is the child who feels this horror.)

Nowhere is this derogatory view of women better illustrated than in the maltreatment of Bertha Pappenheim, the very first "case" presented in Freud and Josef Breuer's famous book *Studies in Hysteria*.[10] In justice to Freud, I must point out that Pappenheim was treated by Breuer, and Freud is responsible only for the analysis of the treatment. (In fact, Freud's case histories reveal a man much more empathetic toward his female clients and more concerned with them as people rather than as stereotypes, than would be inferred from his theory.)

Bertha Pappenheim (1869–1936) was an active welfare worker in Germany and an early champion of equal rights for women, through the beginning of the Nazi takeover. She organized and ran a home for illegitimate children and young girls who had been forced into prostitution. She translated important feminist books like *A Vindication of the Rights of Women* by Mary Wollstonecraft, and she wrote books, pamphlets, and plays of her own on feminist subjects. She was recognized as such an important person in the struggle for justice for women that a German postage stamp was issued in her honor in 1954. At her funeral Martin Buber stated: "I not only admired her but loved her, and will love her until the day I die. There are people of spirit and there are people of passion. Rarer still are people of spirit and passion. But rarest of all is passionate spirit. Bertha Pappenheim was a woman with just such a spirit." A co-worker also praised her: "A volcano lived in this woman; it erupted when someone angered her. . . . She fought only about things that were involved with her ultimate aims. . . . If she had the feeling that she had slid off factual ground and hurt the other person in a personal sense, she would unhesitantly apologize and turn back her assault. . . . She loved people and she needed them."[11]

Bertha Pappenheim was first treated by Breuer at age twenty-one. In Freud and Breuer's description of the treatment, she was given the pseudonym *Anna O.*, and "the case of Anna O." later became one of the best-known case histories in the psychoanalytic literature, possibly the single most famous—in part, perhaps, because later analysts concluded that Breuer had botched her case by failing to recognize that Anna had fallen in love with him (kindly referred to as her "transference") and he with her (less kindly referred to as his "narcissistic countertransference"). In fact, Breuer abruptly terminated treatment (his critics have claimed that he "fled") when Anna falsely claimed that she was pregnant by him. He nevertheless wrote in *Studies in Hysteria* that his treatment of her was a success and that it was the first demonstration of the efficacy of "abreaction," the cure of hysterical symptoms by allowing the patient to talk about the circumstances surrounding their development and thereby come to understand their symbolic significance. (Anna referred to this process as "chimney sweeping"; in fact, this technique was not successful and Breuer did botch the case, although most probably for reasons unrelated to transference or countertransference.)

Breuer was first consulted after Anna had developed an alarming variety of symptoms—paralysis, fatigue, insomnia, periods of amnesia, hallucinations—and alternated moods between her "naughty self" (in which she was angry) and her more usual subdued self. Her father, to whom she was devoted, was dying of a lung abscess. Although the family was very wealthy and could easily have afforded a nurse, Anna and her mother had continually attended to him for many months until two months before Breuer became involved. At this point her mother had become so concerned about Anna's physical and psychological condition that she had forbidden her to see her father any longer—except for very brief periods of time. Breuer described his initial impressions of Anna:

She was markedly intelligent, with an astonishingly quick grasp of things and penetrating intuition. She possessed a powerful intellect which would have been capable of digesting solid mental pabulum and which stood in need of it—though without receiving it after she left school. She had great poetic and imaginative gifts, which were under the control of sharp and critical common sense.[12]

And later:

This girl, who was bubbling over with intellectual vitality, led an extremely monotonous existence in her puritanically-minded family. She embellished her life in a manner which probably influenced her decisively in the direction of her illness, by indulging in systematic daydreaming, which she described as her "private theater." While everyone thought that she was attending, she was living through fairy tales in her imagination; but she was always on the spot when she was spoken to, so that no one was aware of it.[13]

His treatment consisted of talking therapy to locate the experiences—which he believed to be accurately recalled—that preceded the emergence of each of her multitude of symptoms. On fifty occasions, for example, she had not heard another person when she was directly addressed; these mental lapses, said Breuer, were due to her belief that she had had to ignore her father's request for wine one day when she was attending to him.[14] Anticipating later psychoanalytic emphasis on unexpressed sexuality, Breuer noted that "the element of sexuality was extraordinarily underdeveloped in her,"[15] that she was a "Daddy's girl," and that she had become inordinately fond of both a "Dr. B,"[16] whom Breuer brought in on the treatment, and of Breuer himself. Again, although Breuer claimed that his treatment was a success, there is plenty of historical evidence that it wasn't—especially given her subsequent commitment to a sanatorium for almost two years between 1890 and 1892.

Later, when Anna O.'s identity as Bertha Pappenheim became known, professional psychologists and psychiatrists were puzzled: How could someone who had been so sick at age twenty-one become such a fulfilled and vital person later in life? In 1984, Max Rosenbaum and Melvin Muroff solicited the opinions of twelve other practitioners to address this puzzle in a book entitled *Anna O.: Fourteen Contemporary Reinterpretations.*[17] The central question was framed by Rosenbaum in the introduction: "How did this woman, believed to be a hopeless case by Breuer [based on what he was alleged to have concluded later—not his writeup], manage to come out of her deeply pathological condition and lead a reasonably [!] fulfilling life?"[18] Rosenbaum continues: "There are those contemporary experts in psychodynamic theory who express the belief that all her later life was not really a fulfilled life, but an overcompensation for what she had in fact never worked out in treatment. They say that she lived out the problems—her unresolved relationship with her father, her sexual difficulties, her fantasies—and her everyday work activity was merely a masking."[19] John Spiegel mirrors this view when he writes: "It should come as no surprise that when Anna O. finally managed to recover from her illness, she expressed her anger in terms of social protest."[20] In fact, with the important exception of Marion Kaplan, the commentators in the book are roughly split between the opinion that she didn't "recover" at all and the opinion that her subsequent life was simply an extension of her previous illness in a socially acceptable form.

Kaplan, in contrast, analyzes the situation in which Anna "became ill."[21] First, she was imprisoned in her own house. As a girl from a very wealthy family, she was expected to make a proper marriage and not to pursue her intellectual or creative activities. (She was indeed extraordinarily accomplished despite the abrupt termination of her schooling; one of her symptoms, for a time, was to speak only in English—one of four languages in which she was fluent.) Her extremely conservative Jewish upbringing was completely male oriented, and she was expected to become the dutiful wife of an appropriate man, although her father's illness interfered with the type of social life that usually preceded this outcome. So she was alone, except for her dying father and her mother. If the societal emphasis on maleness might have led her to be a "Daddy's girl" anyway, the attitudes of her mother—whom Ernest Jones described as "somewhat of a dragon"[22]—could only reinforce that attachment. And then she was not permitted to see him except for brief periods of time! "This was the most severe psychical trauma that she could have possibly experienced," wrote Breuer and Freud.[23] And then he died.

Living in a sexist prison, is it any wonder that her sexuality was "astonishingly underdeveloped?" That she became attracted to Dr. Breuer and Dr. B—the only men outside her family with whom she had any contact? That she retreated into daydreams and fantasies? What might have happened had Breuer's therapy consisted of a demand on her mother that "for God's sake, let her see her father and let her get out of the house, to see other people and pursue her creative interests!"

There was another, perhaps even darker side to her situation, one treated cavalierly by Breuer. Part of Anna's "treatment" consisted of giving her massive quantities of drugs that would currently be given much more sparingly. At one point Breuer decided, "On those nights when she had not been calmed by verbal utterances it was necessary to fall back upon chloral [hydrate]. I had tried it on a few earlier occasions, but I was obliged to give her five grammes, and sleep was preceded by a state of intoxication which lasted for some hours."[24] Five grams is twice the dosage normally required to make a normal person addicted within thirty days.[25] Later, when she was at the sanatorium, she was—according to its records[26]—given seven to ten centigrams of morphine a day in addition, roughly five to ten times the amount now given for postoperative pain. Like Breuer, the physicians apparently believed that such medications were "necessary" and that they were "obliged" to give them.

(Here we have a parallel with modern practice, in which professionals feel "obliged" to medicate patients to prevent overt symptoms, and 60,000 or so professional psychologists are anxious to shoulder that obligation. Again, I ask: *What is so terrible about psychological symptoms that necessitates assaulting the nervous system of the people manifesting them?* Of course, modern advocates of such therapies claim that we know so much more now than we did in Breuer's day and that drugging patients does not actually harm them—which is what lobotomists claimed about lobotomies, and what hot bath and insulin shock therapists claimed about hot baths and insulin therapy. Those practices were based on an ignorance we have overcome, my critics reply, so I'm being unfair. One particularly distressing aspect of the professional therapy field is the doggedly persistent but sincere belief that whatever the current practice is, it is "enlightened," while past practices were deficient if not outrageous. We learn the specific faults of the past but seem immune to learning the general principle that decade after decade, great new insights and great new therapies turn out to be anything but great. It is not at all unusual for a psychiatrist totally convinced of her own perspective in 1991 to refer to the early 1970s as the "dark ages" of psychiatry.[27])

Bertha Pappenheim did get out of the sanatorium. Its final report indicated that "she continued to be irritated with her family, exhibited hysterical symptoms, and continued to disparage medicine [sic] and science [sic] as modalities of treatment." Further, she was "in 'childish opposition' to her physicians. By the time she had left the Swiss hospital, she was a confirmed addict accustomed to high doses of morphine and chloral. The general feeling of her physicians at the hospital was that she was an unpleasant person who exhibited hysterical behavior and who had neurological symptoms."[28]

How then, did she change so profoundly? Aside from Kaplan's, the psychological analyses presented in Rosenbaum and Muroff's collection—and which are so prevalent in our society—ignore obvious factors to concentrate on esoteric hypotheses. Moreover, they miss the one truly remarkable change in Bertha Pappenheim's life, which was her ability to overcome on her own the addictions thrust upon her by her well-meaning doctors, a story that to the best of my knowledge has never been told. Instead, she is derogated: Her earlier problems are all said to have arisen from her attachment to her father. The temporary success of Breuer was due to abreacting the repressions related to this attachment. Despite her apparent accomplishments in life, she never succeeded in growing up. Due to her unresolved attachment to her father, her accomplishments were not "really" real but were mere manifestations of, defenses against, or sublimations of her illness. She was, according to Freud and Breuer and according to thirteen of the fourteen commentators, simply an hysterical woman who was incapable of becoming a whole person—without psychotherapy.

There was, however, one aspect of Bertha Pappenheim's "character" that didn't change. As Breuer described it, "Even during her illness she herself was greatly assisted by being able to look after a number of poor, sick people, for she was thus able to satisfy a powerful instinct."[29]

While Breuer was addicting Pappenheim to drugs, other less psychoanalytically oriented psychiatrists were attacking women's brains in a more direct and less reversible manner—with lobotomies (see Chapter 2). Freedman and Watts, the main practitioners, justified this procedure on the grounds, "It is better for him [the patient] to have a simplified intellect capable of elementary acts than an intellect where there reigns disorder of subtle synthesis"—whatever that means. "Society can accommodate itself to the most humble laborer, but it justifiably distrusts the mad thinker."[30] And who were these "mad thinkers" to which society could not accommodate itself? "Women were preferred to men, "observes a psychiatric historian," because they could receive the protection of the home after the operation, unlike men who were expected to work outside [it]. Jews were preferred because of the 'solidarity' of their family life. Freeman and Watts also said that lobotomies were more successful on blacks than on whites."[31] Exact figures about the numbers of lobotomies are unavailable. Many hospitals where these operations were performed have since been closed down, and the only figures available are from samples involved in horribly flawed studies. We must take Freeman and Watt's word about their preferred subjects. They preferred people whom they regarded as more infantile to begin with and whose intellects were not important. Once again, women.

Now consider today's obsession with "repressed" past incestuous abuse. Once again, the little girl is Daddy's girl—only this time in a more direct and appalling manner. Once again, she is incapable of growing up the way most men do, as a result. She is flawed for life without realizing it, until that flaw is pointed out by an expert (often on the basis of extraordinarily common symptoms). She is neither mature nor responsible—without intervention from a psychotherapist. It is therefore justified to subject her to an extraordinarily harsh treatment—in this case not assaulting her brain but "helping" her to become alienated from her family, perhaps learning to hate not just the father who committed the act, but the mother who failed to protect her by acceding to the "conspiracy of silence." At best, those who claim the abuse didn't happen—including her siblings—are "in denial" at worst they are psychopaths or even satanists. The only way a woman who has been rendered incompetent by the repressed incest can get her life together is to start all over again, with a realization that all that she had previously valued was nothing but the hollow denial of a victim.

Like Freud and Breuer, and like Freeman and Watts, the people treating women this way today are being paid to do so, often quite handsomely. Like these predecessors, they are convinced that they are helping. Like these predecessors, there is no good evidence that they are doing more good than harm, and some of them are surely doing more harm than good.

A POSSIBLE SOLUTION

Who should be allowed to be a psychotherapist, and what licensing should be involved? Certainly anyone should be permitted to give advice for money. We live in a free society. People who have not been declared legally incompetent should be allowed to spend their own money as they wish. That means that some vulnerable people will be harmed by the incompetent or the exploitative, but that is a price we must pay for the freedom of our society—just as we have higher crime rates than do totalitarian societies, where the state can control and detain people without regard for their liberties. We cannot and should not restrain people from seeking the advice of others simply because we believe they are vulnerable, or that the advice is bad, or that they would be better off seeking advice elsewhere. Moreover, if the people giving the advice wish to refer to themselves as "therapists," we should not restrain them from doing so in order to protect legally competent citizens from making what we believe to be a foolish choice. Psychic readers bilk people, but we should not outlaw psychic reading. Moreover, as we saw in Chapter 2, there is evidence that the personal characteristics of therapists are important in relationship therapies and we cannot presume to evaluate these characteristics for all who advertise themselves as good therapists.

But that does not mean that anyone who calls herself or himself a "therapist" should be reimbursed for what they do by third-party funding, or should be recognized as some sort of expert in a court of law, or should be accorded any particular social status or respect. (The same principle applies to anyone else with a self-assigned label.) Who should? That is, who should be licensed as a psychotherapist?

My answer is based on three simple principles.

1. Licensing should protect the public in fact, not just in rhetoric.
2. Licensed people should be paid on the basis of applying knowledge. The "earn now, learn later if at all" model should be thoroughly rejected. The fact that therapists and other people sometimes provide valuable treatments and sometimes make correct judgments independent of applying knowledge does not imply that they should be paid at an "expert level" for such treatments and judgments.

3. Legal values and procedures should be based solely on knowledge that has survived the scrutiny of skeptical challenge. Intuition has no place in our court system. The fact that intuition is sometimes correct does not justify its presence. No citizen's legal and civil fate should be determined on the basis of someone else's intuition.

The first principle, concerning protecting the public, implies that anyone in the mental health field who has power over people who cannot exercise free choice themselves should be required to have a license. Aides, assistants, and counselors—as well as psychiatrists, psychologists, and social workers—must be licensed when they work in mental hospitals or halfway houses (or in any sheltered living arrangements where clients are physically incapable of leaving or where legal authorities can be summoned to bring back a client who walks away). People who work in such settings must be subject to the ethical and legal rules involved in licensing. Proved abuse of a client in any such situation should be grounds for automatically retracting the license and imposing legal penalties. To accomplish such a change, we must upgrade the position and pay of aides, assistants, and counselors who work in these settings.

The second principle, concerning applying knowledge, implies that only people who can demonstrate that they practice psychotherapy on the basis of scientific knowledge and training should be licensed as mental health experts. Opinion alone should not be enough, no matter how much others making the same claim to the same expertise may agree with that opinion. Whole programs must be licensed on the same basis, which would automatically license those working within them to work there, but not allow such employment as a path to "hanging out a shingle" to engage in a private practice based on anything they please or find useful on an intuitive basis.

Those who are licensed should receive the same remuneration they do currently. They should be eligible for pay from general funds (insurance or government) and accorded the status of "expert" because they have some special knowledge, insight, and skills that others lack.

It might difficult for a licensing board to make a judgment about whether a person or program *actually* applies scientific principles. But it would be no more difficult in principle than making a judgment about whether someone is *actually* a good therapist. Implementation in fact would be more difficult than in principle, however, because in fact licensing boards do not currently make a judgment about whether a candidate for a license would actually provide a valuable service. Instead, such boards rely on credentials and interviews. Moreover, a judgment about whether someone actually applies scientific principles would be more difficult to make than the ones currently made by "peer review boards" evaluating treatment plans. The problem with peer reviews is that they can be—and are—made according to the principle that the treatment is good if it is the same treatment the people on the review boards would provide. In contrast, we should be willing to invest both the money and effort to thoroughly evaluate whether what someone actually does or proposes really does have a scientific rationale. Such money and effort would certainly result in great financial savings, and it could not have a negative effect on quality of treatment.

Finally, the third principle: only those licensed by such rules would be permitted to testify in court about particular people. When they testify, they should be required to provide the evidence and rationale for any conclusion they reach and for any recommendation they make. The presentation of psychological portraits or intuitions should be automatic grounds for disqualification. If the courts are interested in general principles rather than judgments about specific individuals, they should turn to experts in general principles—that is well-recognized researchers. The current system of recognizing someone on the basis of their years of experience who has received a credential based on minimal training is not only absurd, it is a danger to the civil liberties of those about whom judgments are made. Judges are elected or appointed to make such judgments. They are paid to do so. They must be the people who make them.

There should be a *different* type of license for people doing only therapy, who would be neither granted the status of expert nor paid on that basis. The primary purpose of this license would be to protect the confidentiality of those seeking their services and to allow payment from third parties when people who are truly mental health experts believe such therapy is warranted or necessary.

The current research indicates that people with master's degrees who practice behavioral or empathy-oriented therapy are every bit as effective as those with M.D.'s and Ph.D's. In fact, those with bachelor's degrees may even be as effective. Some program directors who employ them have reached similar conclusions.[32] If an M.D.'s or Ph.D.'s wish to be therapists, there is no reason they should not be, provided they are licensed and paid on the same basis as master's degree holders. For starters, people licensed as therapists could be paid at the current rate of independent social workers with an MSW (master of social work). Whether a therapist's services are necessary or desirable for an individual and are subject to third-party payments, however, must be a judgment made by a holder of the other kind of license, a licensed mental health expert. While therapy generally is effective, and while it would be nice to provide therapy to everyone who wishes it on the basis of their own judgment of need or desire, society as a whole should not pay. Again, however, people not judged legally incompetent in our society should be free to pay anyone out of their own funds any amount they wish for advice or therapy.

For future modifications of this special therapist license, more research should be conducted to determine the threshold of intelligence or training that is required for being a therapist who is as effective as most others. Perhaps even a master's degree is unnecessary. Perhaps unemployed college graduates could be as effective as anyone else. I don't know. My point is that money and effort provided "up front" to find out could result in great value and savings later.

The changes should not, of course, be implemented by those already in control of the profession. Again, making them will not be easy, but if the rationale for licensing—protecting the public—is to be realized, they must be implemented. The current licensing procedures protect no one except those licensed.

CHAPTER 7

WHY THE MYTHS ARE BELIEVED

Most mental health practitioners sincerely believe that they are helping their clients, that they have specialized knowledge, and that their
judgments are good ones whether they base them on a modicum of
scientific knowledge or on some harebrained new ideology. Moreover,
whatever it is they do does require extensive training, often prolonged
and expensive. Naturally, they would like to be rewarded with money
and status. As we have seen, the constant repetition of the sentence
"mental illness is just like any other illness" has led to a status for
mental health practitioners comparable to the high status of medical
doctors, who are at least supposed to base their practice on verified
medical knowledge. The rewards associated with this high status have
cumulated to become a major expense for our society, which it generally pays through third-party payments. Yet unlike medical practitioners, well-paid mental health practitioners have hardly caused even a
blip in alleviating society's rate of the distress. For whatever reason
one gains status, however, it leads to wealth, and wealth in turn
increases status, as both the general public and individual legislators
are lobbied to increase status and monetary allotments. Such a self-
augmenting cycle is not unusual in a capitalist society, least of all in
ours, where lobbying has become such an important influence on government spending decisions.

Lobbying is a commonly accepted practice, and it is not my inten-
tion to analyze it or criticize it in this book. What I wish to do instead
is to analyze some of the factors that underlie successful lobbying.
Lobbying can be especially successful when it is done by a large group
that controls considerable amounts of political contribution money or

that can influence a considerable number of votes. The National Rifle Association has been generally successful in its lobbying efforts as the result of such control and influence. But the 64,000 to 90,000 psychologists in this country, along with the 40,000 or so psychiatrists, 150,000 or so social workers, and an undetermined number of other mental health "experts" hardly constitute such a group. Another major way in which lobbying can be successful, however, is by simple persuasion—in particular by providing information and framing issues in a way that will lead legislators to agree with the position of the lobbyist.[1] The desired result is legislators who believe that they are voting in the best interest of their constituents, or even "for the right thing," when they vote the way the lobbyist wishes. Thus, lobbyists for quite small groups can be successful if they are able to make persuasive arguments.

Arguments for enhancing professional psychology can be very persuasive in this regard because they appeal to people's psychological needs and intuitions. Moreover, it is possible to specify exactly which needs and intuitions they satisfy, on the basis of well-established psychological principles. I am not maintaining that those wishing to advance the fortunes of professional psychology and psychiatry are deliberately making use of these principles. (As pointed out by Sechrest, many don't even know them.) Most important, I am not maintaining that those involved in the lobbying have made any conscious decision to use these principles to deceive the public. Like other well-established principles, these do work, in the statistical sense that their application increases the probability of success. What works generally is reinforced at the individual level, and selectively evolves across "generations" of lobbyists or others wishing to advance the cause of mental health professionals.

OUR NEED TO ACCEPT AUTHORITY

The first need to which arguments for enhancing professional psychology appeal is the need for authority. When I originally became involved in psychology, this need was derogated as part of an aberrant "authoritarian personality." Having observed the horror of Nazi Germany, we sought an explanation for why so many people could have followed the wishes of that authoritarian and irrational regime. The standard psychoanalytic explanations didn't work; there was no evidence that those convicted at the Nuremberg war crimes trials suffered from "psychosexual" pathologies any more than other people did, or that their childhood experiences were particularly aberrant. Nor did they appear to be particularly "bloodthirsty" people; they all claimed that they had simply been doing their jobs—even when it meant exterminating people. (When Adolf Eichmann was captured and tried in Jerusalem almost twenty years later, his total lack of pathological emotion about what he had done led Hannah Arendt to coin the phrase "banality of evil.") Nor could standard Freudian psychopathology account for the large-scale passive collaboration of the German people that was so essential to the success of the Nazis. What was there about the German people that had led to this horror? The answer proposed was that their rigid father-oriented upbringing had caused them to develop an "authoritarian personality," characterized by an "intolerance of ambiguity" and passive compliance to authority figures.[2] *Authoritarianism* achieved the status of a psychopathological syndrome in and of itself, to be distinguished from normal psychological functioning; paper-and-pencil scales of it were developed that asked subjects to endorse or reject such statements as "respect for parents and authorities are the most important virtues that children can learn." To accuse someone of being authoritarian became the same sort of insult that accusing someone of being "passive-aggressive" or "sexist" would later become. Authoritarians were thought to be particularly prevalent on the extremes of the political right and left, although they could be found anywhere. Unlike the rest of us, authoritarians were unthinking, gullible, passive sheep who in group settings could be led by accepted authorities to wreak great havoc on the world.

There were problems with this conceptualization from the beginning. First, differences in authoritarianism among people didn't predict differences in their actual behavior very well; the correlations were significant but not large. Second, people who were judged to be authoritarians had a disconcerting habit of endorsing contradictory statements on the paper-and-pencil scales, which was inconsistent with the notion that authoritarianism is a consistent syndrome.

Then in 1963 the late Stanley Milgram changed our thinking about "authoritarianism" by publishing his famous studies on "destructive obedience."[3] In these studies ordinary people were led to administer what they believed to be severe and dangerous electric shocks to others. The victims were actually actors who feigned pain. Milgram challenged the aberrant "authoritarian personality" theory of Nazism by reversing the question, asking in effect not how the Nazis are different from the rest of us but how we are like them.

Individuals' scores on the pencil-and-paper authoritarianism scales did predict to some extent how much shock they were willing to administer, but not nearly as much as the social and physical arrangements between the experimenter urging obedience, the person receiving the shock who was presumably suffering, and the subject. If the subject was in the same room as the person receiving the shock whose (feigned) agony was clear, there was less obedience; more people refused to go on sooner. If the person receiving the shock could not be heard at all, there was more obedience; even if this person could be heard but not seen, over 60 percent of the subjects administered what they believed to be the strongest shock, labeled XXX and "dangerous." If the experimenter who urged the subject to administer the shocks was remote—say, on the other end of a telephone—there was less obedience. If the subject was one of several who had to decide collectively whether to administer the shock, there was much less obedience if at least one urged the others to quit, but much more if all urged continuing. Finally, it made little difference whether the experiment was conducted at Yale University or in a shabbily furnished office in New Haven with a sign that said "Psychology Associates." (Goebbels maintained that the effects of propaganda depend less on a belief in the legitimacy of the source than on the repetition and intensity of the propaganda itself. Subsequent psychological experiments have borne out this contention; experimenters have consistently found that people tend to judge that whatever has been repeated is true—even when the repetition is only of the words in the assertion.[4] Are we, for example, immune to the effects of repetitive news that we know to be "managed" simply because we know that what we are being shown and told is what those managing it want us to see and hear? I know I was not during the recent Gulf War.)

The implication of Milgram's experiments and others that followed is that "authoritarianism" is not such an unusual phenomenon. Perfectly normal people have a tendency to accept authority—even to the point of inflicting pain and possible harm on others, or at least believing they are. In fact, so strong is this tendency that we do not make compelling demands on authorities to prove that they are indeed authorities. Most of the time and in most contexts, most of us do not adopt the "show me" scientific attitude (see Chapter 3).

Moreover, as others have pointed out, we couldn't.[5] Consider how extremely difficult life would be if we did not accept what many authorities tell us is true. Suppose we are feeling sick and we go to our doctor for a diagnosis and treatment. If we were not medically trained, we would have to spend at least two years in medical school to obtain the knowledge necessary to decide on our own whether our doctor's diagnosis was accurate and whether his or her recommended treatment was good—by which time we might be dead. Do we perform our own chemical tests on what we eat and drink to determine whether they are poisonous—or do we accept the authority of the Food and Drug Administration? Of course, authorities make mistakes, and sometimes they even demand that we do awful things, but life would be impossible without accepting what most authorities have to say. It's not just esoteric knowledge that we accept, either, such as what "authoritative" molecular biologists and noted astronomers say. How many of us have really observed for ourselves that the earth is round rather than flat? Have we repeated the experiments of Eratosthenes (of Alexandria, c. 276–193 B.C.) concerning the angle at which sun rays strike the bottom of wells that are a known distance apart?

It's a matter of simple coping with the world. The "completely open mind that questions all authority" is impossible, a myth. Such a mind would never get past "go." To maintain that acceptance of authority constitutes a psychological aberration from normality is silly. My own view is that the unusual position is rejection of authority. Moreover, "the price of liberty is eternal vigilance,"[6] which is not necessarily a happy way to go through life, and can easily become paranoia, or at least "paranoid realism."

It is thus not surprising that we accept the authority of medical doctors. Not only have we been socialized to do so, but because medicine works; "by their fruits shall ye know them." People recover from diseases that just a few generations ago were almost always fatal (like pernicious anemia) or were often fatal (like cholera) or were incurable except for symptom remission (like syphilis). Some diseases—at least, in this country—no longer exist, like polio and smallpox. Our lifespan has increased radically since our grandparents and great-grandparents were children. Now we worry primarily about diseases that occur when something goes wrong with our bodies, often as a result of aging or genetic predisposition—not when something invades them, HIV being an important and devastating exception). A few short generations ago, advice that children should control their fat intake because too much cholesterol might lead to clogged arteries in the fifth decade or beyond of life would have appeared ludicrous. Only a little more than half the children born, even in this country, survived childhood diseases, and for those who did, worrying about one's condition after age sixty-five or so would have meant worrying about a rather improbable event. Thus, there is plenty of evidence available about the *consequences* of modern medicine that would lead us to accept medical people as authorities.

In contrast, there is little evidence that "expertise" in the mental health area has brought about a reduction in the incidence of emotional disturbance and distress. Even great champions of drug therapies maintain that all these drugs do is to control the conditions. The American people appear not only aware of this lack of evidence but judge that the national problem of mental illness is actually getting worse—at least according to a recent Yankelovich poll.[7] We nonetheless maintain a belief in the authority of the purported experts in the mental health field.

How can such a glaring inconsistency persist? For one thing, people are not necessarily consistent in their beliefs. Contradictions often must be pointed out, and even when they are, many people are prone to forget about them. (Consider how long it took for the contradictions arising from the Newtonian view of space and time to lead to Einstein's relativity theories.) In a popular book about the "mature mind" in the late 1940s, Harry Overstreet (on the basis of his general impressions and anecdotes) wrote that the human individual "is a fairly tight-knit pattern of consistency."[8] Careful study indicates that at least in terms of beliefs, people aren't. (Nor are they consistent in terms of behavior—if they were, their future actions would be more predictable than they are; see Chapter 3). We often maintain contradictory beliefs, and the fact that we do not insist on resolving them is no more a sign of psychopathology than is the fact that we accept authority, often without checking it out and often for the worse.

Another example of inconsistency is the usual addendum to the statement that mental illness is just like any other illness—"and nothing to be ashamed of." People were accepting that platitude at the same time they were horrified that Senator Eagleton, whom George McGovern had chosen as his vice presidential candidate in 1972, had undergone electroshock therapy for depression; he was quickly dropped. Nor did those psychiatrists who had previously testified to its virtues stand up and argue publicly that having had such therapy should in no way disqualify the candidate. We repeat that mental illness "is nothing to be ashamed of," yet bills involving permits to purchase firearms have in them a prohibition that firearms should not be sold to former mental patients, even though former mental patients have a rate of violence that is if anything lower than that of the general population. And would you want your daughter to marry one? This is not hypocrisy, it is simple inconsistency. Consequently, nothing prevents people from accepting mental health professionals as authorities on mental illness—while simultaneously believing that they haven't even made a dent in solving the problem.

We make many social judgments on the basis of what we're told and on the basis of our intuition, a conclusion not supported by convincing evidence. There's nothing necessarily bad about intuition; in fact, many of our most profound or interesting insights may arise from it—even, perhaps especially, creative work. The problem is, however, that intuitions may be wrong. In this particular context, our intuition that people who claim to be experts in mental health must necessarily be experts happens to be wrong.

ESPECIALLY AUTHORITIES WHO AGREE WITH US

Our intuitive beliefs about mental illness itself reinforce our acceptance of the authority of mental health experts. A major reason we believe in the experts is that their views so often coincide with popular opinion, indeed, seem to corroborate public opinion. An interesting example of this comes from a study by my former student Von O. Leirer and his colleagues.[9] They compared the predictions that groups of psychiatrists and psychologists made about which new patients in a psychiatric ward would become violent with predictions that high school students made about the same new patients. The predictions were based on an "adjective checklist" form, on which such character-

istics as "emotional withdrawal," "motor retardation," and "hallucina-
tory behavior" were assessed at the time each patient was admitted.
When Leirer presented the same checklist results to totally untrained
high school students and asked them to predict which patients would
become violent, their average judgments were almost identical to the
average judgments of the professionals. Despite the professionals'
expertise, both the professionals' and the high school students' predictions were based on the same stereotype that the "sicker" the patient,
the more likely the patient was to be violent—weighting for example
"emotional withdrawal," the second-best predictor, positively when it
should have been weighted negatively). That fits perfectly with our
social stereotype, as expressed in potential gun control legislation,
that "sickies" are prone to violence. Whether a patient's hospitalization had come as a result of assaulting someone was the fifth most
important variable in the professionals' ratings and the tenth most
important in the students' ratings, while in fact it was the best predictor of future violence.

Like the APA president quoted in Chapter 1, professional psychologists make claims to be experts not only in problems of mental illness
but in knowing what constitutes the good life in general ("We are
teachers . . ."). Again, they have established this authority in part by
reaching "expert" conclusions that are compatible with what people
generally believe anyway. For example, Abraham Maslow's "needs
hierarchy" and Erik Erikson's hierarchy of childhood stages have
become so accepted in our culture that people often refer to them as if
they were established facts. Yet the evidence supporting their existence
is scant. A true hierarchical structure implies fundamental asymme-
tries; it is impossible to reach a higher stage without reaching lower
stages—often at an earlier point in time. The slender research evidence for the existence of these hierarchies could often be restated
with the generalization that "good things in life occur in loose clumps,
as do bad things." That generalization should not be surprising given
the existence of positive feedback between what people do, how they
feel about themselves, and the future opportunities available to them.
George Vaillant, too, discussed his findings about remarkable adulthood changes throughout the male life course in terms of a hierarchy
of increasing "maturity" of their defense mechanisms.[10] Vaillant considers the use of biting humor in a social cause, for example, to be a

more mature defense against one's own hostile impulses than projec-
tion ("*They* are hostile") or denial ("What? *Me* hostile?"). But he does
not show any systematic progression from lower to higher (or regression from higher to lower) of the kind that is required to establish the
existence of a true hierarchy; that is, he does not show that moving up
or down the hierarchy of defenses occurs in sequence, or specify the
life experiences that would hypothetically bring it about.

Some hierarchies do exist. The negative behaviors of aggressive
young boys, for example, fall in a neat hierarchical pattern; they do
not engage in or attempt physical abuse of their parents and siblings
unless they also have "fights" with them using verbal abuse and
humiliation. Without the latter behavior, they do not engage in the
former.[11] My point is, however, that we too readily postulate hierarchies of behavior and feelings (or spiritual "levels") in the absence of
much evidence. When professionals espouse such hierarchies they are
quickly believed and their ideas are acceptable. Hierarchies exist in
almost all societies and organizations, and many major Western
philosophers have proposed that the soul is—or ought to be—hierarchically ordered as well. Plato explicitly proposed that the hierarchies
of the well-ordered soul and the well-ordered society should be identical; the lowest level of the soul consisted of the animal functions (the
producers in a society), the medium level of the spirited functions
(the warriors in a society), and the highest level of the rational functions (the philosopher king rulers of a society). Problems for either an
individual or a society arose when the hierarchy was disturbed by the
"lower" functions disrupting the higher ones. People and societies got
"carried away" by greed (animal desires, the lowest of all) or ambition
(slightly higher) to behave irrationally. Aristotle was a little less keen
about spirited functions, so when he ordered the soul hierarchically,
the progression was from passive ("vegetative") animal functions to
active ones to—once again—reason. The Catholic Church retained
the hierarchical structure of the soul, so that the highest level consisted of the "pure" love of Christ and God, and the lowest level consisted of impure lust for the sensual and material things of the earth—to
the point that a celibacy (or "virginity") and asceticism were common
among devout Christians at a very early date. Freudian psychology
contains two hierarchies: the unconscious, preconscious, and conscious; and the id, ego, and superego. Moreover, these Freudian hier-

archies interact; the defense mechanisms consist of the unconscious part of the ego, even though they were preconscious at the time they were established. Such "spatial paralogic" is appealing to many people for reasons that are not entirely clear (as the reason for the ubiquity of three levels is unclear); what is clear is that people very often code the world in such terms, as Clinton DeSoto and his colleagues have demonstrated.[12] The mental health professionals who discuss life in general often affirm the existence of such hierarchies, usually in terms of quality of "mental health."

Not only are hierarchies of life accepted for their compatibility with the way people normally think, they have the further motivational appeal that they deny the sometimes painful necessity of making tradeoffs in life, of forgoing some valued outcomes or behaviors in favor of others, because achieving a higher state in a hierarchy implies having achieved everything that is valuable in lower ones; hence, people do not have to forgo anything in achieving a higher state. Hierarchies deny, moreover, that societies are not just "higher" or "lower" ("primitive") in relation to one another; some provide political and economic rights to their members (like personal freedom, autonomy, and opportunity for self-expression and accomplishment), while others provide social benefits (like guarantees of employment and minimal physical well-being and safety, a sense of oneness with other living things or even the universe in general). The hierarchical view of societies, in contrast, implies that there are some processes— like spiritual growth, mental health, social progress—that advance in a cumulation of desirable outcomes. In individuals, the hierarchical view implies that a mentally healthy person necessarily one who is loving, treats others well, is socially an activist while internally at ease, accomplishes much in life, is creative, and so on—so that to achieve any of these desired states, all one must do is become mentally healthy. The world would be a very benign place if this myth were true. Unfortunately, the world is what it is—however appealing the myths may be. By perpetuating such a myth in the area of mental health, professionals enhance their acceptance as authority figures.

THE IMPORTANCE OF EVERYDAY ATTRIBUTIONS

Another reason that the authority of mental health professionals is accepted is that they emphasize the importance of personality in explaining *others'* behavior. That again is compatible with what most of us do: "He is an angry person, you are touchy, I just look out for my rights." Here, aggressive behavior is ascribed as a stable personality characteristic to "him," variable behavior to "you," and a reasonableness to "me." As noted in that famous declination, the causes we often hypothesize to explain behavior can be quite different when applied to others from the ones we attribute to ourselves.

These causal attributions vary in a simple but systematic way. As Ned Jones and Richard Nisbett have pointed out, we have a *fundamental attribution error* or *bias* to attribute the behavior of others to personality factors and that of ourselves to situational factors.[13] This bias is not merely self-serving, as in the above example of explaining aggressive behavior. The person who engages in a heroic act—helping others off a burning airplane, diving under the ice to rescue a child—and then maintains that "anyone would have done the same thing" is not merely being modest or even false modesty. When people act themselves, they attend to the environment—to the plight of the people needing help, to an insult, to a competitive threat. The hero or villain is not attending to his or her own heroism or villainy. In fact, it isn't clear that there are internal cues at all about what heroism or villainy feels like, certainly not cues that differentiate my feelings from the feelings of others, to which I do not have access. In contrast, the observer of the heroic or villainous act is primarily attending to the person who is acting, not to that person's environment. The actor seeks causal explanations in the environment, while the observer seeks them in the actor. The observer of an heroic act will quite likely attribute the actor's claim of attending only to "what needed to be done" as due to modesty or false modesty. (It follows, incidentally, that we often worry that the military capacities of a potential enemy country may lead it to take aggressive action, while we rarely worry that our own military capacities might have a similar effect on *us*.) We are biased to attribute causality to the focus of our attention. The professional mental health expert delivers a message perfectly consistent with this bias. What other people do—in particular, the things they do that we don't like—is due to their personality. They suffer from such problems as low self-esteem or repressed hostility. They are not mentally healthy. Thus, we derogate them without having to acknowledge our own judgmental attitudes or anger—as we would, for example, if we were to label them "evil" or "depraved." The icing on the cake is that when *we* do things that we don't like, we attribute our acts to environmental factors, specifically the way in which our parents raised us and our consequent experiences that have stunted our growth up through the hierarchy of mentally healthy states.

THE BELIEF IN THE TYRANNY OF CHILDHOOD EXPERIENCES

But do our childhood environments and experiences really have such a profound causal effect on the rest of our lives? When Alexander Pope wrote that "Just as the twig is bent, the tree's inclin'd,"— changed to "the child is father to the man" by Wordsworth, not Freud—Pope was discussing education, not early childhood experience.[14] As compelling as his analogy is, it is generally not even literally true; trees are bent by consistent forces such as rocks, other trees in the way of their growth, or wind, and in absence of such forces will orient straight toward the sunlight. Moreover, Freudian psychology's claim that adult problems are "caused" by childhood experience can be interpreted in two ways. The first is that some experiences are pathological and will inevitably yield problems; for example, people who have been abused in some way as children *must* suffer as adults. The second is that when problems occur, they take the form of "regression" to childish ways of coping and hence mirror these experiences. For example, if—for whatever reasons including medical ones—people become distressed as adults, the form and type of their distress is likely to mirror the form and type of distress they experienced as children. Compatible with this second interpretation, Freud observed that he knew many people who had experienced the same childhood traumas and pathologies that his patients had but who nevertheless did not become disturbed as adults—a fortunate outcome he often ascribed to "constitutional factors." Nevertheless, our culture has come to accept the primacy of childhood experiences in yielding adult character and personality problems, and this acceptance is widespread. A recent book about the painter and sculptor Max Ernst tells us that "we now *know*, in the light of twentieth-century psychological research, that childhood experiences of the type Ernst suffered are a decisive factor in personality development" (italics added).[15] In a more popular outlet, *TV Guide*, the director of a special television program about the late actor Rock Hudson tells us that Hudson "was shut down as a child. He learned to keep things inside, to create a fantasy world. Even without his career, he would have a tough time maintaining relationships because he never let anyone know who he was. As he became a superstar, his secret became more painful. The result was tortured, twisted, bizarre behavior—promiscuity and alcoholism."[16] Question: How does this director know that Hudson was "shut down as a child," or what he "learned"? In fact, how do we know how we ourselves felt as children, or how we ourselves learned?

THE ROLE OF RETROSPECTIVE MEMORY

For most people, the answer is memory. As has been documented and well-accepted since the publication of Sir Frederick Bartlett's *Remembering* in 1932,[17] however, retrospective memory is a reconstructive process. It is influenced by our *current* ideas about what people are like, our current "scripts" about how people behave, including ourselves, our theories of human change and stability, and in particular our implicit theories about what causes such change and stability.[18] The experiencing of recalling what has happened may be much like observing a moving picture for those of us whose "schematic thinking" is primarily visual or a dialogue for those whose coding is primarily verbal. But the actual process of recalling is that of recalling bits and pieces of the past ("memory traces") and filling in the gaps with what "makes sense" to us now—even though these gaps may be every bit as vivid in our recall as the traces themselves.[19] Our current state influences both the selection of concrete instances and the filling-in process, as do our current theories and assumptions about what the past *must* have been like. Our overall assessments about past periods of our lives—and even about the "feeling tone" involved in them—are especially vulnerable to such influence.

This process is illustrated by an experience of one of the world's most recognized experts on memory research, Elizabeth Loftus:

> An uncle told her that when she was 14, she found her mother's drowned body. That shocked Ms. Loftus. "I said, 'no I didn't find the body, somebody told me about it.'"
> The uncle was adamant about his story. Over the next few days, she says, "I thought to myself, 'My God, maybe I have repressed a

memory. Maybe that's why I'm so obsessed with this topic.'"

Her uncle's claim quickly played with her mind. "I started seeing my mother in the pool, she was face down. I started to picture myself finding the body. I started putting everything into place. Maybe that's why I'm such a workaholic. Maybe that's why I'm so emotional when I think about her even though she died in 1959. And I practically got the memory going, over the next two days."

Then her brother called her and said there had been a mistake. The uncle had double-checked his story. Ms. Loftus had not found the body after all.[20]

This influence also affects our assessments about the past experiences of others. We can be quite certain, for example, that the author of the book on Max Ernst did not directly observe Ernst's childhood, any more than the television director of the Rock Hudson program observed Hudson's childhood. Certainly, they may have read others' descriptions, perhaps even descriptions by Ernst and Hudson themselves, but these descriptions as well would have been influenced by these factors. Consider the description of Hudson. Many of us think that there is something wrong with sexual promiscuity; Hudson was promiscuous. People have things wrong with them as a result of childhood experiences, we believe; thus, it follows that Hudson's childhood must have been somewhat as the director described—and we will believe any information tending to confirm that description. (Note the total absence in the director's analysis of the possibility that Hudson simply enjoyed sex and enjoyed getting drunk. That interpretation doesn't "fit" with our beliefs about people who are promiscuous and alcoholic.)

In June 1986, I was privileged to organize a workshop on retrospective memory for a Social Science Research Council committee meeting on Cognition and Survey Research.[21] Researchers from diverse fields presented their work, and those in attendance discussed its relevance to reaching conclusions on the basis of surveys that treat recalled information as accurate. Let me briefly outline a few examples of what they discussed.

We tend to share a belief that in our culture women suffer more from stress than do men, and that the stresses from which women suffer are more focused on interpersonal events and relations than are the stresses from which men suffer. In fact, many feminist psychology theorists have suggested that the psychology of women is of a much more "relational" type than is that of (competitive, rule-oriented, emotionally insensitive) men.[22] The data supporting these beliefs are primarily based on what women say about themselves and their reactions to past events and behavior.

In her doctoral dissertation at the University of Oregon, Sandra Hamilton was particularly concerned with discovering the differences in what men and women find stressful and in how much they are actually stressed in their day-to-day lives.[23] In her first few studies, she asked her subjects—freshmen men and women at the University of Oregon—to recall what events and problems they had found stressful during the last academic quarter and how they had attempted to deal with them. She developed a list of twenty-eight specific stressful events that were the most common. The women suffered from all these stresses; the men suffered from all of them as well, except for eight that could be termed "interpersonal" and except for concern with weight. The women reported that they had attempted to deal with their stresses by changing their feelings, whereas the men were more prone to report taking action. These gender-differential findings were based on what subjects had recalled. In her final study, instead of relying on her subjects' retrospective memory, Hamilton paid subjects to report to her three times a week over the telephone which stressful events they had experienced the previous day and how they had dealt with them. At each telephone call, a telephone interviewer read to the subject the list of the twenty-eight stressful events in different orders throughout the experiment, asked whether the subject had experienced each, and asked how the respondent had dealt with each that the subject had experienced. The manner of dealing was coded as "internal" (changing feelings) or external (taking action). *The result was that the gender differences totally disappeared*, except for the concern with weight. When the women were considering only events of the previous day, they reported no more stressful events than did the men. The men were every bit as likely as the women to experience the "female" interpersonal stresses. Moreover, both the men and the women had a tendency to deal with these stresses through internal ways rather than external ways, so the differences in coping style disappeared as well. Experiencing stress from interpersonal problems and dealing with them by changing feelings is simply not part of our cultural view of what men are like. Hamilton concluded that in her earlier studies, of longer-term recall, the men had not consciously lied about not having them when they did; rather, their views about themselves at the time when they were engaged in recalling distant events simply didn't cue them to the existence of these stresses. That interpretation is consistent with the other research on retrospective memory.

At the same meeting on Cognition and Survey Research, Peter Lewinsohn and Michael Rosenbaum presented a study of depression in approximately a thousand people in the Eugene-Springfield area of Oregon over a fifteen-month period.[24] The subjects were recruited by mailing out 20,000 requests to a random sample of people asking them if they would be interested in participating in a psychological research study for which they would be paid. Those who agreed gave brief reports about how they felt every few months, and if they indicated in these reports that they were depressed, they were interviewed at length. (In all, 998 people were monitored in this manner.) Lewinsohn and Rosenbaum were primarily interested in the degree to which many phenomena we associate with depression are due to the "state" of being depressed as opposed to the "trait" of being susceptible to becoming depressed. Previous studies that had simply compared depressed and nondepressed people could not distinguish between these two factors. But people who are depressed not only experience depression but are likely to have "depressive traits," such as a negative evaluation of oneself and pessimistic expectations about the future. Nondepressed individuals generally have neither problem. In Lewinsohn and Rosenbaum's study, some subjects were depressed at the beginning of the study but got over it, some subjects were not depressed at the beginning of the study but became depressed during it, and some subjects were not depressed at the beginning, became depressed, and got over the depression during the study. Differences between such people and those who never became depressed at all generally involve the trait of being prone to depression; on the other hand, differences that arose only during the time in which the depressed people were in fact depressed are related to the state of being depressed.

One of the most intriguing and striking differences they found between depressed and nondepressed people concerned recall of how their parents had raised them. The depressed people recalled their parents as being generally much more rejecting than were the parents recalled by the nondepressed people. Had Lewinsohn and Rosenbaum simply compared depressed and nondepressed people, they could easily have concluded that rejecting parental care leads to depression. It turned out, however, that such recall was specific to the times at which the depressed people were in fact depressed. Before they became depressed or after they got over it, their recall of their parents' rejecting behavior was no different from the recall of the subjects who never became depressed. What was happening, apparently, was that the depression itself was "coloring" the recall of childhood (specifically, coloring it "blue," the color that my anthropologist friends assure me is used to describe depression in many if not most cultures). Perhaps the depressed people's recall was actually more accurate when they were depressed than when they were not; without access to knowing what their parents and their childhood experiences were actually like, we cannot tell. There is evidence that at least in the area of assessing the impression they make on others, depressed people are more accurate than are nondepressed people, whose judgments about this effect are colored by a "rosy glow."[25] Nondepressed people—at least, those in college (and that's an important qualification)—believe themselves to be more popular, intelligent, pleasant, and loving than people who interact with them believe they are. (That has led some psychologists to conclude that being realistic is not as important in maintaining mental health as is having "positive illusions."[26])

The Lewinsohn and Rosenbaum result concerning recall of childhood is quite consistent with the finding that depressed people generally have great difficulty in either remembering or anticipating joy, and that the failure to anticipate enjoying normally pleasurable activities ("Now that she's gone, I can't enjoy anything") inhibits depressed people from engaging in them—which in turn can aggravate the depression. In fact, Lewinsohn has developed a behavioral therapy for mild depression that consists of nothing more "profound" than having people keep lists of activities they enjoy (or that they enjoy slightly, given they're depressed), and then consciously making an effort to engage in these activities more often.[27] It works.

Consistent with Lewinsohn and Rosenbaum's findings, George Vaillant presented a case history of a man who when studied as a young adult appeared to be exceptionally well-adjusted but who became involved in alcohol, drugs, and theft (to support his habits) after he graduated from college. He joined Alcoholics Anonymous (AA), gave up these behaviors, and became successful in his profession. Afterward, he recalled his childhood and young adulthood as having been exceptionally disturbed, and he claimed that he had always been a "psychopath" who was now sober and law-abiding only as a result of accepting his own sickness and following the twelve-step AA program, turning himself over to the Higher Power it entails. His recall of his relationship with his mother was now totally different from what it had been observed to be when he was younger. He even vividly recalled her death in a manner that it hadn't occurred, and from the wrong disease. In the man's own view, the AA program was responsible for a single dramatic change in his life, but Vaillant noted that while the change was indeed dramatic, it was preceded by an equally dramatic change from a promising to an addictive one of which the man was unaware, and the man's later memory fit his "life story" of a dramatic change that resulted from espousing AA principles much better than it fit what had actually occurred.

Consider now one of Lewinsohn and Rosenbaum's depressed subjects or Vaillant's AA subject going to a psychotherapist. The therapist may well ask the person to recall childhood experiences and may find that exactly those experiences occurred that the therapist expected. What has happened in such a situation, however, is that the patient and the therapist share the same set of assumptions about the importance of childhood experience on adult development, and perhaps even about exactly what types of childhood problems will lead to exactly what types of adult ones. Because these assumptions bias the memory of the client, the therapist's views of the causative power of childhood experiences are reinforced, while the patients acquire a "good story" about why they are the way they are.[28] It's a compatible relationship, one that leads both the client and the therapist to accept the therapist as an expert. The mechanism is not, however, reality, but the biases of retrospective memory. (When I presented this material to the Pittsburgh Psychological Society, many of the therapists there expressed at least partial agreement, but they then maintained that having a "good story" handy to explain past and current psychological problems might be helpful to their clients in changing their feelings and behavior. My own concern is that such a good story can be more of a trap than a liberator; if people become convinced that some childhood trauma caused their current distress, then, since they can do nothing about the trauma, they can do little about the distress, except to focus on or attempt to "relive the trauma," to the exclusion of addressing the very real adult problem that they may face.[29]) Unfortunately, no research has been conducted on the extent to which the "good story" is a liberator or a trap—at least, none of which I am aware—so the question is unresolved. Even if such a "good story" is liberating, however, we may still question whether it is really the role of the therapist to encourage a belief in a story that is predictably incorrect. Do clients come to therapy to become deluded in the interests of their liberation? Would we really choose to believe an incorrect "explanation" of our own behavior simply because it made us happy—especially if this explanation negated the role of our own deliberate choice in what we did? (Critical value questions like these that transcend therapy per se will be discussed in Part II.)

After the Cognition and Survey Research meeting was completed, Robert Pearson, Michael Ross and I were in the process of writing it up when we discovered many more examples. Women who raised their children quite strictly before the publication of Benjamin Spock's famous "baby book" encouraging permissiveness recalled their practices as being radically more permissive than they in fact were.[30] Women recall their psychological stress during menstruation as having been much greater than their stress was actually rated to be during their period itself, when they were unaware that the stress ratings they were giving would be correlated with the stage of their menstrual cycle.[31] Moreover, the greater their expressed belief that psychological stress was associated with the menstrual period, the more *incorrect* their recall was when compared with their daily stress ratings. People who were asked on five different occasions whether they had "ever been" depressed were remarkably inconsistent in their answers, but when their current state of depression was assessed at the time of their fifth questioning, it was quite positively related to responding that they had been depressed in the past.[32] (Again, the survey researchers couldn't be certain whether the respondents had ever been depressed "in reality," but two inconsistent answers imply that at least one of them is factually incorrect.) Most sadly, before Down's syndrome ("mongolism") was discovered to be due to the presence of a third twenty-first chromosome from conception, women who had Down's syndrome children retrospectively reported having had such a high incidence of "shocks" during early pregnancy that an investigator who collected these reports concluded that the syndrome might be caused by stress in pregnancy.[33] (While the investigator carefully hedged statements about causality in the body of the paper, it was entitled "Some Psychosomatic Aspects of Causality in Reproduction.")

The only way to avoid the biases of retrospective memory in understanding the relationship between childhood and adulthood is to study the life course *prospectively*; that is, to begin with the subjects as children and then observe them throughout life or at least at specific points in later life. What do prospective studies show? They are well summarized by Sandra Scarr, Deborah Phillips, and Kathleen McCartney in an article entitled "Facts, Fantasies and the Future of Child Care in the United States."

> The "romance of early experience" (Scarr & Arnett, 1987) has given us the assumption that infancy provides more potent and pervasive influences than does later experience. Although evidence for modest relations between early experience and later development exists [references omitted], we agree with Kagan's (1979) interpretation of the data, namely that continuity does not imply inevitability. The human organism is surprisingly resilient in the face of deleterious experiences and sufficiently malleable to "bounce back" given constructive inputs. Only the most pervasive and continuous detrimental experiences have lasting effects on development [references omitted].[34]

In other words, people really are like twigs after all: Only continual obstacles will prevent an initial bend in a twig from righting itself in the direction of the sunlight. Scarr and her colleagues' conclusion is supported by careful research studies, by summaries of such studies, and by carefully observed life-course case histories. The point Scarr and her colleagues make is well illustrated in a recent prospective study by Kathy Widom, who examined approximately 2,600 petitions involving child abuse or neglect in order to compare a group of children who appeared definitely to have been abused or neglected by the age of eleven with children of similar socioeconomic background whose parents had never been suspected of abusing or neglecting them.[35] She then examined court records for evidence of arrests in the subsequent twenty years: "In comparison to controls, abused and neglected children had overall more arrests as a juvenile (26% versus 17%), more arrests as an adult (29% versus 21%), and more arrests for any violent offense (11% versus 8%)."[36]

While Widom's article was widely hailed as "at last proving scientifically that abuse leads to criminal behavior," Widom herself was pointed out in her abstract that *"The majority of abused and neglected children do not become delinquent, criminal, or violent"* [italics added].[37] In fact, those who do not are a vast majority. In addition, there is one finding in the article that she does not emphasize but that in my view is of great importance: *"Of those with juvenile offenses, roughly the same proportion of abused and neglected children and controls go on to commit offenses as an adult (53 versus 50%). Similarly, of those with violent offenses as juveniles, approximately the same proportion go on to commit violence as an adult in the abused and neglected group (34.2%) as in the controls (36.8%). Thus, despite significant differences in the extent of involvement in criminal activities, nonabused and nonneglected subjects are just as likely as abused and neglected individuals to continue criminal activity once they have begun"* [italics added].[38]

Now let's look at the proportions of subjects who had arrests as adults but not as juveniles. A little arithmetic reveals that about 16% of the neglected and abused children were arrested only as adults versus about 12.5 percent of the nonabused and nonneglected group. This difference turns out not to be even statistically significant. What is the connection in this sample, then, between childhood and adulthood? The early experiences (as children) increased the probability of later ones (arrests as adolescents), and these in turn increased the probability of still later ones (arrests as adults). Whether the adolescent arrests indicate a personality characteristic or in fact played a direct causative role in being arrested later (such as through labeling) cannot be known from these data, but this issue is not what is important here. What is important is that knowledge of the distant past (in Widom's study, physical abuse by age eleven) does not increase our predictability of the present when it is combined with knowledge of the more immediate past (in Widom's study, arrest as an adolescent). There is no evidence that childhood "abuse and neglect will out," or that it will have some permanent effect on adulthood without first having an effect on adolescence. I'm not maintaining that such an effect is impossible—just that there is no evidence for it in these data, and that the absence of such "incubation" effects is consistent with other findings mentioned in this book and with sensible theorizing.

The same pattern has been found in the prediction of academic achievement. Background variables predict how well students will do their first year in college or professional school. This first year's achievement, in turn, predicts the second year's achievement, but at this point adding in the background variables does not improve the prediction. That finding, as replicated by Marjorie Rice Lewis in her doctoral dissertation at Carnegie Mellon University, is somewhat remarkable in that had some improvement been found, it could have been ascribed to the "error" in the assessment of the first year's achievement.[39] The second year's achievement predicts the third, but now adding in both the background variables and the first year's does not improve prediction, and so on. Again, the past is a far-from-perfect predictor of the future, but the point is that predictions based on the recent past are superior to predictions based on the distant past; viewed prospectively, that principle is the same as the principle that predication is always better the shorter the time period about which it is made. It is also the pattern found in studies of predicting adult psychological problems from childhood problems. Thus, problems such as poor peer relationships in grade school predict adolescent problems such as dropping out of school and juvenile delinquency far better than they predict later adult problems such as depression or schizophrenia.[40] Again, there are no "incubation effects" found in such predictive studies, although there can be trivial exceptions, such as the certainty of the prediction that we will all be dead in three hundred years in comparison with the uncertainty in predictions that we will be alive or dead in ten years.

(A fascinating challenge to this generalization can be found in Elaine Walker's and Richard Lewine's study showing that subjects viewing home movies of children aged five or less could predict which would become schizophrenic.[41] Unfortunately, the investigators did not ask their subjects to predict any other unusual conditions besides schizophrenia, so that "unusual kids" of any kind are picked out as future schizophrenics. Another interpretation is that there really is some physiological difference between future schizophrenics and normal children that people can intuitively judge by viewing these movies, consistent with the view of schizophrenia as a "natural category." If so, physiological differences may have greater predictive power than the psychological ones that are generally believed to have predictive power, such as being "withdrawn" in a school setting. Incidentally, once again, clinical experience was not related to the accuracy of the predictions.)

Why should the results about predictability across time be otherwise? The state of our health in the future, for example, is determined by the state of our bodies at this time plus what happens to them between now and that future time. The fact that our bodies were in different shape six months or six years ago is irrelevant to predicting what shape they will be in in a week, a month, or a year. Past states may in part determine what our bodies are like right now, but adding knowledge of this past state to knowledge of the current state adds nothing to the prediction. Even if we have smoked, quit smoking, and subsequently develop a disease associated with smoking, it is the state of our bodies resulting from the past smoking that is important—not that the past smoking is somehow "catching up" with us. The past is gone and does not catch up with the present or future in some vague manner. In fact, even the physical "incubation" of a disease refers only to the emergence of overt symptoms. During the incubation period from rabies infection to rabid behavior, for example, the bodies of those animals or people infected are continually changing (otherwise, literally nothing would happen); during the period between HIV infection and AIDS symptoms, T-4 helper cells are consistently being destroyed. Why should psychological changes throughout life follow a completely different principle? The answer is that they shouldn't, and the empirical evidence is that they don't.

Nevertheless, our intuition is that they often follow a completely different principle. People who join self-help groups of people sexually abused as children, for example, often confidently assert that people who have been abused but who currently appear not to have suffered from the experience are simply "denying" that they are distressed. The same assertion is found among children of alcoholics who have suffered and either entered therapy or joined such groups. The assertion is, of course, based in part on an availability bias; those with whom these people interact who have had similar experiences have all suffered from them; therefore, everyone who has had similar experiences must suffer as well. The problem with this logic is that the people with whom the person making the generalization interacts are present in that person's experience precisely *because* they are suffering. Otherwise, they would be unlikely to join such groups or enter psychotherapy. In addition, however, many people harbor a deep intuition that "certain things will out"—like the intuition that "what goes around comes around." This intuition simply exaggerates the degree of predictability, order, and justice in the world.[42] Life might be more manageable if the world were just, but that doesn't make it just. This intuition is similar to the intuition of many children—*and a slight majority of adults studied*—that if a small ball is spun within an enclosed spiral it will continue to move in a spiral motion once it comes out of the enclosure.[43] It doesn't; consistent with Newton's laws, it moves in a straight line in the direction it is oriented once it leaves the spiral enclosure. Somehow, our intuitions about the effects of childhood is that any spiraled paths traversed in it must be repeated once it is left.

The "connection" from childhood to later life—that one thing can lead to another, which leads to another and so on—implies that we might expect to find a great deal of change in adulthood, and indeed we do. George Vaillant summarized the results of his studies of his sample of Harvard men throughout their lives as follows:

> First, it is not the isolated traumas of childhood that shape our future, but the quality of sustained relationships with important people. Second, lives change, and the course of life is filled with discontinuities. . . . [A third issue concerns his interpretation of psychopathology, not his direct observation of what happened.] Fourth, human development continues throughout the adult life, and thus, truth about lives remains relative and can only be discovered longitudinally. Retrospective explanations are filled with distortion.[44]

Consistent with Vaillant's emphasis on sustained relationships, Emmy Werner also found that a "sustained relationship" is the most important factor in "how some individuals triumph over physical disadvantages and deprived childhoods," in her thirty-year study of children born on the Hawaiian island of Kauai.[45]

What we find in prospective studies, then, is that our culture tenders a "romance of childhood"—not evidence that childhood experiences radically constrain adult functioning. I suggest a more dramatic phrase: *tyranny of childhood*. Americans marvel at how people from "primitive" cultures accept absurd beliefs on the basis of little evidence, and at how the Germans in an "advanced" culture could have believed all the nonsense about "Aryan superiority." Yet our belief in the tyranny of childhood has little more foundation than a belief in a mountain god. Yes, the professional mental health authorities propagate this belief, but the authorities about mountain gods also propagate beliefs about mountain gods. Acceptance of this belief is to their advantage; after all, if the locus of problems is childhood and its effects are tyrannical, then interminable talking about childhood while paying a handsome fee to the listener must be the only way to escape the tyranny. Again, I am not claiming that mental health professionals propagate this belief deliberately to make money, but again, what works is reinforcing and evolves. Many scientifically oriented mental health professionals, by contrast, have come to understand the misguided intuitions and the distortions of retrospective memory that underlie this belief. They have come to slough it off, and I am suggesting that it is time for the rest of us to do so as well.

In summary, we believe in the authority of mental health professionals because we have continually heard that they are experts, because we are prone to accept what people claiming to be authorities say anyway, because these particular authorities tell us what we already believe, and because they reinforce our bias to attribute undesirable behavior in others to personality characteristics ("mental illness") and in ourselves to environmental circumstances—particularly to the environment in which we were raised as young children and the tyrannical effects it has had on us throughout our lives. These needs and beliefs do not stand up to rational or empirical scrutiny, but they are there. Consequently, we accept even contradictory assertions, we agree, and we license.

We shouldn't. We don't have to. Instead, we should believe the recommendations and research findings of those psychologists and psychiatrists who believe that psychological knowledge should be "given away," to use a phrase from the APA presidential address of one of the last distinguished research psychologists to be elected to that post, George C. Miller.[46]

Part Two

IMPACT ON OUR CULTURAL BELIEFS

The previous chapters have compared the myth of mental health expertise with the research findings. Only Chapter 7 has been speculative, because—unsurprisingly—there have been no direct studies by psychologists of why people hold unjustifiable belief in their expertise. The conclusions in it, however, were based on research. I have tried to avoid simply presenting a "viewpoint" but have acquainted the reader with the published findings or summaries of these findings published in top scientific journals, ironically most usually in those of the American Psychological Association. While I have concentrated on contrasting myth versus fact in professional psychology—because I know it better than other fields—many of these findings have important implications for other claims to professional expertise in allied fields, such as psychiatry and psychiatric social work.

Throughout, I have specifically rejected the approach used in one recent book questioning expertise that: "My comments and conclusions are derived primarily from my personal experiences in the area" because "for every point I make I could have found numerous references in support of my position, as well as numerous references in refutation."[1] But studies supporting the unique efficacy of high-status mental health professionals in psychotherapy, or their unique ability to understand people as evidenced in their ability to predict human outcome, or their unique ability to learn from experience in some ineffable and intuitive manner, simply don't exist. Readers who suspect that my presentation has been biased or one-sided are invited to read the references themselves, to read the studies referenced in the references, or to peruse the *Psychological Abstracts* in a vain search for the "other" literature. It just isn't there. Moreover, while I have referenced my own work occasionally, the overwhelming majority of the work I have discussed has been conducted by others.

Part II, in contrast, presents my own views about psychology and psychotherapy. These views are not based on my "personal experience" in thousands of hours of professional practice (as the author quoted above claims to base his views), although personal experience has not been exactly irrelevant. Rather, they are based on a knowledge of what is going on in the mental health professions and in our society—especially the tendency to "psychologize" all problems as being determined by feelings (not the unconscious drives and needs of Freudian psychology, but the self-image of New Age psychology). As well as leading to a misplaced trust in professionals, undisciplined theorizing of leaders in the mental health professions has led to unjustifiable and pernicious obsessions: obsessions with self-esteem, with the quick attainment of desirable goals, and with an unrealistic sense of security and superiority to other people. These obsessions do not have desirable consequences for our society.

I will use research findings to support my position, but unlike previous chapters, the research will be selectively referenced because there are no circumscribed fields of inquiry relevant to the areas I will discuss. While I have done my best, I cannot claim that my conclusions are supported by the gold standard of being able to respond to the "show me" challenge. I trust, however, that the arguments I will make are supported by enough evidence to merit the reader's serious consideration.

CHAPTER 8

NEW AGE PSYCHOLOGY

No good has ever come from feeling guilty, neither
intelligence, policy, nor compassion. The guilty do
not pay attention to the object but only to themselves, and not even to their own interests, which
might make sense, but to their anxieties.

—Paul Goodman[1]

The M'Naughten decision (British House of Lords, 1843) concerning
the insanity defense for murder held that people who understand the
nature of reality—in particular, what society defines as right or
wrong—are responsible for their actions. Thus, only those who are
mentally incompetent or psychotic at the time they commit a crime
are not guilty by reason of insanity. While this decision is often
ascribed to the "enlightenment" view that "man is the rational animal" or "ruled by reason," it can ultimately be traced to the philosophies of Plato, Aristotle, and the Catholic Church. It embodies both
a "should" and an "is." People's behavior should be ruled by their powers of conscious choice, and the corollary is that such power can hold
sway because we do not mandate that people behave in ways that are
impossible for them.

In contrast, the Durham decision (District of Columbia Court of
Appeals, 1954), enunciated by Judge D. L. Bazelon, held that people
could be ruled not guilty of a crime by reasons of "irresistible impulse."
That decision later led to the acquittal of John Hinckley in the
attempted assassination of President Ronald Reagan. Bazelon himself
has since questioned that decision,[2] but it is still in effect. The problem, as he later pointed out, is in determining whether someone's
impulse to commit a crime was "irresistible." How does a jury reach
that decision concerning someone else's behavior? For that matter,
how could we even decide whether our own impulses are "irre-

229

sistible"? If the mere fact that we act on them makes irresistible by definition, then the Durham decision implies that no one is legally guilty of anything, or responsible for anything good or bad, because it would by definition be impossible for any of us to have acted in any way other than as we did. (As the joke goes, "Anyone crazy enough to want to kill the President must be crazy.") To argue, in contrast, that we can distinguish between impulses that are resistible and those that aren't implies a remarkable power to assess hypothetical counterfactuals about what could have happened but didn't (that are to be legally binding on someone). Moreover, it implies not just the existence of a human volitional process but an understanding of how it functions, an understanding that has eluded philosophers and psychologists ever since it was first considered. In point of fact, what happens when the Durham rule is invoked—as pointed out by Bazelon—is that judges and juries leave this impossible distinction to psychiatric and psychological "experts" to make. They, in turn, simply disagree with each other depending often on who pays them.

As I have emphasized throughout this book, there is no knowledge in psychiatry or psychology that would allow *anyone* to determine whether impulses are "irresistible"—no theory, no valid assessment technique, no evidence of special intuitive discrimination powers of "trained clinicians," nothing. As a former president of the American Psychiatric Association and professor of law and psychiatry asserted after the Hinckley trial, his colleagues who confidently make this distinction in court are best regarded as "a bunch of clowns." The silliness involved in the implementation of the Durham decision, however, is of less concern here than its underlying assumption about what "causes" human behavior. For centuries in Western thought the cause has been believed to be conscious choice based on rational considerations. Such choice, thinkers knew, did not always predominate; animal or spirited needs or "poorly repressed drives" could on occasion overcome its dictates. But they shouldn't—because the only excuse for otherwise condemned behavior was a flaw in this rationality itself. People who "knew better" were held responsible; hence the importance of "moral education." "He didn't know any better" was, in this line of thought, an excuse. "Weakness of the will" was an acknowledged problem when nonrational needs were strong and tempting, but that could be overcome through prayer or contemplation; hence the importance of religion. Feelings were clearly important; while for Plato they were a "distraction," many others recognized their importance. But feelings in and of themselves could not explain behavior or determine it, particularly not in a manner beyond the "conscious control" of the individual. The Durham decision recognized a change in our views. A feeling strong enough to achieve the status of an "irresistible impulse" could in and of itself determine a behavior. Hence the person who experienced this feeling was not responsible. This change mirrored changes in our views of such problems as alcoholism, drug addiction, and crime. (Note that I say "problems," not "evils.") Alcoholism and drug addictions became "diseases," criminality became a "product" of the social environment in which people were raised, and so on. Even many "environmentalists," who stressed the importance of early experience in "molding character," tended to accept the idea that the mediating variable leading to behavior was how adult individuals *felt* about themselves and the world.

In the late 1960s many in the Hippie movement espoused the philosophy that feelings not only were the major determinant of behavior but should be as well: "Make love, not war." People who are feeling good do not need to be imperialists, they thought. If drugs can help to achieve the goal of good feeling, that is fine; by then, using "legal drugs" had become a predominant practice in American culture anyway. Sex provided not only shared physical enjoyment and ecstasy but "enlightenment" as well. The Platonic hierarchy was turned on its head. Evil now resulted from allowing "rationality"—often in the form of a devotion to some "ism" or other—to rule the feelings, which most often involve love. Saint Francis was the only true religious leader. Experiments with strict Eastern asceticism were brief, to be replaced by the "Hinduism" of those gurus who preached satori through peak experiences and free love (like Bagwan Shree Rajneesh in Oregon). Tune in, turn on, drop out; return only later, after the rest of your fellow citizens have achieved similar enlightenment. "You can't love anybody else until you learn to love yourself first," was the maxim, and first things first.

Interestingly, one of the first philosophers to suggest this reversal of the Platonic hierarchy was not an Eastern guru but Bertrand Russell. At age eighty, he decided to write short stories. "I have devoted the first eighty years of my life to philosophy," he wrote, "and propose to devote the next eighty years to another branch of fiction."[3] The stories, the longest of which were "Zahatopolk" and "Faith and Mountains," all had the same theme: Societies had been constructed on the basis of faith in "higher principles"—religious, medical, or rational. Those in charge allowed their sense of justice and duty to "stifle all softer emotions" (a phrase Rudolf Höss, the commandant of Auschwitz, responsible for killing 2,900,000 people also used in his autobiography to describe how his own behavior had been more heroic than despicable.[4]) At some point, however, the sexual attraction of a young man and woman for each other leads them to question their societies' beliefs, and one or both eventually lead a revolution to destroy these beliefs. The sexual attraction is in Russell's implied view good, the "thought" supporting the current social system bad. As one sympathetic character explains to a couple, who are expressing remorse for ever having accepted what they had been brought up to believe: "No, my dear young friends, you need not feel that you have been exceptional in folly, for folly is natural to man. We consider ourselves distinguished from the ape by the power of thought. We do not remember that it is like the power of walking in a one-year-old. We think, it is true, but we think so badly that I often feel it would be better if we did not."[5] Rational thought was important to Russell, but only for determining contradictions—because what can't be true isn't true. Moreover, this function arises not from the power of a single intellect but from collective free criticism and appraisal. The importance of rationality does not, however, imply that it is or should be the determining factor in our lives. Given that we would often be better off if we did not think, the Platonic hierarchy can hardly explain human life; nor should it—or so Russell thought.

Enter the professional psychotherapist. This person deals primarily with feelings. If feelings are predominant, then this person understands not only why people behave as they do but how they should behave. (Recall the APA president's statement that psychologists should be "society's teachers.") The professional's message is perfectly compatible with a feeling-oriented, "do your own thing" expressionist view of how humans function. The move to turn Plato upside down and the expansion of the mental health professions beyond psychiatry are perfectly timed and reinforce each other.

But while the New Age psychology begins with the music of Aquarius, it ends with the puerile harmony of pure selfishness. The actor Paul Newman expressed the problem well in a fall 1991 CBS interview after he and his wife, actress Joanne Woodward, received a Franklin Roosevelt award for helping free people from want. He maintained that the deification of the individual is bad both for us and for our society, and that this deification may have reached the point of no return. If individual feelings are all that matter, why not?

Moreover, a failure to feel just right is to be explained in psychological terms. External problems like economic deprivation or being shot at in a war arouse bad feelings only because they cue areas of psychological maladaptation (John Huston, in his documentary about psychological collapse in combat, bought into that belief). Almost everybody has been abused in some way or other by their parents ("psychological abuse" predominates), and since childhood experience is the determinant of adult feeling, we can only get better by allowing the selfish, bratty "child within" to come out, maybe even in group "therapy" sessions where we grasp teddy bears to facilitate communication with our "inner child."[6] We are blocked, however, not only by our own dependencies but by "codependencies"[7] between everybody except client and therapist, but I confidently expect new treatments for such codependencies to emerge soon. The twelve steps can help, but so can almost anything that gets you to admit how awful you feel and to understand that only by loudly reveling in your unhappiness can you achieve a sort of freedom from these awful feelings. Negative emotions such as guilt "cause" undesirable behavior and therefore should be expunged by whatever means possible, probably some new, unproven, often bogus, technique or other. The widely cited quote from Paul Goodman with which I opened this chapter has become not just descriptive dogma but a moral imperative as well. People shouldn't feel guilty, no matter what they do. There is something wrong with people who experience guilt. Thus, contrary to what people have believed for centuries, guilt following bad behavior is inappropriate; moreover, unlike other punishments, a feeling of guilt is not to motivate us to change our behavior; if we do happen to feel guilty about something, that is an indicator of psychopathology (so we might end up feeling guilty about feeling guilty). Other negative emotions have similarly devastating effects, no matter how they come about. As one questioner on the Oprah Winfrey talk show of November 5, 1991, put it: "Everyone should get therapy."

SELF-ESTEEM

Why should "everyone get therapy"? The New Age answer is that we all suffer from deficiencies in self-esteem, and these deficiencies are responsible for our problems, definitely not vice versa. This belief that human distress can be traced to deficient self-esteem is widespread in our current society. Popular books such as Nathan Branden's *The Psychology of Self-Esteem* have propagated it,[8] and poor self-esteem is often cited as the "root cause" for everything from a failure to learn in elementary schools, to failure in business, to "overachievement," to divorce, or even to "sexual codependency."

For example, Branden wrote in a subsequent article,

> I cannot think of a single psychological problem—from anxiety and depression, to fear of intimacy or of success, to spouse battery or child molestation—that is not traceable to the problem of poor self-esteem.

And later:

> There is overwhelming evidence, including scientific findings, that the higher the individual's level of self-esteem, the more likely he or she will treat others with respect, kindness, and generosity. People who do not experience self-love have little or no capacity to love others. People who experience deep insecurities or self-doubts tend to experience others as frightening and inimical. People who have little or no self have nothing to contribute to the world.[9]

Once again, "if you don't love yourself, you can't love anyone else." If you have "deep insecurities or self-doubts," you not only "have nothing to contribute to the world," you may end up abusing your own spouse and children. (And if you suffer from low self-esteem, that's another reason for feeling bad about yourself.) There are a number of flaws in Branden's reasoning, but before discussing them let me state categorically that there is *no* "scientific evidence" that people who have "deep insecurities and self-doubts" have "nothing to contribute to the world." The most casual reading of biographies indicates that many admirable people, like Abraham Lincoln, often suffered from "deep insecurities and self-doubts," and that many less-than-admirable people suffered from no self-doubts whatsoever, at least until they were caught or disgraced. (For a good first-person account of how a lack of self-doubt can result in disaster, I recommend John Dean's *Blind Ambition*, which is not so much about "ambition" as about mindless arrogance.[10])

The "scientific evidence" to which Branden refers is a *correlation* between the level of self-esteem and the degree to which people engage in personally and socially positive activities and avoid negative ones. My great-grandmother would not be surprised by the existence of this correlation. "Of course," she might say, "it's because people who do rotten things feel bad about themselves and people who do good things feel good about themselves." She might add, "Damned good thing too, or society would fall apart."

She might even note the kind of availability bias that could lead Branden, a psychotherapist, to reach his conclusion: "He sees people who don't feel good about themselves," she might say, "they wouldn't come to him otherwise." She might speculate that alcohol abuse and child molestation are not "traceable" to poor self-esteem, but that the *desire to change* is traceable to the poor self-esteem that results from these behaviors—again, a damned good thing. Here, she would be in agreement with the writer Willard Gaylin, who writes:

> There is so much nonsense there about feelings. All the pop psychologists are misleading people about things like guilt and conscience. Guilt is a noble emotion; the person without it is a monster.[11]

In fact, there's a term for such "monsters": *psychopaths*, we call them, or sometimes *sociopaths*. These are our words for people who do not suffer from negative emotions when they perform antisocial, often violent acts and who do not suffer from "pangs of guilt" afterward. Juries and judges often recommend particularly stiff sentence for those found guilty who show no remorse.

Of course many people who behave in personally or socially destructive ways suffer from lowered self-esteem, and poor self-esteem does constitute a psychological problem in and of itself. But the difference between my great-grandmother's "naive" view and Branden's is that Branden maintains that poor behavior is "traceable" to low self-esteem. In some places in his writings and lectures he says that desirable behaviors are traceable to high self-esteem. My great-grandmother, however, views self-esteem as *following* from what we do. Is either interpretation correct? Is there evidence for either? For answers, we can turn to the report of the California Task Force on the Social Importance of Self-Esteem.

THE TASK FORCE REPORT

At the urging of John Vasconcellos, one of its members, the California State Assembly, established a task force to promote self-esteem, and Governor George Deukmejian signed a bill to fund its work in 1986. The results of the task force's findings were published in a book entitled *The Social Importance of Self-Esteem* in 1989.[12]

In the introduction to the book, the editor sets the tone by suggesting that we already know that high or low self-esteem as a causal variable leads to desirable or undesirable consequences respectively.[13] He writes: "Intuition also tells us that both benign and vicious cycles characterize various levels of self-esteem and their supposed behavioral consequences." His examples; "These [high self-esteem] feelings are reflected in the superior academic and social performance of the child; this feeds positively into a child's self-perception and turns into an upward spiral that may continue throughout life." Further, "Violence sets off a frenzy of greater shame and guilt, which can find expression only in another bout of destructiveness."

He continues:

> Low self-esteem is the causally prior factor in individuals [sic] seeking out kinds of behavior that become social problems. . . . Or, as we say in the trade, diminished self-esteem stands as a powerful *independent variable* (condition, cause, factor) in the genesis of major social problems. We all know this to be true, and it is really not necessary to create a special California task force on the subject to convince us. The real problem we must address—and which the contributors of this volume address—is how we can determine that it is scientifically true.

That is a rather remarkable statement. We "know" something to be true, and what we must now do is to "determine" that it is "scientifically true"—by showing that self-esteem is in fact an important causal variable ("independent variable") predicting behavior ("dependent variable"). There appear to be two types of truth involved here. The first is the type of truth we know prior to seeking evidence and independent of evidence, while the second is the type that arises from evidence. The purpose of the second is to confirm the first. For most of us, however, the purpose of evidence is to determine what is or is not in fact true or to modify our prior beliefs.

The problem faced by the editor and contributors is that what they "know" to be true turns out *not* to be "scientifically true." The editor himself telegraphs this conclusion when he writes: "One of the disappointing aspects of *every* chapter in this volume (at least to those of us who adhere to the *intuitively correct* models sketched above) is how low the association between self-esteem and its consequences are in the research to date" (page 15, italics added). Further; "If the association between self-esteem and behavior is so often reported to be weak, even less can be said for the causal relationship between the two."

But it doesn't matter. Again, the editor: "Why, we ask next, must this causal relationship be regarded as so weak?" (page 17). The answer is given at the beginning of the very next paragraph: "The first answer to this question is based on the common scientific knowledge that correlation does not establish cause."

True—the mere existence of a correlation does not establish causation; it is possible to have correlation without causality. The problem is that except in unusual circumstances not relevant here, causality *does* imply correlation. Therefore, a failure to find correlation implies a lack of causation. In other words, if self-esteem were to "cause" superior or inferior behavior (as in academic achievement), then higher levels of self-esteem should be associated with higher levels of behavior and lower levels of self-esteem with lower levels.

The subsequent chapters continue in a similar vein. The first concerns the association between child maltreatment and self-esteem.[14] At the end of this chapter, the authors list seven conclusions about the associations they found. I would like to list three of them here.

1. "There is insufficient evidence to support the belief in a direct relation between low self-esteem and child abuse."
2. "Low self-esteem should not be perceived as the *primary* cause of

child abuse, especially in light of other factors such as age, employment status, availability of child care, and economic insecurity." (In light of the first conclusion, why should it be considered a cause at all, let alone a "*primary*" one?)

3. "There is no basis on which to argue that increasing self-esteem is an effective or efficient means of decreasing child abuse (by comparison with other techniques)." Nevertheless: "Policy interventions to reduce child abuse that involve increasing self-esteem should be encouraged and should include interventions at the individual, family, group, community, and societal levels."

No comment is necessary.

The next chapter concerns the relationship between self-esteem and academic achievement in schools.[15] This chapter is a remarkable example of how a serious researcher with a preconceived idea can evaluate reams of evidence that fail to support this idea—and in some instances contradict it—yet be able to hypothesize reasons why the evidence is poor and the idea correct.

First, the author notes the importance of differentiating between causality and correlation. The author then reviews studies that simply present correlations and concludes that the average correlation found between various measures of self-esteem and academic achievement is about .17. There are about three hundred studies that lead to this average correlation, which is fairly minuscule. It may, of course, be used to reject the null hypothesis that there is *no relationship whatsoever* between self-esteem and performance, but its small size indicates that attempts to enhance academic performance through enhancing self-esteem would yield minimal success. In fact, even the little success that might arise would not necessarily be due to the causal effect of self-esteem; some other variable—such as hard work—might be the cause, or self-esteem could be a *reflection* of academic achievement.

Aware that correlation does not imply causality, the author notes a single study in which self-esteem was added to other variables in a multiple prediction study of school achievement "that already included factors such as social class and intelligence." (Because the study was omitted from the list of references at the end of the chapter, I cannot cite it myself.) "The self-esteem measure accounted for only an additional 3% of the explained variation in performance."

Then the author asks, "On the face of this evidence alone, would we be better advised to concentrate our limited educational resources on potentially more effective and immediate ways [than enhancing self-esteem] to offset educational failure, such as teaching improved study habits or increasing the amount of time students spend on a task?" (page 29). This question is especially compelling since "The situation is scarcely improved when we consider the research that is attempting to demonstrate experimentally that changes in self-concept lead to improved performance."

One would think that the answer to the rhetorical question posed would be "yes." But the author has another answer: "First, the fact that a sense of personal satisfaction in school and in grade point average are not necessarily correlated is now understandable. Some students, especially those we will later characterize as *over-strivers*, may accomplish extraordinary feats, but, again, for the wrong reasons" (pages 89 and 91). What are the "wrong reasons"? The answer: "These students are driven to succeed simply to avoid failure." (page 91).

Then, in a remarkably circular assertion, the author continues:

> Second, fear-driven successes of the kind just described rarely convince individuals that they are worthy. It may appear that over-strivers possess great self-confidence, as a result of an unbroken string of successes. But given their underlying self-doubt, it *may* take only a few failures to convince them of what they had suspected all along: that they are really not bright enough to be worthy." (page 91; italics added)

The author supplies no independent definition whatsoever of what it means to be an "over-striver" or to achieve as a result of being "fear-driven" rather than as a result of self-esteem. The idea that only a few failures may have awful consequences for "fear-driven over-strivers" is merely hypothesized; no evidence is presented.

In other words, correlations near zero are ascribed to countervailing factors, which are merely hypothesized rather than identified. The reader should be by now familiar with such arguments, for example from Chapter 2, in which we saw that a failure to find any correlation between therapy outcome and the credentials or experience of the therapist is ascribed to various possibilities that are hypothesized but not studied. The vacuum-based "explanation" presented here is, however, particularly implausible. First, the measures of academic success are grades, not Nobel Prizes, and given the standards in our schools, characterizing the achievement of high grades as an "extraordinary feat" is dubious at best. Second, the analysis ignores the single moderately high correlation reported in the chapter itself: an average value of .42 between various achievement measures and the self-perception of performance on *ability scales*.[16] Thus, self-esteem concerning academic ability *is* moderately correlated with actual academic ability. What is not correlated is performance and measures of *general* self-esteem. The author's tortured countervailing-forces-and-wrong-reasons explanation for the lack of the latter correlation ignores the former one, which is most directly interpreted as meaning that students' performance realistically affects their self-esteem about their performance.

The next chapter in the task force report concerns self-esteem and unwanted teenage pregnancy.[17] After an introduction, the chapter is divided into three sections—concerning self-esteem and sexual activity among teenagers, self-esteem and contraceptive use, and self-esteem and unwanted pregnancy. In the first section, the authors review four studies, of which "Only the Jessor and Jessor study includes longitudinal data."[18] In that study, the major finding was that *for males*, higher self-esteem prior to engaging in their first sexual activity was related to *greater* sexual activity in the ensuing teenage years. ("Family values" conservatives should take heed.) Considering all four studies, the authors conclude: "In sum these studies do not support an association between self-esteem and sexual intercourse during the adolescence [except that they do for males—in the "unwanted" direction], perhaps because premarital sexual intercourse can no longer be considered a deviant activity in the culture at large" (page 139). Nevertheless, "low self-esteem may account for the behavior of the female adolescent described above, but this is sheer speculation at this point." Yes, it is mere speculation to try to account for the behavior of the pregnant teenager described above since that pregnant teenager is an entirely *hypothetical* one, and a stereotype to boot. Given the research results, it would be equally valid to speculate that for real adolescents there is a relationship in the opposite direction.

The evidence concerning self-esteem in contraceptive use was a bit more encouraging to this chapter's authors: "there is evidence linking high self-esteem to more effective use of contraceptives among sexually active adolescents. Because none of the studies controlled entirely for the possibility that pregnancy or guilt associated with not using contraception might account for the lower self-esteem reported by the less effective users, any causal inference must be tentative" (page 143). I agree, but we should also consider the somewhat trivial alternative possibility that lower self-esteem might *result* from engaging in the behavior that the adolescents studied generally consider undesirable—risking pregnancy. Finally, the authors consider the relationship between self-esteem and unwanted teen pregnancy. They correctly note that correlational studies conducted *after* pregnancy occurs provide no relevant information about the purported causal role of self-esteem, because a lower self-esteem they found (although, somewhat surprisingly, not found consistently) among pregnant teens could be the result of the pregnancy. Thus, they review three longitudinal studies in which self-esteem was assessed prior to pregnancy. Two find lower self-esteem related to pregnancy, one doesn't. Their conclusion: "Given the disparate results and the differences in design of the studies, reasonable people could justifiably draw different inferences from the data" (page 149). But then they outline their own rules for drawing an inference. "Our approach is to make the strongest case possible, given the research, for the existence of a causal link between self-esteem and teenage pregnancy."

Unwanted teenage pregnancy is an extraordinarily serious problem in our culture. The approach of these authors is, however, to "make the best case possible" for the causal effect of self-esteem—rather than examine the evidence to see whether self-esteem is indeed an important causal variable. Here, they mirror the philosophy of the editor in the introduction. We "know intuitively" what the nature of reality should be, and the point of considering evidence is to demonstrate that what we know intuitively is true is also scientifically true; we do not use evidence to mold or modify our beliefs about reality.

The next chapter examines the causal role of self-esteem in predicting crime and violence.[19] It has none, as the authors themselves admit:

Readers of the last two studies may conclude that these reviews represent the state of the field as healthy. But it is possible to construe them, in concert with the four critical reviews, in a different way:

even reviewers who are completely sympathetic to the intentions of the quantitative studies acknowledge that these studies have produced no results. (page 177)

Later,

the implication of all six of the general reviews is not that the field is healthy but that it is in a state of crisis, and has been for some time. This interpretation has been underlined since the publication of the two positive reviews (in 1976 and 1979). Several thousand quantitative studies later, there are still no results that are both strong and replicated. How many inconclusive studies will be conducted before basic premises are examined?

Nevertheless, the authors proceed to make a "plausible" case for self-esteem as a causal variable. "Public policy does not wait for final proof in other realms, and even a case that is merely plausible should provide grounds for debate and discussion of possible new law and policy in the area of corrections" (page 178). My objection to this approach is that the public is perfectly capable itself of deciding what is "plausible," and that when it turns to expert social scientists for advice it is expecting something more than plausibility—that is, evidence.

The next chapter, on self-esteem and chronic welfare dependency, likewise finds no results in the research literature.[20] The two final chapters concern self-esteem and alcoholism and drug use.[21] There is no evidence in either of these chapters that lower self-esteem plays a causal role in alcoholism or drug use, although *retrospective* reports of female alcoholics and of heroin users of both sexes indicate that they may have suffered from low self-esteem during adolescence. I have already discussed the problems with such retrospective reports.

Having examined all the chapters, we are left with a task force report that does *not* support the basic idea that self-esteem plays a causal role in determining various social behaviors, let alone that government programs designed to enhance self-esteem will have salutary social effects. As the authors of the chapters on academic achievement and on crime and violence asked, isn't it time to look at other causes, to find which *actually* do influence desirable and undesirable behaviors (as opposed to merely reflecting them). Isn't it time to reexamine our premises concerning the role of self-esteem? The negative results in the task force report certainly did not result from any lack of thorough investigation. The author of the last chapter, for one, conducted a library search of such sources as the Psychological Abstracts, the Social Science Index, the Educational Resource Information Center at the University of California, and others, and found more than sixty-five hundred studies that used the word *self-esteem* in their titles. In addition, there were more than thirty thousand journal articles and dissertations that used a variety of terms related to self-esteem, such as *self-concept*, *ideal self*, and *self-image*. If only a few studies had been conducted, we could fault the way they assessed self-esteem, or the outcome measures they used. But self-esteem has been examined "every which way." All that has been discovered concerning global self-esteem are very unimpressive correlations, and they—as well as higher ones involving specific areas of self-esteem—can be easily accounted for on the basis that self-esteem reflects reality. The California task force has performed a valuable service, but not the one it intended. Rather, it created a volume of work demonstrating that the Holy Grail of pop psychology is nothing more than a mirage.

THE GENERIC PROBLEM WITH THE SELF-ESTEEM OBSESSION

One problem with the New Age obsession with self-esteem (aside from the absence of evidence for its validity) is that it discourages action. The purveyors of pop psychology often argue that past failure is due to deficiencies of self-esteem and that these deficiencies will therefore predict future failures. The first problem with this analysis is that it ignores the probabilistic nature of the relationship between past success and future success (see Chapter 1). While past behavior is generally the best predictor of future behavior available to us, it is far from a perfect predictor (see Chapter 3).

A second and pernicious problem is that the obsession discourages *trying* to change one's behavior or life course. Instead, it encourages shoring up self-esteem *first* by running to a therapist or group. Fortunately, many other people in our society are not "psychologically sophisticated" enough to derogate the role of making an effort in behavior change. Athletes and their coaches understand the importance of trying—hard. While a few highly visible ones may seek psychotherapy (or contemplation) following a failure, the vast majority train themselves and "try harder" the next time. They sometimes succeed, and they often do so only with the assurance that if they *don't* try they *won't* succeed. We might well learn more from them than from the New Age psychologists—a great deal more.

New Age psychologists explain not just personal problems but social ones as well in terms of feelings of self-esteem. If children from economically poor areas do not learn much in school, that is because their early experiences do not allow them to feel good enough about themselves. They lack self-esteem, as do the homeless on the streets, the members of the "underclass," and welfare mothers who won't get low-paying jobs (and thereby lose health care for their children that welfare provides). Once again, everyone should get therapy. No one is responsible for themselves or for the situation of anyone else. Since the problem with homelessness is one of feelings and self-esteem, a tax increase to provide housing would not help. People can't help themselves or others without changing feelings *first*; they should worry about actually doing something for oneself or for others later. If "you can't love anyone else until you have learned to love yourself," a self-centered obsession with feeling is the only way to proceed.

Of course, that's all nonsense, and as the California task force report documents, even the *correlations* leading to such interpretations are slight to nonexistent. Our feelings alone no more rule our behavior than does reason alone. Both influence it, just as both genetic and environmental factors influence it. Exactly how do these influences interact in a particular situation? The honest answer to that question is that we don't know, and a psychological expert who claims to know is consciously or inadvertently engaging in fraud. If professionals—or others—knew, then clinical judgment would be superior to actuarial judgment based on the weighing of relevant factors. It isn't (see Chapter 3). Behavior, thought, and feelings are all intimately related, and they are related in different ways in different situations. Moreover, they affect each other. Just as feeling bad about oneself may be an important influence leading to self-destructive or antisocial behavior *on occasion*, such behavior itself may lead us to feel bad about ourselves. This mutually reinforcing relationship holds not just for thoughts, feelings, and behavior but for social interactions as well. I am the way I am in part because of the way you respond to me, and you respond to me that way in part because of the way I am. The attempt to "reduce" or subordinate some of these influences to others is at this point in our knowledge just plain silly. (I'm not maintaining that someday we may not develop a more thorough view of life that leads to such reduction or subordination, but that it certainly does not exist at present.) Moreover, since our knowledge in psychology and related social sciences is highly probabilistic, nonsensical claims expressed in grandiose terms—statements like Goodman's about "no good ever"—clearly lack scientific merit.

THE SELF-ESTEEM OBSESSION AND OUR EDUCATIONAL SYSTEM

The quality of the educational system in the United States is dismal, particularly at the elementary and high school levels. Much has been written about it; decrying its "sorry state" and issuing bold new proposals for "educational reforms," with or without ways to raise the funds to accomplish them, has become almost a ritual for everyone involved—parents, educators, and politicians. Perhaps the greatest indictment comes from the National Commission on Excellence in Education, set up by President Reagan. In its 1983 report, *A Nation at Risk*, this commission concluded: "If a foreign power had attempted to give America the bad education it has today, we would have viewed it as an act of war."[22]

Just a few examples of the results of this system:

1. An estimated 29 million adult Americans cannot locate the United States on a map of the world.[23]
2. An estimated 48 percent of Americans who have been educated through high school but not beyond cannot examine a restaurant menu to compute the cost of a meal from individual items and subsequently determine how much change they should receive if they pay in dollars. Of those who have gone on to complete two to four years of college, an estimated 39 percent cannot compute a 10 percent tip.[24]
3. Among young adults aged twenty-one to twenty-five, an estimated 20 percent cannot read at the eighth-grade level, and 38 percent cannot read at the eleventh-grade level, even though this level is required for understanding most job manuals.[25]

These estimates are all based on national surveys—not on ad hoc samples or informal opinion. The list goes on. While I deliberately picked examples to illustrate the magnitude of the problem, we are all familiar with it.

Many in our culture assume that students' lack of self-esteem is the root cause of our educational failures. In fact, critics too numerous to cite maintain that lowered self-esteem of students resulting from broken homes, welfare dependency, and so on has had such a catastrophic effect on academic work that there is little reason to attempt to make educational reforms directly without prior society wide reforms that will enhance self-esteem (mainly of "them," the poor).

There are, in contrast, only a few careful studies of multiple factors that actually influence academic achievement or lack of it in our schools. One such study was conducted by Richard Felson.[26] He began by acknowledging the well-established correlation between academic achievement in schoolchildren and their level of self-esteem *concerning such achievement* (see the California task force report). Felson correctly noted, however, that such correlations "are difficult to interpret causally because behaviors affect self-concepts as well, and because behaviors and corresponding self-concepts are likely to have common antecedents."[27] He employed a statistical technique called *structural modeling* to assess whether some intervening variable could account for the relationship he himself found between self-esteem and success in the grade-school children he studied.[28] He found that the relationship between their self-esteem and their academic achievement could be entirely accounted for by effort—as assessed by self-reports of the number of hours they worked and "how hard I work." In other words, self-esteem was indeed related to achievement, but the relationship could be explained by the relationship between self-esteem and effort, where effort was the variable most predictive of success. The particular statistical model he used cannot yield firm conclusions about what "accounts for" what, but it can determine which hypotheses about such influences are supported by the data better than others, and here "effort" clearly won. In fact, his results are compatible with the conclusion that another variable related to self-esteem that is often thought to be important in determining performance—test anxiety— had no effect whatsoever on the children's achievement in grades, although it affected their scores on standardized tests.

If effort is that important, how do we help children put it forth? One way, but only one way, is through changing their feelings. Another way is to institute external incentives. For example, Albert Shanker, the president of the American Federation of Teachers, suggested on National Public Radio on November 9, 1991, that establishments such as McDonald's might select its teenaged employees on the basis of their academic accomplishments. Another way is to instill a sense that working hard is the "right thing" to do. Still another way, very much discouraged by New Age psychology, is simply to require it (although this later may be reinterpreted as a form of child abuse). Wise parents may require their children to devote a half hour a day to learning a musical instrument; children who do so originally under threat of punishment may come to find that they actually enjoy it and want to pursue music on their own—a process the late psychologist Gordon Allport termed *functional autonomy.*[29] Behavior originally engaged in to seek external rewards or to avoid external punishments may become intrinsically rewarding in its own right.

The one variable that is of utmost importance in allowing children to put forth effort, no matter what motivates it, is providing them with the *time* to do it. Our school system does not provide time. Compared to countries such as Germany and Japan—and even to what existed in this country a few years ago—we have a shorter school year and a shorter school day. Moreover, the proportion of time in school actually spent in academic work is much smaller in this country than elsewhere. A group of researchers who clocked how much time was devoted to various activities in a Minnesota fifth-grade class discovered that only 64.5 percent of the hours at school were devoted to academic work, as opposed to 91.5 percent in a comparable Chinese school and 87.4 percent in a comparable Japanese one.[30] (The Minneapolis school was chosen because its students came from "native-born, English-speaking, economically sound families" and hence would not experience some of the problems students face in less affluent areas.[31]) Moreover, the teachers whom the researchers interviewed agreed that they face a major problem due to the amount of time devoted to nonacademic functions.

American teachers frequently said that if they could shed some of their nonacademic functions, they could spend more of their time actually teaching. A large amount of classroom time is spent in unproductive activities that can be attributed, in part, to the American teacher being asked to take on too many functions other than teaching, including the role of counselor, family therapist, and surrogate parent.[32]

The problem thus is that the teachers are expected to act *in loco parentis* (acting as parents in the parents' absence) concerning not just educational matters but emotional and behavioral ones as well, particularly "discipline." There is nothing intrinsically wrong with such activity, except that it detracts from time spent on education. After all, if parents won't or can't deal with their children's emotional and behavioral problems, someone else must, and if children can't learn discipline, they disrupt the school time for others. The problem arises, however, when teachers assume that in their role of counselor they must help to establish a child's self-esteem *prior* to teaching the child anything. But if self-esteem (academic self-esteem, anyway) primarily reflects achievement, and achievement results in large part from hard work, then such efforts are misdirected. Ironically, the results that the teachers attempt to achieve as counselors would be better achieved by abandoning that role and instead concentrating on teaching and insisting on standards of performance.

Some teachers' attempts to instill (illusory) self-esteem may be successful, although it is difficult to separate the role of teachers from the role of the general culture in this "success." While a cross-national comparison of children in two good schools in the United States with those in Japan and China indicates that American children are far worse in mathematics *and that their relative inferiority increases over the school years*, they (and their mothers) generally regard themselves as above average or superior in mathematics, while the Asian students don't regard themselves so highly.[33] Worse yet, this comparison found, our students derogate the importance of hard work in achieving skill: "we asked the eleventh graders what they considered most important for doing well in mathematics. Over 60 percent of the Chinese and Japanese students answered, 'study hard.' In contrast, less than 25 percent of the American students said studying hard is important."[34]

These percentages in the Minnesota study actually underestimate the extent of the problem, because the school week is shorter in the

United States than elsewhere. In fact, in the Minneapolis school the absolute amount of time per week spent on academic work (19.6 hours on the average) was approximately half that of the comparable Chinese school (40.4 hours) and the Japanese one (32.7 hours). Add the fact that the school year in the United States is shorter than elsewhere and that schools in this country require less homework (two-thirds of high school seniors report spending less than one hour per night[35]), and we reach a remarkable conclusion: *Our children are spending somewhere between one-third to one-half as much time on schoolwork as are children in our "competitor" countries.* No wonder the assessments of the American educational system are so dismal. What is required is a change in behavior; *changes in feelings or self-concept are just one way of achieving behavioral change* (maybe), and as pointed out by the teachers themselves, attempting to achieve that change in the school setting itself detracts from the time devoted to academic work.

Before proceeding, I want to make clear that I am discussing not just time per se but "time on task." There is certainly nothing wrong with recesses, sports, cultural activities, clubs, assemblies, or even bull sessions. Schools in countries with educational systems far more successful than ours (again, like China and Japan) in fact devote more time than our schools to such activities. The problem is what happens within the classroom. The cross-national comparison mentioned earlier found that American students attend to what is going on 60 percent of the time and the Asian students 80 percent.

Moreover, when teachers are asked what qualities are important for them to have, American teachers rate "sensitivity" first, "enthusiasm" second, "patience" third, "standards" fourth, and "clarity" a distant last. In contrast, Chinese teachers rate "clarity" by far the most important, agreeing somewhat about "enthusiasm," but with little interest in "sensitivity" and "standards" and almost none in "patience"— which apparently they don't need. ("Sensitivity" is the prime virtue of a *counselor*; "clarity" of a teacher.[36]) Nor do I wish to belittle the role of parents, but again this role apparently has its greatest effect by facilitating time spent on task—homework. Thus, second-generation Asian-American students often do well in our schools, encouraged (if not required) to work hard by their parents and siblings, with the striking result that such students form the only group in our country whose academic achievement is *positively* correlated with the number of brothers and sisters they have.[37]

The last finding is important. *Parents make a big difference*, as does the culture of the family, and the culture of the country. Modifying schools can have an effect, but it will be vitiated or exacerbated by parental attitudes and behaviors. (Ideally, it would help to change parents, too, but they are under less social control than are schools—rightfully so in a free society.) The actual research indicates, however, that parental effects are mediated *not* through the enhancement or thwarting of children's self-esteem but through their attitudes toward work and academic achievement, and through their use of rewards and discipline to implement those attitudes. Insofar as schools must compensate for parental negativity and neglect, therefore, they must concentrate on these attitudes, not on the enhancement of self-esteem. If the parents won't reward or discipline, the schools must. That requires upholding standards and communicating the expectation that students will meet these standards. Ironically, as the comparison of American with Asian schools illustrates, the attempts of schools to raise self-esteem directly has the effect of lowering standards.

WHERE DO THE PROFESSIONALS STAND?

Professionals in psychology and psychotherapy clearly benefit from A New Age psychology—it brings them clients. Unfortunately, they in turn contribute to and reinforce that psychology. Having lost sight of scientific skepticism and the need for careful research, the professionals' "view" has become highly compatible with the New Age view. In particular, that very egoism Paul Newman decries has come to be viewed as a necessary component of "mental health." Again, I am not maintaining that professionals deliberately choose to express these views in order to attract clients or to strengthen the economic well-being and status, but that stressing egoism as something desirable will bring in clients and continue in the absence of some reason not to, which in this case would be adherence to the scientific standard of "show me." Without that standard, professional psychology and psychotherapy become a matter of "views" and "schools," with the result that they are highly influenced by cultural beliefs and fads: currently, the obsession with "me." The impact of self-esteem ideology and the school system provides an example of the negative effects of substituting an overall "view" for strict attention to what is going on and a careful analysis of it: in particular, a view that feelings and self-esteem "cause" certain problems, in the absence of evidence. There are unfortunately many other examples, as we will see in the next chapter.

CHAPTER 9

PATERNALISTIC PUT-DOWNS

Clients as Slaves to Therapists, and the Rest of Us as Slaves to Our Feelings

A psychiatrist writes:

> A troublesome aspect of narcissistic countertransference, as many analysts will attest, is that they don't experience themselves as being in that state when they are. Time and time again, while working with preoedipal patients, I have felt like getting rid of one as incurable, or felt that maybe I ought to marry that wonderful female patient or have a homosexual affair with an attractive male, before recognizing that I was being swayed by the induced feelings. Unless you are alert to the possibility that feelings that you experience as your own and that seem to have nothing to do with the patient may actually be the patient's feelings, that danger exists.
>
> Over the centuries, the phenomenon of emotional induction appears to have contributed to society's dismal handling of those suffering from acute mental illness. One explanation of why these individuals have been mutilated, shackled, sexually abused, burned at the stake, even killed, is that they felt that they deserved such treatment and induced those feelings in the people around them.[1]

Why it is that we believe it so necessary to change the behaviors ("alleviate the symptoms") of those we label "mentally ill"? Attempts to do so have produced all the horrors mentioned in the quotation above, and now powerful drugs can produce side effects such as tardive dyskinesia and perhaps other effects of long-term use of which we are currently unaware. I would like to propose a simple answer to this question. For good social and personal reasons, the behavior of people we label "mentally ill" is distressing to the rest of us. We want to end it, fast. Why? *We don't like what they do.* As anyone who has had friends or relatives who are brain injured or severely disturbed can testify, their behavior can range from annoying to infuriating. Even if we love such people, we ourselves cannot avoid becoming irritated or angry—occasionally wishing that they would just go away, bother someone else for a change, or die. Often, moreover, when we are dealing with someone close to us who has previously been quite competent but now is extremely disturbed or brain injured or senile, we have the feeling that this person is *deliberately* "kidding" us and others. "Come off it," we first want to joke, and later shout. Such feelings may be "induced" in us by their behavior in the sense that we react to what they do, but our feelings and our reactions are very much our own. To claim, as the psychiatrist quoted above does, that maltreatment results from feelings that are not really ours but are those of the victim is a remarkable example of "blaming the victim."

We're not supposed to feel angry at the mentally ill. After all, "mental illness is an illness just like any other illness," and certainly brain injury is beyond the individual's control. The appropriate response to someone who is ill is support and sympathy not anger. Of course, people have throughout history felt disgusted by the illnesses of others; terms like *leper, epileptic, cripple,* and *dunce* reflect such feelings; moreover, the response to ill people has often been to "keep them in their place"—away from everyone else. Often, such distancing has been justified as being in the best interests of the person ostracized. (The place for mentally ill people is a mental institution, we are told, to allow them to live elsewhere is to "abandon" them.) Such a response may even be adaptive for a healthy person who wishes to "keep a distance" by preventing exposure to a contagious disease. The adaptation is far from perfect; for example, we kept people with leprosy in leper colonies even though the leprosy in its commonest form is one of the least contagious of all diseases. But adaptive mechanisms tolerate false positives—"Better safe than sorry."

We can make a conscious effort to overcome our aversion to physical illness, but doing the same for mental illness is harder. Normally, we hold people accountable for what they do, and "mental illness" is defined by a person's behavior, at least as it is observed by others. We find it harder to excuse behavior than to excuse a physical condition. That difficulty is as natural as our anger. Professionals who deal with disturbed people are in an even more difficult position. First, their constant contact with such people can exacerbate their negative feelings toward them—even as philosophy guiding the professionals' work is that of acceptance and sometimes "unconditional" acceptance. Second, whatever ambivalent feelings professionals may have, their goal is to be "objective" without letting such feelings interfere with their work. Some observers, such as Jeffrey Masson,[2] have argued that such objectivity is not only a myth but is dangerous for clients because it hides the professionals' own feelings—most important, from themselves. Here, I am less concerned about the effects of "objectivity" than its implications for the difference between the profession of psychology and that of medicine. Medical people, most of us accept, are supposed to be objective; a surgeon need not know the people on whom she or he operates but is expected to do a competent job; how the surgeon feels about that job is secondary to its performance. Moreover, there are standards for what constitutes competent and incompetent surgery. The ethics code of the American Medical Association makes it quite clear that the ethics of using a procedure is based on whether it is known to be the best available, and it prohibits doctors from using useless or outmoded procedures.[3] In professional psychology, in contrast, where the major empirical claim to objectivity is a socially trained consensus concerning diagnosis, the *feelings* of the professional are considered to be paramount.

Given that these feelings are ambivalent, at least for many professionals, they have led them to treat clients as difficult children. The child is infuriating but "can't help it," and it is "our responsibility" to change the child. Such paternalism encompasses acknowledgment and acceptance that certain behaviors are in need of change—and that they may be personally distressing, perhaps even disgusting, to the person attempting to change them. This philosophy is best expressed in the major work concerning ethics that is cited throughout the profession of psychology, Patricia Keith-Spiegel and Gerald Koocher's *Ethics in Psychology: Professional Standards in Cases.*[4] The philosophy is that professional ethics in psychology must be based on the "one-up" relationship the professional has to the client. The client, after all, "opens up" himself or herself to the professional, whether in long-term therapy, in an hour-long session about how to interview for a job, or in taking a vocational interest test. At least, the client *should* open up and presumably will if the professional is effective. The professional, in contrast, does not—or should not—open up to the patient. Thus, the professional and the client have a relationship analogous to that of parent and child. For parents to discuss their own problems with their children would likely be considered to be poor parenting, and in fact, any mention on the part of therapists of their own problems is currently considered an indicator that such therapists are "sick," perhaps suffering from a narcissistic countertransference. This paternalistic, one-up ethic not only resolves the problems raised by the professionals' ambivalent feelings toward their clients but advances the profession. Practicing psychologists have an ethical mandate to be high status professionals.

TWO EXAMPLES OF PATERNALISM

The one-up ethic is applied with the greatest vigor in the area of sexual contact between professionals and clients. Through the early 1970s, during the era of informal, uninhibited, and ad hoc experimentation (including nude encounter groups) in therapy, such contact was not prohibited, even for clients currently in therapy. In 1977, however, the ethics code of the American Psychological Association was rewritten and specifically included a statement that "sexual intimacies with clients are unethical."[5] Some professionals regarded the new rule, Principle 6a, as an explicit acknowledgment that any such contact could only be a matter of exploitation and hence the rule merely acknowledged "what we knew all along." Others saw it as mandating that a clear separation between therapist and client was necessary for good treatment. Still others saw it as a rule to prevent fraud—to prevent the therapist from attempting to achieve a sexual liaison while ostensibly attempting to help independently of the therapist's own wishes (and most usually charging for this help). There was some controversy within the profession when the rule was initiated, but not much. The problem soon arose, however, about who was a "client." Was a former client a "client"? Was a graduate student a "client"? Was a Ph.D. apprentice receiving training in something that didn't work a "client"? Since most states adopted the APA's ethics rules as required for maintaining a license in psychology, this ambiguity led to legal disputes and extreme personal recriminations.

At its spring 1986 meeting, the APA ethics committee "voted 6–1 (Dawes dissenting)" that: "In adjudicating complaints of sexual intimacies under Principle 6a of the Ethical Principles of Psychologists, the Ethics Committee takes a position that, once a person becomes a client, regardless of termination of the professional relationship, all subsequent sexual intimacies with that client are unethical. The policy becomes effective upon the data of this notification to the membership." The new policy was supposed to have been published in the next issue of the *APA Monitor*.[6] Anyone who had ever seen a psychologist in any professional relationship for any reason whatsoever—student, trainee, business person seeking consultation—was to be considered a client.

I objected and wrote a letter of resignation, pointing out the one-down implication for the client of this prohibition, and I sent a copy to the APA's board of directors. The board's lawyers subsequently overturned the policy on the grounds that it "constituted a new rule," and I was persuaded to serve out my term on the ethics committee. Currently, there is a precise prohibition against intimacies for two years after termination of *therapy* (not just *any* professional contact); the statement about later intimacies is vague and ambiguous.

There were, in my view, two reasons to object to this rather sweeping policy. First, when the rule against sexual intimacies was first enunciated in 1977, the multiple reasons for accepting it were ignored in favor of the one-up reasoning of Keith-Spiegel and Koocher.[7] The power and exploitation argument, having placed the therapist on somewhat of a pedestal, simply assumes that the basis of the sexual contact is due to the exploitive tendencies of the therapist (narcissistic countertransference)—as opposed to sexual attraction pure and simple, mutual infatuation, or even "falling in love" (a concept absent from the analyses of most professional psychologists). The one-up status of the therapist also—of necessity—implies a "one down" status for the client. "One-down" status violates another dearly held principle, that of client autonomy,[8] but as we saw in Chapter 6, all of us can tolerate contradictions in our belief systems. The second reason is that the concept of client-for-life is certainly in conflict with the policy that people should not be hesitant about seeking therapy. (In fact, it might even preclude the possibility of a former client holding positions of great responsibility in the future; do we, for example, want to elect a senator or a president who is "under the control" of a therapist seen twenty years earlier?) A final concern was that couples who

share *any* emotionally arousing experience—war, a political campaign, building an organization, or even an exciting research project—are apt to become emotionally involved in a sexual manner, and
therapy can be quite emotionally arousing.

The other ethics committee members and those who supported this
rather extreme policy were decidedly not insensitive to these concerns
when I raised them. Many are, in fact, quite modest people who were
loath to consider themselves on pedestals. Many showed great respect
for their clients' autonomy. One of the chief advocates of total prohibition of sexual contact has written in his papers supporting the position
that it is perfectly natural for therapists to be sexually attracted to
clients.[9] Why then did these people as a group ("Dawes dissenting")
reach such an extreme conclusion concerning former clients? My suggestion is *group polarization*: When a group reaches a decision, the decision
tends to be more extreme than the average positions that its members
take singly; if their average position is on the conservative side of an
issue, the group decision will tend to be more conservative; if the average is on the liberal side, the group decision will tend to be more liberal.
Research psychologists first discovered this phenomenon when they
thought they had observed that, contrary to public perception, groups
are more likely to endorse risky decisions than their members are. But
this "risky shift" phenomenon was shown by Dorwin Cartwright to be
due instead to group polarization.[10] What had happened was that in a
majority of the problems investigated by the original experimenters, the
average group opinion was on the risky side of neutral; hence, the shift
brought about by group polarization led to greater riskiness.

The result was an attempt to establish an official policy based on
the premise that clients are totally under the control of their therapists. Were this paternalistic putdown limited to clients, my concern
would be similarly limited. After all, clients often do choose to be in
therapy (and hence may choose to be regarded in a paternalistic manner, *if* they are aware beforehand that that is the prevailing philosophy). Those who do not choose therapy—like those in institutions—
are often treated in a highly paternalistic manner anyway. This paternalistic philosophy and treatment, however, is extended to the public
in general, and it can affect social policy.

Nowhere is the existence of this extension clearer than in the lobbying efforts of professional psychology (the APA in particular) to

prevent the marketing of home kits for testing for HIV infection. In fact, the profession opposes not just the marketing of such home tests but their even being *considered* by the FDA for *possible* marketing and scientific trials of their use of the kind that are common to other medical products such as drugs and pregnancy testing kits.[11] The APA and allied groups oppose home testing for HIV on the grounds that the current testing system provides counseling to those who are tested both before and after the results are known. The testing is either confidential (with the people in charge of testing protecting the person's identity) or anonymous (without the people in charge of testing knowing the person's identity). Such counseling is not only provided but required. The person wishing to be tested goes to the testing site, is told about the nature of HIV infection and how to take precautions against it, and has blood drawn. At the time the test results are known he or she is given further counseling. Both counseling sessions (the former often in a group setting) are supposed to stress what is currently known medically about HIV infection and AIDS, while the second session (most often conducted on an individual basis) may stress psychological factors as well—particularly for those who test positive. Counseling is also supposed to provide the people being tested with information about where they can obtain further medical or psychological help if they desire it.

Professional psychology, through the APA, supports such counseling, *as do I*. It is clearly desirable. The question, however, concerns people who want to know their HIV status but who do not wish to have the counseling—who do not wish to go to the testing site to interact with other people, possibly in a group setting, or who do not like the current system for *any* reason (even for reasons of "paranoid realism" about promises of confidentiality or anonymity in general). Should they *not be allowed* to discover whether they are infected? There clearly are such people. (I have heard the person who devised the test claim there are 17 million such people, but I am not aware of any good data about their numbers.) In my own view, the policy of refusing even to consider home testing violates the *rights* of such people, much as thirty years or more ago a doctor's decision not to inform a patient that a medical condition was fatal violated that patient's rights. Moreover, many people who are infected have a strong desire to *avoid* infecting others (despite the popular conception that "they" don't care about others, or the highly unusual but well-publicized cases of someone deliberately infecting others,[12]) so that not allowing anyone to be tested who wishes to be can only augment the HIV epidemic. The case against home testing for HIV ("they might not seek medical advice," or "they might commit suicide") is every bit as flimsy as that against home testing for pregnancy and much resembles it. Before proceeding, however, I want to make one aspect of my position perfectly clear: *While I am a member of a National Research Council committee on AIDS (CBASSE-AIDS) that has issued three recent reports,[13] the opinions I will express are completely my own, not those of the committee.*

The basic premise of the opposition to home testing is that it is desirable that people who are tested receive counseling. Again, I agree completely. But the conclusion that therefore testing should not be available without counseling does not follow. The inference is paternalistic. Parents may decide (correctly) that it is more desirable that their children eat healthy foods than junk foods; parents may therefore forbid their children to eat too many junk foods or even deprive them of the opportunity. That's fine for raising children. The problem is, however, that those who would use a home testing kit are not children. They are adults and presumably they have the right to engage in less-than-optimal behavior if they so wish. This right is particularly important in contexts where the determination of what constitutes optimal or desirable behavior is made by "expert" others. (Again, I personally agree with these others, but again, my agreement with them is not the point of my argument.) Adults have the right to ignore expert medical advice and forgo a recommended operation, therapy, or even change in lifestyle if they choose.

The role of the FDA, as we saw in Chapter 5, is clearly to protect people when people cannot reasonably be expected to understand the consequences of their choices. Drugs that have dangerous effects or that have been scientifically proven to be worthless are kept off the market; the rationale is that citizens not trained in medicine (and most probably many of those who are trained in it) cannot look at a pill or liquid or read a few paragraphs about it and subsequently determine the effects it would have on their bodies. Once citizens are told of the consequences—as of a medical procedure explained by their doctor—they do have the right to choose for themselves.

Opposition to home testing represents a radical departure from this philosophy. First, opposition to conducting a scientific study of something's effects is totally unknown for other procedures proposed. Second, the opposition is based not on the presumption that the test would be inaccurate or useless because people wouldn't understand its results, but on the presumption that the test *would* be accurate and that the user *would* understand its results. This opposition involves a total reversal of the rationale for having medical procedures regulated by the FDA.

On what then is the opposition based? It is based on the presumption that the ordinary citizen is *incapable of coping with the results of the test*. The ordinary citizen might not seek appropriate medical advice if the results were positive, we are told. A positive result must be verified by a more specific test, due to the false positive problem brought about by the sensitivity of the test; the ordinary citizen couldn't understand that and would automatically interpret a positive finding as a "death sentence," *even though the citizen would be specifically informed of that necessity*. Moreover, the opponents warn, the ordinary citizen might misinterpret a negative result as implying immunity or might be so devastated by a positive finding that severe psychological problems would result, like depression or even suicide. When pushed, the opposition backs down from such contempt for the mass of citizens; their concern is for the few who couldn't cope. As one spokesperson for APA argued on television, even if a single person were to commit suicide as a result of the test, the test should be banned.

But the same arguments could be made against a home test for pregnancy, or rectal cancer, or hypertension. No doubt some people have become depressed, or even committed suicide, as the result of the availability of such tests. But it's their bodies, and it's their choice. The psychological paternalism of the opposition maintains, in essence, that people should not have the right to information about their own bodies without the guidance of an expert, or the right to make their own choices. This opposition is based in part on the framing of social issues in terms of individual psychology, and in part on an unwillingness to recognize the existence of tradeoffs in any social policy whatsoever. Yes, an individual may commit suicide, but on the other hand, hundreds of thousands of people who are unaware of their

HIV status but who won't follow the current procedures for being tested may inadvertently infect thousands more, perhaps hundreds of thousands.

Finally, we can ask how people *should* cope with being infected with HIV. Indeed, who is to decide how people should cope with the knowledge: the people themselves or the professional?

In addition, there is a utilitarian rule argument for home testing. While the opponents *conjecture* that the negative consequences would outweigh the positive one, they don't know that—and without experimental trials, no one can know that. Our collective experience (at least in this country) has been, however, that allowing people to have access to the information they seek, free of restraint or censorship, has had beneficial social results. In the absence of any reason to the contrary, why should we suppose knowledge of one's HIV status would have negative consequences? Once again, people claiming psychological expertise are making an inference that what is generally true is not true for the specific case under study, without any evidence.[14]

This paternalistic attitude on the part of professional psychologists is not limited to home testing for HIV infection. Whenever there is a tragedy in a schoolyard, or an earthquake, or a terrorist attack, psychologists, psychiatrists, and social workers descend like locusts to the area to help people who are presumably incapable of helping themselves. How badly traumatized are people by such experiences? How much are they helped by the experts? We don't know. In order to find out, it would be necessary to conduct a long-term, perhaps fifty-year prospective study of people who do and do not have such experiences both before and after the experiences occur. Statements such as that of one noted psychiatrist that *half* of people suffer permanent psychological damage from traumatic experiences are simple assertions without any basis in evidence. And such assertions are clearly self-serving. Ever since our species began, people have suffered from traumatic events, from uncertainty about the future, and from negative changes in their life over which they have little or no control. Until the last century, half one's children on the average would die before reaching adolescence. Yet when something so simple as a possibly disturbing movie is shown on television, professional psychologists are willing to set up ad hoc counseling services to deal with the trauma of viewing it. At least, that was proposed—and implemented on a small scale—

in Oregon when *The Day After* was aired. (In my own opinion, *On the Beach* is a much more compelling movie about nuclear holocaust, as are *Testament* and *Threads*, but *The Day After* received wide publicity and hence the attention of people who decide for others what problems they will have after being exposed to certain fiction.) And I again ask: Who is to decide how people *should* cope with such negatives in life? Is calming people down the right way for everyone to cope? Is there no wisdom in the popular office sign of a few years ago, "If everyone else is losing their heads and you remain calm, perhaps you don't understand the situation"? Shouldn't people decide for themselves whether they value psychological comfort or "understanding the situation" more?

· HISTORY

The idea that the ordinary person cannot cope without some sort of help has pervaded professional psychology and psychiatry ever since these became influential fields. Freud believed that neurosis and psychosis resulted not from repression but from the *failure* of repression to hold in check our unacceptable ideas and impulses. Freud's belief involves essentially the same hierarchy as did the philosophies of Plato, Aristotle, and the Catholic Church; in the well-ordered soul, reason (and for the Catholic Church, "pure" love) masters animal impulses (or "venal" love), while in the disordered soul the needs of the "lower" levels overwhelm the higher ones. The main difference was that Freud believed this hierarchy was not justified philosophically but evolved from the animal nature of humans. Moreover, Freud's hierarchical structure was a lot more fragile than those of the earlier thinkers, and it could not be maintained simply by an act of will or by contemplation or prayer. The Freudian idea that people always have to cope with the intrinsic aggressiveness of their nature, even though it may be largely or wholly repressed, was popular after the "civilized" countries of the world fought two bloody world wars against each other in a period of thirty years. Freud's less well-accepted idea of an intrinsic "death wish" suggested an explanation for such slaughter, and with the development of atomic weapons, many believed that we had simply boarded over our Pandora's box of animal impulses with a fragile veneer of civilization. Without the extraordinary luck of having childhood experiences that led us to deal effectively with these impulses, we would be subject to forces beyond our knowledge or control, and some of us might even wipe out the whole human race as a result. That is not a very flattering picture of the average human being.

Some people who believed they were following Freud laid the onus of our sorry state on repression rather than its failure and consequently advocated achieving nirvana through "letting it all hang out" (perhaps through a "primal scream" or two). But most professionals became increasingly enamored of what was called ego psychology. The ego is supposedly part conscious and part unconscious; the unconscious part consists of defense mechanisms that battle to keep the unconscious sexual and aggressive drives and needs of the id from being expressed in socially unacceptable forms. Perhaps the contents of these drives and needs, it was thought, were not as important as the strength of the ego itself and its efficient functioning. Various scales of "ego strength" were developed, including some based on Rorschach responses. Because part of the ego was conscious, more emphasis was placed on the conscious functioning of the human and correspondingly less emphasis was placed on unconscious functioning. This shift in emphasis was paralleled in the movement in academic psychology away from behaviorism toward what is now called cognitive psychology. Behaviorist principles had considered the effect of rewards on people to be automatic; the law of effect was supposed to determine responses, much as, in Freudian psychology, an unconscious need was supposed to lead to a particular behavior once it was "filtered through" the ego. (I do not wish to imply that the behaviorists and early psychoanalytic theorists appreciated the similarity of their thinking or felt any affinity for each other—quite the opposite!) Experiments such as those by Bower and Trabasso, however, led academic psychologists to postulate the existence of a hypothesis-testing, conscious mind that mediates between a stimulus and a response, as if that need were not already obvious from everyday observation.[15] The fact that even dogs can learn such a general response as "helplessness" and failed to learn a simple way to avoid shock in a subsequent situation led academic psychologists away from a stimulus/response view of the behavior of other animals as well.[16]

The focus of ego psychology, by contrast, was on reality, and it held the most important function of the human mind to be "reality testing," that is, the ability to "test" our immediate perceptions and judgments to distinguish between what is real and what is unreal. Such testing did not, however, come about easily. Supposedly, young infants have very little ability to test reality, confusing their own internal needs and impulses with the surrounding external world, so that building up "ego boundaries" is a slow process. The fact that most infants are fed after being hungry leads to a natural association of hunger pangs with nourishment, to the point that later as an adult a person might—as a result of this "childhood omnipotence"—believe that her or his needs influence what happens in the outside world, a form of paranoia. Again, the emphasis was on childhood development, and the resulting adult human—or rather the human ego—was seen as frail. (No wonder so many people could be overwhelmed by negative information from a home medical test, let alone from various tragedies that have beset human life since its beginnings.)

Ego psychology was in part an outgrowth of the psychoanalytic movement, finding its expression in David Rapaport's book *Organization and Pathology of Thought*.[17] It also received impetus from the theorizing and observational investigations of developmental psychologist Jean Piaget and his followers.[18] While Piaget was not psychoanalytically oriented, he agreed that infants and very young children are totally "egocentric," explaining the world in terms of their needs and its reaction to them, and he believed that child development involves an increasing understanding that the world functions according to logic and laws that exist independent of the self. The acme of human development—which occurs through a process of assimilation, incorporating what is "out there" as part of the self, and accommodation, changing the self to be compatible with the world out there—is to appreciate objective reality by thinking like a scientist. Thus, children first learn that objects are not necessarily animate, as their egoism had previously projected, and that they have permanence ("conservation" of matter and number). Then they learn that this conservation can be understood through principles of compensation (the amount of water is the same when poured from a short stout glass into a tall thin one); then that the inanimate external world can be described in terms of systematic laws of motion, force, and cause. Finally they learn that abstract reasoning principles can be used to infer these laws.[19]

Subsequent research has demonstrated that this progression is far from orderly and that Piaget may have confused an appreciation of the world as it is with an ability to verbalize that appreciation. Very young children who are not supposed to understand the permanence of objects, for example, find magic tricks based on defying this permanence surprising and amusing (or distressing).[20] The "orienting" or startle response of children as young as six months indicates a rudimentary understanding of number, if only at the level of "one, two, three, many."[21] Conversely, mature adults very often ignore principles of logic when they are asked to solve everyday problems that they do not specifically regard as involving coherent reasoning.[22] Nevertheless, both the psychoanalytic and the Piagetian beliefs in the importance of childhood-to-adulthood movement from primitive egoism to reality testing had a profound impact on professional psychology, reinforcing the belief in the overriding importance of childhood experience and the view of adult psychopathology as resulting from an inability to grow up, a view that is quite consistent with paternalism. Childhood became not just an experience, but a tyranny with the result that not only clients but everyone is considered fragile—what Paul Meehl has termed the "spun glass model" of the human adult.[23]

At the same time, another group of psychologists developed "behavioral therapy," based on principles of classical and operant conditioning. Their hope was to be able to explain and alleviate psychological distress in terms of certain principles. In order to appreciate this hope, it is necessary to understand the principles.

Classical conditioning, studied by Ivan Pavlov, elicits a "conditioned" response to a previously neutral stimulus when that stimulus is paired with an "unconditioned" stimulus that automatically elicits that response. For example, when a bell is paired with the presentation of food, dogs will begin to salivate whenever they hear the bell. The popular phrase *conditioned response* is a translation from the Russian that might better have been rendered *conditional response*. Thus, the food itself leads the dogs to salivate in an unconditional manner, while salivation that follows the bell is *conditional upon* the bell's being paired with the food. The word *conditioned* in English, by contrast, has connotations of "mindlessness."

Operant conditioning, in contrast to classical conditioning, elicits a new response to a stimulus situation by rewarding that new response. When a dolphin is rewarded with fish after leaping on cue, for example, the dolphin quickly learns to leap whenever the trainer presents the cue. The existence of operant conditioning has been well known for probably tens of thousands of years to animal trainers, and to parents, and in fact to anyone interested in controlling another's behavior. What the behavioral psychologists did, in large part influenced by B. F. Skinner, was to explore such conditioning systematically and develop "laws" (really probabilistic generalizations) governing it. The term *reinforcement* was used in place of *reward* and was more broadly defined as *any* event following a response that would increase the probability of this response in the same stimulus situation. That gave it the advantage of allowing the exploration of events that might not appear to be "rewarding" on an intuitive basis. (Like *conditioning*, the term *reinforcement* has come to have connotations of mindlessness—although the actual phenomenon of operant conditioning simply refers to the conditions under which the probability of a particular behavior is enhanced or diminished.)

Some of the "laws" developed by behavioral psychologists appeared to be particularly important to the development of psychopathology, such as those involving *avoidance conditioning*. In avoidance conditioning, an animal learns how to respond to one stimulus to avoid another, noxious stimulus; for example, a rat or a dog learns to jump over a barrier to escape a noxious electric shock following a bell. In contrast to classical conditioning, jumping over a barrier is not an automatic response to an electric shock, the way salivating is to food. Behavioral psychologists discovered that avoidance conditioning can be permanent. Apparently, the reinforcement it provides is the reduction in anxiety or fear that the noxious stimulus will occur. If the experimenter continues to ring the bell but never presents the shock, the animal has no way to learn that jumping over the barrier is unnecessary, because it jumps over the barrier anyway. Avoidance conditioning may be involved in many phobias, like going outside the house. By avoiding the feared stimulus (going out of the house), whenever it is contemplated, the person experiences a reduction of anxiety, which is a reinforcement. The problem is that the more often the person avoids the phobic object or situation, the greater the number of such reinforcements—with the result that the phobia becomes stronger rather than weaker. (It's not always that simple; for example, many if not most airplane phobics are more frightened of "freaking out" when they start flying than they are of crashes.[24] In fact, phobias often arise when people simply misinterpret physiological and psychological indicators of mild stress as being indicators that they are apt to "fall apart" in some way, perhaps die.)

Such avoidance conditioning involves *negative reinforcement*, which is not to be confused with punishment. The reinforcement consists of removing the noxious stimulus, in this case the internally experienced anxiety. (A strict behaviorist would explain avoidance conditioning without reference to such an internal state, but postulating the anxiety that we all feel when approaching a phobic stimulus or situation yields the most parsimonious explanation.) Such negative reinforcement is also often involved in dysfunctional family interactions, including physical fights. In a negative interaction (the fight), what leads up to the final act—from absenting oneself to yelling to throwing things to physical abuse—is extraordinarily unpleasant to the person who commits the act as well as to everyone else. The act itself ends the negative interaction and hence it also ends the unpleasantness. This act can therefore be extraordinarily reinforcing. (Note that in this behavioral analysis it is not the release of feelings that makes the act rewarding—and hence more likely to be repeated in the future—but what happens as a consequence of it.)

Finally, behaviorists discovered that classical conditioning can occur as the result of a single trial if the unconditioned stimulus evokes an extremely powerful response. (Presumably operant conditioning could occur in a single trial as well if the reinforcement were strong enough.) In a particularly grisly study, men in an alcoholism recovery hospital ward were exposed to a 600-cycles-per-second bell tone a sufficient number of times that they no longer had any reaction to it.[25] Subsequently, experimenters injected the men with scoline immediately after one occurrence of the tone. The scoline, a derivative of curare, caused total skeletal paralysis for about a minute and a half, including an inability to breathe. Henceforth, even though the injection was not repeated, the subjects reacted to the 600-cycles-per-second tone with extreme anxiety (assessed by physiological indicators). This anxiety response never diminished over a period of weeks; if anything it strengthened. (In a "manipulation check," the experimenters determined that all their subjects found the experience to be "horrific to a degree"; in fact, "all the subjects in the standard series said that they thought they were dying." That's quite a unique treatment for alcoholism. The experiment, however, raised no ethical concerns in the research community, while the Milgram studies on destructive obedience, published in the very same journal a year earlier, aroused a storm of protest. My own explanation of this differential response is that the Milgram study involved duping real people into ostensibly "doing evil," while this study simply involved the further victimization of nonpersons—historically consistent with transorbital lobotomy and the overuse of drugs to make such people malleable.)

Some psychologists came to believe that the (*hypothesized*) relationship between traumatic childhood events and adult problems could be accounted for in terms of single trial conditioning. The naive hope was that such principles of classical and operant conditioning could lead to the understanding of human emotional (more strictly, behavioral) distress and to its amelioration. If the effects of reinforcement were brought about automatically through "the law of effect" (that reward and punishment result in behavior and behavior change independent of the person's beliefs about the reward and punishment or about their meaning), the mental health worker should pay particular attention to the new developments in psychology laboratories that led to an expansion and refinement of conditioning principles. Skill was to consist of the systematic application of these principles. As I pointed out in Chapter 4, the law of effect does not work with all the power it was supposed to have, and professional psychologists with a behavioristic orientation began combining behavioral principles with principles postulated by ego psychology that were actually found in cognitive psychology (the "eclectic" approach). Nevertheless, several professionals retained an emphasis on the use of behavioral techniques, sometimes with success.

One example of an eclectic approach is that of Hollinda Wakefield and Ralph Underwager, who designed programs to help impoverished people:

> We focus on behavior, not on feelings. We tell people that they can choose to change their behaviors whether they "feel" like engaging in the new behavior or not—even if they have to pretend for a few minutes. Once they behave in a more effective way, they get some

positive feedback. That makes it easier to keep it up and to feel better. An important fact is that our feelings are affected by the way we behave. It doesn't work very well to try to feel better and then change behavior. . . . We are free to make the cognitive choice to behave in ways that work better for us. We emphasize this principle throughout therapy. We know principles about how people learn.[26]

Other therapists also focus on behavior, such as Peter Lewinsohn does in treating mild depression.[27] In contrast, still other therapists focus on feelings and belief. Perhaps the most successful is that of Aaron Beck and his colleagues, also for dealing with depression.[28] The basic premise is that depression follows from adopting self-defeating *cognitions* (thoughts and habitual ways of thinking) that lead people to avoid fulfilling behaviors, to interpret positive experiences as negative ones, and to blame themselves for outcomes that are partially or totally beyond their control. The purpose of the therapy is to help people establish more *realistic* cognitions, not to help them necessarily feel good about themselves independently of the way they behave. There is the unfortunate complication that in some respects depressives are already more realistic than are nondepressed "normals," who often have a "rosy glow" outlook about their own personalities, capabilities, and social interactions.[29] There is the further complication that, as pointed out by James C. Coyne and his colleagues, depressed people *really are* less capable and likable than are others, at least while they're depressed, and that comparing the "realism" of depressed and nondepressed people about themselves therefore necessarily involves comparing how realistic they are about different realities[30]. Nevertheless, Beck's approach works. Often it is combined with drug treatment, particularly for people who are severely depressed. While the conventional wisdom is that a combination of therapy and drugs works best, there is always the potential, not yet appreciated, for long-term deleterious effects of the drugs.

As behaviorism was abandoned as a system of psychology, therapists became more oriented to clients' thoughts and feelings. Ego psychology led to the conception that the most important aspect of the ego may not be how it appears to function to the outsider but how it appears to function to itself—specifically, whether the individual (ego) has high *self-esteem* and a belief in *internal control* over important outcomes in life. Both high self-esteem and internal control are believed to be important in leading the person to cope successfully with life's problems rather than adopting a passive stance of helplessness. This movement in professional psychology was again paralleled by one in academic psychology, which began to emphasize attribution theory, or "the effect of how we explain events to ourselves." Of particular importance in attribution theory is how we explain our own behavior and our own successes and failures to ourselves—and how these explanations affect our subsequent behaviors. Moreover, as documented by Albert Bandura, the degree to which these attributions lead to a potentially realistic *sense of efficacy* is related to future success in our endeavors to change ourselves.[31]

I have already discussed what both professional and pop psychology maintain about self-esteem. Theories about the importance of self-esteem and belief in internal control have even led to a new conception that appreciation of reality is unimportant or at least of secondary importance in mentally healthy functioning. Let's turn now to the belief in internal control over outcomes.

Employees who believe that they have control over the rewards organizations give them have higher morale than those who don't, and they often work better. The feeling that no matter what you do, it will have no effect, is a debilitating one, and the resulting *learned helplessness* can be pernicious. Alternatives to belief in lack of control, however, include not only belief in partial control but belief in total control. The belief in partial control is more realistic, while total control is perhaps more soothing—although, as I will argue, not always. Certainly, as the wise preacher in Ecclesiastes cautions, "time and chance" are factors in human life, and our ability to predict its course is limited.

The major research on the beneficial effects of perceived control over outcomes, however, has contrasted belief in lack of control with belief in total or near-total control. Specifically, Julian Rotter's most popular scale for assessing believed "locus of control" confounds being "captain of my soul" with being "master of my fate"[32] on the internal control end. For example, the person responding to this scale is asked to choose between endorsing the statement that "becoming a success is a matter of hard work, luck has little or nothing to do with it" and the statement that "getting a good job depends mainly upon being in the right place at the right time."

When I look at this scale myself, I want to answer "neither"—again and again. I believe that both control over self—mastery of one's soul—and luck are important. To endorse the proposition that either luck has "nothing to do with" outcome or is the "main" determinant of it is absurd. More generally, I believe that in later adulthood I can control myself to be able to capitalize on at least some of the lucky breaks that come my way. Nevertheless, given the widespread use of this confounded scale, many professional psychologists believe that it is mentally healthy only to believe in total control, even for occurrences—such as airplane accidents—over which one has realistically no control. Moreover, our culture has accepted this belief; for example, when I ask college students to rank themselves along with nine randomly selected other students in terms of their likelihood of developing multiple sclerosis, which they know cannot be controlled by their behavior, I obtain an average rank of around 7.5. In far more systematic studies, Neil Weinstein has found that people believe they are less likely than other people to develop diseases, including diseases unrelated to personal behavior such as smoking, drinking, or failure to exercise.[33] (The problem with such studies is that people who judge themselves less likely than others to experience negative outcomes could either be underestimating their own likelihood or overestimating the likelihood of others, or both; for example, a recent survey of sexually active college women by Bernard Whitley, Jr. and Andrea Hern indicated that the women were quite accurate about their own probability of becoming pregnant—given the precautions they took—but exaggerated the probability that other college women would become pregnant.[34] Perhaps the instances of unwanted pregnancy among their peers were quite salient to them, while the fact that others took the same precautions they did was not.)

How did the notion that belief in internal control—however unrealistic—is a good thing come about? By studying mainly college students, supplemented by studying people with cancer, although there are important exceptions like Weinstein's community based sample. College students and cancer patients are unique in that those in the first *do* have almost total control over their outcomes while those in the second have almost *no* control, except to follow a medical regimen and hope. Belief in internal control among college students has consistently been found to be related to other indices of mental well-being, while the data on cancer patients are slight.[35] Consequently, I will focus my discussion on the use of college students, a subject population easily sampled by professors engaged in research, but whose life stage and situation may be unrepresentative of the adult population at large.[36]

Admissions committees in colleges are not omniscient, and they occasionally admit students who cannot do as well as other students no matter how hard they try. In general, however, success in academic work, and in sexual and romantic attachments, is dependent on "getting one's act together" to overcome the *largely internal* problems of late adolescence. The college environment itself in general protects students from external problems, although certainly there are exceptions like medical and financial problems. For such "advantaged" people, consequently, it is no wonder that in general belief in control over self and control over outcome are confounded. Compare the situation of a student with that of a forty-year-old minority woman from an impoverished area. Certainly, *she* would understand that her outcomes are influenced both by what she does and by factors beyond her control. Would a Pollyanna confounding of control over self with control over outcome be associated with mental well-being for *her*?

Still using college students, psychologists have recently extended their views ("theory") about how people's beliefs in internal and external control are related to their well-being. A systematic study examined what such students regard as the sources of success and failure. Attributing success to internal control and attributing failure to external, specific, and temporary causes are positively associated with well-being.[37] ("The idiot professor gave a lousy exam.") In his recent book *Learned Optimism*, Martin Seligman reviews this later development and presents evidence that these attributions are associated with well-being and future success for professional athletes as well as for college students.[38] But such people too, are in a "protected" environment in which the vicissitudes of time and chance play a minimal role. Ditto, salespeople (and by the way, university professors with tenure). Few, for example, lose their jobs as the result of executive decisions to build lousy products, take over another company, or shut down a particular plant, although shutting down certain departments within universities has become a phenomenon in the last five or so years, a trend that soon may expand to shutting down entire universities. Superb athletes, however, remain invulnerable in our society—so long as they perform well.

In a televised CNN discussion during jury deliberations in the 1984 New Bedford rape trial, psychologist Lee Salk claimed that one of the worst parts of being victimized is that it destroys one's beliefs that one is superior and invulnerable and that the world is intrinsically just. Salk said that it often takes several years for rape victims to reestablish these beliefs, which are the foundation of mentally healthy functioning. But of course, we are not superior in all respects; we are not invulnerable; and the world is often unjust. Rain falls on the good and on the evil alike. Ironically, research psychologist Melvin Lerner has recently shown that the *delusion* that the world is just can result in totally irrational behavior.[39] People often act as if they were owed some type of "entitlement" from the world at large as the result of being good people.[40] Occasionally this causes them to behave foolishly, such as those who feel invulnerable to HIV infection from unprotected gay sex because "I've been so good about this in general,"[41] others justify morally wrong behavior by the fact that purported entitlement is not fulfilled: "Since I really deserve that, it's okay to cheat."

The culmination of the view that mental health consists of high self-esteem; optimism; feelings of invulnerability and superiority—internal, pervasive, and stable explanations for one's own success, and external, specific, and fleeting explanations for one's own failure—may be found in Shelley Taylor's *Positive Illusions: Creative Self-Deception and the Mentally Healthy Mind*.[42] Accepting the view that "every theory of mental health considers a positive self-concept to be the cornerstone of a healthy ego," Taylor attempts to establish that "in many ways, the healthy mind is a self-deceptive one."[43] Her major argument is that because people who can deceive themselves with positive thoughts about themselves tend to be happy, and because happy people tend to behave in ways we consider to be good and constructive, it follows that people who deceive themselves are more mentally healthier than are those who don't. She bases this argument on statistical association (and low correlations at that), so it is not very compelling. If we were to argue that "all people are animals and all animals are mortal, therefore all people are mortal," the syllogism would be valid (as an argument, whether or not one accepts the premises). But to make the same argument on the basis of statistical association is like arguing that "since most mammals live on dry land, and that since most multicelled animals that live on dry land are insects, it follows that most mammals are insects." Thus, citing the study that concluded that well-adjusted college students have a "rosy glow" in evaluating themselves, as Taylor does, and Alice Isen's work that "positive affect is associated with increased sociability and benevolence"[44] does *not* demonstrate Taylor's point.

What must be established is a direct link between positive illusions and healthy functioning. Does it exist? Is there evidence? Christopher Peterson, Martin Seligman, and George Vaillant discovered in their longitudinal study of Harvard graduates that *pessimism* at age twenty-five does predict medical problems and death between ages forty-five and sixty.[45] But there are other alternatives to pessimism besides positive illusions. The twenty-five-year-olds were asked to respond to open-ended questionnaires about themselves; when the authors analyzed the results, pessimistic explanatory styles were often confounded with good reasons for pessimism (such as "I cannot seem to decide firmly on a career,... this may be an unwillingness to face reality," or "what I feel is characterized more by confusion than by sense"—see their Table 1). What their analysis did *not* confound was pessimism with actual physical health at age twenty-five.

What is associated with physical health, if not optimism? In his later work, Seligman suggests four possible mechanisms, all of which may be important.[46] The first is avoiding learned helplessness, which may affect the immune system. The second is "sticking to health regimes and seeking medical advice." The third is avoiding bad events in life, and the fourth is having *social support* from others, a lack of which Sheldon Cohen and other researchers have shown can exacerbate symptoms of physical illness.[47] Is self-delusion really the only way to avoid learned helplessness, to have reasonable health habits, to avoid bad events, and to have the support of others? Is self-delusion even an important way? Would it be important even if it *were* shown to have a direct correlation, even a low one?

A careful reading of Taylor's book also reveals links between optimism and good outcomes that do not involve illusions—and like Seligman's they all involve actual behavior and experience. For example, she quotes Lee Iacocca explaining his success at Chrysler by advising: "Decide what you want to achieve, and then work tirelessly to achieve it." (Did a "positive illusion" rather than a knowledge of his own abilities lead to his own behavior?) She quotes Thomas Edison's statement that success is "one percent inspiration and ninety-nine percent perspiration,"[48] and so on. We return to the principle, illustrated by the Felson study, that the causative power of the ideas and feelings hypothesized to be so important is mediated by effort. What causes people to make an effort? Is an illusion really the only or the best way to motivate oneself to put forth effort? Why not "desire to do the right thing" or a religious or existential commitment? Why not a rational analysis of a situation that leads to the conclusion that if one does not put forth the effort, one will certainly fail, while putting it forth *might* yield success?

Exercise is a wonderful illustration. As a result of functional autonomy (discussed in the last chapter), it has become very enjoyable for many of us to exercise. What does it matter *why* we exercise? The behavior is more important than the motives for engaging in it; yet these current "theories" of mental health I'm discussing concern only motives and feelings, to which we are viewed as slaves.

Let me rephrase this argument. We are not invulnerable; we are not superior (even by definition, a majority of us can't be); and if there is justice in the world, it arises not from atoms, molecules, and strands of DNA but from the actions of humans, or from some extra dimension of reality postulated by religious or ethical thinkers, or from some combination of these two sources. I am not propounding any special theory on the origin of justice—only arguing that the "just world" belief is false. What goes around doesn't necessarily come around. To believe in personal invulnerability, personal superiority, and a just world can be characterized as just plain silly. We now find that silliness is positively correlated with happiness in some institutional environments that can be characterized as "protected," like colleges and cancer wards; all people therefore should be silly, and those who are not are in need of help. For example, belief that the world is indifferent to our own particular fate is supposedly a symptom of depression requiring therapy. But that's absurd. There is nothing wrong with researchers finding a correlation and reporting it. The problem arises in the *therefore*—in the mindless leap from the *is* to the *ought*. The social fraud in this leap is in the claim that it is justified by some sort of scientific findings, which therapists and writers of pop psychology books and guests on television talk shows make, supported by private testimonials about how this leap has benefited the person recounting it. Those who believe them are guilty not of fraud but of ignorance. I am writing this book in part because I do not want the people in our nation to believe that they should be silly.[49] Preaching that people should be silly has already converted too many. In particular, such preaching encourages people to embrace egoistic individualism.

The mandate psychologists give us today is to be happy, at whatever cost to one's reality testing. We are to adopt what the poet Yevgeny Yevtushenko urges us to forget: "the vulgar, insultingly patronizing fairy tale that has been hammered into your heads since childhood that the main meaning of life is to be happy."[50] Freud, ever the moralist, would be appalled were he to rise from the dead and discover that his intellectual baby has grown into a callow adolescent interested only in his own feelings. Perhaps that adolescent can still become an adult—but only if it rejects its own currently accepted theories of mental health.

EGOISTIC INDIVIDUALISM

The approaches of Freud and his successors do share one common characteristic: They are alike based on a framework of *egoistic individualism*. The egoistic assumption is that a person's interactions with the outside world—including the world of other people—are important only in the way in which they affect the internal structure of that individual. Even psychologists who emphasize the importance of one's relationships with others most often consider these relationships important only in terms of their conscious or unconscious meaning to the individual "object relations" theory. To maintain that interpersonal relationships have a meaning or effect beyond their impact on the individual is considered transcendental nonsense, and object relations theorists can easily "define away" any proposed counterexample by pointing out that since it is the person who is engaged in the relationship, its meaning must be an egoistic one. (As sophomores in college, we often argued that altruism is impossible because people who choose to behave altruistically are by definition doing what they want to do; but by defining "egoism" and "altruism" in a way that makes one universal and precludes the existence of the other, we had left the terms devoid of meaning.)

This egoistic individualism framework is quite consistent with frameworks in other social sciences, like classic economics. Interactions are considered to basically involve trades—of money for goods, goods for money, goods for goods, time for something or other, and so on. In a completely free "market," a person would propose an exchange of A for B only if they valued B more highly than A, and the person accepting the trade would do so only if that person valued A more highly than B.

Thus, any free trade involves a net increase in value for all those involved. Government legislation to protect those who have "no choice" (such as parents who have no choice about sending their seven-year-olds to work in factories to avoid starvation) inhibits this net benefit.

While many of us disagree with this framework, it has a certain appeal and consistency. In the last twenty years or so, however, this economic analysis has been extended to consider *all* social interactions—those of lovers, of spouses, of parents and children—as trades. Thus, these relationships are to be explained in terms of the egoistic gains people accrue from them. Here, economics has merged with *social exchange theory* in social psychology. People do nice things unto others only in the anticipation that these others will reciprocate with nice things for them. As Robert Axelrod, a main proponent of explaining social cooperation in terms of such "reciprocal altruism," has recognized, this view has some implications that people find disquieting: for example, that we should not be cooperative or kind to people who do not have the power to reciprocate, or to older people who may not be around long enough to reciprocate.[51] Political science, too, has adopted a stance of egoistic individualism. The votes and statements of politicians are interpreted as strategies to maximize their chances of election or reelection.

Thus, all these analyses explain the behavior of people "out there" in terms of its effects "in here" on the individual ego. In their view, we strive only for egoistic payoffs. For economists, these payoffs most often involve money; for social psychologists, reciprocity; for political scientists, election; and for many if not most professional psychologists, feelings of self-esteem. The coin is different in each field, but the "nonsatiety of greed" for accumulating these coins is the same.

BUT IS THE CURRENT VIEW CORRECT?

Often, these egoistic individualism analyses are too glib. People do reciprocate kindness, but that does not necessarily imply that the original act of kindness was motivated by a desire for reciprocation. Politicians often vote in ways that please their constituents, but that does not necessarily mean that they do so in order to please them. After all, their constituents elected them in the first place, and politicians who strictly "vote their conscience" would be elected if the majority of voters agree with them and defeated if the majority doesn't. Since social structures attempt to confound social good and altruistic behavior with egoistic incentives (by rewarding work that helps others, by sending people who rob banks to jail), it is difficult to disentangle the motive from the act. In general, inferring motives from consequences is a dubious procedure. My favorite example: At a meeting I attended on resource depletion, a Marxist maintained that because the rich get richer whether there is inflation or depression, they therefore control the political process that brings about such shifts in the economy. The fact that he couldn't find any empirical evidence for such control simply demonstrated how subtle they are. Similarly, the mere fact that most of us are alive and feel all right or better about ourselves does not imply that all our actions are to be explained in terms of striving to survive and feel high self-esteem.

Are people egoistic individualists? A series of experiments with my colleagues John Orbell, a political scientist at the University of Oregon, and the late Alphons van de Kragt, a sociologist, indicate that even college students may not be—unless one is willing to accept an all-encompassing definition of *egoism*. Here, I will briefly describe just one experiment from this series.[52]

Seven people in need of money who do not know each other enter a room and are promised six dollars each. They are then told to anonymously check one of two boxes on a piece of paper. If they check the box marked "keep," they retain the six dollars no matter what other people in the room do; if they check the box marked "give," they lose their six dollars, but the experimenter doubles that amount to twelve dollars and gives two of this twelve to each of the *other* six people in the room. They can only make one choice. No one except the experimenters knows whether each subject chooses to "keep" or to "give."

That choice presents each person with what is termed a *social dilemma*. Each person would receive two dollars from each other person's "give" choice. People who kept their six dollars would receive this six dollars in addition. Hence, the individualistic strategy would be to keep the six dollars, because no matter how many others give away their six dollars, the person who keeps it will be six dollars better off. If everyone keeps the six dollars, however, everyone ends up with only six dollars, while if all seven people give their six dollars away, everyone will end up with twelve dollars (two dollars each of the "give" choices of the other six people). Clearly, giving is the cooperative choice, but it involves sacrifice and risk. What do people do in this experiment?

With only two exceptions we could find in the research literature, previous experimenters who had studied people's choices in such experimental games had simply *assumed* that the only reason subjects would have for cooperation would be the hope of getting others to cooperate in the future, that is, to adopt reciprocal altruism as a norm. Hence, these researchers had devised experiments in which their subjects would have several opportunities to make such a choice. In our experiments, however, reciprocal altruism is not possible. There was no repeat of the choice. Nevertheless, about 80 percent of our subjects cooperated by giving their money away when the group could discuss the problem, and about 30 percent if it couldn't—even though there was no way that any subject could find out what other subjects would choose to do after the experiment was over. We paid the subjects one by one and made sure that each had left the experimental area before we paid the next; moreover, in the discussion conditions, we prohibited any discussion of plans to meet later—although even if they could have arranged a meeting, a subject who chose to keep the six dollars would not necessarily show up. Cooperation and failure of cooperation would thus be equally anonymous.

So why did people give away their six dollars, particularly when they could discuss the problem? Other researchers have suggested that the motives involved conscience, self-esteem, or the pure habit of cooperating—because in other situations cooperation or failure to cooperate is not anonymous. To test these explanations, we modified the experiment to involve two groups. Several groups of fourteen subjects were recruited, saw each other but did not talk in a waiting room, and then were divided into two groups of seven on a clearly random basis (drawing white poker chips versus blue ones from a bookbag). These groups were sent to separate rooms. In half the conditions, they were not permitted to discuss the problem, and their choice was as described above; in half of these they were allowed to discuss the problem. In the other half of the conditions, however, they were told that each "give" choice would generate twelve dollars for the people in the *other* group. Thus, if a person labeled A in one group gave away the money, two dollars was given to B, C, D, E, F, and G in the other group. Again, half of the groups in this "other group benefits" condition were allowed to talk and half were not.

If giving were a matter of habit, or self-esteem, or conscience—perhaps triggered by conversation with others—we would not expect differences in the giving away of the money depending on whether it goes to people in the same room or in the other room. Consistent with our earlier findings, however, we would expect more giving when groups could discuss the problem. What we found, however, was a huge difference in the giving rate that *interacted* with discussion. When the money went to people in the same room, there was again a rate of about 80 percent of giving the money away, but when the subjects couldn't discuss the problem *or* when the money went to the other group, the rate remained at 30 percent. Contrary to the conscience hypothesis, during discussion many people suggested that "it would be great if we all kept our money and they all gave away their money to us"—even though "they" were people just like the group members, from whom they had been separated on a random basis less than ten minutes earlier.

We concluded that our 30 percent "heroes" were acting out of conscience, and that was what they told us on questionnaires collected just before they left. For the majority of subjects, however, the important factor was group identity and solidarity. In effect, discussion led them to replace their natural concern to obtain the best payoff for themselves with a concern that their group obtain the best payoff, but only their own group. If some other group benefited, so what? This interpretation was supported by subsequent findings in similar experiments that increasing cooperative giving by promising works *only* when all group members promise—that is, when there is group solidarity; the fact that there is absolutely no relationship between individual promising and individual choice in the absence of unanimity further supports the group identity interpretation. While about two-thirds of our subjects were students and one-third townspeople, we never found a consistent difference in the rate of cooperative giving between these two groups; nor did we find a gender difference, or a difference based on religious belief or affiliation.

Group identity is not morality. But it is a powerful force in human behavior that has often led people to sacrifice even their lives for the benefit of "us." One need only observe people, without straining to distinguish "apparent" concern for others from "really" motivated concern for what one will gain individually. Like other researchers, we have found that it is extraordinarily easy to create group identity in an experimental laboratory situation.[53] Randomly drawing a blue versus a white poker chip provides little basis for identifying with one group rather than another, certainly none that could be related to internal egoistic needs. But it happens. Social science that ignores the power of group identity (family, ethnic, locale, national)—or that attempts to reduce it to egoistic terms by stretching the definition of "egoism" to accommodate group-oriented behavior—is simply unrealistic.

In fact, egoistic individualism is more a religion than a science. It is not surprising to find it endorsed by a Unitarian minister, Kenneth L. Patton, when he writes: "We seek to understand the shyness behind arrogance, the fear behind pride . . . the anguish behind cruelty."[54] Here is a statement that lousy behavior *must* be due to internal failings, whether they are observed or not. The assumption that behavior we dislike or condemn is due to internal problems is religious, however, not established by empirical science, and while people certainly have a right to their religious beliefs, there is no reason to pay people who espouse egoistic individualism and are labeled "therapists" handsome salaries out of insurance and governmental funds to which we all contribute. Nor to pay any attention in criminal or civil court proceedings to what they say.

Is egoistic individualism even a good religion? I have my doubts. (I'm not discussing Unitarianism, certainly not on the basis of a single statement of a single minister.) Martin Seligman espouses the virtues of an egoistically based optimism, for example, but he also suggests that the current epidemic of depression in this country—and it's a big one—may be due in large part to the focus of the society on the self.[55] In fact, the typical person in this culture has what Anthony Greenwald terms a "totalitarian ego," one obsessed with protecting itself and interpreting information in a way that favors it.[56] But must we have such an ego? Should we? I cannot cite evidence, but I believe that Seligman's suggestion that an excess of egoism creates problems like depression is a good one. Egoism is frail. The ego, after all, *is* subject to harm from forces beyond its control, and it faces an ultimate destiny of disintegration and death. Throughout history people have answered no to the question "is this all there is?" when regarding their own ego's frailty. Perhaps that *is* all there is, but the acceptance of this conclusion as scientific is unjustified, and it may be creating great harm in our culture. Professional psychology's harping on the self—and in particular on how the self feels about the self—as the focus of all desirable or undesirable behavior can only exacerbate that harm.

CHAPTER 10

AUTONOMY AND ADVICE

There is nothing more profitable for a man than to
take good counsel with himself; for even if the event
turns out contrary to one's hopes, still one's decision
was right.

—Herodotus[1]

We can change our lives. To accomplish change, it is not necessary to
feel wonderful about ourselves first. It is not necessary to have a
superb childhood experience, or one we recall as superb. It is not necessary to run to an expensive therapist. It is not even necessary to
have a past history of success at attempts to change. For example,
while people who quit smoking on their own do not have higher success rates than those who enter cessation programs, the success of a
new attempt is unrelated to the number of past failures.[2] It is not at all
necessary to be certain in advance that we will succeed at changing
things, only that we need not be certain of failure. We can follow the
wisdom of Herodotus, echoed in the Old Testament books of Job and
Ecclesiastes. We do not always get our "just deserts" (fortunately, on
occasion), and the belief that we must get our due because we are
superior, invulnerable, and the world is just has the down side of making us miserable by failure, intolerant of others who fail (or have
AIDS[3]), and prone to cheat (which is widespread in our society, from
kindergartens to boardrooms). A sense of self-efficacy can be a great
help, but we are not slaves to feelings of doubt or uncertainty.

Professional psychologists and related mental health professionals,
unfettered by the modesty imposed by actual research findings, would
often lead us to believe we cannot change our lives on our own. As
Aaron Beck, whose work was discussed in the last chapter has said,

The troubled person is led to believe that he can't help himself and must seek out a professional healer when confronted with distress related to everyday problems of living. His confidence in using the "obvious" techniques he has customarily used in solving his problems is eroded because he accepts the view that emotional disturbance arises from forces beyond his grasp. He can't hope to understand himself through his own efforts, because his own notions are dismissed as shallow and insubstantial. By debasing the notions of common sense, this subtle indoctrination inhibits him from using his own judgment in analyzing and solving his problems.[4]

Is our behavior really determined by forces beyond our control? If it is, they are not the "psychological" forces that we have been led in our culture to believe are responsible. There is ample evidence, reviewed in this book, that while *some* psychological forces (better termed influences) are related to human outcomes, they certainly do not determine outcomes. But couldn't our lives be determined nevertheless? After all, all effects must have a cause, and our intuitions about volition (or even free will) must be illusions, must they not?

That type of philosophical determinism is based on the argument that *if* we could figure out all the causes, *then* we could predict the effects. In its traditional religious form, it suggests that because an omnipotent and omniscient God knows the future with certainty, our fate is "predestined." Many religious thinkers have rejected such omniscience as a basis for denying human volition, however, and some nonreligious ones have suggested that the act of knowing enough to predict the future with a high degree of certainty would lead to a change in its nature—at least in human affairs—and that therefore indeterminism rather than determinism is the ultimate principle, again at least for human affairs. Here, I simply point out that the "if" in the argument has never been established and can never be.

A more scientific formulation of the argument would be: "As we approach perfect knowledge, we can predict better and better; therefore, it is reasonable to conjecture that perfect knowledge would lead to perfect prediction." Here, the argument is the same that in an increasingly "perfect vacuum," all objects fall to earth with increasingly uniform acceleration. An analogy in psychology would be: "As we know more and more about a person, we can predict that person's behavior with greater and greater precision; therefore . . ." This premise is demonstrably false, as we saw in Chapter 3. As we know more and more about people, in fact, we often get more and more confused, attending to striking but irrelevant information rather than statistically valid—but predictively weak—information, and our predictions get worse. Will they get better in the future, when we have learned more through more systematic research? That's an empirical question that I cannot answer, and even an affirmative answer would remain only hypothetical and need not change our current views of ourselves.

There is nothing in current psychological knowledge that should lead us—in one way or another—to modify our view of the importance of our own strivings and attempts to change our lives. Even current support for the importance of genetic factors in influencing what we do demonstrates only *influence*; for example, children of alcoholics or schizophrenics are more likely to suffer from the same problems than children without such parents, they are still more likely *not* to become alcoholic or schizophrenic respectively than to suffer from these conditions.

So we have freedom at least insofar as we do not *know* what we will feel or choose to do, and we can change. In order to effect change, however, we must accept the reality of tradeoffs in life. We cannot expect to "have it all" through the successful pursuit of the chimera of perfect "mental health," which will lead to all good outcomes for all of us. Certainly an upbeat, optimistic approach to life is a great aid to activities that involve selling, for example. Blaming oneself for errors and defeats can be pernicious. Is optimism, however, helpful for creating high-quality products? For starters, what is the motive to improve the current ones if everything is okay—in fact wonderful—as is? When things go wrong a "cover your ass" (CYA) philosophy may be helpful in not losing clients, but will it help fix the things that go wrong? Here, I would like to argue, sometimes acknowledging inferiority can have beneficial results.

Our highly successful business competitors, the Japanese, began with an outright admission of the inferiority of their products. As Jack Grayson and Carla O'Dell detail, "what the Japanese did [in 1950] was to acknowledge their shortcomings" at a time when the one Japanese automotive import to the United States was not the Corolla, Honda, Camry, Acura, or Lexus, but the Toyapet, "which could hardly negotiate the hills of San Francisco."[5] The Japanese government assembled approximately 340 research workers, engineers, and plant managers at a conference to address the problem that Japanese products had a well-deserved reputation for inferiority. This conference consisted of an eight-week course given by the American industrial management specialist W. Edward Deming, ignored here at the time but is now somewhat revered as the developer of TQM, and who was earlier given the honor of being named in the Japanese JUSE Deming prize, the most prestigious prize awarded for industrial progress in Japan (granted to only about four people a year). Deming stressed to the Japanese the importance of quality and long-term commitments both to product development and to personnel development, which led to the mutual commitment of workers and companies, for which the Japanese found cultural precedent. We know the results. What is less well known is that an admission of inferiority and failure led to them.

These results were however, not without costs. In many ways the extreme work ethic, competitiveness, and ethnocentrism of Japanese culture makes it unpleasant to us. Just a few years back, there were many stories in this country about the horror of Japanese young people committing suicide when they failed an examination for entrance to higher education and training. Moreover, women have "their place," and retired people are often excluded from the benefits of the Japanese economy; they too accept "their place" in its society. The point is that we can't have everything every way we would like if we are still going to make choices. We cannot be happy about the relative paucity of demands we make on our children in school—as many of us apparently are—and simultaneously bemoan our country's lack of technological competitiveness.[6] Of course, we can try, but not if we are to function in a coherent, autonomous, manner.

The Japanese economic success illustrates another principle—the beneficial effects of being problem-oriented rather than success-oriented. Success is a reward for one's efforts, in terms of money or recognition. But we know from behavioral psychology that the prospect of a distant reward has little effect on behavior. As Albert Shanker, the president of the American Federation of Teachers, points out, telling eighth-graders that they should work hard so that they can go to college five years later and then maybe get a good job after college graduation a few years after that provides remarkably little motivation for hard work. An orientation toward success requires that the rewards that reinforce strivings be provided as quickly as possible—that is, it requires exactly the type of "short-term thinking" that observers of 1980s and 1990s U.S. business practices decry: "success now" through inflated executive incomes, takeovers, financial manipulation.

Moreover, the very nature of the rewards that generally successful people in our culture seek may lead to a self-defeating cycle of strivings that can lead to disaster. Rats in Skinner boxes press levers when this activity is followed by the appearance of food, which they need to survive, or even by "pleasure cutters" in their brains, which are apparently even more reinforcing than food for a starving rat. In our culture, we tend to assume that the major reward for which people strive is money. This may well be true for the 14 percent of our fellow citizens who live in poverty (as reported on CNN, Sept. 4, 1992), or for those who have chosen criminal careers, or for those in the middle class hoping to accumulate enough to buy a decent house in a decent neighborhood and to send their children to college. But is it really the reward for which the "movers and shakers" strive? Almost weekly, we witness the disgrace of some extraordinarily wealthy person in our society from financial dealings, and we ask what could have motivated that person. Such people often have "more money than they could possibly spend"; why would they violate the law or common ethics codes in order to acquire even more?

The answer is social status. In late August 1992, National Football League (NFL) receiver Jerry Rice signed a contract with the San Francisco Forty-Niners for a reported four million dollars a year. An outstanding pass receiver, he had been holding out for this large salary, which became the highest ever given to any player in the NFL who is not a quarterback. None of the sportscasters I heard who reported this signing expressed any opinion about what Rice would do with four million dollars per year, as opposed—for example—to what he would do with $3.5 million. The money's impact on Rice's life was not important to the sportscasters, nor by implication to him. Instead, they all emphasized that this annual salary constituted *recognition* of Rice's excellence, that he was "the best."

The principle here is that once our physical needs are met, the major reward we often seek is social status, which by its very nature involves a comparison of us to other people. Money, titles, even awards of some sort become important mainly to the extent that they constitute and reflect social status, especially for those already wealthy, i. e., those with the most power in our society.

But social status—or rather, self-perceived social status—is a psychological phenomenon and as such is subject to *adaptation level effects*. Just as we adapt to the gray light in a movie theater after originally finding it difficult to see and just as we adjust to the bright light when leaving it after originally being a bit blinded, we come to adapt to whatever our current psychological state happens to be and to experience it as normal, at least for us personally. Thus, people whom others regard as "having it made" may experience dissatisfaction with their lives, while prisoners in a concentration camp may take great pleasure in being able to obtain a simple extra piece of bread, or cultivate a single weed, or draw a simple design on a scrap of paper. As a result of such adaptation, self-perceived social status can place people on what my colleagues the late Philip Brickman and Don Campbell have termed a "hedonic treadmill."[7] Through adaptation level effects, we incorporate our previous rewards into our current status quo; they become, in effect, invisible. Our status quo, which incorporates our previous success, becomes a new "zero point." This incorporation is enhanced when we evaluate our social status, because it involves comparison with others, and those others with whom we have most contact tend to have roughly the same status (evaluated in absolute terms) that we do. Thus the reward of social status results from its *enhancement* rather than from *experiencing* it. And we must run very fast on this particular treadmill, because effective rewards are short-term rewards. So people with millions or hundreds of millions of dollars may "need" more money, but the financial hanky-panky they may engage in to get it can end up costing the rest of us $600 billion or so. That such personal aberrations will occur on occasion as they have in the past is a predictable result of a culturally shared success orientation.

In contrast, an orientation toward the problem, toward "taking good counsel," toward "doing the right thing," does not leave us on a treadmill where only more matters. New and different problems and challenges in life require new and different "good" responses. We don't ask ourselves (unless we happen to be Ben Franklin striving for "moral perfection") whether our wisdom in meeting these problems and challenges is "on the increase," as we ask ourselves whether our success in a job or profession is "keeping pace". When we take pleasure in taking good counsel and behaving well, it is because we have done so here and now. We do not judge whether we have behaved ethically in a particular situation by comparing our "level of ethicality" to that of others. Many craftspeople and poets do not take pleasure in the results of their efforts because these results are better than others' results, but because they are what they are. (Those who do not have this orientation find themselves on the treadmill, often regarded by others as unpleasant egoists.) Crafting our lives rather than seeking rewards has long been recommended by many moral philosophers. Psychological research supports that recommendation. Free of social comparison and adaptation level effects, it works.

A problem orientation, as opposed to a success orientation, can have intellectual benefits as well as psychological ones. Robert J. Sternberg is considered by many cognitive psychologists to be one of the world's foremost researchers in the area of "nonacademic intelligence" and creativity. As he and his graduate student Todd L. Lubart summarize their past findings: "It has been found again and again that people do their most creative work when their motivation is (a) task-focused rather than goal focused and (b) intrinsic rather than extrinsic. These people care deeply about what they are doing and not just what it will get them."[8]

Optimism and a success orientation have also had a profound effect on American politics that is not without costs. As Martin Seligman has shown in systematic studies, election results, even upsets and opinion shifts, are related to the optimism and good feelings that politicians express in their speeches.[9] Consider the phenomenal political success of Ronald Reagan. Whatever one thinks of his presidency, it is clear that his appeal was greatly enhanced by his extraordinary optimism and remarkably high level of self-esteem—even if the latter was largely based, as Garry Wills has suggested, on a memory that was often incapable of distinguishing between what had happened and what he wished had happened.[10] Is such a view of life and of oneself, however, a good one for actually running a country? Consider Reagan's optimistic conclusion that economic growth stimulated by a massive tax cut would lead to more government revenues than would be lost by the cut—and the resulting deficit, which our *children* must shoulder.

In personal life as well, there are tradeoffs. If feeling good were our ultimate goal, then why do we not all take drugs? Many people do; some take illegal ones; more take legal ones. But we will have to sacrifice some of their good feelings to achieve a more drug-free society. Ironically, a major belief in our culture is that we and our children take drugs because we do not feel good *enough*, particularly about ourselves, although researchers who actually study drug use conclude that the poor self-esteem problems of drug users follows rather than precedes the use itself.[11] I suggest that we question that view by—with Yevtushenko—questioning whether the "main meaning of life is to be happy." The reader need not question it, but what I urge the reader to do is to think and make autonomous choices about such matters, without automatically accepting the assumption that feelings determine everything else in life, or that egoistic individualism is all there is. Connections to other people and "taking good counsel" with oneself may be more important, even with, as John F. Kennedy put it, "a clear conscience as our only sure reward."

If someone is upset to the point of feeling unable to cope, however—which is quite different from being upset to the point of not being completely certain that one can—then therapy is a good option. Some therapists—such as those quoted most approvingly in this book—base their help on systematic principles of behavior and theory derived from careful research studies and an analysis of their implications. Ironically, these are often not the high-priced people; they are usually associated with universities, and since their treatments are systematic, they often involve a number of paraprofessionals in their "teams." In addition to many already mentioned in this book, those at the Oregon Social Learning Center in Eugene, Oregon are a good example; they use behavioral and cognitive principles to deal with "out-of-control" children, and they have succeeded by training not only the paraprofessionals but also the parents themselves to apply the principles involved.

Many—perhaps most—therapists, however, consider themselves "eclectic."[12] That means that they attempt to use whatever they find to be "best" in their experience. The problem, of course, is how do they determine what is best? They themselves decide—on the basis of limited experience, with all the problems of trying to learn from it discussed in Chapter 4. Nevertheless, they often succeed in helping people. Their experience, credentials, and costs, however, are not related to their success. The person seeking such a therapist should feel free to "shop," just as that person would shop for any other service. People should try to find a therapist who is empathetic and whose philosophy about life is compatible with theirs. (Recall the Hester et al. study in which people with alcohol problems were helped much more by a program consistent with their belief that the problem was a bad "habit" or a "spiritual disease.")

Moreover, there is no reason for abandoning one's own views of what is important in life for those of a therapist. While constructs such as "love" or "deserved guilt" may not be in many therapists' repertoires, they may nevertheless be important ones to the person seeking therapy, and there is no reason to abandon them due to a false belief in the omniscience of the therapist. There is nothing wrong with intuitions in helping to decide how to run one's own life (as opposed to using them—unchecked—as a basis for running a profession). When working with a therapist who functions on an intuitive basis, there is no reason for clients to abandon their own intuitions for those of the therapist without considering such a change with great seriousness. Therapy is a probabilistic process—or at least its success is—and the possibility that the client is right and the therapist wrong is always important. Moreover, therapy involves values, and there is no reason for clients to abandon theirs. Many people believe that an important way to get over depression, for example, is to "do something for someone else." The therapist, in contrast, may view learned optimism as the best way. To the best of my knowledge, these two ways have not been compared. Even if they were, however, and learned optimism was found to be superior in general, the results would once again be only about a statistical trend. I would certainly not argue for "going against the base rates" of a statistical trend for a medical choice or a governmental policy, but when a choice involves personal values, a person may well decide to do so. A particular depressed person may, for example, find learned optimism distasteful and helping others not only rewarding but ethically superior.

Suppose the person's distress is very serious—of the type diagnosed as psychosis or extreme depression. Here I urge caution. Many experts will state that they "know exactly what to do" to "cure" the person involved. While there is evidence that experts agree with each other (as many have done historically about a lot of procedures that didn't work or created harm), the evidence of the validity of their judgments is far from encouraging. There is a dilemma here, because while the culture mandates that a true expert should "exude confidence," and while we have come to expect that of an expert, any confidence exuded in this area is clearly unrealistic. That leaves the potential client, or the relatives and friends of the potential client, in a bind. Should they trust the person who appears to know what he or she is doing, however questionable the basis of such confidence? Or should they trust the person who appears doubting and indecisive?

I have no good answer. I do, however, have some specific advice along the lines of being conservative. First, try to make a judgment about what to do with yourself or someone else on the basis of the actual behavior involved—not on the basis of the purported insight of a mental health expert independent of that behavior, especially not an insight based on a projective test that only the expert "knows how to interpret." Second, systematic studies using the scientific gold standard of random assignment have demonstrated that people who can be treated either in hospitals or in outpatient facilities do better if they are assigned to the outpatient facilities.[13] Avoid hospitalization unless it is clearly necessary—again, on the basis of current behavior. Be cautious about drugs and their dosages. We simply don't know the long-term effects of many drugs, although we do know that some can be disastrous—can lead to tardive dyskinesia. The therapist who says "take this drug the rest of your life" has undoubtedly seen people who stopped taking the drug and who experienced subsequent problems but is unaware of how many people given this advice have thrown the drugs down the toilet when they felt better and experienced no subsequent ill effects. Only scientific studies can address the problems of long-term effects, and these studies themselves must be long term. Finally, if hospitalization and consequently drugs are the only option, be aware of the power of the aides in mental hospitals. Insist—both for the good of the person involved and for the good of all others—that it is they who should be licensed and regulated, not just the gurus.

The advice to be cautious and to be concerned primarily about those who have the true control over mental clients' lives is about how to cope with truly debilitating emotional distress. It exists, and it can sometimes be related to prolonged experiences that have emotionally scarred people, or to "natural-like" conditions that may have a genetic or physiological base. People experiencing such distress, however, are unlikely to be reading this book, and because such people—fortunately—constitute a minority in our society, the person reading this book is unlikely to be one of them. My advice for the general reader, therefore, is to remain consistently aware that those factors and experiences that scientific psychology has found to be important for most people in life are better termed "influences" than "causes." It is simply not true that optimism and a belief in one's own competence and prospects for success are *necessary* conditions for behaving competently. Good feelings may help, but they are not necessary. Moreover, we do not need to believe that in general we are superior, we are invulnerable, and the world is just. (Show me someone who truly believes that—or who has no self-doubts at all—and I'll show you a nitwit.) It is not true that we are slaves to our feelings or to our childhood experiences, which are often inaccurate reconstructions of what actually happened anyway. More important, we do not have to feel wonderful about ourselves and the world in order to engage in behavior that is personally or socially beneficial. If we don't feel so wonderful, there is no shame in seeking a little help from our friends (or a therapist), but there is also no necessity for seeking the services of a high-priced professional who claims to have insights that the research shows are no better than insights inferred from general principles. Nor is it necessary to join a "recovery" program, or some updated version of EST that can convince us that we have failed to obtain perfect selfishness because our parents and everyone else have abused us in some direct or subtle way. Most important of all, there is no evidence that for the majority of people a change in internal state and feeling is necessary prior to behaving in a beneficial way. There is, in contrast, good evidence that changing our behavior will change our internal state and feelings. Just do it.

NOTES

PART ONE: THE CLAIMS OF THE MENTAL HEALTH EXPERTS VERSUS THE EVIDENCE

1. This statement was made by two jurors who found the second defendant in the 1991 North Carolina Little Rascals Day Care Center sex abuse trial guilty, a verdict that led to a sentence of life in prison. The interviews in which the jurors made the statement were shown on public television, in an evening program aired on WQED in Pittsburgh, PA, July 22, 1993.
2. P. C. Stern. (1993). A second environmental science: Human-environment interactions. *Science*, 260, 1997–1999.

CHAPTER 1: INTRODUCTION

1. D. P. Rice, S. Kelman, L. S. Miller, and S. Dunmeyer, *The Economic Costs of Alcohol and Drug Abuse and Mental Illness: 1985*, report submitted to the Office of Financing and Coverage Policy of the Alcohol, Drug Abuse, and Mental Health Administration, U.S. Department of Health and Human Services (San Francisco, CA: Institute for Health and Aging, University of California, 1990), p. 81.
2. See, for example, D. Yankelovitz, "Public Attitudes Toward People with Chronic Mental Illness," prepared for the Robert Wood Johnson Program in Mental Illness, April 1990.
3. National Research Council, "News Briefs: Mental Health," *News Report*, April–May 1992, p. 26.
4. J. Adler and D. Rosenberg, "Dr. Bean and Her Little Boy," *Newsweek*, April 13, 1992, pp. 56–57.
5. Rice et al., *Economic Costs*, p. 164.
6. Ibid., p. 164.
7. See J. R. Wilder, S. E. Mahood, and M. B. Greenblatt, *Pennsylvania Family Law Practice and Procedures Handbook*, 2nd ed. (Norcross, GA: Harrison Co., 1989).
8. J. L. Kohout, M. M. Wicherski, T. J. Popanz, and G. M. Pion, *Salaries in Psychology 1989*. Office of Demographic, Employment, and Educational Research, American Psychological Association, 1200 17th Street N.W., Washington, DC 20036.
9. R. Boyer and D. Savageau, *Places Rated Almanac: Your Guide to Finding the Best Place to Live in America* (Chicago: Rand McNally Co., 1985).

10. American Psychological Association, *Directory of the American Psychological Association*, 1959 ed.

11. American Psychological Association, *Directory of the American Psychological Association*, 1989 ed.

12. *Encyclopedia of American Associations* (Cole Research Company, Detroit Book Tower, 1959, 1989).

13. Rice et al., *Economic Costs*, p. 81.

14. G. M. Pion, "Psychologists Wanted: Employment Trends over the Past Decade," in R. R. Kilburg, ed., *How to Manage Your Career in Psychology* (Washington, DC: American Psychological Association), pp. 229–246.

15. R. B. Reich, *The Work of Nations: Preparing Ourselves for the Twenty-first Century* (New York: Alfred A. Knopf, 1991), p. 192. Reich makes the point that the fastest-growing professions are those involving "symbolic manipulation," as opposed to creation or production.

16. Both the last two figures are from T. H. Dial, R. Tebbutt, G. M. Pion, J. Kohout, G. VandenBos, M. Johnson, P. H. Schervish, L. Whiting, J. C. Fox, and E. I. Merwin, "Human Resources in Mental Health," in R. W. Manderscheid and M. A. Sonnenschien, eds., *Mental Health, United States 1990* (DHHS 9DM 90-1708) (Washington, DC: U.S. Government Printing Office, 1990), pp. 196–260.

17. Others, such as Charcot and Janet, had previously treated psychologically distressed people with "talk" therapy, or hypnosis. In fact, Freud's main interest after neuropsychiatry was in hypnosis. Still others, such as Adolf Meyer and later Alfred Adler, proceeded with verbally oriented psychotherapy quite independently of Freud's psychoanalytic ideas.

18. Lowell Kelly gave his last speech at the American Psychological Association in 1984. Since he had suffered the physical disabilities of aging he first rehearsed his speech with a tape recorder. Unfortunately, he apparently did not realize that people talk much faster into a recorder than to a responsive audience, and he never finished the speech before the audience. He documented how rapidly and severely clinical practice had divorced itself from its research base, but at the end he had to blurt out his conclusion that "the bubble will burst." For the rest of that convention he was deeply honored and even given an award, but his message was ignored.

19. G. M. Pion, "Psychologists Wanted," p. 232.

20. Ibid.

21. A. Howard, G. M. Pion, G. D. Gottfredson, P. E. Flattau, S. Oskamp, S. M. Pfafflin, D. W. Bray, and A. Burstein, "The Changing Face of American Psychology: A Report from the Committee on Employment and Human Resources," *American Psychologist*, 41 (1986): 1311–1327, 1313.

22. Ibid., p. 1315.

23. Personal letter, July 21, 1991.

24. S. C. Hayes, "An Interview with Lee Sechrest: The Courage to Say 'We Do Not Know How,'" *APS Observer*, 2, no. 4 (1989): 8–10, 8.

25. "Recommended Graduate Training Program in Clinical Psychology," report of the Committee on training in clinical psychology of the American Psychological Association submitted at the Detroit meeting of the American Psychological Association, September 9–13, 1947, published in *American Psychologist*, 2 (1947): 539–558, 549.

26. W. F. Anderson, "Human Gene Therapy," *Science* 256 (1992): 808–813, quote on p. 812.

27. For a discussion of the (invalid) medical belief in the "doctrine of signa-
tures," by which the medicinal value of a particular substance or procedure
could be assessed by its similarity to the condition it was meant to alleviate,
see R. Nisbett and L. Ross, *Human Inference: Strategies and Shortcomings of
Social Judgment* (Englewood Cliffs, NJ: Prentice-Hall, 1980), chap. 6.

28. J. Larkin, J. McDermott, D. Simon, and H. Simon, "Expert and Novice
Performance in Solving Physics Problems," *Science*, 209 (1980): 1335–1342.

29. They did—the American Psychological Society, which had slightly over
13,500 members by 1992.

30. K. Fisher, "Graham: 'A Product of My Times,'" *APA Monitor*, 19 (1988): 5.

31. P. Scott, *The Jewel in the Crown* (New York: William Morrow, 1966; reprint-
ed by Avon, 1979). At the time, this novel was being serialized on public
television. A major theme is the myopic British exploitation of India.

32. W. B. Arthur, "Positive Feedback in the Economy," *Scientific American*, 262
(1990): 92–99, quote on p. 92.

33. See, for example, R. A. Smith, "Advocacy, Interpretation, and Influence in
the U.S. Congress," *American Political Science Review*, 78 (1984): 44–63.

34. J. B. Matarazzo, "Psychological Assessment Versus Psychological Testing:
Validation from Binet to the School, Clinic, and Courtroom," *American
Psychologist*, 45 (1990): 999–1017.

35. Ibid., p. 1016.

36. Ibid., p. 1015.

37. Ibid.

38. Ibid.

39. Ibid.

40. Ibid., p. 1016.

41. In 1986 the National Academy of Sciences issued a book edited by Neil J.
Smelser and Dean R. Gerstein entitled *Behavioral and Social Sciences: Fifty
Years of Discovery* (Washington, DC: National Academy Press) that summarized these findings. In 1988 the academy issued another book entitled *The
Behavioral and Social Sciences: Achievements and Opportunities* (Washington,
DC: National Academy Press), also edited by Gerstein and Smelser, but this
time with R. Duncan Luce and Sonja Sperlich as well. The interested reader
can find a great deal of material in these volumes concerning advancements
in the social and behavioral sciences.

42. See, for example, P. S. Holzman and S. Matthysse, "The Genetics of
Schizophrenia: A Review," *Psychological Science*, 1 (1990): 279–286.

43. For a fascinating account of the inability to predict adult alcoholism from
childhood problems once genetic factors have been controlled for statistically, see G. E. Vaillant and E. S. Milofsky, "The Etiology of Alcoholism: A
Prospective Viewpoint," *American Psychologist*, 37 (1982): 494–503.

44. For a brief nontechnical review of this "accepted wisdom" regarding drug use
and psychotherapy for depression—as well as opposing views—see D.
Goleman, "Critics Challenge Reliance on Drugs," *New York Times*, October
17, 1989, pp. C1, C6. For a slightly longer nontechnical discussion, see M.
Shuchman, and M. S. Wilkes, "Dramatic Progress Against Depression," *New
York Times Magazine*, October 7, 1990, p. 2, pp. 12–32.

45. For a recent discussion of attributions in depressed individuals, as well as the
relationship between such attributions and susceptibility to subsequent
depression, see S. Peterson, and A. J. Stunkard, "Cognates of Personal
Control: Locus of Control, Self-efficacy, and Explanatory Style," *Applied and*

Preventive Psychology, 1 (1992): 111–118. Also see comments on this article in the same journal issue by M. E. P. Seligman (pp. 119–120), A. Bandura (pp. 121–126), and J. P. Rotter (pp. 127–129).

46. Unsurprisingly, I recommend my own book: R. M. Dawes, *Rational Choice in an Uncertain World* (San Diego: Harcourt Brace Jovanovich, 1988).

47. R. W. Pearson, M. Ross, and R. M. Dawes, "Personal Recall and the Limits of Retrospective Memory in Surveys," in J. Tanur, ed., *Questions About Questions: Inquiries into the Cognitive Bases of Surveys* (New York: Russell Sage Foundation, 1992), pp. 65–94.

48. M. Conway, and M. Ross, "Getting What You Want by Revising What You Had," *Journal of Personality and Social Psychology*, 47 (1985): 738–748; and M. Ross, "The Relation of Implicit Theories to the Construction of Personal Histories," *Psychological Review*, 96 (1989): 341–357.

49. S. C. Hayes, "The Emperor's Clothes: Examining the 'Delusions' of Professional Psychology: The Healthy Skepticism of David Faust," *Scientist Practitioner*, 1 (1991): 22–25.

50. R. M. Dawes, "Comments on Walster and Cleary," *American Statistician*, 25 (1971): 56.

51. For a comparison of trip-by-trip versus lifetime probabilities and their questionable impact on persuading people to use seat belts, see P. Slovic, B. Fischhoff, and S. Lichtenstein, "Accident Probabilities and Seat-belt Usage: A Psychological Perspective," *Accident Analysis and Prevention*, 10 (1978): 281–285.

52. An unfortunate exaggeration in an otherwise excellent review article by C. Anderson and B. Weiner, "Attribution and Attributional Processes in Personality," Forthcoming in G. Caprara and G. Heck, eds., *Modern Personality Psychology: Critical Reviews and New Directions*.

53. Ibid.

54. K. Fisher, "Graham: 'A Product of My Times,'" *The APA Monitor*, 19 (1988): 5.

55. S. Taylor, *Positive Illusions: Creative Self-Deception and the Healthy Mind.* (New York: Basic Books, 1989), p. 227.

56. See A. J. Ayer, *Language, Truth, and Logic* (New York: Dover, 1935/1947).

57. See M. Rosenbaum and M. Muroff, eds., *Anna O.: Fourteen Contemporary Reinterpretations* (New York: The Free Press, 1984).

58. See G. P. Gardner, (chair), National Committee on Excellence in Education, *A Nation At Risk: The Imperative for Educational Reform.* A Report to the Nation and the Secretary of Education, U.S. Department of Education, 1983. See also H. W. Stevenson, S. Lee, and J. W. Stigler, "Mathematics Achievements of Chinese, Japanese, and American Children," *Science*, 231 (1986): 693–699.

59. Rice et al., *Economic Costs*, p. 157. See also M. R. Burt, *Over the Edge: The Growth of Homelessness in the 1980s* (New York and Washington, DC: Russell Sage Foundation and Urban Institute Press, 1991), chap. 2.

60. American Psychiatric Association, *Task Force Report: Tardive Dyskinesia* (Washington, DC: American Psychiatric Association, 1980). P. R. Breggin, "Brain Damage, Dementia and Persistent Cognitive Dysfunction Associated with Neuroleptic Drugs: Evidence, Etiology, Implications," *The Journal of Mind and Behavior*, 11 (1990): 425 [179]–464 [218].

61. J. Rubin, "Drugs for Treating Behavior Problems: How Safe Are They?" *American Psychologist*, 45 (1990): 985–986.

62. R. L. Balster, "Comment on Comment by Rubin," *American Psychologist*, 45 (1990): 986.
63. S. Moses, "Training in Prescribing Planned by the Military," *APA Monitor*, 21 (July 1990): 30–31.
64. N. Youngstrom, "On Privileges Issue Field Is Tilting to 'Yes,'" *APA Monitor*, 21 (June 1990): 12–13.

CHAPTER 2: PSYCHOTHERAPY: THE MYTH OF EXPERTISE

1. S. C. Hayes, "An Interview with Lee Sechrest: The Courage to Say 'We Do Not Know How,'" *APS Observer*, 2, no. 4 (1989): 8–10, 8.
2. S. Freud, *An Analysis of a Case of Hysteria* (New York: Collier Books, 1963).
3. G. E. Vaillant, *Adaptation to Life* (Boston: Little, Brown and Co., 1977).
4. H. H. Strupp, "Psychotherapy: Research, Practice, and Public Policy (How to Avoid Dead Ends)," *American Psychologist*, 41 (1986): 120–130, 123.
5. E. Meehan, "Social Indicators: Policies and Inventories," paper presented at the meeting of the Public Choice Society, New Haven, March 1974. Or see E. J. Meehan, *The Thinking Game: A Guide to Effective Study* (Chatham, NJ: Chatham House, 1988).
6. Pointing out examples of success constitutes such flawed evidence for the efficacy of therapy that the APA Ethics code when I was a member of its national ethics committee specifically forbade "testimonials" about successful therapy as a way for a therapist to advertise her or his effectiveness. Principle 4, dealing with public statements, has since been revised. Compare, for example, the principle about public statements (number 4) in the 1981 Ethics Code, in *American Psychologist*, 36 (1981): 533–638, with that same principle in American Psychological Association, Ethical Principles of Psychologists, amended June 2, 1989, *American Psychologist*, 45 (1989): 390–395. During my service on that committee, however, the Federal Trade Commission (FTC) came to the conclusion that such a prohibition constituted restraint of trade and information. The public, the FTC contended, had a right to decide for itself that such testimonials were worthless, or—if the APA felt so strongly that they were worthless and misleading—it could educate the public about its reasons for reaching this conclusion. It never did. The prohibition had to be dropped. (I personally am on the side of the FTC *and* of education.)
7. E. T. Gendlin, "What Comes After Traditional Psychotherapy Research?" *American Psychologist*, 41 (1986): 131–136.
8. See R. M. Dawes, *Rational Choice in an Uncertain World* (San Diego: Harcourt Brace Jovanovich, 1988), pp. 84–89. For an excellent journal article, see L. Furby, "Interpreting Regression Toward the Mean in Developmental Research," *Developmental Psychology*, 8 (1973): 172–179.
9. K. McKean, "Decisions: Two Eminent Psychologists Disclose the Mental Pitfalls in Which Rational People Find Themselves When They Try to Arrive at Logical Conclusions," *Discover*, June 1985, 22–31.

10. *Behavior Today*, 3 (May 16, 1977). There are some statistical ways to attempt to understand whether change over time after an intervention such as psychotherapy is simply due to regression effects or to the intervention. See D. T. Campbell and J. C. Stanley, *Experimental and Quasi-Experimental Design for Research* (Chicago: Rand McNally and Co., 1963). One of these ways is to predict functioning at a subsequent time from functioning at the initial time that therapy was begun and then look at the *discrepancy* between the predicted later functioning and the actual functioning. For example, in assessing whether an educational program has an effect on people who have scored particularly badly (or well) on a test of achievement at one point in time, their scores at the second point can be predicted from those at the first point and then an assessment can be made of whether their scores in general are higher than this predicted value. Technically, such a discrepancy is termed a *residual* score, as opposed to a *discrepancy* score. (Thus, doing *as well* may indicate effectiveness for a high scoring group, because the prediction is that in general they will do less well at the second point in time.) Another method is to use an entire set of variables to predict functioning at the second point in time and again look at discrepancies. See R. W. Mee and T. C. Chau, "Regression Toward the Mean and the Paired Sample T Test," *American Statistician*, 45 (1991): 39–42. Here, the statistical model predicting what *would* have happened without the intervention provides the hypothetical counterfactual. Both these and other methods, however, rely on strong statistical assumptions, and all that can be done is to demonstrate that the results do not "significantly" violate these assumptions (see Chapter 1), not that the assumptions are necessarily met. It is, moreover, always possible that even though no significant violations are found examining one set of assumptions, additional tests of other assumptions would find such violations.

11. E. J. Posavac, and T. Q. Miller, "Some Conceptual Problems Caused by Not Having a Conceptual Foundation for Health Research: An Illustration from Studies of the Psychological Effects of Abortion," *Psychology and Health*, 5 (1990): 13–23. See also R. M. Dawes, letter to the editor, *Chronicle of Higher Education*, February 28, 1990, p. B4.

12. Coronary Drug Project Research Group, "Influence of Adherence to Treatment and Response to Cholesterol on Mortality in the Coronary Drug Project," *New England Journal of Medicine*, 303 (1980): 1038–1041.

13. P. Meier, "The Biggest Public Health Experiment Ever: 1954 Field Trials of the Salk Poliomyelitis Vaccine," in J. Tanur, F. Mosteller, W. H. Kruskel, R. F. Link, R. S. Pieters, and G. R. Rising, eds., *Statistics: A Guide to the Unknown* (San Francisco: Holden Day, 1972).

14. "Psychosurgery," *Time*, November 30, 1942, p. 42.

15. "Mass Lobotomies," *Time*, October 15, 1952, p. 86.

16. "Psychosurgery," *Time*, November 30, 1942, p. 42.

17. Ibid., p. 100.

18. "Mass Lobotomies," *Time*, October 15, 1952, p. 86. Lobotomies on a smaller scale and other forms of psychosurgery have nevertheless continued. The commonly accepted definition of *psychosurgery* is the destruction of brain tissue for the *primary* purpose of achieving behavioral or psychological change—not of alleviating pain or reducing seizures, even though success in such an endeavor would yield behavioral and psychological changes as well. A National Commission for the Protection of Human Subjects report pub-

lished in 1977 was able to report on psychosurgery (to treat such problems as obesity) conducted after 1970. As earlier, the evaluations of the results of such surgery were inadequate. As the commission noted in its tables reporting the results of these studies, "In the vast majority of instances, results of surgery were summarized by neurosurgeons and/or associated psychiatrists and are based on subjective (or poorly defined) criteria." See K. J. Ryan, *Psychosurgery: The National Commission for the Protection of Human Subjects of Biomedical and Behavioral Research*, DHEW Publication No. 105J 77-0002 (Washington, DC: U.S. Department of Health, Education, and Welfare, 1977), tables 19 (I-76) and 20 (I-79) of the appendix.

19. J. M. Masson, *Against Therapy: Emotional Tyranny and the Myth of Psychological Healing* (New York: Atheneum, 1988), chap. 5.
20. H. Bakwin, "Pseudodoxia Pediatrica," *New England Journal of Medicine*, 232 (1945): 691–697.
21. Ibid., p. 692.
22. M. L. Smith and G. V. Glass, "Meta-analysis of Psychotherapy Outcome Studies," *American Psychologist*, 32 (1977): 752–760.
23. That the two groups are normally distributed on the outcome measures (the standard "bell-shaped" distribution) and that sampling is independent.
24. For some striking comparisons, see, for example, R. Rosenthal, "How Are We Doing in Soft Psychology?" *American Psychologist*, 45 (1990): 775–776.
25. R. M. Dawes, "Comment: Quandary: Correlation Coefficient and Contexts," in L. Montada, S. H. Filipp, and M. J. Lerner, eds., *Life Crises and Experiences of Loss in Adulthood* (Hillsdale, NJ: Erlbaum, in press), pp. 521–529.
26. A. A. Lazarus, "If This Be Research," *American Psychologist*, 45 (1990): 670–671.
27. J. T. Landman and R. M. Dawes, "Psychotherapy Outcome: Smith and Glass' Conclusions Stand Up to Scrutiny," *American Psychologist*, 37 (1982): 504–516.
28. J. S. Berman and N. C. Norton, "Does Professional Training Make a Therapist More Effective?" *Psychological Bulletin*, 98 (1985): 401–407.
29. H. H. Strupp and S. W. Hadley, "Specific Versus Nonspecific Factors in Psychotherapy," *Archives of General Psychiatry*, 36 (1979): 1125–1136.
30. D. M. Stein and M. J. Lambert, "On the Relationship Between Therapist Experience and Psychotherapy Outcome," *Clinical Psychology Review*, 4 (1984): 127–142; and B. Smith and L. Sechrest, "The Treatment of Aptitude X Treatment Interactions," *Journal of Consulting and Clinical Psychology*, 59 (1991): 233–244.
31. W. R. Miller and R. K. Hester, "Inpatient Alcoholism Treatment: Who Benefits?" *American Psychologist*, 41 (1986): 794–805.
32. K. L. Howard, S. M. Kopta, M. S. Krause, and D. E. Orlinsky, "The Dose-Effect Relationship in Psychotherapy," *American Psychologist*, 41 (1986): 159–164.
33. K. S. Ditman, G. G. Crawford, E. W. Forgy, H. Moskowitz, and C. Macandrew, "A Controlled Experiment on the Use of Court Probation for Drunk Arrests," *American Journal of Psychiatry*, 124 (1967): 64–67.
34. Strupp and Hadley "Specific Versus Nonspecific Factors," p. 1136.
35. M. J. Lambert, D. A. Shapiro, and A. E. Bergin, "The Effectiveness of Psychotherapy," in S. L. Garfield and A. E. Bergin, eds., *Handbook of Psychotherapy and Behavior Change*, 3rd ed. (New York: John Wiley, 1986), pp. 157–212, 175.

36. D. Mazza, "Comment on Miller and Hester's "Inpatient Alcoholism Treatment: Who Benefits?" *American Psychologist*, 43 (1988): 199–200.

37. Berman and Norton, "Does Professional Training Make a Therapist More Effective?" p. 404.

38. See R. M. Dawes, "Monotone Interactions: It's Even Simpler Than That," *Behavior and Brain Sciences*, 13 (1990): 128–129; and W. F. Chaplin and R. M. Dawes, "The Interpretation and Evaluation of Statistical Interactions in Psychotherapy Outcomes," in preparation.

39. Smith and Sechrest, "Aptitude X Treatment Interactions" (in preparation).

40. P. Lafferty, L. E. Beutler, and M. Crago, "Differences Between More and Less Effective Psychotherapists: A Study of Select Therapist Variables," *Journal of Consulting and Clinical Psychology*, 57 (1989): 76–80. See also J. S. Berman, R. C. Miller, and P. J. Massman, "Cognitive Therapy Versus Systematic Desensitization: Is One Treatment Superior?" *Psychological Bulletin*, 97 (1985): 451–461.

41. R. K. Hester, W. R. Miller, H. D. Delaney, and R. J. Meyers, "Effectiveness of the Community Reinforcement Approach," paper presented at the twenty-fourth annual meeting of the Association for the Advancement of Behavior Therapy, San Francisco, November 2, 1990.

42. J. D. Frank, *Persuasion and Healing*, 2nd. ed. (Baltimore, MD: Johns Hopkins University Press, 1973); and H. H. Strupp, "Psychotherapy: Can the Practitioner Learn from the Researcher?" *American Psychologist*, 44 (1989): 717–724. Others such as Otto Rank and Sándor Ferenczi have previously stressed the importance of the relationship.

43. For a critique of such vague assertions, see N. D. Schaffer, "Multidimensional Measures of Therapist Behavior as Predictors of Outcome," *Psychological Bulletin*, 92 (1982): 670–681.

44. W. R. Miller, C. A. Taylor, and J. C. West, "Focused Versus Broad-Based Behavior Therapy for Problem Drinkers," *Journal of Consulting and Clinical Psychology*, 48 (1980): 590–601.

45. This idea is neither original nor recent. For example, Otto Rank wrote in 1929: "The modern neurotic has thus completed the human process of internalization which reaches its peak in psychological self-knowledge, but also is reduced to an absurdity. He [sic] needs no more knowing; *only experience and the capacity for it may yet be able to save him*" (italics added). In O. Rank, *Will Therapy and Truth and Reality* (New York: Alfred A. Knopf, 1964): p. 94.

46. For an explanation of "sunk costs" and their potential power in leading to irrational decisions, see Dawes, *Rational Choice*, chap. 2.

47. For an excellent description of such positive feedback, see the award-winning paper of M. Maruyama, "The Second Cybernetics: Deviation-Amplifying Mutual Causal Processes," *American Scientist*, 51 (1963): 164–179.

48. P. M. Lewinsohn, D. O. Antonuccio, J. L. Steinmetz, and L. Teri, *The Coping With Depression Course* (Eugene, OR: Castalia Press, 1984).

49. G. L. Paul and A. A. Menditto, "Effectiveness of Inpatient Treatment Programs for Mentally Ill Adults in Public Psychiatric Facilities," *Applied and Preventive Psychology*, 1 (1992): 41–63, quote on p. 56.

50. M. Rothbart and M. Taylor, "Category Labels and Social Reality: Do We View Social Categories as Natural Kinds?" forthcoming in G. Semin and K. Fiedler, eds., *Language and Social Cognition* (in press).

51. W. F. Chaplin, O. P. John, and L. R. Goldberg, "Conceptions of States and

Traits: Dimensional Attributes with Ideas as Prototypes," *Journal of Personality and Social Psychology*, 54 (1988): 541–557.

52. L. Wittgenstein, *Philosophical Investigations* (New York: Macmillan, 1953).
53. G. Lakoff, *Women, Fire, and Dangerous Things* (Chicago: University of Chicago Press, 1987).
54. G. Vaillant, *Adaptation to Life* (Boston: Little, Brown and Co., 1977).
55. Ibid., p. 353.
56. See T. S. Szasz, *The Myth of Mental Illness: Foundations of a Theory of Personal Conduct.* rev. ed. (New York: Harper and Row, 1974); and J. M. Masson, *Against Therapy: Emotional Tyranny and the Myth of Psychological Healing* (New York: Atheneum, 1988).
57. J. T. Englehardt, Jr., "Typologies of Disease: Nosologies Revisited," in K. F. Schaffner, ed., *Logic of Discovery and Diagnosis in Medicine* (Berkeley, CA: University of California Press, 1985), pp. 56–71.
58. H. Schulsinger, "A Ten Year Follow-Up Study of Children of Schizophrenic Mothers: Clinical Assessment," *Acta Psychiatrica Scandinavica*, 53 (1976): 371–386; and R. M. Dawes, "An Unexpected Correlate of Psychopathology Among Children of Schizophrenic Couples," *Journal of Psychiatric Research*, 6 (1968): 201–209.
59. S. Hamilton, M. Rothbart, and R. M. Dawes, "Sex Bias, Diagnosis, and DSM-III," *Sex Roles*, 15 (1986): 279–284.
60. For an interesting paper about the psychological and social correlates of high uric acid that accompany the tendency to develop gout, see S. V. Kasl, G. W. Brooks, and W. L. Rodgers, "Serum Uric Acid and Cholesterol in Achievement Behavior and Motivation," *Journal of the American Medical Association*, 213, no. 7 (1970): 1158–1164, and no. 8 (1970): 1291–1300.
61. A. Siebert, "Should Schizophrenia Be Facilitated Instead of Treated?" paper presented at the Western Psychological Association convention, San Jose, CA, April 1985.
62. L. Thomas, "Chapter 84: Humanities and Science," in L. Thomas, *A Long Line of Cells: Collected Essays* (New York: Viking Penguin, 1990), pp. 345–352, 348.
63. To assure statistical stability of our results, we require a ratio of sample size to number of items or predictors of at least 10 to 1; here, the ratio is 3.1 to 1 *in the wrong direction.* (The fact that only 11 items were retained still leaves the number of items examined equal to 399; 399 − 11 = 388 items have simply been given effective weights of zero.) The 11-item scale was then "cross-validated" [sic] with a new set of 33 offenders but the same 37-person comparison sample, which does not constitute the type of new comparison necessitated when items or variables are chosen in the post hoc manner of the test developer.
64. According to a communication from the APA publication board on February 14, 1991, approximately 30 percent of APA members subscribe to one or more scientific journals. That figure includes research and academic members as well as professional practice members. Since that time, dues have been raised and one journal of the member's choosing is provided along with the increased dues.

CHAPTER 3: PREDICTION AND DIAGNOSIS:
MORE MYTHS OF EXPERTISE

1. P. E. Meehl, "Causes and Effects of My Disturbing Little Book," *Journal of Personality Assessment*, 50 (1986): 370–375, 372–373.
2. 15,509 of 44,901 surveyed, according to a communication from Janet Cole of the American Psychological Association's ODEER Office on February 22, 1991.
3. The principle of Ockham's razor, first proclaimed by William of Ockham in the fourteenth century.
4. P. A. M. Dirac, "The Evolution of the Physicist's Picture of Nature," *Scientific American*, 208 (1963): 45–53.
5. See any encyclopedia description.
6. I. M. Klotz, "The N-Ray Affair," *Scientific American*, 242 (1980): 168–173.
7. W. Revelle, "Personality, Motivation, and Cognitive Performance," in R. Ackerman, R. Kanfer, and R. Cudeck, eds., *Learning and Individual Differences: Abilities, Motivation, and Methodology* (Hillsdale, NJ: Erlbaum, 1989), pp. 297–341.
8. H. J. Einhorn, "Accepting Error to Make Less Error," *Journal of Personality Assessment*, 50 (1986): 387–395.
9. L. T. Hoshmand, and D. E. Polkinghorn, "Refining the Science—Practice Relationship and Professional Training," *American Psychologist*, 47 (1992): 60.
10. W. G. Chase, and H. A. Simon, "The Mind's Eye in Chess," in W. G. Chase, ed., *Visual Information Processing* (London: Academic Press, 1973), p. 215.
11. P. E. Meehl, *Clinical Versus Statistical Prediction: A Theoretical Analysis and Review of the Literature* (Minneapolis: University of Minnesota Press, 1954).
12. J. Sawyer, "Measurement and Prediction, Clinical and Statistical," *Psychological Bulletin*, 66 (1966): 178–200.
13. R. M. Dawes, D. Faust, and P. E. Meehl, "Clinical Versus Actuarial Judgment," *Science*, 243 (1989): 1668–1674.
14. B. Lubin, R. M. Larsen, and J. D. Matarazzo, "Patterns of Psychological Test Usage in the United States: 1935–1982," *American Psychologist*, 39 (1984): 451–454; and C. Piotrowski and J. W. Keller, "Psychological Testing in Outpatient Mental Health Facilities: A National Study," *Professional Psychology: Research and Practice*, 20 (1989): 423–425.
15. See S. R. Hathaway and P. E. Meehl, *An Atlas for the Clinical Use of the MMPI* (Minneapolis: University of Minnesota Press, 1951); and W. G. Dahlstrom, G. S. Welsh, and L. E. Dahlstrom, *An MMPI Handbook: Revised Edition* (Minneapolis: University of Minnesota Press, 1982).
16. L. R. Goldberg, "Simple Models or Simple Processes? Some Research on Clinical Judgments," *American Psychologist*, 23 (1968): 483–496.
17. R. F. Bloom and E. G. Brundage, "Predictions of Success in Elementary School for Enlisted Personnel," in D. B. Stuit, ed., *Personnel Research and Test Development in the Naval Bureau of Personnel* (Princeton, NJ: Princeton University Press, 1947), pp. 233–261.
18. T. M. Gehrlein and R. L. Dipboye, "In Search of Validity in the Selection Interview," poster presented at the second annual convention of the American Psychological Society, Dallas, TX, June 8, 1990.
19. G. F. Dreher, R. A. Ash, and P. Hancock, "The Role of the Traditional

Research Design in Underestimating the Validity of the Employment Interview," *Personnel Psychology*, 41 (1988): 315–327.

20. R. A. DeVaul, F. Jervey, J. A. Chappell, P. Carver, B. Short, and S. O'Keefe, "Medical School Performance of Initially Rejected Students," *Journal of the American Medical Association*, 257 (1957): 47–51.

21. R. M. Milstein, L. Wilkinson, G. N. Burrow, and W. Kessen, "Admission Decisions and Performance During Medical School," *Journal of Medical Education*, 56 (1981): 77–82.

22. S. Oskamp, "Overconfidence in Case Study Judgments," *Journal of Consulting Psychology*, 63 (1965): 81–97.

23. J. S. Carroll, R. L. Winer, D. Coates, J. Galegher, and J. J. Alibrio, "Evaluation, Diagnosis, and Prediction in Parole Decision Making," *Law and Society Review*, 17 (1988): 199–228.

24. D. Gottfredson, L. T. Wilkins, and T. B. Hoffman, *Guidelines for Parole and Sentencing* (Lexington, MA: Lexington Books, 1976).

25. For example, see P. D. Werner, T. L. Rose, J. A. Yesavage, and K. Seeman, "Judgment of Dangerousness in Patients on an Acute Care Unit," *American Journal of Psychiatry*, 142 (1984): 263–266.

26. See J. Monahan, "The Prediction of Violent Behavior: Toward a Second Generation of Theory and Policy," *American Journal of Psychiatry*, 141, (1984): 10–15. For a striking example, see H. J. Steadman, "Follow Up on Baxstrom Patients Returned to Hospitals for the Criminally Insane," *American Journal of Psychiatry*, 130 (1973): 317.

27. R. E. Inwald, "Five Year Follow-up Study of Departmental Terminations as Predicted by Sixteen Pre-employment Psychological Indicators," *Journal of Applied Psychology*, 73 (1988): 703–710.

28. D. A. Leli and S. B. Filskov, "Clinical-Actuarial Detection and Description of Brain Impairment with the W-B Form 1," *Journal of Clinical Psychology*, 37 (1981): 623–629.

29. D. Faust, K. Hart, and T. J. Guilmette, "Pediatric Malingering: The Capacity of Children to Fake Believable Deficits on Neuropsychological Testing," *Journal of Consulting and Clinical Psychology*, 56 (1988): 578–582.

30. D. Faust, K. Hart, T. J. Guilmette, and H. R. Arkes, "Neuropsychologists' Capacity to Detect Adolescent Malingerers," *Professional Psychology: Research and Practice*, 19 (1988): 508–515.

31. E. D. Bigler, "Neuropsychology and Malingering: Comment on Faust, Hart, and Guilmette (1988)," *Journal of Consulting and Clinical Psychology*, 58 (1990): 244–247.

32. T. J. Guilmette, D. Faust, K. Hart, and H. R. Arkes, "A National Survey of Psychologists Who Offer Neuropsychological Services," *Archives of Clinical Neuropsychology*, 5 (1990): 373–392.

33. H. J. Einhorn, "Expert Measurement and Mechanical Combination," *Organizational Behavior and Human Performance*, 7 (1972): 86–106.

34. L. Goldman, E. F. Cook, D. A. Brand, T. H. Lee, G. W. Rouan, M. C. Weisberg, D. A. Acampora, C. Stasiulewicz, J. Walshon, G. Terranova, L. Gottlieb, M. Kobernick, B. Goldstein-Wayne, D. Copen, K. Daley, A. A. Brandt, D. Jones, J. Mellors, and R. Jakubowski, "A Computer Program to Predict Myocardial Infarction in Emergency Department Patients with Chest Pain," *New England Journal of Medicine*, 318 (1988): 797–802.

35. K. L. Lee, D. B. Pryor, F. E. Harrell, R. M. Califf, V. S. Behar, W. L. Floyd, J.

J. Morris, R. A. Waugh, R. E. Whalen, and R. A. Rosati, "Predicting Outcome in Coronary Disease," *American Journal of Medicine*, 80 (1986): 553–560.

36. A. L. Brannen, L. J. Godfrey, and W. E. Goetter, "Prediction of Outcome from Critical Illness: A Comparison of Clinical Judgment with a Prediction Rule," *Archives of Internal Medicine*, 19 (1989): 1083–1086.

37. G. C. Sutton, "How Accurate Is Computer-Aided Diagnosis?" *Lancet*, October 14, 1989, pp. 905–908.

38. W. H. Beaver, *Empirical Research in Accounting: Selective Studies* (Chicago: University of Chicago, Graduate School of Business, Institute of Professional Accounting, 1966); and E. B. Deacon, "A Discriminant Analysis of Prediction of Business Failure," *Journal of Accounting Research*, 10 (1972): 167–179.

39. R. C. Blattberg and S. J. Hoch, "Database Models and Managerial Intuitions: 50 percent Model 50 percent Manager," *Management Science*, 36 (1990): 887–899.

40. See W. A., Knaus, D. P. Wagner, and J. Lynn, "Short-term Mortality Predictions for Critically Ill Hospitalized Adults: Science and Ethics," *Science*, 254 (1991): 389–394.

41. P. E. Meehl, "Causes and Effects of My Disturbing Little Book," *Journal of Personality Assessment*, 50 (1986): 370–375.

42. D. Faust and J. Ziskin, "The Expert Witness in Psychology and Psychiatry," *Science*, 241 (1988): 31–35.

43. R. D. Fowler and J. D. Matarazzo, "Psychologists and Psychiatrists as Expert Witnesses," *Science*, 241 (1988): 1143–1144.

44. J. Bales, "APA Rebuts Criticism of Clinical Witnesses," *APA Monitor*, September 1988, p. 17.

45. R. M. Dawes, D. Faust, and P. E. Meehl, "Clinical Versus Actuarial Judgment," *Science*, 243 (1989): 1668–1674.

46. J. Shanteau, "Psychological Characteristics and Strategies of Expert Decision Makers," *Acta Psychologica*, 68 (1988): 203–215.

47. L. R. Goldberg, "The Effectiveness of Clinicians' Judgments: The Diagnosis of Organic Brain Damage from the Bender Gestalt Test," *Journal of Consulting Psychology*, 23 (1959): 25–33.

48. R. M. Dawes, "Comment: Quandary: Correlation Coefficients and Contexts," forthcoming in L. Montada, S. H. Filipp, and M. J. Lerner, eds., *Life Crises and Experiences of Loss in Adulthood* (Hillsdale, NJ: Erlbaum, 1993), pp. 521–529.

49. Bigler, "Neuropsychology and Malingering."

50. The statistical prediction is superior, but neither prediction is very good in most studies—so, as a dean of an education school once objected, "twice nothing is nothing." He made that remark after hearing the results of a study I had conducted demonstrating that a unit-weighted average based on three characteristics of applicants to graduate school (standardized undergraduate grade point average, standardized Graduate Record Examination scores and a standardized rating of the selectivity of the applicant's undergraduate institution) predicted later faculty ratings with a correlation coefficient of .48, whereas the prior average ratings of the admissions committee members predicted it with a correlation of only .19. See R. M. Dawes, "A Case Study of Graduate Admissions: Application of Three Principles of Human Decision Making," *American Psychologist*, 26 (1971): 180–188.

51. See R. M. Dawes, *Rational Choice in an Uncertain World* (San Diego: Harcourt Brace Jovanovich, 1988), chap. 11.
52. M. J. Lerner, "Integrating Societal and Psychological Rules of Entitlement: The Basic Task of Each Social Actor and Fundamental Problem for the Social Sciences," *Social Justice Research*, 1 (1987): 107–125. I also recommend his excellent *The Belief in a Just World: A Fundamental Delusion* (New York: Plenum Press, 1980).
53. S. S. Wilks, "Weighting Systems for Linear Functions of Correlated Variables When There Is No Dependent Variable," *Psychometrika*, 8 (1938): 23–30; R. M. Dawes and B. S. Corrigan, "Linear Models in Decision Making," *Psychological Bulletin*, 81 (1974): 95–106; H. Wainer, "Estimating Coefficients in Linear Models: It Don't Make No Nevermind," *Psychological Bulletin*, 83 (1978): 312–317; H. Wainer, "On the Sensitivity of Regression and Regressors," *Psychological Bulletin*, 85 (1978): 267–273; and D. A. Bloch and L. E. Moses, "Non-Optimally Weighted Least Squares," *American Statistician*, 42 (1988): 50–53.
54. A. Tversky and D. Kahneman, "Judgments Under Uncertainty: Heuristics and Biases," *Science*, 185 (1974): 1124–1131; R. Hamil, T. D. C. Wilson, and R. E. Nisbett, "Insensitivity to Sample Bias: Generalizing from Atypical Cases," *Journal of Personality and Social Psychology*, 39 (1980): 578–589; and Dawes, *Rational Choice*, chap. 6.
55. Dawes, *Rational Choice*, chap. 5; and A. Tversky and D. Kahneman, "Judgments of and by Representativeness," in D. Kahneman, P. Slovic, and A. Tversky, eds., *Judgments Under Uncertainty: Heuristics and Biases* (London: Cambridge University Press, 1982).
56. P. E. Meehl, "Why I Do Not Attend Case Conferences," in *Psychodiagnosis: Selected Papers* (New York: Norton, 1973).
57. D. Faust, "Declarations Versus Investigations: The Case for the Special Reasoning Abilities and Capacities of the Expert Witness in Psychology/Psychiatry," *Journal of Psychiatry and Law*, 13 (1986): 33–59.
58. See F. L. Schmidt, J. E. Hunter, K. Pearlman, H. R. Hirsh, P. R. Sackett, N. Schmidt, M. L. Tenopyr, J. Kehoe, and S. Zedeck, "Forty Questions About Validity Generalization and Meta-analysis with Commentaries," *Personnel Psychology*, 38 (1985): 697–798.
59. R. M. Dawes, "A Case Study of Graduate Admissions: Application of Three Principles of Human Decision Making," *American Psychologist*, 26 (1971): 180–188.
60. Dawes and Corrigan, "Linear Models in Decision Making."
61. L. R. Goldberg, "Admission to the Ph.D. Program in the Department of Psychology at the University of Oregon," *American Psychologist*, 32 (1977): 663–668.
62. Dawes, *Rational Choice*, p. 219.

CHAPTER 4: EXPERIENCE: THE MYTH
OF EXPANDING EXPERTISE

1. American Psychological Association, *Report of the Task Force on the Evaluation of Education, Training, and Service in Psychology* (Washington, DC: American Psychological Association, 1982).
2. H. N. Garb, "Clinical Judgment, Clinical Training, and Professional Experience," *Psychological Bulletin*, 105 (1989): 387–392.
3. Ibid.
4. D. Faust, T. J. Guilmette, K. Hart, H. R. Arkes, F. J. Fishburne, and L. Davey, "Neuropsychologists' Training Experience, and Judgmental Accuracy," *Archives of Clinical Neuropsychology*, 3 (1988): 145–163, 145.
5. R. M. Dawes, "Experience and Validity of Clinical Judgment: The Illusory Correlation," *Behavioral Sciences and the Law*, 7 (1989): 457–467. Much of the material presented in this chapter of the book may also be found in this 1989 article.
6. B. Franklin, *Poor Richard's Almanac.* (1757; New York: David McKay, 1973), p. 31.
7. N. J. Ehrlich, "Toward a Taxonomy of Automobile Driving," *Perceptual and Motor Skills*, 22 (1966): 759–762.
8. For a discussion of such common ground and its importance in human communication, see H. H. Clark, R. Schreuder, and S. Buttrick, "Common Ground and the Understanding of Demonstrative Reference," *Journal of Verbal Learning and Verbal Behavior*, 22 (1983): 245–258.
9. F. Restle, "Selection of Strategy and Cue Learning," *Psychological Review*, 69 (1962): 329–343; and G. Bower and T. Trabasso, "Reversals Prior to Solution in Concept Identification Tasks," *Journal of Experimental Psychology*, 63 (1963): 438–443.
10. D. E. Dulany and D. C. O'Connell, "Does Partial Reinforcement Disassociate Verbal Rules and the Behavior They Might Be Presumed to Control?" *Journal of Verbal Learning and Verbal Behavior*, 2 (1963): 361–372.
11. See, for example, H. Wakefield and R. Underwager, "Sexual Abuse Allegations in Divorce and Custody Disputes," forthcoming in *Behavioral Science and the Law*; and R. M. Dawes, *Rational Choice in an Uncertain World* (San Diego: Harcourt Brace Jovanovich, 1988), chap. 6.
12. R. M. Dawes, D. Faust, and P. E. Meehl, "Clinical Versus Actuarial Judgment," *Science*, 243 (1989): 1668–1674.
13. Again, the reason for research involving randomized comparisons is to provide these hypothetical counterfactuals as best possible. In custody cases a rational procedure would have been to do the research *first* and *then* apply its results to an actual setting, rather than make the judgments in an applied setting first and subsequently argue that one can tell from "experience" that such judgments were valid without ever having conducted the research required to reach that conclusion. For example, we could easily *test* mental health experts' judgments in custody cases by randomly choosing cases to be judged with or without these experts' input and then evaluating—on a blind basis—whether the outcomes for the children of cases involving expert input were better than the outcomes for the children in the control cases. Or if we believe that such experimentation would be inappropriate in a legal context, we could at the very least evaluate whether outcomes in instances where the experts made a very strong or confident recommendation were superior to

those in which their recommendations were more tentative, if there are in fact a reasonable number of such recommendations to evaluate them.

14. Reported in T. Morganthau, S. Agrest, N. F. Greenberg, S. Doherty, and G. Raine, "Abandoned," *Newsweek*, January 6, 1986, pp. 14–19.

15. C. M. Harding, J. Zubin, and J. S. Strauss, "Chronicity in Schizophrenia: Fact, Partial Fact, or Artifact?" *Hospital and Community Psychiatry*, 38 (1987): 477–486, quote on p. 481.

16. See H. J. Einhorn and R. Hogarth, "Confidence in Judgment: Persistence of the Illusion of Validity," *Psychological Review*, 85 (1978): 395–416.

17. J. C. Naylor and E. A. Schenck, "The Influence of Cue Redundancy upon the Human Inference Process for Tasks of Varying Degrees of Predictability," *Organizational Behavior and Human Performance*, 3 (1968): 47–61; and J. C. Naylor and R. D. Clark, "Intuitive Inference Strategies in Interval Learning Tasks as a Function of Validity Magnitude and Sign," *Organizational Behavior and Human Performance*, 3 (1968): 378–399.

18. H. N. Garb, "Clinical Judgment, Clinical Training, and Professional Experience," *Psychological Bulletin*, 105 (1989): 387–396.

19. T. Szasz, *The Myth of Mental Illness: Foundations of a Theory of Personal Conduct*, rev. ed. (New York: Harper and Row, 1974).

20. R. Brown, "Schizophrenia, Language and Reality," *American Psychologist*, 28 (1973): 395–403.

21. P. E. Meehl and A. Rosen, "Antecedent Probability and the Efficacy of Psychometric Signs, Patterns, or Cutting Scores," *Psychological Bulletin*, 52 (1955): 194–201; G. B. Melton, "Bringing Psychology to the Legal System," *American Psychologist*, 42 (1987): 488–495; K. R. Murphy, "Detecting Infrequent Deception, *Journal of Applied Psychology*, 72 (1987): 611–614; R. M. Dawes, "A Note on Base Rates and Psychometric Efficiency," *Journal of Consulting Psychology*, 26 (1963): 422–424; and R. M. Dawes, "Representative Thinking in Clinical Judgment," *Clinical Psychology Review*, 6 (1986): 425–441.

22. A. Tversky and D. Kahneman, "Judgments Under Uncertainty: Heuristics and Biases," *Science*, 185 (1974): 1124–1131; and A. Tversky and D. Kahneman, "Judgments of and by Representativeness," in D. Kahneman, P. Slovic, and A. Tversky, eds., *Judgments Under Uncertainty: Heuristics and Biases* (London: Cambridge University Press, 1982).

23. L. Furby, M. R. Weinrot, and L. Blackshaw, "Sex Offender Recidivism," *Psychological Bulletin*, 105 (1989): 3–30.

24. See Einhorn and Hogarth, "Confidence in Judgment," pp. 395–416.

25. See, for example, S. Strack and J. C. Coyne, "Confirmation of Dysphoria: Shared and Private Reactions to Depression, *"Journal of Personality and Social Psychology*, 44 (1983): 798–806.

26. F. C. Bartlett, *Remembering: A Study in Experimental Social Psychology* (Cambridge: Cambridge University Press, 1932).

27. R. W. Pearson, M. Ross, and R. M. Dawes, "Personal Recall and the Limits of Retrospective Questions in Surveys" [forthcoming], in J. Tanur, ed., *Questions About Questions: Meaning, Memory, Expression, and Social Interaction in Surveys* (New York: Russell Sage Foundation), pp. 65–94.

28. B. Fischhoff, "Hindsight ≠ Foresight: The Effect of Outcome Knowledge on Judgment and Uncertainty," *Journal of Experimental Psychology: Human Perception and Performance*, 104 (1975): 288–299. B. Fischhoff, "For Those Condemned to Study the Past: Reflections on Historical Judgment," in

Kahneman, Slovic, and Tversky, *Judgment Under Uncertainty.*
29. C. Camerer, G. Loewenstein, and M. Weber, "The Curse of Knowledge in Economic Settings: An Experimental Analysis," *Journal of Political Economy,* 97 (1989): 1232–1254.
30. E. R. Loftus, K. Donders, H. G. Hoffman, and J. W. Schooler, "Creating New Memories That Are Quickly Assessed and Confidently Held," *Memory and Cognition,* 17 (1989): 607–616.

CHAPTER 5: LICENSING:
THE MYTH OF PROTECTING THE PUBLIC

1. American Association of State Psychology Boards, *Entry Requirements for Professional Practice of Psychology: A Guide for Students and Faculty* (undated, obtained in 1990) American Association of State Psychology Boards, P. O. Box 4389, Montgomery, AL 36101.
2. American Psychological Association, Office of Demographic, Employment and Educational Research, *1989 Salaries in Psychology* (American Psychological Association 1990), table 5, pp. 18–19.
3. R. G. Frank and J. R. Lave, "The Effect of Benefit Design on the Length of Stay of Medicaid Psychiatric Patients," *The Journal of Human Resources,* 21 (1986): 321–337.
4. E. Goffman, *Asylums* (Garden City, NY: Doubleday and Co., 1961).
5. D. L. Rosenhan, "On Being Sane in Insane Places," *Science,* 179 (1973): 250–258.
6. Ibid., p. 251.
7. Ibid., p. 256.
8. See B. Lubin, R. M. Larsen, and J. D. Matarazzo, "Patterns of Psychological Test Usage in the United States," *American Psychologist,* 39 (1984): 451–454. Also see C. Piotrowski, and J. K. Keller, "Psychological Testing in Outpatient Mental Health Facilities," *Professional Psychology: Research and Practice,* 20 (1989): 423–425.
9. American Psychological Association, "Ethical Principles of Psychologists (Amended June 2, 1989)," *American Psychologist,* 45 (1990): 390–395, 390–391.
10. According to a communication from the APA publication board on February 14, 1991, approximately 30 percent of APA members subscribe to one or more scientific journals. That figure includes research and academic members as well as professional practice members. Since that time, dues have been raised and one journal of the member's choosing is provided along with the increased dues.
11. American Psychological Association, *Casebook on Ethical Principles of Psychologists* (Washington, DC: American Psychological Association, 1987).
12. U.S. Department of Justice, National Institute of Justice, *NIJ Reports,* no. 207 (January/February 1988), p. 4.

13. See the APA's own "Statement on the Use of Anatomically Detailed Dolls in Forensic Evaluations," adopted by its Council of Representatives on February 8, 1991: "Neither the dolls nor their use are standardized or accompanied by normative data. There are currently no uniform standards for conducting interviews with the dolls."

14. Ibid.: "Therefore, in conformity with the *Ethical Principles of Psychologists*, psychologists who undertake the doll-centered assessment of sexual abuse should be competent to use these techniques."

15. S. C. Hayes, "An Interview with Lee Sechrest: The Courage to Say 'We Do Not Know How,'" *APS Observer*, 2, no. 4 (1989): 8–10.

16. Ibid., p. 9.

17. A. H. Roberts, "Biofeedback: Research, Training, and Clinical Roles," *American Psychologist*, 40 (1985): 938–941.

18. N. E. Miller, "Learning of Vascular and Glandular Responses," *Science*, 163 (1969): 434–445.

19. J. Kamiya, "Operant Control of EEG Alpha Rhythm and Some of Its Reported Effects on Consciousness," in C. Tart ed., *Altered States of Consciousness* (New York: John Wiley, 1969).

20. Roberts, "Biofeedback," p. 939.

21. Ibid.

22. J. Morrow, and R. Wolff, "Wired for a Miracle," *Health*, 23 (1991): 64–69, 84.

23. Roberts, "Biofeedback."

24. Ibid., p. 939.

25. Ibid.

26. Ibid., pp. 939–940.

27. Ibid., p. 940.

28. See Lubin, Larsen, and Matarazzo, "Patterns of Psychological Test Usage," and Piotrowski and Keller, "Psychological Testing."

29. Ibid.

30. Ibid.

31. L. J. Chapman and J. P. Chapman, "Associatively Based Illusory Correlation as a Source of Psychodiagnostic Folklore," in L. Goodstein and R. Lanyon, eds., *Readings in Personality Assessment* (New York: John Wiley, 1971).

32. L. R. Goldberg, "Objective Diagnostic Tests and Measures," *Annual Review of Psychology*, 25 (1974): 343–366.

33. J. E. Exner, Jr., *The Rorschach: A Comprehensive System*, 2nd ed., vol. 1 (New York: John Wiley, 1986). Also see a review of Rorschach "validity" by K. C. H. Parker, R. K. Hanson, J. Hunsley, "MMPI, Rorschach, and the WAIS: A Meta-analytic Comparison of Reliability, Stability, and Validity," *Psychological Bulletin*, 103 (1988): 367–373. The six studies indicating validity of the Rorschach evaluate such hypothetical constructs as "adaptive regression" and "developmental level" of those tested. Even the most cursory reading of the articles, however, reveals that the actual assessment of these constructs is based on form level—that is, the degree to which what the subjects see in the blots can be seen by others who are presumably normal (that is, psychologists).

34. F. C. Shontz and P. Green, "Trends in Research on the Rorschach: Review and Recommendations," *Applied and Preventive Psychology*, 1 (1992): 149–156, 150.

35. Ibid., p. 152.

36. T. C. Wade and T. B. Baker, "Opinions and Use of Psychological Tests," *American Psychologist*, 32 (1977): 874–882, 874.
37. T. A. Widiger and M. Schilling, "Towards a Construct Validation of the Rorschach," *Journal of Personality Assessment*, 44 (1980): 450–459, 450.
38. The materials quoted in this section have been taken from the second through the eighth *Mental Measurement Yearbooks*, all edited by Oscar K. Burros. The second and third were published in New Brunswick, NJ, by Rutgers University Press; the fourth through the eighth were published in Highland Park, NJ, by Gryphon Press; the years were 1949, 1953, 1959, 1965, 1972, and 1978. Each yearbook in which the Rorschach was reviewed includes at least one positive and one negative review. The positive reviews cite *possible* validity and clinical use; the negative reviews cite studies that fail to confirm the possibilities that have been suggested— often, ironically, in previous "positive" reviews. The theme of the positive reviews across the years is a repeated one of "Well, the studies indicate that the Rorschach doesn't do this, so it must do that." There is a fascinating alternation between these reviewers' proposing that the content of what is seen is important and their proposing that the structural characteristics (size, use of color, movement) of what is seen are important. Any current recent claims for Rorschach validity—beyond its use as a disguised intelligence test or as a method of evaluating overall aberrance on the basis of seeing many percepts that others cannot—must be viewed in the light of decades of negative evidence.
39. L. J. Cronbach, "Assessment of Individual Differences," *Annual Review of Psychology*, 7 (Stanford, CA: Annual Reviews, 1956): 173–196, quote on 184.
40. P. Goldenthal, S. N. Berk, J. I. Eidelson, L. Knauss, and J. F. McBreaty, "Ethical Issues in Child Custody Evaluations," *Pennsylvania Psychologist Quarterly* (February 1991): 14–15, 15.
41. J. Ziskin and D. Faust "Coping With Psychiatric and Psychological Testimony, 4th ed. (Marina del Rey, CA: Law and Psychology Press, 1988).
42. P. E. Meehl, "Psychology: Does Our Heterogeneous Subject Matter Have Any Unity?" *Minnesota Psychologist* (Summer 1986): 3–9, 4.
43. For a good example of definitional ambiguity when attempting to summarize the results of many studies, see A. Browne and D. Finkelhor, "Impact of Child Sexual Abuse: A Review of the Research," *Psychological Bulletin*, 99 (1986): 66–77.
44. I have witnessed such interviews on television, for example in mid-April 1991 on the CBS *Morning News Show*.
45. W. Maltz, "Adult Survivors of Incest: How to Help Them Overcome the Trauma," *Medical Aspects of Human Sexuality* (December 1990): 42–47.
46. D. Rabinowitz, "From the Mouths of Babies to a Jail Cell: Child Abuse and the Abuse of Judgment: A Case Study," *Harper's* May 1990, pp. 52–63. Also see L. Manshel, *Nap Time: The True Story of Sexual Abuse in a Suburban Day-Care Center* (New York: Zebra Books, Kensington Publishing Co., 1991). Unlike Dorothy Rabinowitz, Lisa Manshel is totally convinced that the children were abused in the manner alleged *despite the fact that every single child she describes (with pseudonyms) originally denied that any abuse occurred*—Evan on page 15, Paul on page 16, Sean on page 17, Joey on page 26, Allison on page 36, Nina on page 38, Lucy on page 39, Robert on page 43, Julie on page 61, Kevin on page 68, Lewis on page 78, and Lou on page 125.

For empirical research evidence that children can in fact recount experiences that never occurred, see S. J. Ceci and M. Bruck, "Suggestibility of the Child Witness: A Historical Review and Synthesis," *Psychological Review, 113* (1993): 403–439. This research is also summarized in D. Goleman, "Studies Reveal Suggestibility of Very Young Children, the *New York Times*, June 11, 1993. One of the studies reported did in fact involve sexual content, specifically whether or not a genital examination was included in a physical exam. Thirty-eight percent of children not given a genital examination were led to state that they had been given one—in this case through the use of anatomically detailed dolls, an interview method to be discussed shortly.

47. R. D. Hicks, "Police Pursuit of Satanic Crimes," *Skeptical Inquirer*, 14 (1990): 276–286 (part I), 378–389 (part II).

48. J. F. Victor, "Satanic Cult 'Survivor' Stories," *Skeptical Inquirer*, 15 (1991): 274–280.

49. Rabinowitz and Manshel agree about the nature of the accusation and the facts of the subsequent trial of Kelly Michaels, the accused abuser, although they reach different conclusions concerning her innocence. Also see D. Nathan, "Victim or Victimizer: Was Kelly Michaels Unjustly Convicted?" *Village Voice*, August 2, 1988, pp. 31–39.

50. U. Neisser, "Snapshots or Benchmarks?" in U. Neisser, ed., *Memory Observed: Remembering in Natural Settings: Selections and Commentary by Ulric Neisser* (San Francisco: W. H. Freeman, 1982), pp. 43–48, example p. 45.

51. F. C. Bartlett, *Remembering: A Study in Experimental and Social Psychology* (Cambridge: Cambridge University Press, 1932); and R. W. Pearson, M. Ross, and R. M. Dawes, "Personal Recall and the Limits of Retrospective Questions in Surveys," J. Tanur ed., *Questions About Questions: Meaning, Memory, Expression, and Social Interaction in Surveys* (New York: Sage Press, in press).

52. R. Underwager and H. Wakefield, *The Real World of Child Interrogations*. (Springfield, IL: Charles Thomas, 1990).

53. R. Reinhold, "After Seven Years, Not Guilty," *Pittsburgh Post-Gazette*, 63 (January 19, 1990): 1–2.

54. The list is combined from two in Underwager and Wakefield, *Real World*. Many of these same symptoms appear as those of suffering from repressed memories of childhood abuse, according to Maltz, "Adult Survivors of Incest."

55. See Underwager and Wakefield, *Real World*, p. 27.

56. Referenced in B. W. Boat and M. D. Everson, "Interviewing Children with Anatomical Dolls," *Child Welfare*, 67 (1988): 337–352.

57. S. White and G. Santilli, "A Review of Clinical Practices and Research Data on Anatomical Dolls," *Journal of Interpersonal Violence*, 3 (1988): 430–442.

58. G. M. Realmuto, J. B. Jensen, and S. Wescoe, "Specificity and Sensitivity of Sexually Anatomically Correct Dolls in Substantiating Abuse: A Pilot Study," *Journal of the American Academy of Child and Adolescent Psychiatry* 29 (1990): 743–746.

59. G. Wolfner, D. Faust, and R. M. Dawes, "The Use of Anatomically Detailed Dolls in Sexual Abuse Evaluations: The State of the Science," *Applied and Preventive Psychology*, 2 (1993): 1–11.

60. See, for example, A. B. Sivan, D. P. Schor, G. K. Koeppl, and L. D. Noble, "Interaction of Normal Children with Anatomical Dolls," *Child*

Abuse and Neglect, 12 (1988): 295–304; D. Glaser and C. Collins, "The Response of Young, Non-sexually Abused Children to Anatomically Correct Dolls," *Journal of Child Clinical Psychology*, 30 (1989): 547–560; M. D. Everson and B. W. Boat, "Sexualized Play Among Young Children: Implications for the Use of Anatomical Dolls in Sexual Abuse Evaluations," *Journal of the American Academy of Child and Adolescent Psychiatry*, 29 (1990): 736–742.

61. American Psychological Association, "Statement on the Use of Anatomically Detailed Dolls in Forensic Evaluations," APA Council of Representatives, February 8, 1991.

62. American Medical Association, Council on Ethical and Judicial Affairs, *Current Opinions* (Chicago: American Medical Association, 1989). On the polygraph, see American Medical Association, AMA *Policy Compendium: Current Policies of the AMA House of Delegates through the 1988 Interim Meeting* (Chicago: American Medical Association, 1988), p. 172.

63. Supposedly an accurate conclusion can be reached by combining a cue with no known incremental validity with other cues whose accuracy it does not increment.

64. T. J. Horner, M. J. Guyer, and N. M. Kalter, "Prediction, Prevention, and Clinical Expertise in Child Custody Cases in Which Allegations of Child Sexual Abuse Have Been Made: III. Studies of Expert Opinion Formation," *Family Law Quarterly*, 26 (1992): 141–170.

65. Understanding that reliability is a necessary—although not sufficient—condition for validity, psychiatrists and professional psychologists have developed diagnostic manuals that are meant to result in consistent diagnoses on the basis of a psychiatric interview. People can be trained to make the same diagnoses. The validity of the diagnoses, however, is determined by the degree to which they form part of a theoretical understanding of the problem, allowing us to predict and intervene to make desired changes. That is what's lacking. See, for example, D. Faust and R. A. Miner, "The Empiricist and His New Clothes: DSM-III in Perspective," *American Journal of Psychiatry*, 143 (1986): 962–967.

66. R. Klein, *In re Hawaii v. McKellar*. Criminal No. 85-0553 (Circuit Court, First Circuit Court Hawaii), Order Granting Defense Motion, January 15, 1986.

67. Guidelines for the Clinical Evaluation of Child and Adolescent Sexual Abuse. American Academy of Child and Adolescent Psychiatry, approved by Council of the AACAP, June 10, 1988, modified December 14, 1990.

68. For a discussion of the courts' rulings, especially in *Youngberg v. Romeo*, see D. N. Bersoff, "Judicial Deference to Nonlegal Decisionmakers: Imposing Simplistic Solutions on Problems of Cognitive Complexity in Mental Disability Law," *SMU Law Review*, 46 (1992): 329–372.

69. D. Cartwright, "Determinants of Scientific Progress: The Case of Research on the Risky Shift," *American Psychologist*, 28 (1973): 222–231.

70. The reaction of the children, many of them now adolescents, to the jury verdict of innocence in the McMartin case is described in Reinhold, "After Seven Years, Not Guilty." See this or any other newspaper account.

71. K. Krajick, "Justice: Genetics in the Courtroom," *Newsweek*, January 11, 1993, p. 64.

72. E. Fiore, *Encounters: A Psychologist Reveals Case Studies of Abduction by*

Extraterrestrials (New York: Bantam Doubleday Dell Publishing Co., 1989). Fiore has a license to practice psychology in California, issued 6/26/74 and good through 9/30/92.

73. Ibid., in unpaginated preface.
74. Ibid., p. 61.
75. Attempts to show that memory is less malleable under hypnosis than in the normal working state have not been successful. See, for example, P. W. Sheehan and D. Stalham, "Hypnosis, the Timing of Its Introduction, and Acceptance of Misleading Information," *Journal of Abnormal Psychology*, 98 (1989): 170–176.
76. J. E. Mack, "Mental Health Professionals and the Roper Poll," in B. Hopkins, D. M. Jacobs, and R. Westrum, *The UFO Abduction Syndrome: A Report on Unusual Experiences Associated with [sic] UFO Abductions, The Roper Organization's Survey of 5,947 Adult Americans* (Las Vegas: Bigelow Holding Co., 1992), p. 7.
77. Ibid., p. 8.
78. Ibid., p. 15.
79. Ibid., p. 50.
80. See S. J. Gould, "This View of Life," *Natural History*, 102 (1993): 14–21, in which he discusses paleontologists' "increasing sensitivity to the many elements of randomness and contingency that make any particular (evolutionary) pathway—including the route to *Homo sapiens*—utterly unpredictable and unlikely ever to arise again if the tape of life could be replayed."
81. H. Wakefield and R. Underwager, "Recovered Memories of Alleged Sexual Abuse: Lawsuits Against Parents," *Behavioral Sciences and the Law* (in press).
82. E. Bass and L. Davis, *The Courage to Heal* (New York: Harper and Row, 1988), p. 22.
83. Ibid.
84. B. F. Loftus, "The Reality of Repressed Memories," *American Psychologist* 44 (1993): 518–537. Also see P. Monaghan, "Professor of Psychology Stokes a Controversy on the Reliability and Repression of Memories," *Chronicle of Higher Education*, September 23, 1992, p. A9.
85. National Center on Child Abuse and Neglect, Children's Bureau, Administration for Children, Youth, and Families, Office of Human Development Services, *Executive Summary: Study of National Incidence and Prevalence of Child Abuse and Neglect: 1988* (U.S. Department of Health and Human Services). Also see A. J. Sedlak, *Technical Amendment to the Study Findings—National Incidence and Prevalence of Child Abuse and Neglect: 1988* (Westat, 1988).
86. L. M. Williams, "Adult Memories of Childhood Abuse: Preliminary Findings from a Longitudinal Study," *The APSC Advisor* (Summer, 1992): 19–21.
87. J. L. Herman and E. Schatzow, "Recovery and Verification of Memories of Childhood Sexual Trauma," *Psychoanalytic Psychology*, 4 (1987): 1–14.
88. But they are supposed to "evaluate" parents before reaching a "decision." Again, see Guidelines for the Clinical Evaluation of Child and Adolescent Sexual Abuse.
89. C. Wasserman, "FMS: The Backlash Against Survivors," *Sojourner*, November 1992, p. 18.
90. Ibid.

91. Wakefield and Underwager, "Recovered Memories."
92. American Psychological Association, "Model Act for State Licensure of Psychologists," *American Psychologist*, 42 (1987): 686–703, quoted on pp. 697 and 700.

CHAPTER 6: A PLETHORA OF EXPERTS AND WHAT TO DO ABOUT THEM

1. L. Whiting, "State Comparison of Laws Regulating Social Work," National Association of Social Workers, May 1992.
2. H. Wakefield and R. Underwager, "Uncovering Memories of Alleged Sexual Abuse: The Therapists Who Do It." *Issues in Child Abuse Accusations*, 4 (1992): 197–213.
3. See G. W. Albee, "No More Rock Scrubbing," *Scientist Practitioner*, 1 (1991): 26–27.
4. See R. C. Kessler and W. J. Magee, "Childhood Family Violence and Adult Depression," available from Ronald C. Kessler, Institute for Social Research, University of Michigan, Box 1247, Ann Arbor, MI 48106-1248.
5. See the work of Bernard Weiner, such as his *An Attributional Theory of Motivation and Emotion* (New York: Springer-Verlag, 1986) and his "On Sin Versus Sickness: A Theory of Perceived Responsibility and Social Motivation," *American Psychologist* (in press).
6. See, for example, L. R. Caporael, "Ergotism: The Satan Loosed in Salem?" *Science*, 192 (1976): 21–26.
7. See, for example, "Satanic Ritual Abuse: The Current State of Knowledge," *Journal of Psychology and Theology*, 20, no. 3 (Special Issue, Fall 1992). For accounts of investigations, see K. V. Lanning, *Investigator's Guide to Allegations of "Ritual" Child Abuse* (Quantico, VA: National Center for the Analysis of Violent Crime, 1992), available from FBI Academy, Quantico, VA 22135, (800) 634-4097, free, in single copies. For a more general account, see former police officer R. D. Hicks, *In Pursuit of Satan: The Police and the Occult* (Buffalo, NY: Prometheus Books, 1991). For a sociological account, see J. S. Victor, *Rumors of Evil: The Satanic Scare and the Creation of Imaginary Deviance* (Peru, Il: Open Court, 1993).
8. At least one clinical psychologist believes in the existence of "breeders" of two million babies a year to be sacrificed—and that the Satanists are in control of the police and FBI. See B. Siano, "All the Babies You Can Eat," *Humanist*, March/April 1993, pp. 40–41. For another bizarre belief among professionals—that satanists are poisoning not the wells but the air-conditioning systems of the Los Angeles County Hall of Administration with diazonon—see J. Okerblom and M. Sauer, "Probe of 'Ritual-Abuse' Therapy Urged," *San Diego Union-Tribune*, January 18, 1993, pp. B1, B10.
9. See, for example, J. E. Singleton, "Enemy Is Domestic for Women," *USA Today*, August 6, 1992, p. 12A.
10. J. Breuer and S. Freud, *Studies on Hysteria*. Translated from the German and

edited by James Strachey in collaboration with Anna Freud, assisted by Alix Strachey and Alan Tyson (New York: Basic Books, by arrangement with the Hogarth Press, Ltd., first published in 1957).

11. Quoted in L. Freeman, *The Story of Anna O.* (New York: Walker and Company, 1972), pp. 174–175.
12. Breuer and Freud, *Studies on Hysteria*, p. 21.
13. Ibid., p. 22.
14. Ibid., p. 36.
15. Ibid., p. 21.
16. Ibid., p. 31.
17. M. Rosenbaum and M. Muroff, eds., *Anna O.: Fourteen Contemporary Reinterpretations* (New York: The Free Press, 1984).
18. Ibid., p. xi.
19. Ibid.
20. J. P. Spiegel, "The Case of Anna O.: Cultural Aspects," in Rosenbaum and Muroff, *Anna O*, pp. 52–58, 57.
21. M. A. Kaplan, "Anna O. and Bertha Pappenheim: An Historical Perspective," in Rosenbaum and Muroff, *Anna O.*, pp. 101–117.
22. Referenced in M. Rosenbaum, "Anna O. (Bertha Pappenheim): Her History," in Rosenbaum and Muroff, *Anna O.*, p. 13.
23. Breuer and Freud, *Studies on Hysteria*, p. 26.
24. Ibid., p. 30.
25. R. Berkow, *The Merck Manual of Diagnosis and Therapy, Fourteenth Edition* (Rahway, NJ: Merck Sharp and Dohme Research Laboratories, 1982), p. 1426.
26. Referenced in Rosenbaum, "Anna O. (Bertha Pappenheim)," p. 7.
27. Phrase attributed to psychiatrist Judith Herman in J. Hawkins, "Rowers on the River Styx," *Harvard Magazine*, 93 (March–April 1991): 43–52.
28. Reported in Rosenbaum, "Anna O. (Bertha Pappenheim)," p. 7.
29. Breuer and Freud, *Studies on Hysteria*, p. 21.
30. W. Freeman and J. W. Watts, *Psychosurgery* (Springfield IL: Charles C. Thomas, 1942).
31. A. Kucharski, "History of Frontal Lobotomy in the United States, 1935–1955," *Neurosurgery*, 14 (1984): 765–772, quote on p. 767.
32. V. Follette, "An Ecological Approach to Treatment: An Interview with Scott Henggeler," *Scientist Practitioner*, 3 (1993): 10–17.

CHAPTER 7: WHY THE MYTHS ARE BELIEVED

1. R. A. Smith, "Advocacy, Interpretation and Influence in the U.S. Congress," *American Political Science Review*, 78 (1964): 44–63.
2. T. W. Adorno, E. Frenkel-Brunswick, D. J. Levinson, and R. N. Sanford, *The Authoritarian Personality* (New York: Harper and Row, 1950).
3. S. Milgram, "Behavioral Study of Obedience," *Journal of Abnormal and Social Psychology*, 67 (1963): 371–378.
4. L. Hasher, D. Goldstein, and T. Toppino, "Frequency and the Conference of Referential Validity," *Journal of Verbal Learning and Verbal Behavior*, 16

(1977): 107–112; and I. Begg, V. Armour, and T. Kerr, "On Believing What We Remember," *Canadian Journal of Behavioral Science*, 17 (1985): 199–214.

5. See, for example, S. P. Stich, and R. E. Nisbett, "Justification and the Psychology of Human Reasoning," *Philosophy of Science*, 47 (1980): 188–202.

6. John Philpot Curran, Speech Upon the Rights of Election (1790), in J. Bartlett, *Familiar Quotations* (Boston: Little, Brown, and Co., 1904), p. 855.

7. See, for example, D. Yankelovitch, "Public Attitudes Toward People with Chronic Mental Illness," prepared for the Robert Wood Johnson Program on Mental Illness, April 1990. The perception is accurate, especially concerning children. See, for example, V. R. Fuchs and D. M. Reklis, "America's Children: Perspectives and Policy Options," *Science*, 255 (1992): 41–46.

8. H. Overstreet, *The Mature Mind* (New York: W. W. Norton, 1949), p. 73.

9. V. O. Leirer, P. D. Warner, T. L. Rose, and J. A. Yesavage, "Predictions of Violence by High School Students and Clinicians," paper presented at the annual convention of the Oregon Psychological Association, Salem, OR, 1984.

10. G. E. Vaillant, *Adaptation to Life* (Boston: Little, Brown and Co., 1977).

11. G. R. Patterson, and R. M. Dawes, "A Guttman Scale of Children's Coercive Behaviors," *Journal of Consulting and Clinical Psychology*, 43 (1975): 594.

12. C. B. De Soto, M. London, and S. Handel, "Social Reasoning and Spatial Paralogic," *Journal of Personality and Social Psychology*, 2, (1965): 513–521.

13. E. E. Jones, and R. E. Nisbett, "The Actor and the Observer: Divergent Perceptions on the Causes of Behavior," in E. E. Jones, D. E. Kanouse, H. H. Kelley, R. E. Nisbett, S. Valins, and B. Weiner, eds., *Attribution: Perceiving the Causes of Behavior* (Morristown, NJ: General Learning Press, 1972).

14. A. Pope, in Bartlett, *Familiar Quotations*, p. 230; and W. Wordsworth, from "My Heart Leaps Up When I Behold." In Bartlett, *Familiar Quotations*, p. 469.

15. E. Quinn, *Max Ernst*. Translated from the French by Kenneth Lyons (Barcelona: Ediciones Poligrafa, S. A., 1984). Quotation appears on p. 29, attributed to Diane Waldman, p. 16, but no reference is given; instead, the reader is referred to something termed *Ecritures*, "thanks to a system of dates and sub-titles introduced by the author."

16. Dennis Turner, the director of a television movie about Rock Hudson's life, October 8, 1990, as quoted in S. Littwin, "Will America be Shocked by 'Rock'?" *TV Guide*, 37, no. 1 (1990): 14–17, 15.

17. F. C. Bartlett, *Remembering: A Study in Experimental Social Psychology* (Cambridge: Cambridge University Press, 1932).

18. R. W. Pearson, M. Ross, and R. M. Dawes, "Personal Recall and the Limits of Retrospective Memory in Questions in Surveys," in J. Tanur ed., *Questions About Questions: Inquiries into the Cognitive Bases of Surveys* (New York: Sage Press, 1991), pp. 65–94.

19. E. F. Loftus, K. Donders, H. G. Hoffman, and J. W. Schooler, "Creating New Memories That Are Quickly Assessed and Confidently Held," *Memory and Cognition*, 17 (1989): 607–616.

20. P. Monaghan, "Professor of Psychology Stokes a Controversy on the Reliability and Repression of Memories," *Chronicle of Higher Education*, September 23, 1992, p. A9.

21. The meeting took place at the Center for Advanced Research in Behavioral and Social Sciences, Palo Alto, CA, June 26–28, 1986.

22. C. Gilligan, *In a Different Voice: Psychological Theory and Women's Development* (Cambridge, MA: Harvard University Press, 1982).

23. S. Hamilton, *A Comparison of Coping Styles in Male and Female Young Adults* (Unpublished doctoral diss., University of Oregon, 1986).

24. P. M. Lewinsohn, M. Rosenbaum, "Recall of Parental Behavior by Acute Depressives, Remitted Depressives, and Nondepressives," *Journal of Personality and Social Psychology*, 52 (1987): 611–619.

25. P. M. Lewinsohn, W. Chaplin, and R. Barton, "Social Competence and Depression: The Role of Illusory Self-perceptions?" *Journal of Abnormal Psychology*, 89 (1980): 203–212.

26. S. E. Taylor, *Positive Illusions: Creative Self-deception and the Healthy Mind* (New York: Basic Books, 1989).

27. P. M. Lewinsohn, D. O. Antonuccio, J. L. Steinmetz, and L. Teri, *The Coping with Depression Course* (Eugene, OR: Castalia Press, 1984).

28. The "good story" is one in which the hero engages in a quest (like the "quest for fire") and must overcome a series of obstacles while engaging in this quest—obstacles often embedded within each other. Many good stories have two other components; first, the hero—being particularly virtuous—receives some unexpected and magical or almost magical help along the way, like the sword in the stone, the electronic gadgetry from the little man in the James Bond movies, the instructions about how to achieve internal enlightenment in *The Return of the Jedi*, the twelve steps of Alcoholics Anonymous, or the particular insights of the psychotherapist. Second, the hero in overcoming the obstacles experiences an unanticipated change in herself or himself— always one for the better, even if it ultimately costs the hero her or his life. In therapy we are told, for example, that "people come to therapy with me because they are frustrated in their neurotic desires, but after achieving insight they seek much healthier goals in their lives." Even our theories of human evolution tend to follow the good story line. Humans were physically weaker than the species with which they competed for food, but in their quest for survival they were granted an almost magical advantage—upright posture, speech, tool use, fire use, or even face-to-face intercourse, leading adults to look at each other during lovemaking and thereby developing the same bonding for each other that adults of closely related species do for infants. The result was something unanticipated at the beginning of the quest: human civilization (and nuclear weapons). See M. Landau, "Human Evolution as Narrative," *American Scientist*, 72 (1984): 262–268.

29. See C. Tavris, "Beware the Incest-Survivor Machine," *New York Times Book Review*, January 3, 1993, p. 1; in particular, see Tavris's comments about one purported incest survivor's anger at her son, who whined to be taken out for fast food, screamed and cursed her, and threw his shoe. This survivor-mother "realized" that her perfectly appropriate reaction of anger to her son's obnoxious behavior was really anger directed at her father, who had incested her.

30. L. C. Robbins, "The Accuracy of Parental Recall of Aspects of Child Development and of Child Rearing Practices," *Journal of Personality and Social Psychology*, 66 (1963): 261–270.

31. C. McFarland, M. Ross, and N. DeCourville, "Women's Theories of Menstruation and Biases in Recall of Menstrual Symptoms," *Journal of Personality and Social Psychology*, 57 (1989): 522–531.

32. C. S. Aneshensel, A. L. Estrada, M. J. Hansell, and V. A. Clark, "Social Psychological Aspects of Reporting Behavior: Lifetime Depressive Episode Reports," *Journal of Health and Social Behavior*, 28 (1987): 232–246.

33. D. H. Stott, "Some Psychosomatic Aspects of Causality in Reproduction," *Journal of Psychosomatic Research*, 3 (1958): 42–55.
34. S. Scarr, D. Phillips, and K. McCartney, "Facts, Fantasies and the Future of Child Care in the United States," *Psychological Science*, 1 (1990): 26–33, 27. Their references are to S. Scarr and J. Arnett, "Malleability: Lessons from Intervention and Family Studies," in J. J. Gallagher, ed., *The Malleability of Children* (New York: Brooks, 1987): pp. 71–84; and to J. Kagan, "Family Experience and the Child's Development," *American Psychologist*, 34 (1979): 886–891.
35. C. S. Widom, "The Cycle of Violence," *Science*, 244 (1989): 160–166.
36. Ibid., p. 162.
37. Ibid., p. 160.
38. Ibid., p. 163.
39. M. Lewis-Rice, *Marketing Post-Secondary Educational Programs With Implications for Higher Education Administration* (Unpublished doctoral diss., Carnegie Mellon University, 1989).
40. J. G. Parker and S. R. Asher, "Peer Relations and Later Personal Adjustment: Are Low-Accepted Children at Risk?" *Psychological Bulletin*, 102 (1987): 357–389.
41. E. Walker and R. J. Lewine "Prediction of Adult-Onset Schizophrenia from Childhood Movies of the Parents," *American Journal of Psychiatry*, 147 (1990): 1052–1056.
42. M. J. Lerner, *The Belief in a Just World: A Fundamental Delusion* (New York: Plenum Press, 1980). See R. M. Dawes, *Rational Choice in an Uncertain World* (San Diego: Harcourt Brace Jovanovich, 1988), chap. 12.
43. M. McCloskey, "Naive Theories of Motion," in D. Gentner and A. S. Stevens, eds., *Mental Models* (Hillsdale, NJ: Lawrence Erlbaum Associates, 1983), pp. 299–324.
44. G. E. Vaillant, *Adaptation to Life* (Boston: Little, Brown and Co., 1977), p. 29.
45. E. E. Werner, "Children of the Garden Island," *Scientific American*, 206 (1989): 106–111.
46. G. A. Miller, "Psychology as a Means of Promoting Human Welfare," *American Psychologist*, 24 (1969): 1063–1075: "For myself, however, I can imagine nothing we could do that would be more relevant to human welfare, and nothing that could produce a greater challenge to the next generation of psychologists, than to discover how best to give psychology away" (p. 1074).

PART II: IMPACT ON OUR CULTURAL BELIEFS

1. R. A. Gardner, *Sex Abuse Hysteria: Salem Witch Trials Revisited* (Cresskill, NJ: Creative Therapeutics, 1991), p. 2.

CHAPTER 8: NEW AGE PSYCHOLOGY

1. P. Goodman, "Reflections on Racism, Spite, Guilt, and Violence," *New York Review of Books*, 10, no. 10 (1968): 18–23, 22.

2. D. L. Bazelon, "Psychiatrists and the Adversary Process," *Scientific American*, 230, no. 6 (1974): 18–23.

3. B. Feinberg, *The Collected Stories of Bertrand Russell* (New York: Simon and Schuster, 1972). Quote from back cover.

4. R. Hoess, *Commandant at Auschwitz: Autobiography* (London: Weidenfeld and Nicholson, 1959).

5. B. Feinberg, *Short Stories of Bertrand Russell*, p. 132.

6. For a report from a "participant observer" (that is, infiltrator) in one such group, see D. Nathan, "Cry Incest," *Playboy* 39, no. 10 (October 1992): 84ff.

7. For a humorous and scathing view of the codependency movement from someone who attended multiple meetings in several locations, see W. Kaminer, *I'm Dysfunctional, You're Dysfunctional* (Reading, MA: Addison-Wesley, 1992.)

8. N. Branden, *The Psychology of Self-Esteem* (Toronto, New York, London, Sydney, Auckland: Bantam Books, 1969).

9. N. Branden, "In Defense of Self," *Association for Humanistic Psychology Perspectives* (August–September 1984): 12–13.

10. J. W. Dean III, *Blind Ambition* (New York: Simon and Schuster, 1976).

11. In an interview in the March 23, 1990, issue of *Publishers Weekly*.

12. A. M. Mecca, N. J. Smelser, and J. Vasconcellos, *The Social Importance of Self-Esteem* (Berkeley: University of California Press, 1989).

13. N. J. Smelser, "Self-Esteem in Social Problems: An Introduction," in Mecca, Smelser, and Vasconcellos, *Social Importance of Self-Esteem*, pp. 1–23.

14. B. Bhatti, D. Derezotes, S. O. Kim, and H. Specht, "The Association Between Child Maltreatment and Self-Esteem," in Mecca, Smelser, and Vasconcellos, *Social Importance of Self-Esteem*, pp. 24–71.

15. M. J. Covington, "Self-Esteem and Failure in School: Analysis and Policy Implications," in Mecca, Smelser, and Vasconcellos, *Social Importance of Self-Esteem*, pp. 72–124.

16. B. C. Hansfeld and J. A. Hattie, "The Relationship Between Self Achievement/Performance Measures," *Review of Educational Research*, 52 (1982): 123–142.

17. S. B. Crockenberg, and B. A. Soby, "Self-Esteem and Teenage Pregnancy," in Mecca, Smelser, and Vasconcellos, *Social Importance of Self-Esteem*, pp. 125–164.

18. S. L. Jessor and R. Jessor, "Transition from Virginity to Non-virginity Among Youth: A Social-Psychological Study over Time," *Developmental Psychology*, 11 (1975): 473–484.

19. T. J. Scheff, S. M. Retzinger, and M. T. Ryan, "Crime, Violence, and Self-Esteem: Review and Proposals," in Mecca, Smelser, and Vasconcellos, *Social Importance of Self-Esteem*, pp. 165–199.

20. L. Schneiderman, W. M. Furman, and J. Weber, "Self-Esteem and Chronic Welfare Dependence," in Mecca, Smelser, and Vasconcellos, *Social Importance of Self-Esteem*, pp. 200–247.

21. R. Skager, and E. Kerst, "Alcohol and Drug Use and Self-Esteem: A Psychological Perspective," in Mecca, Smelser, and Vasconcellos, *Social Importance of Self-Esteem*, pp. 248–293; H. H. L. Kitano, "Alcohol and Drug

Use and Self-Esteem: A Sociocultural Perspective," Mecca, Smelser, and Vasconcellos, *Social Importance of Self-Esteem*, pp. 294–326.

22. G. P. Gardner (chair), National Commission on Excellence in Education, *A Nation at Risk: The Imperative for Educational Reform* (Washington, DC: U.S. Government Printing Office, 1983), p. 5.

23. G. Grosvenor, "Super Powers Not So Super in Geography," *National Geographic, 176* (1989): 816–821.

24. U.S. Congress, Office of Technological Assessment, *Worker Training: Competing in the New International Economy*, OTA-ITE-457 (Washington, DC: U.S. Government Printing Office, 1990), p. 160.

25. Ibid., p. 154.

26. R. B. Felson, "The Effects of Self-Appraisal of Ability on Academic Performance," *Journal of Personality and Social Psychology*, 47 (1984): 944–952.

27. Ibid., p. 944.

28. This technique suggests upper bounds on the influence of distant variables—such as attitude prior to working at school—and lower bounds on the importance of the influences that "mediate" these—such as hard work in this example. See H. F. Gollob, and C. S. Reichardt, "Interpreting and Estimating Indirect Effects Assuming Time Lags Really Matter," in L. M. Collins and J. L. Horn, eds., *Best Methods for the Analysis of Change* (Washington, DC: American Psychological Association, 1991), 242.

29. For a discussion of Allport's conception of functional autonomy, see N. J. Ehrlich, *Psychology and Contemporary Affairs* (Belmont, CA: Woodsworth, Brooks/Cole, 1972).

30. H. W. Stevenson, S. Lee, and J. W. Stigler, "Mathematics Achievement of Chinese, Japanese, and American Children," *Science* 231 (1986): 693–699.

31. Ibid., p. 694.

32. Ibid., p. 698.

33. H. W. Stevenson, *A Long Way to Being Number One: What We Have to Learn from East Asia*. Federation of Behavioral, Psychological, and Cognitive Sciences: Science and Public Policy Seminar, March 20, 1992.

34. Ibid., p. 14.

35. Gardner, *Nation At Risk*, p. 19. The commission also found an average of twenty-two hours per week devoted to academic work in high school.

36. Stevenson, *Long Way to Being Number One*.

37. N. Caplan, M. H. Choy, and J. K. Whitmore, "Indochinese Refugee Families and Academic Achievement," *Scientific American*, 266 (1992): 36–42.

CHAPTER 9: PATERNALISTIC PUT-DOWNS: CLIENTS AS SLAVES TO THERAPISTS

1. H. Spotnitz, "The Case of Anna O.: Aggression and the Narcissistic Countertransference," in M. Rosenbaum and M. Muroff, *Anna O.: Fourteen Contemporary Reinterpretations* (New York: The Free Press, 1984): 132–140, 137.

2. J. M. Masson, *Against Therapy: Emotional Tyranny and the Myth of Psychological Healing* (New York: Atheneum, 1988).

3. American Medical Association, *Current Opinions: The Council on Ethical and Judicial Affairs of the American Medical Association* (Chicago: American Medical Association, 1989), Principle 2.19.

4. P. Keith-Spiegel, and G. P. Koocher, *Ethics in Psychology: Professional Standards in Cases* (Hillsdale, NJ: Lawrence Erlbaum Associates, 1985). While the book itself emphasizes many other concerns than the "one-up" position of the professional psychologist (and hence the "one-down" position of the client), that concern was the one most commonly referenced by other committee members when I served on the national ethics committee of the American Psychological Association from 1985 through 1987.

5. American Psychological Association, "Ethical Principles of Psychologists (Amended June 2, 1989)," *American Psychologist*, 45 (1990): 390–395, 390–391.

6. See R. M. Dawes, "The Philosophy of Responsibility and Autonomy Versus That of Being One-up," paper presented at the annual convention of the American Psychological Association, Washington, DC: August 24, 1986.

7. Keith-Spiegel and Koocher, *Ethics in Psychology*.

8. Ibid.

9. K. E. Polk, P. Keith-Spiegel, and B. G. Tabachnick, "Sexual Attraction to Clients: The Human Therapist and the (Sometimes) Inhuman Training System," *American Psychologist*, 32 (1986): 752–760.

10. D. Cartwright, "Determinants of Scientific Progress: The Case of Research on the Risky Shift," *American Psychologist*, 28 (1973): 222–231.

11. P. Freiberg, "AIDS Home Test Kits Will Get a Second Look," *APA Monitor*, July 1990, p. 35.

12. For a study of gay men, see T. J. Coates, R. D. Stall, S. M. Kegeles, B. Lo, S. F. Morin, and L. McKusick, "AIDS Antibody Testing: Will It Stop the AIDS Epidemic? Will It Help People Infected with HIV?" *American Psychologist*, 43 (1988): 859–864. For a study of IV drug users, see D. DesJarlais, "Effectiveness of AIDS Educational Programs for Intravenous Drug Users," background paper prepared for the Health Program, Office of Technology Assessment, U.S. Congress (Washington, DC: U.S. Government Printing Office, 1987).

13. C. F. Turner, H. G. Miller, and L. E. Moses, eds., *AIDS, Sexual Behavior, and Intravenous Drug Use* (Washington, DC: National Academy Press, 1989); H. G. Miller, C. F. Turner, and L. Moses, eds., *AIDS: The Second Decade* (Washington, DC: The National Academy Press, 1990); S. L. Coyle, R. F. Boruch, and C. F. Turner, eds., *Evaluating AIDS Prevention Programs* (Washington, DC: National Academy Press, 1991).

14. The ubiquity of counterinductive inferences, in fact this phrase itself, is detailed in P. E. Meehl, "Why I Do Not Attend Case Conferences," in P.E. Meehl, ed., *Psychodiagnosis: Selected Papers* (New York: W.W. Norton and Co., 1977), pp. 225–302.

15. G. W. Bower and T. Trabasso, "Reversals Prior to Solution in Concept identification Tasks," *Journal of Experimental Psychology*, 63 (1963): 438–443.

16. For full reference list for the animal experiments on learned helplessness, see M. Seligman, *Helplessness: On Depression, Development, and Death* (San Francisco: W. H. Feeeman, 1975).

17. D. Rapaport, *Organization and Pathology of Thought* (New York: Columbia University Press, 1951).

18. See, for example, J. Piaget, *The Construction of Reality in the Child* (New York: Basic Books, 1954), and I. E. Sigel and F. H. Hooper, eds., *Logical Thinking in Children* (New York: Holt, Rinehart and Winston, 1968).

19. See B. Inhelder and J. Piaget, *The Growth of Logical Thinking from Childhood to Adolescence* (New York: Basic Books, 1958).

20. For a discussion of surprise in young children, see W. R. Charlesworth in D. Elkind and J. H. Flavell, *Studies in Cognitive Development* (New York: Oxford University Press, 1969), pp. 257–314.

21. See P. Starkey, E. S. Spelke, and R. Gelman, "Detection of Intermodal Numerical Correspondence," *Science,* 222 (1983): 179–181.

22. See R. M. Dawes, "An Interpretive of Inhelder and Piaget," in *Proceedings: Third Invitational Interdisciplinary Seminar on Piagetian Theory and Its Implications for the Helping Professions* (Los Angeles: UAP, Children's Hospital of Los Angeles, 1975).

23. Meehl, "Why I Do Not Attend Case Conferences." The "spun glass theory" is discussed on pp. 252–255.

24. See, for example, D. H. Barlow, *Anxiety and Its Disorders: The Nature and Treatment of Anxiety and Panic* (New York: Guilford Press, 1985).

25. D. Campbell, R. D. Sanderson, and S. G. Laverty, "Characteristics of a Conditioned Response in Human Subjects During Extinction Trials Following a Single Traumatic Conditioning Trial," *Journal of Abnormal and Social Psychology,* 68 (1964): 627–639.

26. H. Wakefield and R. Underwager, "Discovering a Life That Works," *IPT Newsletter,* Fall 1989, pp. 2–6, 6.

27. P. M. Lewinsohn, D. O. Antonuccio, J. L. Steinmetz, and L. Teri, *The Coping with Depression Course* (Eugene, OR: Castalia Press, 1984).

28. A. T. Beck, *Cognitive Therapy and the Emotional Disorders* (New York: New American Library, 1976).

29. P. M. Lewinsohn, W. Michel, W. Chaplin, and R. Barton, "Social Competence and Depression: The Role of Illusory Self-perceptions?" *Journal of Abnormal Psychology,* 89 (1980): 203–212.

30. See, for example, S. Strack and J. C. Coyne, "Social Confirmation of Dysphoria: Shared and Private Reactions to Depression," *Journal of Personality and Social Psychology,* 44 (1983): 798–806.

31. A. Bandura, "Self-Efficacy Mechanism in Human Agency," *American Psychologist,* 37 (1982): 122–147.

32. See J. Rotter, "Generalized Expectancies for Internal Versus External Control of Reinforcements," *Monographs of the American Psychological Association,* 80 (1966) (whole issue no. 609); and J. Rotter, "Some Problems and Misconceptions Related to the Construct of Internal Versus External Control of Reinforcement," *Journal of Consulting and Clinical Psychology,* 43 (1975): 56–67. See also W. E. Henley, "Invictus" (1875) in H. Felleman, ed., *The Best-loved Poems of Americans* (New York: Doubleday, 1936).

33. N. D. Weinstein, "Unrealistic Optimism About Susceptibility to Health Problems: Conclusions from a Community-Based Sample," *Journal of Behavioral Medicine,* 10 (1987): 481–500.

34. B. E. Whitley, Jr., and A. L. Hern, "Perceptions of Vulnerability to Pregnancy and the Use of Effective Contraception," *PSPB Bulletin,* 17 (1991): 104–110.

35. See S. E. Taylor, R. Lichtman, and J. Word, "Attribution, Belief About Control, and Adjustment to Breast Cancer," *Journal of Personality and Social Psychology,* 46 (1984): 289–503.

36. On life stage, see D. O. Sears, "College Sophomores in the Laboratory: Influences of a Narrow Data Base on Psychology's View of Human Nature," *Journal of Personality and Social Psychology*, 51 (1986): 515–539. On situation, see R. M. Dawes, "Discovering 'Human Nature' Versus Discovering How People Cope with the Task of Getting Through College: An Extension of Sears's Argument," paper presented at the annual convention of the American Psychological Society, Washington, DC, June 16, 1991.

37. For a review, see C. Anderson and B. Weiner, "Attribution and Attributional Processes in Personality," forthcoming in G. Caprara and G. Heck, eds., *Modern Personality Psychology: Critical Reviews and New Directions*.

38. M. E. P. Seligman, *Learned Optimism* (New York: Alfred A. Knopf, 1991).

39. M. J. Lerner, *The Belief in a Just World: A Fundamental Delusion* (New York: Plenum Press, 1980).

40. M. J. Lerner, "Integrating Social and Psychological Rules of Entitlement: The Basic Task of Each Actor and Fundamental Problem of the Social Sciences," *Social Justice Research*, 1 (1987): 107–125.

41. R. S. Gold, M. J. Skinner, P. J. Grant, and D. C. Plummer, "Situational Factors and Thought Processes Associated with Unprotected Intercourse in Gay Men," *Psychology and Health*, 5 (1991): 1–20.

42. S. E. Taylor, *Positive Illusions: Creative Self-Deception and the Healthy Mind* (New York: Basic Books, 1989).

43. Ibid., p. 227; p. xi.

44. A. M. Isen, "Toward Understanding the Role of Affect in Cognition," in R. Wyer and T. Scrull, eds., *Handbook of Social Cognition* (Hillsdale, NJ: Erlbaum, 1984), pp. 174–236, quote on p. 189.

45. C. Peterson, M. E. P. Seligman, and G. E. Vaillant, "Pessimistic Explanatory Style in a Risk Factor for Physical Illness: A Thirty-five Year Longitudinal Study," *Journal of Personality and Social Psychology*, 55 (1988): 23–27.

46. Seligman, *Learned Optimism*.

47. S. Cohen, "Psychosocial Models and the Role of Social Support in the Etiology of Physical Disease," *Health Psychology*, 7 (1988): 269–297.

48. Iacocca and Edison are quoted in S. E. Taylor, *Positive Illusions: Creative Self-deception and the Healthy Mind* (New York: Basic Books, 1989), p. 60.

49. Richard P. Bentrell, in the June 1992 issue of the *Journal of Medical Ethics*, has humorously proposed that happiness might be a new category of pathology to be included in the American Psychiatric Association's *Diagnostic and Statistical Manuals*. The proposal is based on the idiotic lack of realism that is considered to be not just a correlate of happiness but a necessary condition for achieving it.

50. Y. Yevtushenko referenced in *Chronicle of Higher Education*, June 12, 1991, p. B3.

51. R. Axelrod, *The Evolution of Cooperation* (New York: Basic Books, 1984).

52. For full review of the experiments, see R. M. Dawes, "Social Dilemmas, Economic Self-Interest, and Evolutionary Theory," In D. R. Brown and J. E. K. Smith, eds., *Recent Research in Psychology: Frontiers of Mathematical Psychology: Essays in Honor of Clyde Coombs* (New York: Springer-Verlag, 1991). Or see R. M. Dawes, A. J. C. van de Kragt, and J. M. Orbell, "Cooperation for the Benefit of Us—Not Me or My Conscience," in J. Mansbridge, ed., *Beyond Self-Interest* (Chicago: University of Chicago Press, 1990).

53. These other researchers include R. M. Kramer, and M. B. Brewer, "Social Group Identity and the Emergence of Cooperation in Resource

Conservation," in H. Wilke, D. Messick, and C. Rutte, eds., *Psychology of Decisions and Conflict, 3, Experimental Social Dilemmas* (Frankfurt am Main: Verlag Peter Lang, 1986), 205–234; H. Tajfel, *Differentiation Between Social Groups: Studies in the Social Psychology of Intergroup Relations* (London: Academic Press, 1978); A. P. Witt, *Group Efficiency and Fairness in Social Dilemmas: An Experimental Gaming Effect* (Doctoral diss., Rijksuniversiteit, Groningen, 1989).

54. K. L. Patton, in Unitarian Universalist Association, *Hymns for the Celebration of Life* (Boston: The Beacon Press, 1964).

55. Seligman, *Learned Optimism*, pp. 63–65.

56. A. G. Greenwald, "The Totalitarian Ego: Fabrication and Revision of Personal History," *American Psychologist*, 35 (1980): 603–618.

CHAPTER 10: AUTONOMY AND ADVICE

1. Quoted in E. Kasner and J. Newman, *Mathematics and the Imagination* (London: Bell and Sons, 1949), p. 239.

2. See, for example, S. Cohen, E. Lichtenstein, J. O. Prochaska, J. S. Rossi, E. R. Gritz, C. R. Carr, C. Y. Orleans, V. J. Schoenbach, L. Biener, D. Abrams, C. DiClemente, S. Curry, G. A. Marlatt, K. M. Cummings, S. L. Emont, G. Giovino, and D. Ossip-Klein, "Debunking Myths About Self-Quitting," *American Psychologist*, 44 (1989): 1355–1365. "As is apparent from Figure 1, there is little relation between [number of] previous attempts to quit [smoking] and probability of success on the current attempt" (p. 1362).

3. V. Murphy-Berman and J. J. Berman, "The Effect of Respondents' Just World Beliefs and Target Person's Social Worth and Awareness-of-Risk on Perception of a Person with AIDS," *Social Justice Research* 4 (1990): 215–228.

4. Quoted in M. E. P. Seligman, *Learned Optimism* (New York: Alfred A. Knopf, 1991), p. 73.

5. C. J. Grayson and C. O'Dell, *American Business: A Two-minute Warning* (New York: The Free Press, 1988), p. 309.

6. At least in Minnesota. Again, see H. W. Stevenson, S. Lee, and J. W. Stigler, "Mathematics Achievement of Chinese, Japanese, and American Children," *Science*, 231 (1986): 693–699, 697.

7. P. Brickman and D. T. Campbell, "Hedonic Relativism and Planning the Good Society," in M. H. Appley, ed., *Adaptation-Level Theory: A Symposium* (New York: Academic Press, 1971).

8. R. J. Sternberg and T. I. Lubart, "Buy Low and Sell High: An Investment Approach to Creativity," *Current Directions in Psychological Science*, 1 (1992): 1–5, quote on p. 4.

9. M. E. P. Seligman, "Predicting Depression, Poor Health, and Presidential Elections," paper presented at the Science and Public Policy Seminar of the Federation of Behavioral, Psychological, and Cognitive Sciences, February 27, 1987.

10. G. Wills, *Reagan's America: Innocents at Home* (Garden City, NY: Doubleday, 1987).
11. M. Newcomb, "Losing the Drug War: Are We Too Addicted to the Quick Fix to Seek the Ultimate Fix?" Science and Public Policy Seminar, Federation of Behavioral, Psychological, and Cognitive Sciences, September 7, 1990.
12. J. O. Prochaska and J. C. Norcross, "Contemporary Psychotherapists: A National Survey of Characteristics, Practices, Orientations and Attitudes," *Psychotherapy: Theory, Research and Practice*, 20 (1983): 161–173. See also S. L. Garfield and R. Kurtz, "A Study of Eclectic Views," *Journal of Consulting and Clinical Psychology*, 45 (1977): 78–83, or more recently A. Zook II and J. M. Walton, "Theoretical Orientations and Work Settings of Clinical and Counseling Psychologists: A Current Perspective," *Professional Psychology Research and Practice*, 20 (1989): 23–31. After some years in relative limbo, psychoanalysis is now almost tied with eclecticism as a favored orientation. This resurgence may have resulted from the growth (both absolute and relative) of the professional schools.
13. C. A. Kiesler, "Mental Hospital and Alternative Care: Noninstitutionalization as Potential Public Policy for Mental Patients," *American Psychologist*, 37 (1982): 349–360.

INDEX

training
  in biofeedback techniques, 143–45
  licensing requirement of, 139–43
treatment
  bias in, 41–43
  decision to seek, 70–71
  randomized experiments in evaluat-
    ing, 47–48
  studies evaluating efficacy, 50–54
  See also drug therapy; hypothetical
    counterfactual
trends, statistical, 28–30
Tversky, Amos, 126

understanding
  clinical prediction as, 79–82
  elements of, 76
  intuitive, 7–9
  predictability as test of, 77–79, 101
  See also knowledge
Underwager, Ralph, 157, 159, 269
unlicensed practitioners, 178

Vaillant, George, 69, 188
  defense mechanism theory, 39–40,
    206–7
  definition of mental health, 66
  example of predictive behavior,
    215–16
  on predictability, 222, 274

validity
  of actuarial prediction, 89–91
  of doll play, 159–62
  incremental, 161
  of interviews, 86–90
  of knowledge, 76–77
  of psychological assessment,
    23–25
  of retrospective memory, 130,
    170–75
van de Kragt, Alphons, 278
Vasconcellos, John, 236

Wakefield, Hollida, 157, 159, 269
Walker, Elaine, 220
Watts, J. W., 193–94
Weinstein, Neil, 272
Werner, Emmy, 222
West, JoAnne, 60
White, Sue, 159
Whitley, Bernard, Jr., 272
Widom, Kathy, 218–19
Wittgenstein, Ludwig, 65
Wood, R. W., 78
Woodward, Joanne, 233

Yevtushenko, Yevgeny, 276, 290

Ziskin, Jay, 24, 94–95, 153
Zubin, Joseph, 120